TEMPLES OF ANCIENT EGYPT

TEMPLES OF
ANCIENT
EGYPT

EDITED BY BYRON E. SHAFER

AUTHORS

DIETER ARNOLD

LANNY BELL

RAGNHILD BJERRE FINNESTAD

GERHARD HAENY

BYRON E. SHAFER

CORNELL UNIVERSITY PRESS *Ithaca, New York*

First published 1997 by Cornell University Press.

Printed in the United States of America

Library of Congress Cataloging-in-Publication Data

Temples of ancient Egypt / authors, Dieter Arnold . . . [et al.] ;
edited by Byron E. Shafer.
     p.   cm.
Includes index.
ISBN 0-8014-3399-1 (alk. paper)
1. Temples—Egypt.   2. Rites and ceremonies—Egypt.   3. Egypt—Religion.
I. Arnold, Dieter, 1936–   .   II. Shafer, Byron E. (Byron Esely), 1938–   .
BL2450.T43T47   1997
299'.31—dc21   97-23851

Cornell University Press strives to utilize environmentally responsible suppliers and
materials to the fullest extent possible in the publishing of its books. Such materials
include vegetable-based, low-VOC inks and acid-free papers that are also either
recycled, totally chlorine-free, or partly composed of nonwood fibers.

Cloth printing   10   9   8   7   6   5   4   3   2   1

CONTENTS

MAPS

PREFACE

This study of ancient Egyptian temples and rituals complements the exploration of the religious world undertaken in *Religion in Ancient Egypt: Gods, Myths, and Personal Practice* (Cornell University Press, 1991). Here, as for that book, the catalyst has been the symposium on ancient Egypt sponsored by Charles and Elizabeth Holman and held at Fordham University in New York City. It brought the authors together at the Lincoln Center campus on February 28, 1992, and they have now developed and refined their lectures into the present chapters.

The topic for the 1992 symposium was suggested and promoted by Gerald M. Quinn, the Dean of Fordham's College at Lincoln Center, a classicist, and a dear friend and colleague of Martha and Lanny Bell. In November 1991, Gerry and Martha died in a tragic highway accident. The symposium, at which Lanny lectured, was dedicated to their memory—as is this publication. *Requiem aeternam dona eis, Domine.*

The authors' intention has been to present in a form accessible to students and scholars alike a summation of current knowledge about ancient Egyptian temples and rituals and an exposition of our individual, specialized understandings and insights. Dieter Arnold, Lanny Bell, and Gerhard Haeny bring to their topics a wealth of field experience at Egypt's temple sites and of expertise in archeology, architecture, and epigraphy. Ragnhild Bjerre Finnestad and I bring to our topics a training and expertise in the field of religious studies that few Egyptologists possess. Several of us also introduce anthropological perspectives that are otherwise unrepresented or underrepresented in Egyptological literature.

In the transliteration of Egyptian hieroglyphs, I have followed the individual author's preference for style, even though that has produced some inconsistency from chapter to chapter. In the English spelling of Egyptian words and names, I have standardized the forms across the book with but few exceptions (notably Seti/Sety and *Akhmenu/Akh-menu*).

The chapters were completed on differing timetables. Chapters 2 and 5 reached near-final form in 1993; Chapters 1 and 4, during 1994; and Chapter 3, in 1995. The editor expresses his heartfelt gratitude to the authors for their hard work, flexibility, and genial spirit throughout the multiple drafts!

BYRON E. SHAFER

New York, New York

TEMPLES OF ANCIENT EGYPT

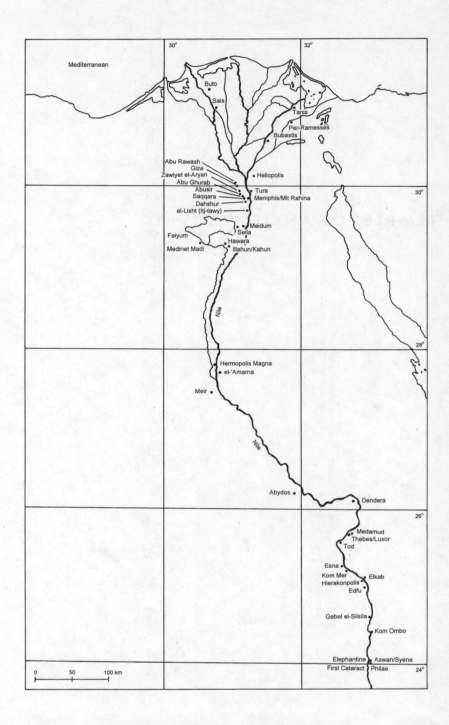

Egypt from the First Cataract to the Mediterranean. Drawn by Carol Meyer

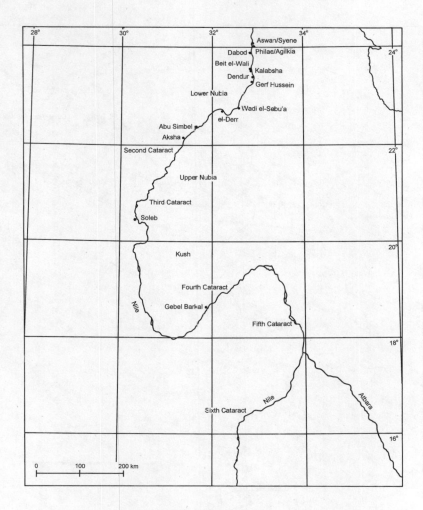

Nubia and Kush. Drawn by Carol Meyer

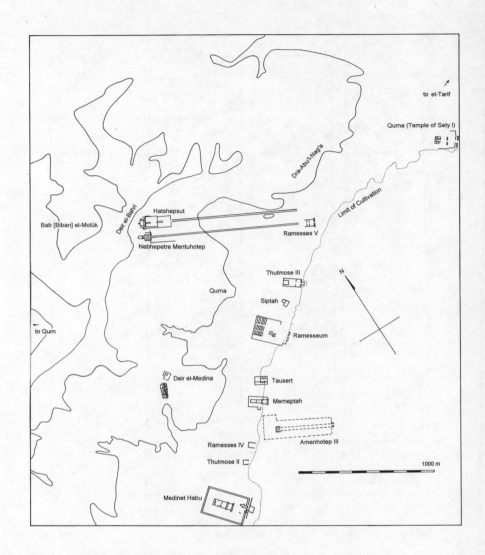

to el-Tarif

Qurna (Temple of Sety I)

Dra-Abu'l-Nag'a

Limit of Cultivation

Bab [Biban] el-Molûk

Deir el-Bahri

Hatshepsut

Nebhepetre Mentuhotep

Ramesses V

Thutmose III

Qurna

Siptah

N

to Qurn

Ramesseum

Deir el-Medina

Tausert

Merneptah

Amenhotep III

Ramesses IV

Thutmose II

1000 m

Medinet Habu

West Bank of Thebes. Drawn by Carol Meyer

1

TEMPLES, PRIESTS, AND RITUALS: AN OVERVIEW

BYRON E. SHAFER

Temples

Ancient Egyptian society comprised the gods, the king, the blessed dead, and humanity, a community that encompassed earth, sky, and netherworld.[1] These three realms converged in temples and cohered in rituals. There the power of creation was tapped, chaos was bridled, and cosmic order was renewed. There a hierarchy of relationships and values was negotiated and maintained. There beings were transformed and even transposed between realms.

Temples and rituals were loci for the struggle between order and chaos. At creation, the existent came into being amid the dark, inert, unbounded waters of the nonexistent (called Nun) and took a multiplicity of forms in space and time.[2] At creation, the cosmos existed in perfect harmony with the Creator's intention, the pristine state Egyptians called *maˤat*, order.[3] But the nonexistent surrounded the existent and, true to its unbounded nature, penetrated the boundaries of the existent. The cosmos came to be shot through with "uncreated" elements representing the nonexistent. Some, like ground water and sleep, manifested the beneficent, regenerative aspect of the nonexistent; but others, like desert and darkness, manifested its hostile, threatening aspect—*isfet*, disorder, chaos.[4] According to Jonathan Z. Smith, chaos is a sacred power, a creative challenge to order that is never completely overcome, a source of possibility and vitality that stands over against order but is inextricably related to it.[5] Smith's observation is certainly true of ancient Egypt, where the sacred opposition between order and chaos found perpetual place in temples and rituals.

Temples and rituals were loci for the creative interplay of sacred space and sacred time. Sacred space is "a place of clarification (a focusing lens) where men and gods are held to be transparent to one another"[6] and "a point of communication, the 'paradoxical point of passage from one mode of being to another.'"[7] In sacred space, one is oriented to the cosmos and immersed in primordial order; there one experiences truth and renews life.[8] Over time, such space appears unchanged and unchanging, "stable enough to endure without growing old or losing any of its parts."[9]

What has been said of sacred place can, for the most part, be said of sacred time as well.[10] It is a moment, or season, or cycle of such clarification and communication, orientation and immersion, experience and renewal. Time, however, is not so stable a dimension of order as space.[11] Egyptians experienced time as a spiral of patterned repetitions, a coil of countless rebirths. The purest moment of sacred time was the first, the moment of creation, when the existent and its order emerged from the nonexistent and its aspect of disorder. Subsequently, time, as a component of order, proved vulnerable to chaos. So, for example, the intervals between sunrise and sunset came to change from day to day and season to season, and the beginning of each new 365-day year came to rotate slowly backward relative to the seasons and the heliacal rising of the star Sirius.[12] Because of order's ongoing vulnerability to chaos, Egyptians needed to conceive of creation not as a single past event but as a series of "first times," of sacred regenerative moments recurring regularly within the sacred space of temples through the media of rituals and architecture.

Scholars have traditionally divided ancient Egyptian temples into several types, the two principal being "divine" (the residence of a god or gods) and "mortuary" (the place of rituals, offerings, and sacrifices for a deceased king).[13] However, "divine" and "mortuary" can mislead in at least three ways: first, insofar as they suggest that a temple's cultic practices were limited either to care for the gods or to concern for the deceased king; second, insofar as they suggest that the recipient of mortuary rituals was not divine; and third, insofar as they suggest that ancient Egyptians saw the functions, plans, symbols, and rituals of "divine" and "mortuary" temples as quite separate and distinct. Dieter Arnold shows in Chapter 2 that the practices and meanings of the royal cult complexes of Dynasties 1 through 12 extended far beyond what "mortuary temple" implies. They were spaces for performing the rituals and erecting the symbolic architecture that transformed the king into a divine being. They were places for effecting and displaying his power and his associations with other gods, which spanned the

BYRON E. SHAFER

three realms or worlds. Arnold also notes that the temple of King Men-tuhotep (Dynasty 11) was the site of a *joint* cultus for the king and the god Amun-Re. This linking of royal and divine cultuses in so-called mortuary temples became standard in New Kingdom Thebes. As Gerhard Haeny and Lanny Bell state in Chapters 3 and 4, the royal temples on the west bank of the Nile also served the cultus of Amun.[14] They were called "*hwt*–King's name–*m–pr*–Amun" ("Temple of King X of the Temple-domain of Amun").[15] During Amun-Re's procession in the Beautiful Festival of the Valley, they became stations for his barque.[16] Furthermore, parts of royal temple complexes served the cultuses of the gods Re and Hathor.[17]

The category "divine" temple can be as misleading as "mortuary." True, "divine" temples, of which every sizable town had at least one, were residences—indeed, estates—for gods, but what happened in and through them had much to do with kingship, the state, the economy, and themes of death.[18] First, as Ragnhild Bjerre Finnestad states in Chapter 5, "divine" temples symbolized not only the realms of sky and netherworld but also the world of Egypt; what took place in them had as much to do with king and people as with gods. The temples were integral to the political, economic, and social structures of the nation and were a central feature of the state's organization.[19] Religion and politics were, as Jan Assmann has said, "aspects or dimensions of one single, indivisible theopolitical unity."[20] What the world needed was not "salvation" but the preservation of order through governance; and governance was provided *jointly* by god and king.[21] The king was both Lord of the Rituals and administrator of land and fertility; and the temples, with their vast estates, were a focus of these governing functions.[22] Second, Bell demonstrates that the Luxor "divine" temple (Dynasty 18 and later) was a cultic place for both Amun and the *ka* of the king. Bell's groundbreaking study of the royal *ka* in Egypt reaches conclusions that remind me of Alfred Adler's statement about the king of the Moundang of Léré (Chad): "the king is not one of, or the first among, the religious dignitaries but rather, one might say, the minister of a cult whose object he himself partially incarnates. . . . [H]e is the receptacle of an atemporal power that fell first upon the founding hero of the dynasty and has been passed down to the present king via all the sovereigns who have preceded him."[23] At Luxor, the king of Egypt was, as it were, both Lord of the Rituals (priest) and Lord of the Cultus (god). Third, Finnestad describes how the "divine" temple was full of *mortuary* symbolism, life and death being reciprocal states of existence. Indeed, during and after Dynasty 21 kings could be buried in the precincts of certain "divine" temples.[24] Assmann has argued that the mortuary cultus was never purely a family cultus and was always a component of official religion. The king presented offerings not only to the gods but also to the transfigured dead; he was not only the priest in the cultus of the gods but also the lord of the sacrifice in the cultus of the dead. And a portion of the offerings presented before the gods was distributed to the tombs of private persons.[25]

For all these reasons, one should not divide the principal temples of ancient Egypt into the categories "mortuary" and "divine"; the temples' functions and symbolic representations were on the one hand too varied and on the other hand too intertwined. Inasmuch as "mortuary" cult complexes like the pyramids served the god of the state embodied in the king, they were part of the divine cultus.[26] Inasmuch as the sanctuary of cult complexes like Edfu symbolized the place of the sun god's death as well as birth, "divine" temples had a significant mortuary aspect.[27] Therefore, when appropriate, I use the unmodified terms "temple" or "cult complex" to describe all cultic enclosures and structures; and when it is important to distinguish one type of cultic assemblage from another based on its *primary* function or symbolism, I use "royal cult complex" and "divine cult complex," usually for those assemblages that have been called "mortuary temple" and "divine temple," respectively.[28] "Divine cult complex" describes temples with cultuses of gods, including temples where a cultus of the divine king (usually living) existed alongside the *primary* cultus of another god. "Royal cult complex" describes temples with a cultus of the divine king (usually deceased), including those temples where a cultus of another god existed alongside the *primary* or *coequal* cultus of the divine king.

Our knowledge of ancient Egyptian temples is limited to what can be deduced or inferred from the surviving evidence. Much earlier than divine cult complexes, royal cult complexes were constructed of stone (a durable, archeologically favorable material) rather than of reed, wood, and mud brick (perishable, archeologically frustrating materials). Arnold describes and discusses numerous royal cult complexes from Dynasties 1 through 12, but there are few extant remains of divine cult complexes from the same periods.[29] Representations of reed shrines on archaic cylinder seals and ebony and ivory tablets attest to the early existence of divine cult complexes, as do traces of constructions found at Abydos, Hierakonpolis, and Saqqara. The reed shrines are larger versions of domestic huts. Their cultic function is clear, for depicted at the entrance of the enclosure are two poles with banners. This symbol was later used in hieroglyphs for the word *nṯr*, meaning "god" or "divine."[30] Through the Old Kingdom, shrines for the gods remained modest in scale and materials, particularly in contrast to the royal cult complexes described by Arnold.[31] When the stone construction and decoration of divine cult complexes began in the Middle Kingdom, they remained relatively modest in scale. Assmann believes that the rites at the royal cult complexes were the official national cultus dur-

4 BYRON E. SHAFER

ing the Old Kingdom and that the national cultus began to be located in divine cult complexes only in Dynasty 11.[32]

In the New Kingdom, divine cult complexes assumed the general architectural plan that characterized them from then onward.[33] Their rectangular sacred area was separated from the surrounding secular space by an outer enclosure wall, usually of mud brick. Egyptians saw the wall as a boundary between order and disorder; temples were fortresses against chaos. In relatively late temples, the mud bricks of enclosure walls, shaped and molded from the formless slime of the Nile, were arranged in wavelike courses, alternately concave and convex, clearly symbolizing the waters of Nun.[34] Decorations on the gateways set into enclosure walls were typically apotropaic; scenes of the king's victories in battle and prowess in the hunt were meant to frighten away enemies and ward off evil, preserving the sacred order of the temple from the threat of chaos.

Within the enclosure wall, three zones of increasing sacredness were defined. From the perimeter inward extended a large open courtyard, the area of tertiary sacredness. Therein were located priests' quarters, small shrines, gardens, workplaces, storage facilities, slaughter yards, areas for processing the offerings, and a pond for ritual lustrations.[35] Every Egyptian—king, priest, or commoner—could enter this area.

The king and priests, after purificatory lustrations, could go through a door or gateway into the zone of secondary sacredness, the open-air court(s) within the walls of the temple proper; on some ritual occasions, at least during the New Kingdom, representative commoners were admitted as well.[36] The gateway was usually a pylon, a pair of high trapezoidal towers linked at the top by a bridge decorated with solar images. The exterior faces of the towers sloped toward the interior, receding from bottom to top; like the outer enclosure wall, they displayed apotropaic scenes of the hunt and battle. The pylon represented the mountain peaks that flanked the eastern horizon at the mouth of the cavern from which the sun rose each day.[37] In addition, the gateway probably symbolized the vagina and (re)birth.[38] Here began the axial path that led inward to the womblike sanctuary of the principal god and symbolized the daily course of the sun.[39] The path's sun symbolism was signaled by the east-west orientation typical of it and by the solar decorations along its route. The Creator had instituted the course of the sun to govern the cosmos, developing order and dispelling disorder along its path; and as a parallel phenomenon the Creator had instituted kingship to govern the earth.[40] Thus it was significant that the first station(s) along the axial way, the large open-air court(s) inside the gateway, displayed both the arc of the sun and statues or pillars of the king. There, too, were erected, at least as early as the Middle Kingdom and with special frequency in the Late Period, statues of persons privileged by the king perpetually to enjoy the gods' presence and to participate in the temple's offerings.[41]

During festivals, the image of the principal god was carried out of the sanctuary in the deck-shrine of the god's ceremonial barque. In the open-air court, the god might meet visiting gods. There, too, at least during the New Kingdom, common people might first glimpse the principal god's shrine.[42] They could also pour water libations and offer prayers to or through the gods, kings, and prominent persons represented by statues; and amulets and divine figurines, which mediated a sense of god's presence, became especially potent after being worn or carried into the court.

From the large open-air court, the king and certain select priests could pass farther inward to the zone of primary sacredness—the dark, roofed rooms at the rear of the temple proper. The first room was the hypostyle hall—a monumental, enclosed, basilica-like ceremonial space whose roof rested on numerous rows of close-set columns.[43] The columns, many more than were needed to bear the weight of the roof, represented marsh plants, and their capitals were usually sculpted as papyrus umbrels or lotus flowers. This dimly lit hall, through which everyone going to the sanctuary of the principal god had to pass, was the swamp between the dark, chaotic, unbounded primeval waters of Nun and the mound of creation; it was a transition point—a liminal space—between the disorder of the nonexistent and the order of creation.[44] After the hypostyle hall came a chamber with small tables and stands on which priests presented the many offerings and sacrifices. Adjoining it was the room where the divine barque was installed atop a platform. During festival processions, this portable boat, carried on priests' shoulders, transported the sacred image of the temple's principal god. The image, made of precious metal, was not inanimate. The mystical rituals performed when the statue was installed in the sanctuary had transubstantiated it; it *was* the god, although the god was neither confined to it nor limited by it. When not in ritual procession, the image and the shrine that encased it dwelt in a small, dark, otherwise unprepossessing room. But because the statue was the very being of god, this residence was the heart of the temple, the focus of cosmic order, and the matrix of creative power: the holy of holies.[45]

As described, the basic plan of a divine cult complex was relatively simple and straightforward, but temples were often greatly expanded as time went by. Indeed, few were ever completed. This resulted in large part from individual kings' desire for personal display. Yet Erik Hornung hypothesizes that from the First Intermediate Period onward kings also desired to "extend the existing."[46] The boundary between the created and the uncreated was fluid, and the existent's encounter with the nonexistent was both threatening and rejuvenating. So, Hornung argues, "we find the yearning

BYRON E. SHAFER

for limitation side by side with the desire to transcend and dissolve all boundaries."[47] By expanding a divine cult complex, a king resolved this tension creatively, simultaneously transcending old limits and establishing new ones.[48] As each king pushed the perimeter of walls and courtyards farther and farther into what had previously been secular space, the area of the sacred was greatly extended. The boundaries of cultic space could be transcended and newly delimited in other ways as well. During the Late Period, as Hornung observes, "the Egyptians extended the stage for worship to include several different levels by adding shrines on the temple roof as well as subterranean crypts."[49]

The ritual founding of a temple site—demarcating its borders, consecrating its land, and renewing creation—lasted from seven to fifteen days. It was performed by the king (or in his stead a priest of the highest rank), assisted by lector priests who recited the requisite formulas. The basic elements of the ritual are clear, but their exact sequence is disputed.[50] The ceremonies may have started at night, under a canopy of stars like Ursa Major and Orion (whose positions helped to orient the temple and its axis) and beneath a new moon (whose reappearance—light emerging from darkness—symbolized rebirth and fresh beginnings). After the temple site had been designated and laid out, the king, aided by the goddess Seshat (played by one of her priests), drove stakes into the four corners of the plot and connected them with a measuring cord. The king and his retinue followed the lines established by the extended cord and, using a hoe, hacked a foundation trench deep enough to expose a seepage of groundwater, which represented the beneficent, regenerative aspect of the encircling Nun. The king molded mud bricks, shoveled sand into the trench to establish purity and to form a boundary between the mud bricks and the ground water, and deposited models of carpentry and brick-making tools and other foundation offerings at sites along the trench. He set either mud bricks at the four corners of the temple or, if constructed of stone, the cornerstone.[51] He also buried the heads of a sacrificial goose and bull.

When the divine cult complex had been built, it was turned over to the principal god in a month-long series of rituals that infused it with the energy of creation.[52] The king, or his priestly representative, purified the temple with natron and whitewash and performed an Opening of the Mouth ritual in every room, giving the temple a life of its own and making it cultically operative.[53] The climax was the installation of the principal god's very being, the cultic image, in the holy of holies. The rituals concluded with a banquet for the priests and for the artisans who had built and decorated the cult complex.

A consecrated divine cult complex symbolized many things, including the island of creation, the "radiant place," the cosmos, and the body of god.[54] At the time of First Creation, the point of land that emerged from the dark, unbounded waters of Nun was a low mud island, and there, on a mound, the first primeval temple was built as the house of god.[55] Symbolizing this, a temple's foundation reached down to groundwater, and its axial way sloped upward through the hypostyle hall (the primeval swamp) to the mound on which the sanctuary of the divine image stood.[56] The temple was also *akhet* (3ḫt), the "radiant place"—the horizon over the eastern mountains where the sun rose in the morning and over the western mountains where it disappeared at night, the land to which the blessed dead journeyed. As *akhet*, the temple was the place where heaven, earth, and netherworld touched.[57] The temple was also the cosmos in microcosm. The enclosure wall and sacred lake were Nun, the sanctuary was the place of First Creation, the hypostyle hall and the bases of walls were the liminal swamp, the columns were plants, the ceilings were sky, the floors were earth, the vaults were netherworld, the pylon was the mountains of the eastern horizon, and the axial way was the path of the sun. The temple was also the body of god and could be personified, especially in the Ramesside Period, as a divine figure of human form.[58] Its symbolizing of the body of god is implicit in its symbolizing of the cosmos, for, as Finnestad argues in Chapter 5, the cosmos is the Creator's divine body. To be in the temple—whether through priestly service or limited "public" access—was to experience the body of god, to commune with god physically and sacramentally.

The temple was a branch of cosmic government and participated in the ordering of the universe by sun and king. It served pharaonic governance by maintaining the cosmos ritually. It also served by playing a vital economic role.[59] Egypt's economy was a complex mixture of peasant exchanges, state redistribution, and a relatively small but dynamic private sector that involved both local and regional marketing.[60] Peasants for the most part engaged in subsistence agriculture and local barter and trade.[61] The families of the many state officials, workers, priests, and soldiers participated in the private sector to increase their wealth, but their basic source of support was the state system for distributing to them local agricultural produce (taxation) and food grown on government estates.[62] The temples, with their landholdings, storehouses, workshops, and transport ships, were part of the state system, particularly from the New Kingdom onward.[63] They had many personnel—priests, officials, scribes, artists, sculptors, artisans, metalworkers, butchers, bakers, brewers, weavers, herders, fowlers, sailors, beekeepers—and large numbers of serfs growing food for them on the landholdings.[64] Sometimes a parcel of temple land was given to a soldier or worker in exchange for a fixed percentage of the yield.[65] The income from a temple's land supported its own priests, workers, and serfs and other state workers, such as those in the necropolises, for most of the food offered to the gods by king, devotees, and temple estates was consumed not by the gods but by the families of priests and workers. On festival days, the offerings were large enough to feed some of the populace as well.[66] Temples engaged in one other type of economic arrangement that should be mentioned. Individuals granted land, offerings, or services to a temple in exchange for its supplying and maintaining their mortuary cultus.[67]

Priests

In many societies, kingship is the office that, by virtue of degree of legitimate force, exercises the greatest dominance while priesthood is the office that, by virtue of degree of ritual purity, enjoys the highest status.[68] In ancient Egypt, kingship not only exercised the greatest control but also enjoyed the highest status. The king stood at the apex of the juridical and sacerdotal systems. In fact, on the walls of the principal chambers of divine cult complexes the king is the only priest depicted. In the reliefs and accompanying texts, it is the king who builds and consecrates god's house; it is he who each dawn is purified with water, fumigated with incense, purged by natron, dressed, anointed, and equipped with the insignia of royal office.[69] It is he who then prays, brings offerings, and makes sacrifices to god; it is he who intercedes, rejoices, and dances before god; it is he who bathes, purifies, and adorns god. In theory, the king was the sole priest. In reality, there were many vicars of his sacerdotal power.

In theory, all priestly appointments were the king's to make. In reality, he handpicked persons to fill significant posts at major centers like Memphis, Heliopolis, and Thebes, he conferred priesthood on persons he wished to reward, and he bestowed benefices on the wealthy who bartered for them. Otherwise, he delegated the naming of priests to the vizier, a high priest, or a collegium of priests. Then, too, by tolerance of the state, many priests inherited their office from their fathers, who declared the sons to be their deputies and successors. Many times, tension must have arisen between the systems of priesthood by appointment and priesthood by inheritance.

Egypt had no separate priestly class.[70] In the Old and Middle Kingdoms, almost all men of prominence acted as priests several months a year and served elsewhere in the power structure the rest of the time.[71] Because of this, religion and state were intertwined inseparably. And because priests were beholden to the king for both their majority-time civil positions and their minority-time sacred positions, cult complexes wielded little power independent of the king. Full-time priesthood first became widespread in the New Kingdom, but even then the majority of priests served part-time.[72]

Relatively few saw priesthood as their primary role, and few received formal training as ritual specialists.[73] Kings frequently complained about having to instruct priests in forgotten rites.[74]

For many priests the daily beholding of god was a religious experience of continuing awe and wonder. But for some the primary concern was secular: the comfortable life provided by redistributed offerings and land allotments. Texts tell us of a priest who sold holy animals for personal profit (Dynasty 20) and of a struggle for priestly income that led to murder (Dynasty 26).[75] To help guard against corruption, the initiation ceremonies for priests probably included vows to maintain purity and integrity and to obey cultic regulations and ethical principles. Assmann suggests that the forty-two declarations of cultic and moral righteousness spoken by a deceased person before gaining admittance to Osiris's hall of judgment (Book of the Dead, chap. 125) originated in oaths sworn by priests during their initiation.[76] Among the deceased's declarations, pertinently enough, were: "I have not stolen the god's-offerings" and "I have not killed men."[77]

Priestly initiation included, in addition to such vows, purifications, an anointing of hands with oil, and a festal introduction to god.[78] Strict purity regulations for those priests on duty in the temples existed from earliest times; such regulations demarcated the sacred from the secular, preserved order, and fended off chaos.[79] By the Late Period, the requirements included circumcision, shaved heads and bodies, multiple daily lustrations, natron chewing, and linen clothing; and the prohibitions included no sexual intercourse and no eating of proscribed foods (the list of which varied from region to region, god to god, and office to office).[80]

The priestly title *ḥm-nṯr*, Servant of God, occurs from the end of Dynasty 1 onward. The *ḥm-nṯr* prepared offerings, performed rituals, had access to the sanctuary of the divine image, and controlled entrance to the temple. In the Old Kingdom, a local government official was often commissioned as *ḥm-nṯr* and given the task of administering a local divine cult complex, its lands, and its work force.[81] In only a few cases was the position a sinecure.

Some Old Kingdom divine cult complexes with many Servants of God (*ḥmw-nṯr*) had a High Priest or Overseer called *jmj-r3 ḥmw-nṯr*.[82] High priests of the most important temples were often sons or sons-in-law of the king, and several high priests were also Vizier, the king's second-in-command. In Dynasties 4 through 6, the office of High Priest and Overseer of the Estate was sometimes held by more than one person at a time.[83] In a number of temples, the office bore a distinctive title. At Heliopolis, the special title was at first *m33 wr*, One Who Sees the Great. By the end of the Old Kingdom, it was *wr m3w*, Greatest of Seers. The High Priest of Memphis bore the title *wr ḥrp(w) ḥmwt*, Greatest of the Masters of Craftsmen. The principal god of Memphis was Ptah, the god of artisanry; perhaps the High Priest originally directed the craft guilds.[84] Both Ptah and Sokar, another Memphite god, had associations with funerary religion, and the High Priest is also called *Sem*-priest, a title from the mortuary cultus. Like the *Sem*-priest, he wore a sidelock of youth and a panther skin. In addition, he often wore a distinctive necklace, the s^ch, whose pendant was a stylized jackal with human hands. The High Priest of Hermopolis was called *wr djw*, Great One of the Five, for the cultus there focused on Thoth and the four dyads of primeval gods known as the Ogdoad. The High Priest of Bubastis, site of a famous school of medicine, was called *wr zwnw*, Great One of Physicians.

In Old Kingdom royal cult complexes (including sun temples), the *ḥmw-nṯr* were organized into five phyles or companies.[85] Each phyle had two subgroups led by a *shḏ*, Inspector, and each of the ten subgroups served the royal cult complex in rotation for one thirty-day month.[86] Some members of off-duty subgroups farmed the temple estate; others worked in the state bureaucracy and probably assigned retainers to farm in their stead.[87]

Numerous women of the Old Kingdom elite had the title *ḥmt-nṯr*, Servant (f.) of God.[88] Most served the goddesses Hathor or Neith. But some queens were Servant (f.) of a male god like Thoth, and queens and princesses could be Servants (f.) of God (*ḥmwt-nṯr*) in the mortuary cultuses of their deceased husbands and fathers.[89] It is not clear what functions the *ḥmwt-nṯr* performed. The equivalent male title, *ḥmw-nṯr*, is rarely associated with the cultus of Hathor, so perhaps the *ḥmwt-nṯr* of Hathor fulfilled the roles ascribed above to *ḥmw-nṯr*.[90] Even in the Hathor cultus, however, priestesses were under the authority of a man.[91] The *ḥmwt-nṯr* were also associated with music making and with a god's *ḥnr*—usually translated "hareem" but properly "musical troupe."[92] The few depictions extant show the women of the *ḥnr* dancing, singing, and rattling sistrums. The female head of the *ḥnr*, the *wrt-ḥnr*, held a high-ranking position in the temple. She was in charge of musical training and practice and was responsible for the quality of musical performance during rituals. Perhaps she also had authority over male musicians.[93] As Gay Robins says, "The priest who officiated before the deity's statue was a man, but much of the musical accompaniment was provided by women."[94]

The *ḥmw-nṯr*, Servants of God, were assisted by a second category of clergy, the *W^cb*-priests, who performed the lesser tasks requisite to maintaining the temples and rituals. Their leader was called Great *W^cb* (*w^cb ^c3*). *W^cb*-priests handled ritual instruments and cultic objects, so they had to be pure.[95] They were not allowed to enter the sanctuary or to feed themselves in the offering hall, however. They consumed their rations in the zone of tertiary sacredness between the enclosure wall and the temple proper.

From at least Dynasty 5, a $W^c b$-priest could be promoted to hm-ntr at either the same temple or a different one.[96] Women, so far as we know, were not called $W^c bt$-priestess during the Old Kingdom. However, in a few texts they perform $w^c b$-service for Hathor and receive the same compensation as a $W^c b$-priest.[97] The $W^c b$-priests of the goddess Sakhmet may have functioned as doctors.[98] Sakhmet assaulted humanity with illness and disease but also healed humanity from maladies. Egyptians thought of her $W^c b$-priests as immune to her dangers and conductive of her benevolence.

A third category of priest, quite a high one, is met as early as Dynasty 2. It is hrj-$hb(t)$, Lector Priest—the skillful reader who carried the ritual book and recited the formulas of cultic performance.[99] No woman held this title. Perhaps elite and royal women were unable to read, or perhaps their ability went unacknowledged.[100] The distinctive garb of the hrj-$hb(t)$ was a broad band worn diagonally from the shoulder across the breast. The earliest Lector Priests were members of the royal family or highest nobility. The title was claimed by High Priests of Heliopolis and by some Nomarchs and Overseers of Priests, Inspectors of Priests, and Great $W^c bs$.[101] The titles Chief Lector Priest (hrj-$hb[t]$ hrj-tp) and Senior Lector Priest (hrj-$hb[t]$ $smsw$) may have connoted not so much degree of command as length of service.[102]

A number of persons associated with royal cult complexes were called $hntj$-$š$. Most scholars see them as laypersons and translate the term as "tenant landholder." However, Ann Macy Roth, following Paule Posener-Kriéger, finds that in papyri from Abusir (Dynasty 5 and early Dynasty 6) $hntjw$-$š$ perform the same duties as Servants of God, save for particular functions relative to the divine image and transporting offerings to and from the temple.[103] She concludes that hmw-ntr served the deceased king's divine aspect while the $hntjw$-$š$ served his human aspect.

Finally, some priests were not associated with temples. These were the mortuary priests who served cultuses at tombs.[104] The mourning of a father, the preparation and interment of his corpse, and his ongoing mortuary cultus were surrounded by elaborate rituals in which the relationship of the living son to the deceased father was central. In the mythology of Horus and Osiris, son Horus (the living king) acted as mortuary priest for father Osiris (the deceased king); and in the mortuary cultus of the deceased king, his son, the oldest living prince, played a crucial role. In this role, the prince was called *sem*.[105] Sons probably also conducted the earliest burial rites for nonroyal men, but as early as Dynasty 1 the mortuary cultuses for private persons could be conducted by professional mortuary priests.[106] In Dynasty 3, the title *sem* came to be applied to the priest wearing a sidelock of youth and panther skin who played the role of oldest living son in the Opening of the Mouth ceremony and other burial rituals.

Besides the *Sem*-priest, mortuary priests came in many types. Each received the usufruct from part of the cultus's endowment, and both the office and the usufruct could be passed on to a descendant or descendants. The topics of funeral rituals, of mortuary observances not connected to temples or temple festivals, and of the priests who conducted them fall outside the focus of this volume, however, and will not be discussed.

During the Middle Kingdom, few changes occurred in the categories of priest. The civil administrator known as Mayor or Town Governor, *ḥ3tj-ꜥ*, regularly filled the office of High Priest or Overseer of the Servants of God at the local divine cult complex, so government and temple were still closely linked.[107] At Kahun, the government-constructed community that built and maintained the royal cult complex associated with the pyramid of Senwosret II, a papyrus mentions categories of priests and the offering portions assigned to each. The Overseer of the Servants of God received ten portions; the Chief Lector Priest (perhaps the only full-time priest) received six; the month's Lector Priest, four; the month's Regulator of the Phyle (*mtj-n-z3*), three; the month's three Watersprinklers (*jbḥw*), two portions each; the month's two *Wꜥb*-priests for the cultus of the king's statues, two portions each; and the month's Temple Scribe, one and one-third portions.[108]

Servant (f.) of God, *ḥmt-nṯr*, remained a common title into the Middle Kingdom, although its use diminished throughout the period. A few persons had the title *Wꜥbt*-priestess, and women remained essential to the *ḥnr*, the musical troupe. Some in the *ḥnr* bore the title Chantress, *šmꜥt*. Three stelae from early in the period recognize distinctions between priests and priestesses, between male and female singers, and between male and female musicians.[109]

In the early New Kingdom, government and temple were still linked through the joint office of Town Governor and Overseer of the Servants of God. The joint office ended during the reigns of Hatshepsut and Thutmose III (mid-fifteenth century B.C.E.). The High Priest or Overseer came to be a trusted prince, official, or priest who received the office as a benefice and bore the title *ḥm-nṯr tpj*, First Servant (or Prophet) of God. Later in the period, accession to High Priest frequently occurred by divine oracle or family inheritance rather than by royal appointment.[110] The High Priest of Karnak became particularly powerful and independent. His distinctive title was *wn ꜥ3wj(n) pt*, Opener of the Gate of Heaven (that is, opener of the doors of the divine image's shrine).

Overseeing the distribution of offerings to all the temples of the land was the Chief of the Servants of God of Upper and Lower Egypt. From time to time he convened an assembly of representatives from each temple. Assemblies might meet with the king, receive his instructions on matters like royal cultuses and new construction, accompany him on a journey, celebrate the royal jubilee (*Sed*-festival), or discuss problems shared by priests, like revenues and repairs.[111] Until Thutmose IV, the Chief of the Servants of God of Upper and Lower Egypt was the High Priest of Karnak. After that, to counteract the accumulation of priestly power at Thebes, the office went to a government official or to the High Priest of Memphis.[112]

In addition to the First Servant, or High Priest, the chain of command at large New Kingdom temples could include a Second, Third, and even Fourth Servant (or Prophet) of God.[113] All were full-time priests. As a rule, the *ḥmt-nṯr*, Servant (f.) of God, is not found during the New Kingdom. We know of two exceptions, however, and both these women held the prestigious rank Second Servant of God, one in the cultus of Mut and the other, Queen Ahmose-Nefertari, in the cultus of Amun.[114] Ahmose-Nefertari later held the priestly title God's Wife.

The three earliest attestations of God's Wife occur in Dynasties 10 and 12 and denote nonroyal women who served the gods Min, Amun, and Ptah respectively.[115] The first royal God's Wife was Ahmose-Nefertari, who was the daughter, most probably, of Kamose (the last king of Dynasty 17), the wife of Ahmose (the first king of Dynasty 18), and the mother of Amenhotep I. Beginning with her, the title was linked exclusively with the cultus of Amun. The God's Wife who succeeded Ahmose-Nefertari was Hatshepsut, daughter of Thutmose I and wife of Thutmose II. When Hatshepsut herself became king, her daughter, Nefrure, became God's Wife. From Thutmose III through Thutmose IV, the God's Wife was related to the royal family only by marriage. From Amenhotep III to the end of Dynasty 18, the God's Wife was not related to the royal family. Beginning with Aset, the daughter of Ramesses VI (Dynasty 20), the God's Wife was an unmarried daughter of a king or of a High Priest of Karnak. When the Persians conquered Egypt in 525 B.C.E., the office of God's Wife of Amun disappeared for several centuries.[116]

The costume of the God's Wife, including her short wig and thin fillet, was similar to that worn by priestesses in the Middle Kingdom.[117] She could be called *dw3t-nṯr*, Worshiper (f.) of God, a title borne by priestesses of Hathor during the Old Kingdom.[118] In reliefs, she was shown standing alongside male priests and performing priestly functions elsewhere depicted in royal iconography: she purifies herself in the sacred lake, stands before the god, adores him, plays for him her sistrum, presents him *maꜥat*, and calls him to the meal; she marches in procession, conducts foundation rites, burns the image of an enemy in execration rites, and attends the presentation of clothing to Wadjit. In other scenes—types normally associated with the legitimation of a king—gods purify her, crown her, embrace her, suckle her, and offer her life.[119]

The God's Wife was also called God's Hand, a title related, in all probability, to the concept that the Creator had masturbated the gods Shu and
Tefnut into being. Both titles—God's Wife and God's Hand—doubtless
had sexual connotations, but the implications of this for the priestess's ritual role are not clear. Robins conjectures that the God's Wife was somehow
to sexually stimulate the Creator to continue the First Creation so that fertility did not flag and the cosmos did not subside into chaos.[120]

As the First, Second, Third, or Fourth Servant of God officiated at the daily and festival rituals, the Chief Lector Priest, ḥrj-ḥb(t) ḥrj-tp, or, in large
temples, the Second, Third, or Fourth Lector Priest, recited the appropriate
prayers, spells, and incantations. Lector Priests also presided at oracles and
divinations. A third priestly rank was jt-nṯr, Father of God.[121] When the divine image processed through the temple courtyards and into the world
outside the enclosure wall, Fathers of God marched in front, sprinkling the
route with purifying water.[122] They also functioned as temple craftsmen.
A fourth rank was Wˤb-priest. In the New Kingdom, these priests were divided into four phyles that rotated in month-long terms of service. Wˤb-
priests carried the divine image during processions. Some also functioned
as horologists, fixing the time for the daily rites and the festivals by studying the stars.[123] Tomb biographies of officials who served as Wˤb-priests in
their youth suggest that such priests graduated from temple schools.[124]
When not on monthly duty, Wˤb-priests filled administrative positions in
the temple. Some, along with other off-duty New Kingdom priests, distinguished themselves from nonpriestly administrators by wearing no wig
(thereby displaying their shaved heads) and by wearing simple, old-fashioned clothing.[125] These fashions spread widely among off-duty priests in
the Late Period.[126]

The title Wˤbt-priestess is not used in extant New Kingdom materials,
but most wives of Wˤb-priests served as temple singers and sistrum play-
ers. The women, like their husbands, were organized into phyles for
month-long service. To supervise them was a prerogative of the High
Priest's wife.[127]

A special category of New Kingdom priest tended the mortuary statues
of deceased kings and their families in both the royal and divine cult complexes. This was the ḥnk, Supplier.[128]

Statistics from Dynasty 19 give some sense of the various sizes of New
Kingdom divine cult complexes, the various numbers of their personnel,
and the various scales of their economies. On the one hand, the temple of
Anubis at Faiyum had six permanent priests and four phyles with eleven
part-time personnel each.[129] On the other hand, the three largest divine
cult complexes in the time of Ramesses III were of much greater scale:[130]

	Karnak	Heliopolis	Memphis
Male personnel	81,322	12,963	3,079
Beasts	421,362	45,544	10,047
Fields	924 sq. miles	170 sq. miles	11 sq. miles
Gardens	433	64	5
Market towns	65	103	1
Work yards	46	5	–
Boats	83	3	2

During the Third Intermediate Period (Dynasties 21–25) and the Late Period (Dynasties 25–30), the categories of priests remained basically the same—Servant of God (ḥm-nṯr), Lector Priest (ḫrj-ḥbt), Father of God (jt-nṯr), and Wʿb-priest—and the priestly purity regulations reached their zenith. During Dynasty 21, the High Priest of Amun at Karnak became the virtual governor of southern Egypt, and a royal woman, Henut-tawy, held two revived priestly titles: ḥmt-nṯr, Servant (f.) of God (in the cultuses of Mut and Onuris-Shu), and dw3t-ḥtḥr, Worshiper (f.) of Hathor. In Dynasty 22, queens and princesses were called God's Mother of Khonsu or similar titles, and kings sought to regain control of Thebes by installing their sons as the High Priest of Amun.[131] The latter did not work well, for several sons used the office as a base for rebelling against their fathers and establishing collateral dynasties. A civil war erupted, and the resultant disintegration and weakness led to a division of power: Dynasty 22 retained control of the Delta, and Dynasty 23 struggled against various descendants of the royal High Priests of Amun for control of Thebes. When the kings of Dynasty 23 succeeded in their struggle, they suspended the office of High Priest of Amun and installed as chief priest of Thebes the God's Wife of Amun. The perpetual celibacy of this unmarried daughter of the king assured that no rival collateral line would trouble him or his successors.[132] In Dynasty 25, the title ḥmt-nṯr ḥtḥr, Servant (f.) of the God Hathor, was revived, as was the office of First Servant of the God Amun at Karnak.[133] The latter office was filled uniquely by a woman, however—the heir-apparent to the supreme rank of God's Wife.[134] Dynasty 26 fostered a return to the past and revived a number of priestly categories and titles from the Old Kingdom.[135] The Persian invasion of 525 B.C.E. ended this dynasty, and the offices of God's Wife of Amun and High Priest of Amun temporarily disappeared. The latter was revived sometime during Dynasties 28 to 30; Dynasty 30 renewed the archaizing trend begun by Dynasty 26.

As for the staffing of individual temples in the Third Intermediate Period and Late Period, the larger temples, beginning in Dynasty 22, added part-time Servants of God to assist the full-time First through Fourth Servants of God. The additional ḥmw-nṯr were, like the lower ranks of priests, organized into phyles for month-long service, and the Old and Middle

Kingdom office of *mtj-n-z3*, Regulator of the Phyle, reappears. Priests continued to receive payment in kind for their services, that is, land allotments from the temple estates (which were then leased to tenants for a portion of the crop) and daily rations of bread, beer, geese, and beef. The allotments and rations of part-time priests were small, so they supported themselves by accumulating positions at several temples. For the most part priests passed on their posts to descendants, but sometimes the appearance that priestly office was granted by royal appointment was maintained. In time, the installation of priests was put in the hands of the council of priests.[136]

Smaller temples were often staffed by one Servant of God and four small phyles of *W^cb*-priests—for example, the temple of Amun-Re at Teuzoi, whose phyles had twenty men each. Teuzoi's income of emmer wheat was divided into one hundred rations. The Servant of God received twenty, and each of the eighty *W^cb*-priests received one.[137]

A rich and diverse body of evidence exists for priesthood in the Ptolemaic Period—hieroglyphic texts, numerous demotic texts, and, for the first time, Greek papyri. Only rarely, however, does the content of all three types intersect.[138] Hieroglyphic texts offer remarkably lengthy priestly titles, demotic scribes mention only principal titles, and Greek papyri use Greek titles without indicating the corresponding Egyptian terms. Egyptian and Greek equivalents are therefore difficult to determine, but the following links can be made. *Prophḗtēs* (Prophet) was the highest rank among the *ḥmw-nṯr*, Servants of God, and included the High Priest and other senior leaders of the temple. The *(Hiero)stolistḗs* (Dresser [of the Sacred]) was apparently a Servant of God who tended and clothed the divine statue in the holy of holies and assisted the Prophets. A priest who was *Hierogrammateús* (Scribe of the Sacred) was a Servant of God responsible, as the title suggests, for temple education, writing, and bookkeeping. The best-known Scribes of the Sacred are Manetho and Chaeremon. The *Pterophórās* (Wing-wearer) was a *ḥrj-ḥbt*, Lector Priest, who recited the liturgies while adorned by a head band with ostrich feathers. The *Hōrológos* (Time-teller) was a priest-astronomer who fixed the times of ritual celebrations by studying the stars; he probably belonged to the category *W^cb*-priest. The *Pastophóros* (Shrine-bearer) was a *W^cb*-priest who bore sacred objects in processions.

During the Ptolemaic Period, the high-level priests were full-time personnel, but part-time service was common in the lower ranks of the clergy and in the smaller temples and necropolises. In 238 B.C.E., Ptolemy III Euergetes added a fifth phyle of priests, leading to a major reorganization of priestly schedules and, in some temples, to the addition of a Fifth Prophet.[139] Because income from the temples and funerary chapels was a major source of disposable wealth, priests often accumulated positions.[140] For example, a Lector Priest of the necropolis of Siut had two other jobs and incomes: a quarter-time job and income as Lector Priest of the nearby necropolis of Shashotep and a twelfth-time job and income as Scribe of the Divine Books of the necropolis of Siut. He bequeathed to his sons the three jobs, daily food rations from two temples, and monthly meat and oil rations.[141]

The succession to office among the high clergy was now always heredi-tary, and it was regularly so among other priests. Because of the hereditary principle and the relatively early age of death in the ancient world, some successors to important priestly positions were quite young. Psenptais III was fourteen years old when he became High Priest of Ptah at Memphis in 76 B.C.E., and the son who succeeded him in 39 B.C.E. was only seven years old.[142] The High Priest of Ptah at Memphis was the most prominent cleric in Egypt during the Ptolemaic Period, and it was he who placed the dou-ble crown of Upper and Lower Egypt on the monarch's head.[143] Doubtless it was also he who convened and presided over the priestly synods that met for up to four months at a time.

Women priests had some prominence in the Ptolemaic Period. At Thebes, the office of God's Wife of Amun was renewed, and in other cul-tuses a senior woman was identified as the god's consort, protectress, or mother.[144] The wives of the High Priests of Memphis were prominent priestesses whose lives and families were recorded in funerary stelae.[145] Several women were given the priestly title $w^c bt$ or $w^c bt \, hmt$; they were per-haps temple musicians. In any event, female singers and musicians con-tinued to play essential roles in the cultus.

About priests in the Roman Period we have sparse information. Rome exercised strict control over Egyptian temples through newly developed institutions, and data about the indigenous Egyptian clergy are fragmen-tary.[146]

Rituals

Ritual is central to religion, but there are differing explanations of what it is, what it does, and how it works. I present my understanding of these matters before describing specific ancient Egyptian rituals.[147]

- Ritual is action or practice, not thought; it is deed, not just indirect com-munication. Ritual may incorporate thought, but within participants it generates consent to actions more than belief in concepts.[148]
- In ritual performance, authority is vested in the office of the officiant, rather than in his or her person.[149]
- Ritual is so contextualized and situational that similar practices in dif-ferent cultures probably do not have the same meanings.[150] Indeed, two

performances of the same ritual within the same culture—even at the same location—are not identical, no matter how rigidly the ritual is prescribed or how minutely it is choreographed. Details of participation, setting, stimuli, and enactment vary, and meanings fluctuate accordingly.[151]

• Ritual engages the right hemisphere of the brain—associated with visual-spatial relationships and holistic, nonverbal perceptions—more than the left hemisphere—associated with analytic thought and discrete, verbal perceptions. Ritual's primary mode of consciousness reinforces (and perhaps underlies) the unity and solidarity that its participants experience.[152]

• Ritual treats the outer limits of our "zone of uncertainty," where we confront "direct, experiential evidence of the essentially transcendental quality of our being and our world," the "mysteries of death, pestilence, catastrophe, change, fertility, birth, growth, origin, failed expectations, and the like."[153]

• However, ritual is not *primarily* a catharsis for unresolved personal or societal neuroses (pace Sigmund Freud and René Girard) nor *primarily* a source of psychological security in the midst of a dangerous world (pace Bronislaw Malinowski)—although ritual may provide catharsis and security.[154]

• Ritual starts with an ordinary event (like a bath or a meal) and changes various of its components (like the size, place, or timing of the gathering, the quality or quantity of the elements, and the intensity, formality, or routineness of the experience), thereby distinguishing the ritual event from mundane events and privileging it as sacred. A ritual event is best observed against the backdrop of mundane events, discerning "what it echoes, what it inverts, what it alludes to, what it denies."[155]

• The smallest unit of ritual is the symbol. A symbol may relate to an object, activity, need, relationship, dynamic, word, value, norm, belief, gesture, time, place, or configuration.[156]

• A ritual symbol typifies, represents, or recalls something other than itself through some corresponding trait(s)—such as an analogous quality (white/cleanness), a natural association (blue/sky), a mental link (fish/Christianity), or a cultural convention (in Belgium: chrysanthemums/funerals; in the United States: chrysanthemums/college homecomings).[157] Most symbols are specific to their culture, but some are widely shared, perhaps because their analogous quality or natural association is commonly perceived.

• Ritual is suffused by creative tension between clarity and opacity, order and chaos. Its actions are, for the most part, choreographed and describable, but its symbols are open, supple, multivalent, indirect, and variously apprehended. Participants perform the same ritual actions without necessarily experiencing, inferring, affirming, or consenting to the same things.[158]

- Ritual symbols have manifest meanings (of which the subject is fully conscious), latent meanings (of which the subject is marginally conscious), and hidden meanings (of which the subject is not conscious). They also have exegetic meanings (the tenor attributed to them), operational meanings (the meaning derived from their use and ritual context), and positional meanings (their place within the gestalt of symbols). Outside interpreters can learn parts of these meanings from the oral and written testimonies of indigenous interpreters (insofar as they are available); and they can infer parts of these meanings from the symbols' characteristics, associations, and contexts (symbolic, linguistic, material, cultural, conceptual, and actional).[159]

- Ritual symbols are infused with the sacred. They elicit profound emotions, moods, and motivations; they instigate important actions.[160]

- Ritual symbolism images the cosmos. It also indexes the social hierarchy, communicating rank and privilege through elements like place, duration, richness of materials, number of officiants, and level of participation.[161]

- Ritual *is* power, not simply an instrument of power.[162] Ritual legitimates the social order, but first it generates and shapes that order. Ritual does so by assertion, not force, by negotiation, not compulsion. Ritual effects social change as well as social conformity.[163]

- Ritual, as power, comprises techniques and practices that direct people's actions without compelling them. It embodies relationships of power; it places its participants in the order of things and gives them a sense of efficacy within it. Ritual offers a "redemptive hegemony," an ordering of power, a pattern of dominance and subjugation, of constraint and possibility, that strengthens people to act—willingly, self-interestedly, effectively—within the perceived system.[164]

- In accomplishing this, ritual sets up binary oppositions—e.g., *(a)* light/dark, *(b)* good/evil, *(c)* order/chaos, *(d)* life/death, *(e)* corporate/individual, *(f)* convened/dispersed, *(g)* higher/lower, and *(h)* inner/outer. Ritual does *not*, in the end, resolve these oppositions.[165] Instead, it maintains and multiplies them, configuring them into a loosely integrated whole with its own hierarchy of dominance and influence— e.g., from highest to lowest, "*(c), (d), (b), (a), (g), (h), (e), (f)*." Ritual privileges one side of the oppositions and forms a taxonomy—e.g., order-life-good-light-higher-inner-corporate-convened. By invoking several elements of the taxonomy—e.g., order and inner—it can imply the others.[166] The ritual environment of privileged oppositions, with its numerous symbols and congruent activities, produces ritualized bodies—

both individual and group—that have internalized the environment's principles. These bodies are empowered to move appropriately—both inside the ritual context and outside it, within the world of shifting power relationships—between the poles of adherence and resistance, subscription and obstinacy, subordination and insubordination. Insofar as the bodies are resistant, obstinate, or insubordinate, they structure, circularly, a new ritual environment with an adjusted set of symbols and activities, which proceeds to reconfigure, circularly, the ritualized bodies that structured it; and the cycle goes on. Ritual does all of this without seeing what it is doing and "without bringing what it is doing across the threshold of discourse or systematic thinking."[167]

- Ritual is an arena for revising tradition while seeming to perpetuate it. An otherwise traditional performance can challenge, renegotiate, or replace part of the existing order by altering some elements within itself: a participant, an action, a setting, a symbol, an opposition, a hierarchy, a material, a quantity, a route, a rubric. Tradition survives through revision in ritual; indeed, it thrives on it.[158]
- Rituals have life spans. "They surge and subside. . . ." They "deteriorate" and "must be raised up constantly from the grave of book, body, memory, and culture."[169]

The stability and cohesiveness that Egypt enjoyed for most of its three thousand years resulted to a significant degree from the effectiveness of rituals at its temples and tombs. In rituals, the sacred was contacted, the three realms were integrated, power was ordered, and the social hierarchy was negotiated without forced compliance and usually without overt opposition. Rituals were not the king's instrument for imposing social solidarity or belief; they were a dynamic, creative arena in which social solidarity was experienced and social consent was generated.[170] Rituals were more than an instrument of the king's power for legitimating his position and controlling people's experience of the worlds; rituals were themselves a form of power that permitted and facilitated the revision and renewal of relationships between the gods, the king, the dead, and the living, a form of power that permitted and drew strength from the ebb and flow of the parties' adherence and resistance, subscription and obstinacy, subordination and insubordination.[171] Many of Egypt's officials were part-time priests. Inside the temple their bodies were ritualized; outside the temple they interacted with the world. Influenced by outside experiences, the priest-officials renegotiated the rites and relationships of power inside the temple. The renegotiated rites and relationships then re-ritualized the priest-officials' bodies, and the cycle began anew. Through ritual power, changes in the relative strength of king, nomarchs, nobility, priests, artisans, and peasants were worked out.[172] Through ritual power, shifts in the balance of the king's "divinity" and "humanity" were accommodated. Through ritual power, alterations in the ranking of the gods were effected. Through ritual power, access to the next world and integration into it were handled both for the king and for a progressively larger percentage of the people. In short, through ritual power, Egypt was able to change while remaining the same.[173]

Rituals were intrinsic to the temple's daily services and periodic festivals.[174] Egyptians came to believe that ritual regulations and formulas had been established by the gods and that Thoth was the overseer of their implementation and proper use.[175] Daily offerings were presented at both divine and royal cult complexes from at least the Old Kingdom onward.[176] Illustrations of the morning ritual at divine cult complexes become numerous from the New Kingdom onward.[177] For the morning ritual, Winfried Barta reconstructs the following sequence:[178]

1. Before sunrise the king, or the priest officiating in his stead, bathes in the sacred pool (or in water drawn from it), receives a censing, and chews natron. After these purifications, he vests and equips himself and consecrates the gifts that lie prepared in the Hall of Offerings. At sunrise he enters the sanctuary, lights a torch to dispel the darkness, and censes the chamber.[179]
2. The king/priest mounts the platform of the shrine of the divine image, breaks its seals, slides its bolt, and opens its doors.
3. He unveils the face of the divine image, and the deity comes into appearance, into view—a high point of the ritual.
4. Seized by awe and dread, the king/priest prostrates himself before the image and kisses the earth.
5. He intones a hymn of greeting and adoration, circumambulates and censes the god, and offers myrrh, fragrant oil, and a figure of the goddess Maʿat.
6. The king/priest places the divine image on the ground atop pure, freshly strewn sand, and he purifies the empty shrine.
7. After embracing the god as a sign of close communion, the king/priest removes the oils, cosmetics, and clothing used to adorn the image the previous morning and purifies the god with incense and water.
8. The king/priest dresses the deity with a head-band and cloths of linen—white, blue, green, and red.
9. He ornaments the god with neck collar, pectoral, and insignia of divinity—another high point of the ritual.
10. He anoints the god with oils, applies green and black eye make-ups, and dresses the god in an outer garment.
11. The king/priest again strews the floor with pure sand, circumambulates the statue, censes it, and further purifies it with water and various kinds

of natron. He returns the god to the shrine and then, with libations and censings of incense and myrrh, purifies the trays of food and other offerings that represent the tablefuls standing outside the sanctuary in the Hall of Offerings.[180] He invites the god to receive the gifts and recites the offering list and formulae, placing each item on the altar individually. Then he presents the god with the *ankh- ('nḫ-)* signs and *ib*-heart, symbolizing the transfer of life force from the food to the god. He pays the god homage, intones hymns, and closes and seals the doors of the shrine. The food is removed for distribution.

12. The king/priest brushes away all footprints, extinguishes the torch, and closes the sanctuary doors until the next morning.[181]

The daily gifts to the gods listed on temple walls were diverse.[182] They included "bread of different kinds; several qualities of beer of different strength; meat of . . . oxen and cows, . . . goats, gazelles, antelopes; birds of different species like geese and water fowls; fruits like dates, grapes, figs, pomegranates; vegetables especially onions, garlic, leek; honey; milk and wine; grease, oil, perfumes, and incense; lamps and wicks; wax, salt; natron; cloth; jewellery and royal insignia."[183] The offerings arrived at the temple as "taxes" paid to the state, as donations from royal or private persons, or as produce from royal or temple estates and enterprises.

Most offerings expressed the thanksgiving of the king and all Egypt for the god's past bounty: *do quia dedisti,* "I give because You have given." They also expressed the petition of the king and all Egypt for the god's ongoing, future gifts of life and order: *do ut des,* "I give so that You may (continue to) give."[184] The god's gifts included life breath, light, air, nourishment, succor, freedom, security, and life in the next world.[185] Compared to these, any human offering of gratitude, no matter how grand, was small indeed; yet the king and Egypt desired that their gifts should bring god happiness and encourage god's continuing benevolence. The latter desire, of course, moved the wheel of motivation from thanksgiving to petition, from *do quia dedisti* to *do ut des.*

Most offerings symbolized the very things the king and Egypt sought in return for them—life, stability, prosperity, health, joy, food, and, in the case of the king, sovereignty, divine status, and millions of years.[186] In short, most offerings symbolized life and order. In fact, they *were* life and order. Here we encounter the rich multivalence of rituals and symbols. Offerings symbolized life (*'nḫ, ankh*) and order (*m3't, ma'at*); they were life and order; and as life and order they were consubstantial with god.[187]

Offerings, as *ankh,* were consubstantial with god. That such a large proportion of them consisted of food makes their link to life force clear. Texts speak of the animal's thigh and heart as awakening life and transmitting life force to the god.[188] Such texts help us understand the symbolism of presenting the *ankh*-signs and *ib*-heart to god during the offering ritual. A god was not immortal in the absolute sense; a god's life force needed replenishment.[189] Of course, the life force that was returned to god in offerings had previously come from god, the source of life force. Thus offerings to god were consubstantial with god.[190] The circular flow of life from god to king/Egypt to god and back again prevented the cosmos from winding down. Offerings were more than gift giving; they were reciprocal creation. From the Old Kingdom onward, Egyptians used a symbol from the royal mythology of Horus, Seth, and Osiris to describe this mystery; they called offerings the Eye of Horus.[191] Osiris, slain by his brother Seth, was brought back to life by his son Horus, who presented his eye to Osiris as an offering meal—the eye being, in the complicated way of myth, both Horus's body part and Osiris's daughter![192] Thus Osiris was revived by consuming the part of his son that was his daughter; in other words, he was revived by consuming his own substance.

Offerings, as *ma'at*, were consubstantial with god. Like all symbols, the Eye of Horus was multivalent. It represented life; it also represented order. It was the eye snatched away by Seth, restored to wholeness by Thoth, and returned to Horus (who then offered it to Osiris); it was reestablished order, sound and perfect again.[193] Offerings were repeatedly called *ma'at* or symbolized by the image of Ma'at, daughter of the Creator and sister of the king.[194] *Ma'at* was a gift of god's self through acts of creation, an image of offerings' consubstantiality with god, an image of order's circular flow from god to king/Egypt to god and back. As noted before, offerings were more than gift giving; they were reciprocal creation. They were the king and Egypt acting with god to prevent the cosmos's return to chaos.[195]

Most offerings symbolized and were a part of the self of god; most offerings also symbolized and were a part of the selves of the donor and the officiant.[196] Offerings symbolized the donor and the donor's desire to bridge the worlds of god and humankind.[197] But more than that, as Marcel Mauss has observed, "to give something is to give a part of oneself. . . . [O]ne gives away what is in reality a part of one's nature and substance. . . . "[198] That many offerings to god presented the donor's self is shown by the Instruction for Merikare (lines 128–29):

> The loaf of the upright is preferred
> To the ox of the evildoer.[199]

That many offerings to god presented the officiant's self is shown by the frequent practice of offering not the material object itself but its model or name.[200] In temple offering reliefs, the king is omnipresent as both donor and officiant. Sometimes he presents a statue of himself.[201] Sometimes he presents his name, an inseparable part of his identity.[202] What clearer representations of the offering as the self of the donor and self of the officiant could there be? The scene of royal name offering is typical of those Ramesside kings having the word *maʿat* in their prenomen—like Ramesses II: User-Maʾat-Reʿ, "The *Maʿat*-order of Re Is Powerful."[203] The king, the recipient of the Creator's daughter-*maʿat*, offers part of his self, which is also part of god's self, in a reciprocal act of creation.

Not all Egyptian offerings represented life and order. Rituals establish binary oppositions, so some offerings represented death and disorder. Animals like the goose, gazelle, and goat could symbolize confusion and disorder. To help rid the land of chaos, they or their representations were sacrificed, sometimes as wholly burnt offerings (frequently so from the Late Period onward).[204] Such sacrifices were ritual enactments of the apotropaic scenes of hunting and battle carved on many temple walls.[205]

The huge majority of offerings were not consumed in fire but were circulated. They provisioned the priests of the temple's principal god, the gods and priests of the subsidiary cultuses, the royal and private statues in the temple area and their attendants, and (especially during the great festivals) private mortuary cultuses outside the temple.[206] The distributed wealth of the ritual offerings reinforced the prosperity of the upper classes, most of whose families were connected to priesthood; and both the sequence of the distributions and the portions assigned indexed the families' rank and honor.[207] But there must have been religious as well as socioeconomic meaning to partaking of god's food, particularly since the food symbolized life, order, the self of god, and the selves of donor and officiant. Those Egyptians sharing in the food must have experienced a sense of privileged communion with god and king that shaped their ritualized bodies and enhanced their feelings of unity, efficacy, and power.[208]

Temple rituals were integral not only to daily services but also to festival observances (*ḥbw*). Festivals arose from an astronomical, agricultural, mythological, or political phenomenon. Some were observed monthly; most were held annually; a few were celebrated at longer intervals or irregularly.[209] Some festivals were observed transregionally at a number of temples—usually in localized forms and often at differing times based on local astronomical sightings or calendars. Some were observed by two or more temples together, celebrating a connection between their gods.[210] But most were observed at a single temple. Some festivals, called *ḥbw nw pt*, were celebrated according to the astronomically determined sidereal calendar or according to the phases of the moon.[211] The great majority, called *ḥbw tp trw*, were celebrated according to the calendar of three four-month seasons—Inundation (*3ḫt*), Emergence (*prt*), and Harvest (*šmw*).[212]

Some of the principal transregional *ḥbw tp trw* were, in calendar order:

- First Month of Inundation: Opening the Year (New Year's Day); the *W3g-*festival, associated with Osiris, the constellation Orion, and mortuary feasts; the Festival of Thoth; and the Festival of Intoxication, associated with Hathor[213]
- Second Month of Inundation: the *Opet*-festival[214]
- Fourth Month of Inundation: the Festival of Hathor, involving boat processions and visits to the cult complexes of deceased kings; the Festival of Sokar, a great procession by sledge and boat—including visits by Sokar, god of the necropolis, to royal cult complexes—which was the centerpiece of an eleven- to thirteen-day series of festivals and, in the Ptolemaic Period, became linked to Osiris festivals celebrated at Abydos[215]
- First Month of Emergence: on the first day, the Festival of *nḥb-k3w,* which came to be observed in the New Kingdom and later as the First Day of the Year *(tpj rnpt);* at the end of the month and into the next, boat processions of various gods
- First Month of Harvest: the Festival of the Departure of Min, wherein the king led the fertility god Min, a white bull, and statues of deceased kings to a threshing floor, then circumnavigated the floor, released a pigeon or goose on all four sides, cut up a sheaf of grain, and offered the grain to Min[216]
- The Five Extra Days: successive day-long celebrations of the births of Osiris, Horus, Seth, Isis, and Nephthys; various apotropaic rites (the days were considered unlucky)

A few of the most significant local festivals were, in calendar order:

- First Month of Inundation: at Abydos, the Great Departure, an Osiris festival which along with other Abydene mortuary festivals later influenced the transregional Sokar rites of the Fourth Month of Inundation, refocusing them on Osiris
- First Month of Emergence: at Edfu, the Festival of the Coronation of the Sacred Falcon[217]
- Second Month of Emergence: at Edfu, the Festival of Victory[218]
- Second Month of Harvest: at Thebes, the Beautiful Festival of the Valley[219]
- Third Month of Harvest: at Edfu and Dendera, the Festival of the Reunion *(ḥb n sḫn)*[220]

Among the royal festivals were Ascension to the Throne and Coronation, Birth of the God-King, Temple Founding, Running about of the Apis Bull (symbolizing the king's powers of fertility), White Hippopotamus Hunt, and Climbing for Min. From the Early Dynastic Period probably until at least the reign of Senwosret I (Dynasty 12), there was a Festival of the Followers of Horus, a biennial convocation of gods and king at tax-collection time.[221] Numerous local festivals developed for individually divinized deceased kings such as Mentuhotep Nebhepetre (Dynasty 11), Senwosret II (Dynasty 12), and Amenhotep I (Dynasty 18).[222] And then there was the *Sed*-festival, wherein the king's divine powers were renewed and regenerated amid an assembly of gods and priests.[223]

The rituals of the *Sed*-festival originated in predynastic times and were celebrated throughout Egyptian history. Typically, a king first observed the festival after thirty years of rule and then triennially; however, a number of kings followed an idiosyncratic pattern. Elements of the rituals are known, but their exact sequence and content are a mystery (which the kings intended) and a topic of scholarly debate (which the kings did not intend). The central episode of the festival was the ritual death and rebirth of the king.[224] Many scholars suppose that in prehistorical times a king whose powers had waned was put to death and replaced by a strong young successor whose vigor had been proven through some test, perhaps a hunt. But in the historical periods, the death of the king was always figurative, symbolized by his temporary disappearance or by the burial of his *ka*-statue.[225] When the king reappeared, he demonstrated that his reinvigorated self was fit by running three or four laps of a ceremonial course.[226] He was escorted to the double throne, which was set between two rows of shrines, one for the gods of Upper Egypt and one for the gods of Lower Egypt.[227] There he was crowned King of Upper and Lower Egypt. The courtiers swore allegiance to him, and the gods blessed him.[228] The king gave offerings to the gods. He visited the chapels of Horus and Seth and received four arrows of victory. To ward off enemies, one arrow was shot toward each cardinal point.

In theory, the king led all festival celebrations. In fact, someone else presided at most nonroyal festivals. From the Middle Kingdom onward, the king honored high state officials by appointing them festival leaders.[229] Festival offerings were larger and more elaborate than those of the daily cultus, which permitted the provisioning of greater numbers of people.[230]

Most festivals featured a joyful procession of god. The enshrined image was mounted on a barque borne by priests, or sometimes on a sledge. It was enveloped in incense and accompanied by dancers, singers, and instrumentalists. The procession started from the sanctuary of the temple and followed a route to the roof or the inner and outer courts. Often the route then went outside the temple. Barque stations stood along the way—for example, in a forecourt, at points along the outside road, and at a quay.

At such stations, rest was taken, rites and offerings were performed, and mythological scenes were sometimes dramatized. In most processions, the populace could glimpse the shrine. In many, they could address questions for oracular reply to the god who was within.[231]

A New Kingdom hymn to Amun captures the colorful scene of gods, priests, and people on a festival day:

> [Amun] has founded the two lands in their place,
> the temples and the sanctuaries.
> Every city is under his shadow,
> so that his heart can move in that which he has loved.
> People sing to him under every roof,
> every foundation stands firm under his love.
> They brew for him on festival days,
> they pass the night still wakeful at midnight.
> His name is passed around above the roofs,
> song is made to him at night, when it is dark.
> The gods receive sacrificial bread through his life-giving power,
> the power of the strong god who protects what is theirs.[232]

A Glance Forward

The chapters that follow treat both specific examples of the great temples of ancient Egyptian state religion and specific problems in studying them. Chapters 2 and 3 focus on royal cult complexes in the Old and Middle Kingdoms and in the New Kingdom.[233] Chapters 4 and 5 focus on divine cult complexes in the New Kingdom and in the Ptolemaic and Roman Periods.[234] The coverage is broad but, given the limitations of space, not exhaustive.

Dieter Arnold argues that the royal cult complexes of the Old and Middle Kingdoms played a key role in the king's deification, both through the rituals performed there (notably the *Sed*-festival and royal *ka*-statue rites) and through the everlasting symbolic architecture erected there (notably the artistic and structural recollections of the archaic "fortress of the gods," where the king and the gods called "Followers of Horus" gathered to enact the *Sed*-festival and to seal their contract of mutual support). Arnold describes the architectural development of the royal cult complexes from Dynasties 1 through 12 and links the changes in their composition, size, style, and orientation to shifts in religious roles, concepts, and emphases (notably those related to the increasing prominence and power of the sun god Re) and to local traditions. Arnold observes that aboveground royal funerary architecture was first decorated with relief scenes in Sneferu's Bent Pyramid (Dynasty 4), that a mortuary cultus section, as distinct from a statue sanctuary, first appeared in the pyramid temple in Dynasty 5, that valley and pyramid temples were never sites of burial rites, and that the royal cult complex of Mentuhotep Nebhepetre at Deir el-Bahri (Dynasty 11) offers the first evidence of a joint cultus for king and god (Amun-Re).

As evidenced by architectural plans, decorative motifs, and priestly titles, a joint cultus for the king and god(s)—most often, Amun-Re, but sometimes Osiris or Ptah—was a main feature of the New Kingdom royal cult complexes studied by Gerhard Haeny. Relief scenes in several temples depict a formal, mystic union of king and god that was expected to endure for millions of years. Indeed, many royal cult complexes were called "Mansions of Millions of Years."[235] New Kingdom royal cult complexes perpetuated earlier associations with the king's claim to divinity, ka-statue rites, and festal celebrations (here, the Feast of the Valley and the *Opet*-festival). Under the influence of political and regional circumstances, developments in religion, and the Egyptian predilection for expressing the same in differing forms, Mansions of Millions of Years varied greatly in architectural plan and decoration. They also were built on both the west and east banks of the Nile. Haeny believes that the origin of Mansions of Millions of Years lay in the ka-statue chapels of earlier times, places where gods offered the king a life of millions of years in return for his offerings to them and where the king, during that eternity, expected to receive, greet, and commune with various gods-in-procession.

Lanny Bell treats New Kingdom divine cult complexes, focusing on one that was also called a Mansion of Millions of Years—the Luxor Temple. Bell describes its construction, decoration, functions, and rites and its relationships with other temples. Bell also presents a detailed discussion of divine kingship and the royal *ka*, concepts intrinsic both to his chapter and to Chapters 2 and 3. He describes the royal *ka* as the immortal creative spirit of divine kingship, the divine aspect of a mortal king. Bell elaborates on two celebrations prominent in Chapter 3 as well—the Festival of the Valley, which was both a state festival for reintegrating kings and the national god and a family festival for strengthening the bonds between people and their deceased ancestors; and the *Opet*-festival, Luxor Temple's principal celebration, in which the Creator was regenerated the national god was reborn, the king was identified with the royal *ka* and bestowed with Amun-Re's powers, and order was re-created. During the *Opet*-festival, common people were admitted to parts of Luxor Temple to see the miraculous effects both of the rites they could witness and of those they could not; during the rest of the year, they were admitted to parts of the temple to supplicate the gods and receive oracular advice. In appendices, Bell discusses Luxor Temple during the reign of the heretic king, Akhenaten, and describes various life-bestowing ritual objects.

Ragnhild Bjerre Finnestad discusses the divine cult complexes of ancient Egypt's last six hundred years, temples richly reflective of pharaonic tradition despite their late date and Greek and Roman patronage. Texts on their walls express much more explicitly than do earlier temples the structures' religious meanings. The temple symbolized the world of Egypt and the world of the gods, a cosmos embodying the Creator and unfolding as pantheon. It was the living form of the Creator, the Creator's cultic body. Its combination of solar and mortuary aspects symbolized the reciprocal states of life and death in a world of repeating transformations. Finnestad also describes the temples' major rituals—for example, the daily morning ceremony, in which coming-into-being attended the seeing, appearing, and coming-out of god, as the world took form in god's light; and the Coronation of the Sacred Falcon at Edfu, in which the king was fused with Horus, and kingship was integrated into divine cultus. Finnestad goes on to discuss the temples' vital roles in land utilization and in transmitting to society-at-large a comprehensive and normative body of knowledge for understanding the world and conducting life. Finally, she considers the old cultuses' new social contexts and finds that in the Ptolemaic and Roman Periods ordinary Egyptians had the opportunity for a variety of contacts with temples and shared the major tenets of the worldview they presented.

2

ROYAL CULT COMPLEXES OF THE OLD AND MIDDLE KINGDOMS

DIETER ARNOLD

The meaning of the buildings in the royal cult complexes of the Old and Middle Kingdoms is so multilayered that it cannot be accurately expressed by the conventional term "mortuary temple," which captures but one aspect of the much larger whole. The overall architectural program of the complex not only provided a burial place for the king but more importantly supplied a framework for the rites that transformed the human and mortal king into an immortal and divine being.[1] The king's supernatural powers could range from mere magical capabilities to divine kingship and union with the gods.[2] His transformation could be achieved by complicated rituals like the *Sed*-festival, or it could be set in motion by erecting everlasting symbolic architecture that guaranteed the continuity of the king's divine rule.[3]

In principle, all Egyptian temples contributed to the deification of the pharaoh. The complexes surrounding the royal burial were especially suited to this purpose, because their connection to the royal tomb opened the gates into another world and addressed eternity. One should not forget, however, that the accommodation of the king's burial was not the prima-

The author owes important contributions to discussions with Gerhard Haeny, James Allen, and especially Felix Arnold on the *Sed*-festival rituals, the chapels of the gods, the presentation of palm leaves, and the Mansions of Millions of Years. The author is very grateful to Adela Oppenheim for numerous suggestions concerning the content and form, and to Byron E. Shafer for editing the manuscript.

ry reason for the construction of a royal funerary complex. On the contrary, the royal burial needed a cult complex because of the important role played by the buildings in the process of the king's deification.

The priests and builders of the cult complexes drew upon the rich repertoire of forms developed in archaic Upper Egypt and the Delta and refined by the sophisticated schools of Heliopolis and Memphis, allowing a considerable variety of frameworks. Older monuments that were still standing remained an important source of information and were frequently visited and studied by priests and scribes. This tendency to search for old prototypes meant that once architectural forms had developed, they rarely disappeared completely. They were periodically revived and integrated into new buildings.

Now, with most of the ceremonies lost and the decoration of the temple walls destroyed, we have only a limited ability to reconstruct and understand the complex fusion of rituals, religious symbolism, and architectural forms that shaped the development of the cult complexes.[4] Recent studies of pyramid temples have profited from new excavations of ancient structures, relief fragments, and statues. Of great importance is the contemporary evaluation of the so-called Abusir Papyri, documents discovered since 1893 but not yet published comprehensively.[5]

The First and Second Dynasties:
Funerary Enclosures and Fortresses of the Gods

The earliest sacral buildings connected to the burials of Egyptian kings are the so-called funerary enclosures at Abydos, located about one mile northeast of the actual royal tombs of the First Dynasty.[6] Seven such monumental brick constructions have been discovered not far west of the ancient town and temple of Osiris: two of them still stand to a height of 10–11 m and enclose spaces of about 65 × 122 m; of the other five, only foundations remain.[7] These structures consisted of large, rectangular brick walls decorated with niches on the north, west, and south sides and more elaborate panels on the main, east side (figs. 1–2). The two primary entrances to these funerary enclosures were placed at the south end of the east side and in the north wall.[8] Smaller secondary gates passed through the west and south walls. "Palace facade" is the Egyptological term used to describe these paneled walls, a name which implies that the monument represented the royal palace and served as a symbol for royal power. Except for a small brick building with a paneled facade (the so-called palace) behind the southeast entrance, the large interior courts appear to have been empty.[9]

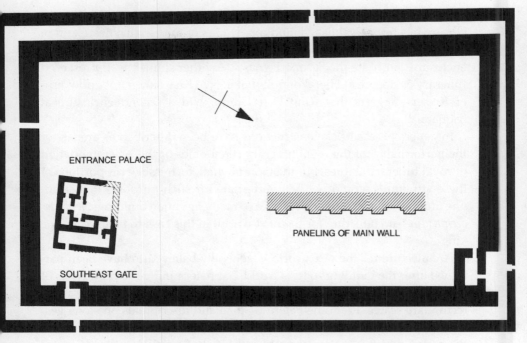

ENTRANCE PALACE

PANELING OF MAIN WALL

SOUTHEAST GATE

FIG. 1. Plan of funerary enclosure F of Khasekhemwy at Abydos, called the Shunet el-Zebib. Drawing by Josiane d'Este-Curry.

FIG. 2. Funerary enclosure of Khasekhemwy at Abydos, called the Shunet el-Zebib. Photo by David O'Connor.

With the help of seal impressions, the identity of the owner of each enclosure has been established, and most kings of the First Dynasty and at least two of the Second Dynasty are represented at Abydos.[10] No funerary enclosures postdate the Second Dynasty. Another similar, well-preserved funerary enclosure at Hierakonpolis belongs to Khasekhemwy, and Werner Kaiser suggests that King Den/Udimu had a second enclosure at Saqqara.[11]

In general, these brick constructions have been described as arenas for the performance of the royal funerary ceremonies or the accommodation of royal funerary statues, but the monumental, fortresslike proportions of these structures would not be appropriate for such purposes.[12] Instead, one must assume that they were, like so many Egyptian buildings, *Jenseitsarchitektur*—architecture for the next world, in this case to be used by the king.

Architecture for the next world is generally believed to have been patterned after the buildings of this world, but determining the prototypes of the enclosures is difficult because the remains of early nonfunerary architecture are scarce. From the Palermo Stone and inscriptions on stone vessels, we learn of a building that Egyptologists have called the "fortress of the gods," which played a key role in the early Egyptian state.[13] In hieroglyphic texts such structures are depicted as rectangular fortified enclosures surrounding the name of individual buildings (fig. 3).[14] The following examples are attested:

smr-ntrw: "the companion of the gods," of King Djer
jswt-ntrw: "the seats of the gods," of King Den
q3w-ntrw: "the mound of the gods," of King Qaᶜa
ḥwt-ntrj-ntrw: "the house of natron of the gods," of an unknown predecessor of King Ninetjer
rn-ḥrw/rn-ntr: "nurse of Horus/nurse of the god," of King Ninetjer
qbḥw-ntrw: "libations of the gods," of King Djoser[15]
nmtwt-ntrw: "procession of the gods," probably of King Sekhemkhet

These names indicate that the fortresses of the gods were gathering places for groups of gods, who were not yet the deities familiar from later periods of Egyptian history, but were predominantly divine powers who appeared in animal and other shapes. Collectively, the powers were known as the *šmsw-ḥr,* the Followers of Horus—that is, adherents of the king as the earthly manifestation of the ancient sky and falcon god. Local shrines or shelters belonged to individual deities in the area of the country in which the divinity was particularly venerated. The Horus-king apparently had these gods undertake boat journeys from their home provinces in order to

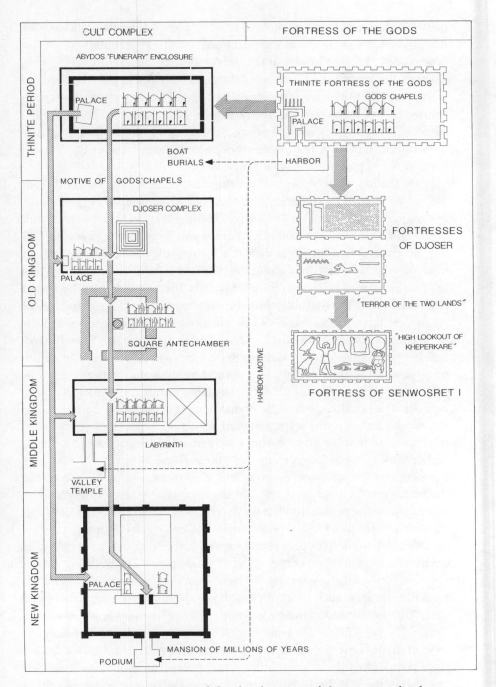

Labels within figure:

THINITE PERIOD

ABYDOS "FUNERARY" ENCLOSURE

PALACE

THINITE FORTRESS OF THE GODS

GODS' CHAPELS

PALACE

BOAT BURIALS

HARBOR

OLD KINGDOM

MOTIVE OF GODS' CHAPELS

DJOSER COMPLEX

PALACE

FORTRESSES OF DJOSER

"TERROR OF THE TWO LANDS"

SQUARE ANTECHAMBER

"HIGH LOOKOUT OF KHEPERKARE"

FORTRESS OF SENWOSRET I

MIDDLE KINGDOM

HARBOR MOTIVE

LABYRINTH

VALLEY TEMPLE

NEW KINGDOM

PALACE

MANSION OF MILLIONS OF YEARS

PODIUM

FIG. 3. Schematic representation of the development of the aspects of palaces, chapels of the gods, and landing stages from the fortresses of the gods to the Mansions of Millions of Years. Drawing by Dieter Arnold.

gather in the fortress of the gods.[16] Sacred emblems, animals, standards, or flags, which are depicted in the traditional artistic representations of the processions of the Followers of Horus, symbolized the deities.[17]

Extensive remains of a fortress of the gods have not yet been adequately explored.[18] But a few structures that could be the remains of such fortresses have been traced at Hierakonpolis, Heliopolis, and perhaps even Abydos.[19] After the Second Dynasty, the fortresses of the gods lose their importance, though a few more seem to have been built in the Middle Kingdom and possibly the New Kingdom.[20]

From the hieroglyphic signs depicting fortresses of the gods and from the appearance of the funerary enclosures at Abydos and Hierakonpolis, one may conclude that a typical fortress of the gods stood on the west bank of the Nile with its main gate placed at the south end of the east side, facing the river. When the gods visited a fortress they would have arrived from the east side, at a quay along the Nile or a canal.[21] An allusion to this landing stage may be seen in the boat burials discovered in 1991 by David O'Connor along the east side of the funerary precinct of Khasekhemwy at Abydos.[22] Boat burials were also found along the approaches to the funerary precincts of Khufu, Khafre, Unas, and Senwosret III.[23] Even the frequent representations of boats and boating scenes in the decorative programs of the later valley and pyramid temples may reflect the traditional role of the royal cult places as assembly points for royal and divine barques. The boat journeys of the divine powers of the whole country were apparently linked to the collection of taxes, an event that took place every other year, so that the gods' barques arrived at the fortress of the gods together with treasure-laden ships from throughout Egypt.[24] The status of the king and the safety of the gods and their treasure may have dictated the buildings' fortresslike shape, but their military character may also be explained by the possibility that they were used as arenas for the delivery, display, and ritual killing of prisoners of war and desert animals.[25]

According to hieroglyphic representations, the fortress's paneled walls enclosed a large, mainly empty court. A single palacelike building, possibly used by the king as a temporary residence, may have stood directly behind the entrance; such an arrangement is indicated by the remains of one such structure in the funerary enclosure of Khasekhemwy at Abydos (figs. 1–2).[26] The presence of the king may also have been indicated by a sacred mound in the court of the funerary enclosure, the so-called high sands that have been detected not only in the funerary enclosure of Khasekhemwy, but also in the temples of Hierakonpolis and Heliopolis, and probably in the temple complex of Osiris at Abydos.[27] From this mound, the king, or his symbol in the shape of the standard of Horus, would have dominated the surrounding assembly of the gods, and this may be the source for the

FIG. 4a. Alabaster statue base from Mit Rahina in the shape of a fortress of the gods, perhaps originally bearing a Horus falcon. Drawing by Dieter Arnold, following Ludwig Borchardt's hypothesis.

image of the "Horus falcon on his palace" that is omnipresent in Egyptian iconography (figs. 4a, 4b).[28]

Another structure that may have existed in the fortress of the gods was the shrine of the Upper Egyptian crown, represented by the vulture goddess Nekhbet, who presided over the other powers.[29] Neither Nekhbet's shrine nor shrines of the other Followers of Horus have been found in the funerary enclosures of the early period. One might suggest that these gods were represented by standards or banners, which would leave only postholes in the pavement, a feature difficult for excavators to distinguish.

During the lifetime of a king, the gods apparently assembled in the fortress of the gods to take part in the distribution of the incoming commodities and to establish a contract with the king, whereby the king would provide the gods with offerings and a cultus and they would "follow" him as his powerful adherents.[30] This periodic ceremony would have been one motive for constructing a similar installation for the other world, namely the funerary enclosure.

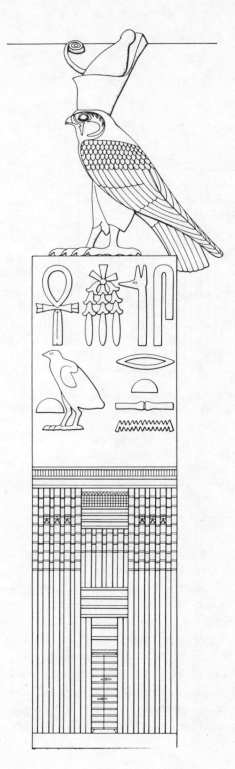

Fig. 4b. A representation of "Horus Falcon on His Palace" from the pyramid complex of Senwosret I, el-Lisht. Drawing by William P. Schenck.

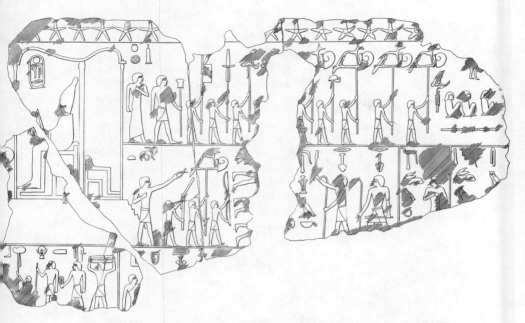

FIG. 5. The enthroned King Niuserre (Dynasty 5) and the procession of the standards during the *Sed*-festival. Relief from the king's solar temple at Abu Ghurab. From Friedrich Wilhelm Freiherr von Bissing and Hermann Kees, *Die kleine Festdarstellung*, vol. 2 of *Das Re-Heiligtum des Königs Ne-woser-Re (Rathures)*, ed. Friedrich Wilhelm Freiherr von Bissing (Leipzig: Hinrichs, 1923), pl. 11.

Numerous representations attest that the assembly of the Followers of Horus played another, even more important role during the *Sed*-festival (fig. 5).[31] This ceremonial regeneration of the king's divine powers was carried out, ideally, thirty years after his coronation or appointment as official successor to the throne.[32] Apparently the rites of this renewal of the royal reign were also performed in the fortress of the gods, where the gods again arrived in the boats that play an important role in this ceremony.[33] The gods were then escorted by the priests of their home towns, who gave the festival the aspect of a synod of priests.[34] These powerful rites, which influenced the nature of Egyptian kingship until the end of pharaonic rule, could culminate in a ceremonial death and rebirth of the aging king.[35] The *Sed*-festival certainly represented an even more important motive for the construction of the funerary enclosures, for these unique ceremonies were believed to regenerate the king's life and reign not only in this world but also in the next. Even as late as the reign of Senwosret I, the *Sed*-festival was celebrated in a fortress of the gods, the name of which ("Senwosret I Is Viewing the Two Lands from the Height") was still written inside a fortresslike hieroglyph.[36]

List of Royal Tombs and Funerary Enclosures of the First and Second Dynasties
(about 3185–2715 B.C.E.)[37]

First Dynasty:

King	Tomb	Enclosure
Menes/Narmer	Abydos B 17/18	(unknown)
Aha	Abydos B 10	(unknown)
Djer	Abydos O	Enclosure A
Djet	Abydos Z	Enclosure B
Meritneith	Abydos Y	Enclosure C (?)
Den/Udimu	Abydos T	Enclosure C (?)
Semerkhet	Abydos U	Western mastaba (?)
Adjib	Abydos X	Western mastaba (?)
Qa'a	Abydos Q	Enclosure G (?)

Second Dynasty:[38]

King	Tomb	Enclosure
Hetepsekhemwy	Saqqara	(east of Unas)
Raneb	Saqqara	(unidentified)
Ninetjer	Saqqara	(south of Djoser)
Sekhemib	unknown	
Peribsen	Abydos P	Enclosure E ("Middle fort")
Khasekhemwy	Abydos V	Enclosure F (Shunet el-Zebib) Hierakonpolis fort

The Djoser Complex at Saqqara

The Djoser complex (figs. 6–9) is generally believed to have been the first
Egyptian royal funerary monument constructed in stone.[39] Its plan is attributed to the famous architect and scholar Imhotep. The monument consists of a 277 × 544 m stone enclosure with one true gate at the south end
of the east side and fourteen mock gates distributed along all four sides
(fig. 6); unlike the funerary enclosures of Abydos, the walls have projecting,
paneled towers.[40] Two royal tombs are enclosed: the main one lay under the
Step Pyramid, while the "south tomb" was placed under a monumental
mastaba along the south wall of the enclosure (fig. 7). The subterranean
chambers of both tombs are similar in size and architectural expenditure
and seem to belong to the same ruler, providing an important example of
multiple burials, a typical phenomenon in Egyptian funerary monuments.
Underground galleries in both tombs, decorated with green tiles that imi-
tate reed structures, are believed to represent the kind of prehistoric-style
residence that the king would use in the next world.

The original superstructure of Djoser's tomb used the preexisting flat
shape of a mastaba; it was transformed into a stepped pyramid only in
stages, suggesting that the idea of a stepped tomb was being created.[41] The

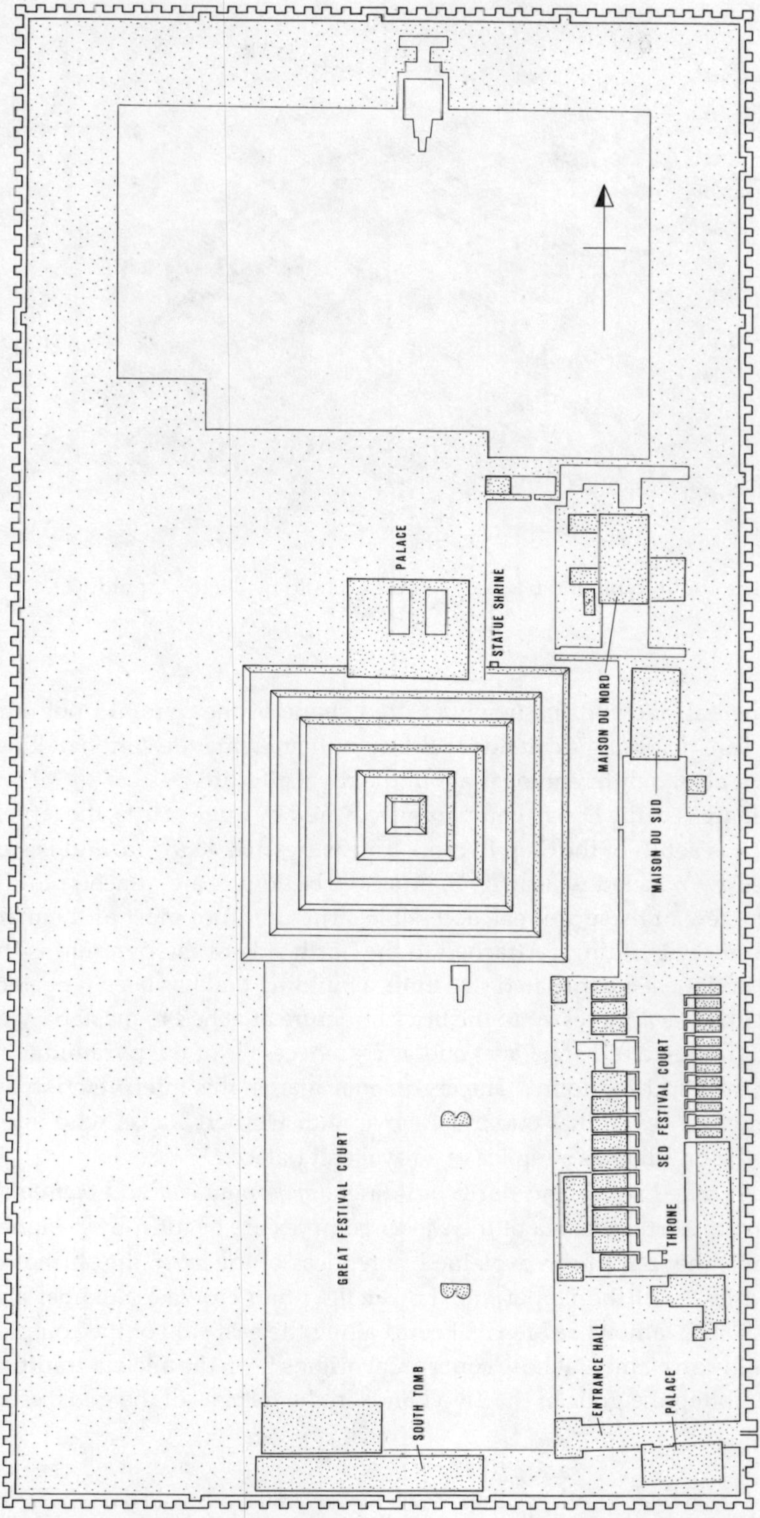
PALACE
STATUE SHRINE
MAISON DU NORD
MAISON DU SUD
GREAT FESTIVAL COURT
SED FESTIVAL COURT
THRONE
ENTRANCE HALL
PALACE
SOUTH TOMB

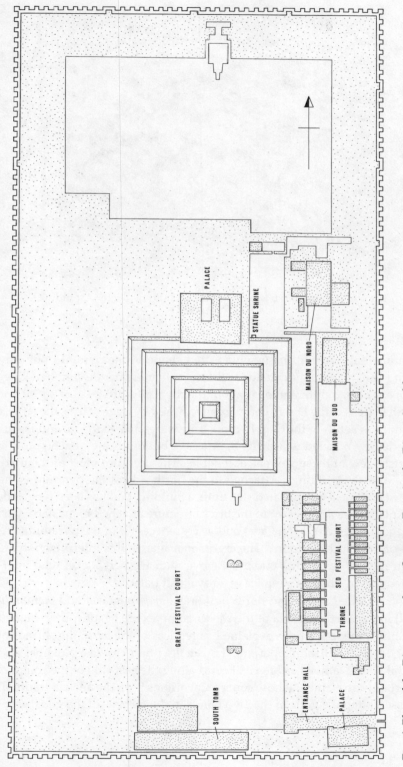

FIG. 6. Plan of the Djoser complex at Saqqara. Drawing by Dieter Arnold.

FIG. 7. The south tomb of the Djoser complex. Photo by Dieter Arnold.

monumental size and the newly created shape of the pyramid not only point to an increasing demand for the monumental manifestation of kingship, but also to different ideas about the royal afterlife.[42]

Other areas of the Djoser complex are covered by huge courts, the largest of which is south of the Step Pyramid, measures 108 × 187 m, and is surrounded by paneled walls (fig. 8). Massive buildings are attached to the courts; a few of these are real, accessible structures, but most of them are huge dummy buildings. Attached to the north side of the pyramid is the largest and most complicated structure, a building that has been repeatedly explained as a successor to the brick structure attached to mastaba 3505 at Saqqara (reign of King Qaʿa) and as a predecessor of the pyramid temples of the Old Kingdom.[43] The arguments against this interpretation are so strong, however, that one must agree with Herbert Ricke, who interpreted the building as a replica of a royal cult palace.[44]

The so-called south and north buildings (*maison du sud* and *maison du nord*) in the northeast area of the Djoser complex are beautifully designed structures that have been explained as replicas of the *iterti*, the shrines of the goddesses of the Upper and Lower Egyptian crowns, Nekhbet and Wadjit.[45] The famous *Sed*-festival court along the east side of the complex is certainly an element whose conceptual origins lie in the ancient tradition of assembling the gods of the Two Lands in the fortress of the gods, espe-

FIG. 8. The great court of the Djoser complex with the horseshoe-shaped cairns in the center. Photo by Dieter Arnold.

cially during the *Sed*-festival; surrounding the court are twenty-five to thirty shrines of at least three different types for the divinities (fig. 9). The close relationship of the court to the *Sed*-festival is also attested by the discovery of a monumental platform that supported a double throne, a feature well known from numerous representations of the rites. Seven statues of the king found in the area also contribute to the requirements of *Sed*-festival architecture.[46]

The number of royal statues in the Djoser complex is remarkable, especially since there are no indications of statue rituals. Instead, one might suggest that the sculptures represent the king living in his palace in the other world. Some statues apparently emphasized the king's divine aspect by placing prostrate foreigners with their heads protruding from the statue base under his feet.[47] An especially important and well preserved sculpture is the seated limestone figure sealed in a limestone chamber that leans against the northern side of the pyramid.

Finding an overall explanation for the Djoser complex is difficult since the only inscriptions and relief decoration consist of six scenes placed in the underground corridors.[48] In the Djoser complex, the architect Imhotep apparently united basic elements found in the royal funerary architecture of Abydos with the traditions of Memphis. The royal Abydene tomb may be reflected in the south tomb; the Memphite tomb, in the north tomb un-

FIG. 9. The *Sed*-festival chapel court in the Djoser complex at Saqqara. Photo by Dieter Arnold.

der the stepped pyramid. The enclosure wall either represents the Abydene or the Memphite funerary enclosure, both of which originated in the fortress of the gods. The paneled brick building, originally found near the entrances to the funerary enclosures at Abydos, is reduced to a paneled stone chapel placed south of the entrance hall of Djoser (fig. 6). The shrines for the Upper and Lower Egyptian crowns were perhaps transformed into the south and north buildings. The prominent installations connected with the *Sed*-festival, which dominate many parts of the complex, may also have their roots in older structures. The earlier, primitive shelters of the Followers of Horus were transformed into solid chapels arranged in two long rows with a throne dais between them (fig. 9). The large court south of the pyramid has been explained as a festival court used for several rituals, including the king's dedication of the field, which symbolized his revivification and newly restored power.

Perhaps later builders believed Imhotep's large-scale architectural model was too much of a pastiche to warrant further development. In any event, the funerary complexes of the short-lived successors of King Djoser were greatly simplified and consisted of paneled enclosures that omitted all the interior buildings except the stepped pyramid and the southern tomb.[49] These simplified complexes laid the groundwork for the funerary structures of the Fourth Dynasty.

List of Royal Funerary Enclosures of the Third Dynasty (2715–2630 B.C.E.)[50]

Nebka (Horus Sanakht)	(unidentified)
Djoser (Horus Netjerykhet)	Complex at Saqqara
Djoserteti (Horus Sekhemkhet)	Complex southwest of the Djoser complex at Saqqara
Horus Khaba (?)	Layer pyramid at Zawiyet el-Aryan
Huni (Horus Qahedjet)	(unidentified)[51]

Because the history of the Third Dynasty is still so problematic, the possibility remains that more rulers and funerary complexes lie undiscovered.[52]

The New Era

Just as the builders of the Djoser complex transformed the mastaba into a stepped pyramid, the architects of the cult complex of Meidum transformed the stepped pyramid into the first true pyramid, a structure that would house the burial chambers of kings until the end of the Middle Kingdom.[53] The more earthly and organic stepped shape was rejected in favor of the more "heavenly" abstract aspects represented by the true pyramid. This majestic building, dated to the early years of King Sneferu, towered over a funerary complex that differed considerably from those of the Third Dynasty: the large and elaborate Djoser complex was replaced by a small, rectangular, and nearly empty court. The axis of the new complex was rotated ninety degrees, so that it was oriented east-west rather than north-south; this realignment from the northern to the eastern sky may indicate that the sun cultus had become more important. In front of the east side of the pyramid, a tiny cultic area appears (fig. 10) consisting of a chapel with two corridors or antechambers that open into a narrow court with two 4.2 m high round-topped, uninscribed (unfinished) stelae.[54] This creation is of great importance, since for the first time a cultic installation is directly connected to a royal tomb; no altars or offering places have been found in any of the earlier funerary complexes. Unfortunately, we have no indication as to the type of rituals enacted here. The rituals may have been directed to the pyramid itself as a kind of manifestation of the king.[55] But the ceremonies could also have been an early mortuary cultus, which addressed the spirit of the king as it left the tomb.[56]

South of the pyramid are ruins that may be the remains of a pyramid-shaped secondary tomb, perhaps a successor to Djoser's south tomb. In the same area, a fragment of a royal stela was found that is similar to stelae from the secondary pyramid associated with the Bent Pyramid. Another building, located along the canal, was joined to the cult area by means of a long causeway. Based on later parallels, the unexcavated building can probably be identified as a statue or valley temple.[57]

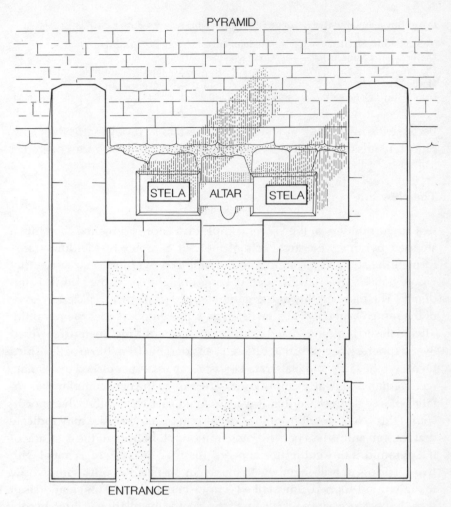

PYRAMID

STELA   ALTAR   STELA

ENTRANCE

FIG. 10. Plan of the cult place at the east side of the pyramid of Sneferu at Meidum. Drawing by Dieter Arnold.

From Djoser to Sneferu there was a tremendous change in the meaning, and consequently the form, of the royal funerary complex. Loosely arranged over a large area, the Djoser complex housed a diverse collection of royal tombs, temples, cult places, palaces, and whatever may be hidden behind these structures. Buildings used in this world for displays of royal power were duplicated for use in the afterlife as a kind of *Sed*-festival architecture.[58] At Meidum, this layout was replaced by a rigorously organized, symmetrical, centralized complex dominated by one single gigantic monument—the pyramid. Such radical changes under King Sneferu reflect a correspondingly major, perhaps revolutionary, change in the concept of the royal afterlife and possibly in religion in general.

At that moment the role of the king was apparently expanded so that he was no longer simply a manifestation of Horus. Instead, he became identified with the sun god and joined the daily cycle of death and resurrection.[59] From the Pyramid Texts of the Sixth Dynasty (which contain much older religious beliefs, see below), it becomes clear that the pyramid was not just a tomb, but that it had evolved into the site of a mystery that allowed the dead king to unite with the *ba* of the sun god.[60] A belief that the most dramatic action occurred underground, in the interior of the pyramid and without the help of priests or rituals, may explain why the cult places attached to all three of Sneferu's pyramids were simple structures.

The Transition in the Fourth Dynasty

The pyramid complexes of the Fourth Dynasty at Dahshur and Giza are dominated by the increasing size and importance of the pyramid, the place where the mystery of royal regeneration was enacted.[61] One cannot ignore, however, the vigorous development that occurs after King Sneferu not only in the funerary apartments of these pyramids but also in the structures surrounding the pyramids, where we see the emergence of the first monumental funerary *temples* (fig. 11).

Beginning with the Bent Pyramid, a prototype for the royal statue temple is attached to the causeway in the desert valley (fig. 12).[62] The 27 × 48 m large stone building contained an open court with a pillared portico and six statue shrines at the rear. Housed in the statue shrines were sculptures of Sneferu wearing the red, white, and double crowns. It is not a coincidence that statue cultuses also appear in contemporary private mastabas, where ceremonies were performed in the first real cult chambers.[63]

Sneferu's statue temple is of great importance because it is the first preserved example of aboveground royal funerary architecture decorated with reliefs. Primarily, the scenes show the divine king as lord of the temple, accompanied by the gods and performing ceremonies; in the entrance passage and court, long processions of the nomes and Sneferu's estates are reminiscent of the delivery and distribution of goods at the royal palace. The seeming maturity of the decorative program presupposes the existence of older prototypes, while the somewhat clumsy composition of the reliefs might indicate that the medium was of fairly recent origin.[64] It is worth noting, however, that the first relief decoration appears a few generations earlier in private tombs, though the subjects differ from those used in the royal sphere.[65]

In front of the east side of the Bent Pyramid, a small cult place is preserved (fig. 12), similar to but simpler than that of the pyramid of Meidum (fig. 10).[66] It is also flanked by a pair of 10 m high stelae, inscribed with the

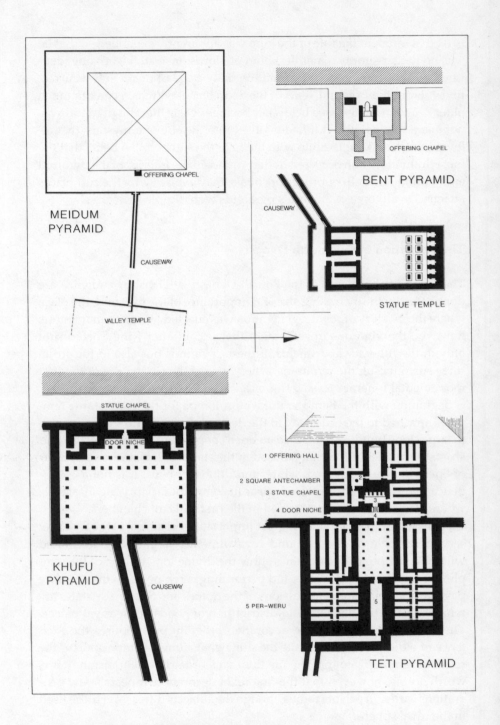

MEIDUM
PYRAMID

OFFERING CHAPEL

CAUSEWAY

VALLEY TEMPLE

BENT PYRAMID

OFFERING CHAPEL

CAUSEWAY

STATUE TEMPLE

STATUE CHAPEL

DOOR NICHE

KHUFU
PYRAMID

CAUSEWAY

1 OFFERING HALL

2 SQUARE ANTECHAMBER

3 STATUE CHAPEL

4 DOOR NICHE

5 PER-WERU

TETI PYRAMID

FIG. 11. Schematic representation of the development of pyramid temples from the Fourth to the Sixth Dynasties. Drawing by Dieter Arnold.

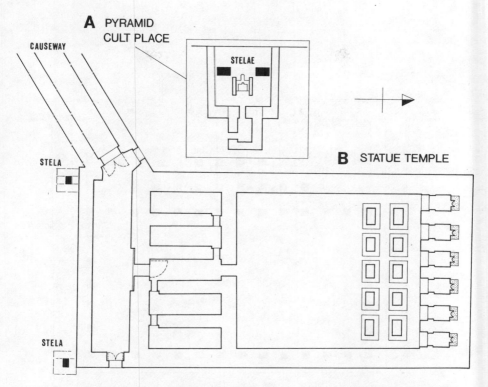

FIG. 12. Plans of the statue temple and the pyramid cult place of the Bent Pyramid of Sneferu at Dahshur. Drawing by Dieter Arnold.

names and titles of Sneferu. Since the addition of stelae to these two pyramids is unique, Rainer Stadelmann suggests that the stelae underline the nature of the pyramid of Meidum and the Bent Pyramid as secondary tombs or cenotaphs.[67]

During recent excavations of Sneferu's North Pyramid at Dahshur (the so-called Red Pyramid), remains of the cult place were discovered at the east side of the pyramid.[68] After the king's death, the unfinished stone building was completed in brick—and is thus poorly preserved. However, the remains do allow us to conclude that two major elements found in the pyramid temple of Sneferu's successor, Khufu (fig. 11), were first developed here, namely the pillared court and a statue sanctuary behind it.

The pyramid temple of Khufu can be reconstructed only from the remains of the foundations, some foundation pits for pillars, and parts of the court's basalt pavement (figs. 11, 13).[69] The temple was 52.5 m wide but only 40 m deep; the front part of the building was dominated by a huge pillared court, while the back contained a *Breitraum* (broad room) for the

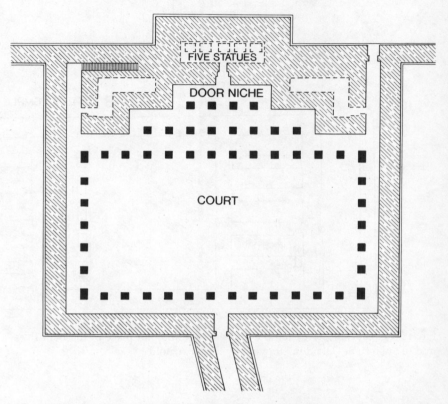

FIVE STATUES

DOOR NICHE

COURT

FIG. 13. Plan of the pyramid temple of Khufu at Giza. Drawing by Josiane d'Este-Curry.

cult statues. The court and the cult chamber were separated by a door niche. The rear wall of the pillared court in front of the statue shrines is not straight but forms a deep central niche that allows space for two more rows of pillars. In the temples of later kings this door niche, called "gate of Nut" by Herbert Ricke, was decorated with scenes of goddesses nursing the young king and of gods welcoming him (fig. 28).[70]

The combination of pillared court and door niche with statue shrines in the back is consistently repeated in Egyptian funerary architecture, surviving until the gigantic Theban tombs of the Late Period.[71] In the latter, the ancient pillared court seems to be retained in the form of an open, underground light well (*Lichthof*). An offering table for the mortuary offering was a feature of the light well, which served as the juncture between the realms of day and night, symbolized by Re and Osiris. In the rear wall of the court, a high, deep vaulted niche leads into the interior parts of the tomb, which contained the statue shrines and burial apartments.

From evidence provided by a few tantalizing relief blocks and fragments found mainly in the court of the Khufu cult area, we can infer that parts of the temple were decorated.[72] The decorative program, similar to that in the statue temple of Sneferu at the Bent Pyramid, included processions of estates and *Sed*-festival rituals, further establishing the functional relationship of the pyramid temple's court to the *Sed*-festival rituals.

Remains of the valley temple of Khufu exist but are now covered by the modern town of Nazlet el-Sammân; excavation would provide an important contribution to our understanding of the development of the pyramid complex during the Fourth Dynasty.[73]

When Khufu's successor Djedefre died, his cult complex at Abu Rawash was hastily completed in brick; only a *per-weru* hall and a court surrounded by storerooms are recognizable.[74]

Both the valley and pyramid temples of Khafre are much better preserved and have been fully excavated (figs. 14, 15).[75] The gigantic limestone buildings (valley temple, 44.6 × 44.6 m; pyramid temple, 56 × 111 m) were cased in granite and had granite pillars and architraves. Located on the bank of a canal, the valley temple consisted of an enormous quay and platform that allowed boats to land in front of the building, a transverse entrance hall with two gates, and a T-shaped interior pillared hall.[76] Sockets in the alabaster pavement indicate the installation of twenty-three seated statues, of which important remains have been found. Completely preserved is the famous statue of Khafre with the falcon behind his head, which shows the king being transformed into Horus (fig. 16).

The traditional explanation that a valley temple served as a landing stage and embalming house for the body of the deceased king is no longer accepted.[77] There is reason to speculate, however, that the valley temples of the Old Kingdom were somehow connected to the earlier tradition of the fortresses of the gods. In the valley temple, the dead king would have met the gods, who arrived there in their barques to celebrate festivals with the king. The Abusir Papyri of the Fifth Dynasty mention several of these occasions.[78] For example, during the Festival of the God of the Netherworld, the god Sokar traveled in a huge boat from the Lake of Abusir along a canal through the necropolis, where he visited a succession of mortuary complexes.[79] Because of the great number of mortuary temples and the shortage of time, the god could only land briefly at every valley temple. The festivals of Hathor and of Min, god of fertility and recreation, also included river processions connected with visits to the dead kings' cult complexes. It has even been suggested that the spectacular ceremony of erecting and climbing a mast in honor of Min, enacted by participants

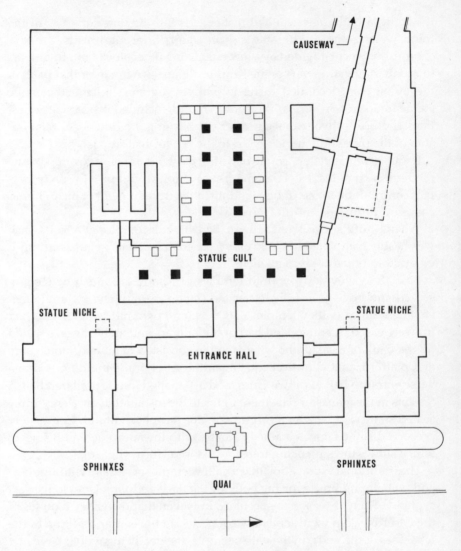

CAUSEWAY

STATUE CULT

STATUE NICHE

STATUE NICHE

ENTRANCE HALL

SPHINXES

SPHINXES

QUAI

FIG. 14. Plan of the valley temple of Khafre at Giza. Drawing by Dieter Arnold.

wearing feather headdresses, took place in the court of the mortuary temple.[80] Also depicting the idea of the unification of the king with visiting divinities are the numerous group statues of the king with one or two deities found in the valley temple of Menkaure.[81] The tradition of attaching some sort of valley temple to a sanctuary continued with the so-called quay or podium placed in front of many later temples, for example at Karnak, Philae, Dendur, and Kalabsha.[82]

For geographical reasons, the valley temple and the pyramid complex

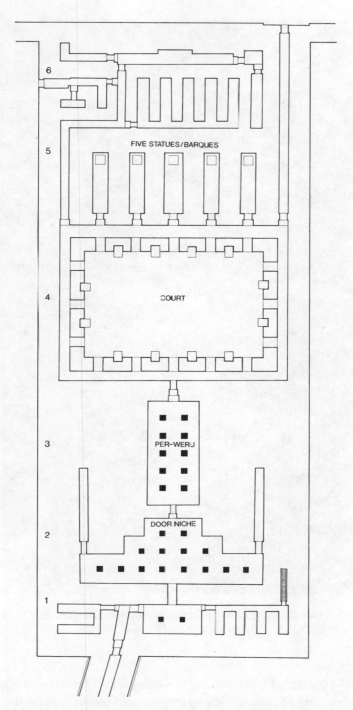

FIVE STATUES/BARQUES

COURT

PER-WERJ

DOOR NICHE

FIG. 15. Plan of the pyramid temple of Khafre at Giza. Drawing by Dieter Arnold.

FIG. 16. Statue of Horus-enfolded Khafre. Photo from the archive of the Egyptian Department, The Metropolitan Museum of Art, New York.

had to be separated, but in exiting the valley temple and then ascending to and reentering the upper temple, one was not meant to walk through an open area. Instead, the conceptual and ritual unity of the complex was maintained in the closed space of a so-called causeway (fig. 17). This link-

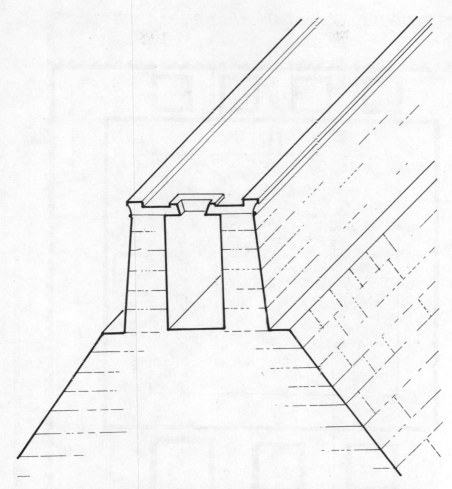

Fig. 17. Reconstruction of the causeway of Niuserre at Abusir. Drawing by Dieter Arnold.

ing of valley temples to pyramid complexes by monumental causeways began with King Sneferu (figs. 11, 12) and continued until the Middle Kingdom (fig. 18). Unlike the sphinx avenues of the New Kingdom, the causeways were narrow, were roofed and thus dark inside, and had decorated walls. In order to keep the connection between valley temple and mortuary temple well protected and ritually pure, the causeway was sealed off from the outside world, a necessity emphasized in the evil-averting relief scenes of later causeways.

A 494.6 m long causeway rising along a natural rock ridge connected the valley temple of Khafre to the pyramid temple. The pyramid temple of Khafre is arranged from east to west in six units (fig. 15). The first unit

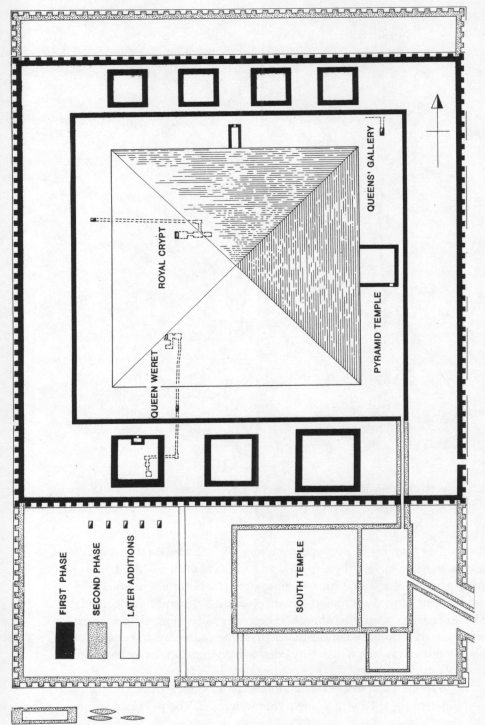

FIRST PHASE

SECOND PHASE

LATER ADDITIONS

QUEENS' GALLERY

ROYAL CRYPT

QUEEN WERET

PYRAMID TEMPLE

SOUTH TEMPLE

FIG. 18. Plan of the funerary complex of Senwosret III at Dahshur. Drawing by Dieter Arnold.

consists of a vestibule and several unexplained chambers. The second is a *Breitraum* with a door niche leading into two corridorlike lateral chambers used for unidentified cultic rituals. Huge breaches cut into the rear walls of the chambers could indicate that the stone robbers who dismantled the temple tried to move out especially heavy monuments, perhaps colossal shrines or statues. The third unit is a pillared passage that anticipates the *per-weru* halls of the Fifth Dynasty. Fourth is the wide pillared court that the excavator believed to have been surrounded by standing statues of the king. If his reconstruction is correct, the statues would clearly have marked the court as an area used for *Sed*-festival ceremonies.[83]

Five gigantic parallel halls comprise the fifth and main unit. Their shapes suggest that they housed barques that could have been up to 7 m long. Such large barques could not have been brought into the temple through the causeway entrance, but could only have been either stationary or carried through the court and *per-weru* into the door niche.[84] We can only speculate about the types of barques and the kinds of statues they held, though one would expect that morning and evening barques for the king's sky journey would be among them.[85]

The sixth and last unit of Khafre's pyramid temple consists of a group of rooms arranged along a passageway, obviously storerooms with a final corridor along the end wall. A flat and wide recess in the west wall of the corridor has been explained as the location of a false door, but the existence of a false door with a corresponding mortuary cultus in the pyramid temple of Khafre remains doubtful (see n. 98). The temple of Khafre still represents the type with only a statue sanctuary (Ricke's *Verehrungstempel*); a section for the mortuary cultus was introduced into the royal complex only in the Fifth Dynasty. In consequence, one could expect that it was mainly statue rituals that were performed in Fourth Dynasty royal pyramid temples.

The most important statue ritual is probably attested in the Old Kingdom Abusir Papyri, but it is better known from the so-called Ramesseum Papyri of the Middle Kingdom and from representations in the Mansions of Millions of Years of the New Kingdom.[86] These rites involved the mock burial of a *ka*-statue of the "old" king (possibly performed at the satellite pyramid; see below), followed by the king's rebirth. Borne in procession on a sledge, the revived *ka*-statue was taken down to the valley temple, accompanied by two emblems composed of a papyrus flower carrying a sun disk with two serpents. The two emblems, named "he who ascends to the sun" and "he who unites with the sun," represented two manifestations of the revived king.[87] From the valley temple, the procession of the *ka*-statue continued by boat to an unidentified annex of the mortuary complex, perhaps in the later Old Kingdom to a sun temple. Dramatized by this ritual was the daily cycle of death and rebirth that the king underwent in the pyramid and that constituted a crucial part of the *Sed*-festival.

Khafre's valley temple (fig. 14) and most of the rooms of his pyramid temple (fig. 15) had walls of granite and were therefore undecorated. The walls of the pyramid temple's court might have been of limestone and might therefore have been decorated.[88] The causeway walls were definitely limestone, but they do not seem to have had relief work.

The cult complex and pyramid of Menkaure were left unfinished, and consequently undecorated, at the king's death. Instead of limestone and granite, the temple was completed with cheap brickwork in a simplified fashion.[89] The pyramid temple consisted of the *per-weru* hall and a court, which was embellished with a paneled wall decoration instead of the pillars originally planned; this time-honored paneling was certainly meant to recall the ancient fortresses of the gods. The door niche returned to the position it occupied in the temple of Khufu, namely the rear wall of the court. Whereas Khafre's temple had had five statue/barque sanctuaries, Menkaure's had only one, which possibly housed a seated alabaster colossus of the king with a barque standing in front of it.[90] Later, probably under Shepseskaf, a mortuary chapel was added between the west wall of the temple and the pyramid in order to make the temple conform to the latest developments in sacral architecture (see below).[91]

The valley temple of Menkaure has practically the same elements as the pyramid temple: an entrance hall (*per-weru*), a large court, a door niche with two rows of columns, a central shrine, and groups of side chambers along the east wall and in the northwest and southwest corners. Found in the valley temple was a unique assemblage of royal sculptures, among them at least eight of the famous Menkaure triads, which each show the king with two deities or nome figures (Egyptian Museum, Cairo, and Museum of Fine Arts, Boston).[92] The triads were probably arranged in the eight portico chapels in conformity with the geographic associations of the particular divinities; a pair statue of Menkaure and his queen might have stood in the central shrine.

Remarkable is the reduction in size and complexity from Khafre's pyramid temple to that of Menkaure. A corresponding reduction in the size of the pyramids certainly indicates a changed attitude toward the cultus of the king.

List of Cult Complexes of the Fourth Dynasty (2630–2510 B.C.E.)[93]

Sneferu	Meidum E1—E3
	Bent Pyramid (Dahshur)
	Red or Northern Stone Pyramid (Dahshur)
	Pyramid of Seila

Khufu	Giza
Djedefre	Abu Rawash (unfinished)
Khafre	Giza
Menkaure	Giza (unfinished)
Nebka (?)	Zawiyet el-Aryan (unfinished)
Shepseskaf	Saqqara (Mastabat el-Fara'un)

Individual Solutions at the Transition between the Fourth and Fifth Dynasties

More spectacular changes characterize the mortuary precinct of Shep-seskaf, the last king of the Fourth Dynasty (fig. 19).[94] Instead of following the Fourth Dynasty royal cult complexes, the king built a gigantic masta-ba-like structure. The base of this structure was probably paneled, suggesting that the building was meant to represent an ancient funerary palace surrounded by the enclosure wall of a fortress of the gods.

The replacement of the pyramid as a place of royal divinization by a funerary palace in which the king was thought to "live" is remarkable.[95] In order to allow the king's continued existence, the monument had to be provided with a new structure, a real funerary chapel attached directly to the east side of the building.[96] Just as the old funerary palaces were surrounded by false doors, this room must have had a false door standing at the west wall. No fragments of the wall decoration of the room remain, but the subsequent development of royal funerary chapels and contemporary private tombs indicates that the dominant theme of the reliefs was offerings brought to the king. Lavish food offerings brought by long lines of courtiers and offered by priests were received by the king, who was probably depicted seated before an offering table; a lengthy offering list would have accompanied the scene.

The (temporary) abandonment of a royal pyramid, together with the introduction of a funerary chapel that probably had a false door and offering scenes, is of great importance. For the first time, the king is shown as a mortal who needs food and supplies, a development that suggests a diminishing of the king's godliness and a greater emphasis on the humanity of the ruler. Such trends can also be observed in written sources that refer to this time.[97] Although the reintroduction of the funerary palace in the royal cult complex did not survive Shepseskaf, the newly established mortuary chapel and false door remained an essential part of the royal pyramid temple.[98] For the development of the funerary complex from the Fourth to the Fifth Dynasties, see fig. 20.

King Userkaf returned to the pyramid tradition but reshaped his cult

FIG. 19. The funerary palace of Shepseskaf, called the Mastabat el-Fara'un, at Saqqara. Photo by Dieter Arnold.

complex (figs. 21, 22). The recently developed royal funerary chapel was attached directly to the east side of the pyramid, while the older statue cult temple, which had been placed in the east since King Sneferu's time, was transferred to the south side of the pyramid. This southern temple was entered through a *per-weru* hall that led into a large pillared court (fig. 22). The door niche was separated from the court by a straight wall, an innovation that would characterize the plan of all later pyramid temples. The statue cult room, located in the center of the south wall, may have housed a colossal royal statue, the head of which is still preserved.[99] We can state that for the first time since the reign of Khufu the pyramid complex was definitely decorated with wall reliefs, a few of which have been preserved.[100] Some of the subjects of the reliefs (spearing of fish, hunting of birds) indicate that they belonged to the decorative program of the *per-weru* hall; others (boating scenes, sailors) could have originated from the causeway or the passage in front of the door niche.

The new spirit and naturalistic elements that characterize the reliefs of Userkaf and his successors (as well as those of the contemporary private mastaba tombs) reflect the increasing importance at the beginning of the Fifth Dynasty of the cultus of Re.[101] Userkaf was the first king to build a sun temple near the royal cult complex, creating a tradition that lasted to the end of the Fifth Dynasty.[102] Solar aspects played an important role in

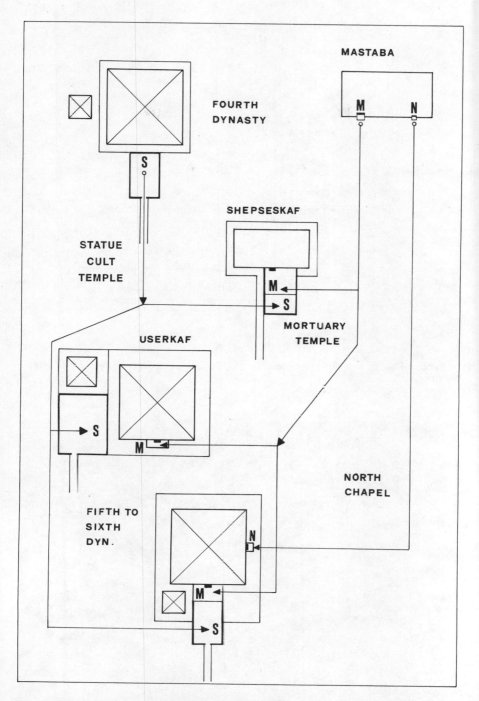

FIG. 20. Schematic representation combining the statue cult temple (S), the mortuary temple (M), and the north chapel (N) during the transition from the Fourth to the Fifth Dynasties. Drawing by Dieter Arnold, following Peter Janoši.

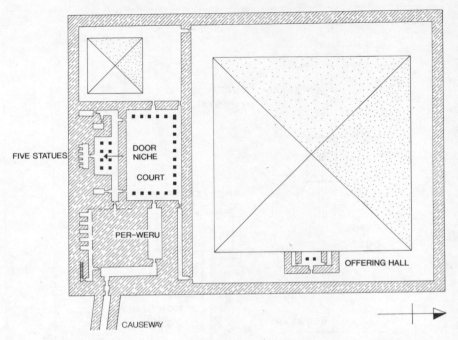

FIG. 21. Plan of the funerary complex of Userkaf at Saqqara. Drawing by Josiane d'Este-Curry.

FIG. 22. The court of the statue cult temple at the pyramid of Userkaf at Saqqara. Photo by Dieter Arnold.

the deification of the king from the beginning of the Fourth Dynasty, but by the beginning of the Fifth Dynasty that tendency had become so dominant that solar cult installations needed independent structures separated from the funerary complexes.[103] At present, we cannot identify installations for a *separate* sun cultus within the pyramid complexes of the Third and Fourth Dynasties.[104] There is, however, a possibility that such a sun cultus was introduced to the pyramid temples of the later Fifth Dynasty and after. At the pyramid temples of Unas (fig. 23), Teti (figs. 11, 24), Pepi I, and Pepi II, the east wall takes the shape of two truncated towers. The great thickness of these structures indicates that they towered over the temples behind them. In the pyramid temples of Sahure and Djedkare (and in the Twelfth Dynasty, of Amenemhat II), these constructions grew into massive, quadrangular mastabas with a side length of 22 m. The podiums would have made ideal elevated platforms for the obelisks associated with the sun temples or the ritual spaces needed for sun cult ceremonies.

The Fifth and Sixth Dynasties

Under King Sahure, priests and architects designed a new ground plan for the pharaoh's cult complex that served as the prototype for at least nine of the mortuary temples of the Fifth and Sixth Dynasties (figs. 23–27).[105] During this period the religious ideas and cultic practices associated with the pyramid temples became highly complex, while the elaborate ground plans and richly decorated walls of the structures reached the pinnacle of their development. The turbulent evolution characteristic of earlier periods slowed; for the first time one can speak of a kind of standardized pyramid complex copied by successive kings (figs. 23–24). We even have indications that the architects of this period enacted some strict building guidelines, which were probably favored by the hereditary office of the royal master builder.[106] All pyramid temples from Sahure to Pepi II are, with only minor variations, based on the same ground plan.[107] Remains of wall reliefs indicate that the decorative programs also followed rigid rules, although artists were allowed some individual expression.

Again we have the upper and the lower temples connected by a causeway (fig. 17). Beginning with Sahure, or possibly with Userkaf, the inside walls of the causeways were decorated with reliefs. Several different types of scenes covered the long causeway walls. Representations of royal lions and griffins (lions with falcon heads) and of royal victories seem designed to protect the cult complex from hostile elements. Processions of tribute and offering bearers, ships arriving with building materials, and market scenes represent supplies being delivered to the successor of the ancient

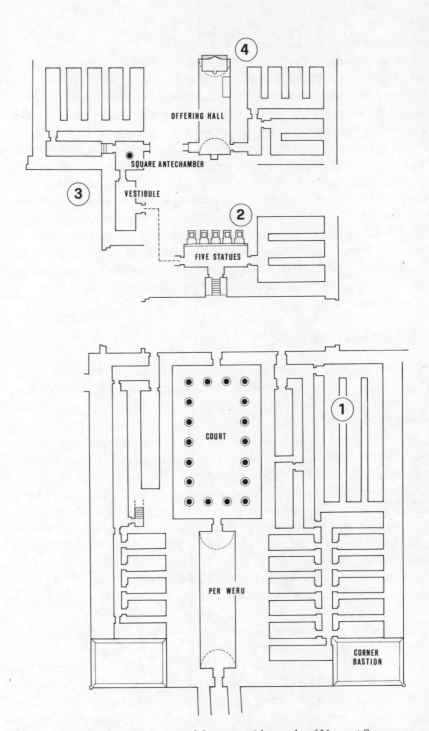

FIG. 23. Schematic representation of the pyramid temple of Unas at Saqqara, separating the four major areas. Drawing by Dieter Arnold.

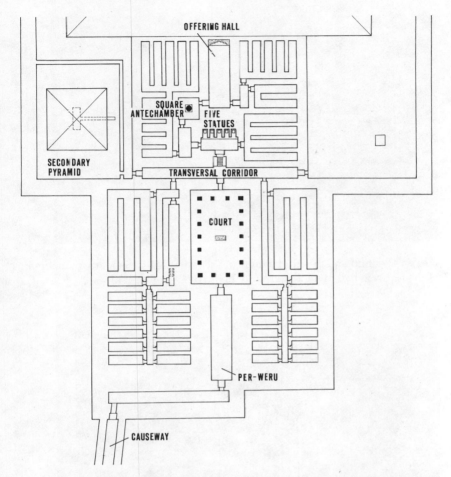

OFFERING HALL

SQUARE ANTECHAMBER

FIVE STATUES

SECONDARY PYRAMID

TRANSVERSAL CORRIDOR

COURT

PER-WERU

CAUSEWAY

Fig. 24. Plan of the pyramid temple of Teti at Saqqara. Drawing by Dieter Arnold.

fortress of the gods and being transported up the causeway to the royal tomb or funerary enclosure. That these latter scenes depict actual activities is demonstrated by the ample number of storerooms placed along the north and south sides of the funerary temple, where they are often arranged in groups of five with two stories (figs. 23–24). Some rooms probably contained implements used in the mortuary cultus, but most of them were meant to house grave goods used to sustain the king's afterlife.

At the front of the now standardized upper temple, one finds the impressive *per-weru* hall—a vaulted, decorated passage 5 m wide and 20 m long (fig. 25). The walls of the *per-weru* hall of Pepi II are decorated with large scenes of the ritual hippopotamus hunt and bird catching and a depiction of the king's inevitable triumph over his human enemies. The up-

FIG. 25. Pyramid and pyramid temple of Djedkare-Isesi at Saqqara, with remains of the *per-weru* hall in the foreground. Photo by Dieter Arnold.

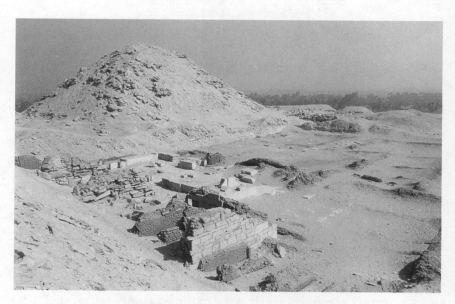

FIG. 26. Pyramid temple of Neferirkare with pyramid of Niuserre at Abusir. Photo by Adela Oppenheim.

FIG. 27. Pyramid and pyramid temple of Sahure at Abusir. Photo by Adela Oppenheim.

per temple's central court is surrounded by the traditional pillars or sometimes by columns, the latter originating during the reign of Sahure (fig. 27).[108] The side walls of the court in Sahure's pyramid temple show four scenes of the king's military victories and four of the collection of booty.

A north-south transversal corridor runs behind the central court (fig. 24), with doors at each end connecting it to the inner pyramid court; the long walls of this passage provide space for extensive relief decoration. In the pyramid temple of Sahure, the east wall is dominated by two immense compositions showing a maritime expedition to the Canaanite/Syrian coast. On the north half of this wall, we see twelve ships departing from the king's presence; on the south half, we see the return of the fleet with (captured?) foreigners. In the corresponding corridor of the temple of Pepi II, the traditional triumph scenes are accompanied by depictions of religious ceremonies, such as the climbing of the mast in honor of Min and divinities meeting or embracing the king. Unfortunately, only a few traces remain of the depiction of the Sed-festival.

Opening in the center of the rear (west) wall of the transverse corridor is the wide door niche (figs. 11 [Teti], 28) with steps that lead up to the rear part of the pyramid temple and into the statue sanctuary that held the five royal statues. Between the statue sanctuary and the offering hall are two or three rooms (fig. 24), the most western of which is a square chamber with

FIG. 28. Reconstruction of the door niche of the pyramid temple of Pepi II at Saqqara. Drawing by Dieter Arnold.

a high ceiling and a central column or pillar. All four walls of this so-called square antechamber are decorated with the well-known *Sed*-festival motif of the king meeting with fifty Upper and forty-eight Lower Egyptian gods, who stand in front of their individual chapels (fig. 29).[109] In the lowest register, the king receives the homage of his bowing courtiers. This crucial part

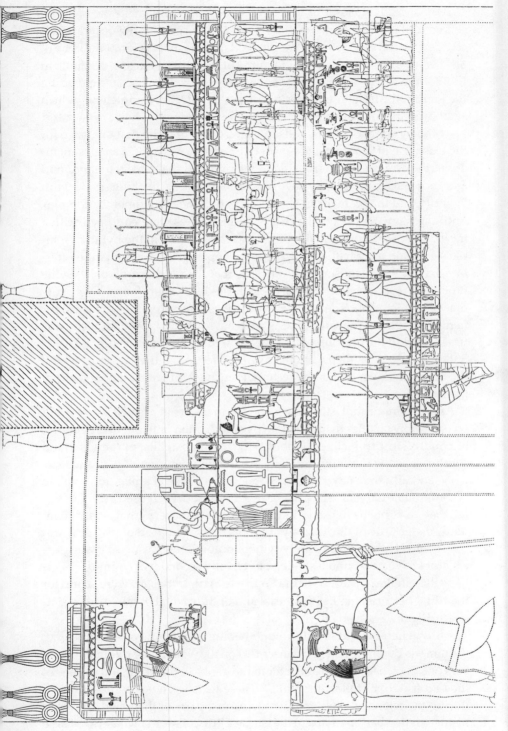

Fig. 29. Representation of the Upper Egyptian gods in the square antechamber of the pyramid temple of Pepi II. From Gustave Jéquier, *Le monument funéraire de Pepi II*, vol. 2, *Le temple* (Cairo: IFAO, 1938), pl. 50.

of the *Sed*-festival is performed in a chapel court similar to the one preserved in the Djoser complex (figs. 3, 6). The purpose of the decoration is clarified by the inscription: "We [the gods] give you [the king] millions of *Sed*-festivals."[110] In the pyramid temple of Pepi II, the narrow vestibule in front of the square antechamber shows unexpected wall scenes including the smiting of human enemies and the slaughter of an antelope, which symbolize the king's supremacy over his enemies.

At the pyramid of Djedkare-Isesi (fig. 25), we find the first evidence for the existence of the so-called northern or entrance chapel, a small sanctuary in the center of the north side of the pyramid that covers the pyramid entrance. Such chapels may have been built by the earlier kings of the Fifth Dynasty, and they remain an important part of the royal funerary complex until the reign of Amenemhat III.[111] These chapels were equipped with a false door and decorated with the same scenes found in the pyramid temple's main offering hall, giving them the appearance of a miniature offering chapel. Peter Janoši rightly suspects that the northern chapel was the functional successor of the northern false-door niche found in private mastabas (fig. 20N). The northern niche was integrated into the royal funerary complex at the same time as the main southern false-door niche was transferred to the offering hall of the royal mortuary temple (fig. 20M).[112] Still observed was the traditional axial connection of the main niche with the burial chamber and of the secondary niche with the entrance (shaft) of the tomb.

Another important structure needing mention is a satellite pyramid considerably smaller than the main pyramid, often only one-fifth the size, but more steeply inclined (about 63°).[113] The satellite pyramids stand southeast of the main pyramid, inside the inner enclosure wall (figs. 20, 24). Generally, they have no cult chapel, and a burial chamber too small to accommodate either a sarcophagus or a human burial. If used at all for burial, they can only have been a kind of secondary place, perhaps used to inter a small statue of the king, a part of his body, or a form of his spirit; but they could also have been purely symbolic monuments, especially since excavators have not found a single object in any secondary pyramid.[114] Perhaps the satellite pyramids of the Fourth to Sixth Dynasties were stages for the ritual performances of the burial and of the revival of the royal *ka*-statue during the *Sed*-festival.[115]

A few generations after Sahure, another important innovation appeared: the famous Pyramid Texts, first inscribed on the walls of the pyramid chambers of King Unas (fig. 30) and later in the tombs of the kings and queens of the Old Kingdom following him.[116] These texts were not entirely created during the reigns of Unas and his successors; parts of them had an earlier history, dating back perhaps to the earlier Fifth or Fourth Dynasty.[117] These

FIG. 30. The pyramid texts in the pyramid of Unas. Photo by Dieter Arnold.

texts are a unique source for understanding Old Kingdom religion and the conception of the royal afterlife. The question of their relevance to royal funerary architecture and actual cult ceremonies has led Egyptologists to controversial theories.[118] But it is generally accepted that parts of the Pyramid Texts reflect the burial of the king, his existence in the tomb, and his participation in the daily journey of the sun.[119] At sunset, according to these texts, the "old" king enters his crypt as the god Re-Atum, a manifestation of the evening sun. The king spends the night in the tomb, which represents the netherworld, and is there united with Osiris, in the form of the king's own mummy. Recently, I. E. S. Edwards has theorized that the royal stone sarcophagus was thought of as the body of the sky goddess Nut, the mother of Osiris, a concept Edwards traces back to Khufu, the first king buried in a stone sarcophagus.[120] At sunrise, the king is reborn and leaves his sarcophagus as the young sun god Khepri. The god-king departs from his resting place through the antechamber of the crypt and starts a new cycle of life, ascending to the sun as the mature sun god Re-Harakhti.[121] This interpretation suggests that the close association of the deceased king with the eternal cycle of the sun did not begin with the royal tombs of the New Kingdom but had already been formulated in the Old Kingdom.[122]

After the offering hall was introduced into the pyramid temple at the beginning of the Fifth Dynasty, the false door that leaned against the pyramid enabled the dead king to leave his crypt to receive his food offering. Information about this ritual is provided by the Pyramid Texts and the Abusir Papyri, the latter being archival remains from the mortuary temples of Neferirkare and Neferefre. The papyri also include lists of daily services, special festivals, inventories of temple furnishings and equipment, registries of accounts, letters, and even "passports" for the staff. It is remarkable that neither the Abusir Papyri nor the temple wall decorations mention the burial of the king; the papyri only give us a picture of the temple activities carried out *after* the king's burial. This gap, as well as other evidence, make it quite clear that the burial rites were not performed in the temple.[123] Further, the funeral procession did not land at the valley temple, did not ascend the causeway, and did not make use of the upper temple. The route along which the funeral was conducted and the stage for the funerary ceremonies are unknown.

The pyramid temples were neither empty shells nor purely symbolic architecture, effective by their simple existence. They were used intensively for a variety of religious ceremonies. For example, an offering service for the king was performed every morning and evening.[124] Central to the daily services were the five statues of the king in the Chapel of the Five Niches (fig. 23), three of which showed the king as Osiris, seated and wearing the Red and White Crowns; the other two have not yet been identified.[125] The priests opened the doors of the five shrines one by one and performed on the statues the ancient ritual of the Opening of the Mouth, a ceremony that brought the cult images to life and allowed them to partake of food offerings. Clothes were offered to the king, probably by being shown to the statue, and a symbolic anointing was performed. Then the priests apparently presented the royal food offering in a separate room, the large offering hall in front of the false door (figs. 24, 26). Disassociating the Chapel of the Five Niches from the offering hall continued the older architectural and ceremonial tradition of constructing the statue temple and the mortuary offering temple as separate buildings for discrete rituals (figs. 11, 21—Bent and Userkaf pyramids). After the offering ceremonies, the offering mats were rolled up and sealed in a chest, and the *še*-basin of copper was placed in front of the statues of the king for the *qebeḥu*-purification by water. After the water had been used, it apparently was poured into the drainage basin in the east wall of the offering hall, and the basin was sealed in its chest. Then the food offering was removed and distributed to the priests, who had to show documents proving that they were entitled to it.

During the day, the temple was full of activity as the guards and priests-in-charge performed their daily duties. Astronomer priests climbed the roof to measure the time and determine the exact beginning of the next cycle of morning ceremonies. Others guarded the doors of the storerooms and other secured places, including the Chapel of the Five Niches and the offering hall. In the evening, after the king had returned from his sky journey and reentered the pyramid, the gates of the temple could be closed. The normal daily service was often interrupted or intensified by festival ceremonies, several of which are mentioned in the Abusir Papyri. The festivals of Sokar, Hathor, and Min have already been discussed, and several more are attested.

Besides the Abusir Papyri, a key source for our understanding of the pyramid temples are their decorations and inscriptions; important groups of reliefs have been found in the temples of Sahure and Pepi II, though not enough to reconstruct their complete decorative programs.[126] From the Sahure temple, which is considered to be well preserved, only 1–2 percent of the original wall surface has survived (fig. 27)! Even so, we are able to gain a shadowy idea of the subjects depicted and of their distribution through the temple. Originally, all interior walls except those in storerooms were decorated with reliefs, but not the temple's exterior walls. Unlike temples of the New Kingdom and Ptolemaic Period, these temples have no building inscriptions or short texts to indicate the name and purpose of the rooms. The subjects and distribution of the reliefs must, however, bear some relationship to the purpose of the architecture.[127] But in what way is one to read and interpret the reliefs? Unlike the ritual scenes under the great lists of the offering hall, these rarely portray identifiable ceremonies. The king, for example, is represented in the *per-weru* hall as fowling or hunting hippopotamus. The reliefs do not mean that such actions took place in the *per-weru* hall or that ritual killings of animals or enemies of the king were symbolically reenacted in that hall. Instead, the motifs demonstrate the funerary complex's role as a place for displaying royal power and victory in both this world and the other, and they stress the importance of such royal aspects for the room in which they appear.

The motif of foreign captives is repeated on statues showing kneeling prisoners of war with their arms drawn back and lashed at the elbows.[128] These limestone statues, about 84 cm high, represent the traditional enemies of Egypt, namely, African, Libyan, Asiatic, and perhaps Puntite tribes, and appear in great quantities in several pyramid temples. Long lines of statues of prisoners were probably placed along the causeway and *per-weru* walls and perhaps even in the pillared court and transverse corridor—that is, in all places where battle and triumph scenes were depicted. The wall decoration and the statues represented the king's power over enemies, an aspect of the pyramid temple whose origins lay in the earlier fortresses of the gods.

List of Pyramid Complexes of the Fifth and Sixth Dynasties (2510–2195 B.C.E.)[129]

Fifth Dynasty:	Userkaf	Saqqara
	Sahure	Abusir
	Neferirkare	Abusir (unfinished)
	Shepseskare-Ini	Abusir (unexcavated)
	Neferefre	Abusir (unfinished)
	Niuserre-Izi	Abusir
	Djedkare-Isesi	Saqqara-South
	Unas	Saqqara
Sixth Dynasty:	Teti	Saqqara
	Pepi I Merire	Saqqara-South
	Merenre	Saqqara-South (unexcavated)
	Pepi II Neferkare	Saqqara-South

The Middle Kingdom

With the end of the Old Kingdom, many important changes took place in Egyptian culture and religion, and they certainly must have affected the royal cult complex. Because of the heavy damage most of these buildings have suffered, we know even less about them than about their Old Kingdom predecessors.

During the Eleventh Dynasty, local rulers of Thebes built their tombs at el-Tarif, at the northern end of the Theban necropolis. These so-called *saff*-tombs were constructed as oversized local private tombs and did not contain exclusive royal cult installations. The earliest true royal cult complex of the Middle Kingdom was that of Mentuhotep Nebhepetre at Deir el-Bahri (fig. 31). It differs essentially from the preceding royal *saff*-tombs and shows no formal similarity to the Old Kingdom temples (fig. 32). The temple rises on a high platform in a large court that occupies the west end of the desert valley of Deir el-Bahri. The front of the temple is grouped around a massive 11 m high core building, which, foundation inscriptions tell us, was dedicated to the god Montu-Re. Behind this building we find the entrance to the tomb passage and a large hall of eighty-two octagonal pillars; the subjects of the hall's wall decoration indicate that it continued the tradition of an offering hall.

Two features that show post–Sixth Dynasty changes seem especially important.[130] In the rear part of the temple, the wall reliefs follow the old prototype depicting the king at an offering table with an offering list and offering bearers. In the center of the hypostyle hall, between the pillars, a sanctuary was added for the *Sed*-festival of the king; it housed a colossal royal cult statue (fig. 32, right) supplemented (later?) by a smaller image of Amun-Re. The wall decoration of this sanctuary illustrates the first impor-

Fig. 31. The temples of Mentuhotep Nebhepetre (foreground) and Hatshepsut (background) at Deir el-Bahri. Photo by Dieter Arnold.

tant changes. No longer is the king the sole recipient of the cultus, but rather he enacts the ceremonies for Amun-Re.[131] In other words, for the first time a god intrudes into the main sanctuary of a royal cult complex. The Mentuhotep Temple is no longer a mortuary temple, if indeed there ever was one; it has been transformed into the site of a joint cultus where the king and the god are united in the same statue. This uniting of the king and the gods will play an important role in the mortuary temples of the New Kingdom, the Mansions of Millions of Years (see Chapter 3). The close connection between the royal cultus, the Mansion-of-Millions-of-Years aspect, and the *Sed*-festival is further emphasized by a long row of royal statues added to the causeway and forecourt of the temple, probably for the observance of the *Sed*-festival celebrated in the king's thirty-ninth year.[132]

The second important change in the Mentuhotep Temple is also found on the wall decoration of the same sanctuary, where the ancient motif of the enthroned king surrounded by the chief gods of Upper and Lower Egypt (Nekhbet, Seth, Horus, and Wadjit) is accentuated by an innovative motif demonstrating an important change in the status of the king: the gods present him with bundles of palm branches, the symbol for endless years.[133] (For a slightly later example, see fig. 33). In the Old Kingdom, the king had been the lord of the pyramid complex, and his cultus had been the center of the temple; now he is reduced to a human ruler dependent on

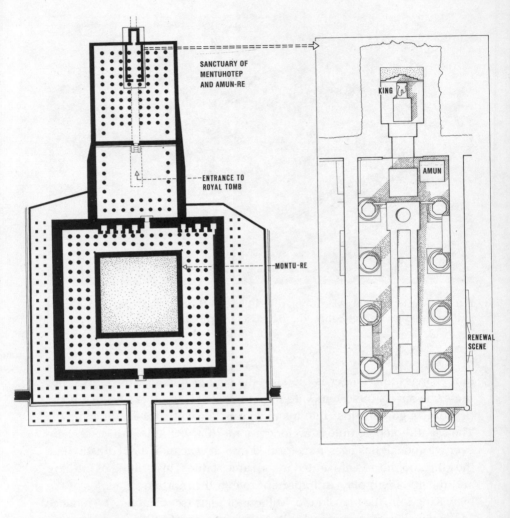

FIG. 32. Plan of the funerary complex of Mentuhotep Nebhepetre at Deir el-Bahri. *Inset:* the sanctuary of Amun-Re and the king. Drawing by Dieter Arnold.

the gods' goodwill. His immortality is no longer innate; it has to be bestowed on him by the gods.

During the reign of Amenemhat I, the royal residence moved from Thebes back to the Memphite area. In the vicinity of modern el-Lisht, the king founded the capital of *Jt-t3wj* (Itj-tawy), where he renounced the provincial Theban tomb tradition in favor of a pyramid complex in the Memphite style of the Sixth Dynasty. Political conflicts apparently prevented the architects of Amenemhat I from studying the ancient guidelines used to construct pyramid precincts, resulting in a number of unique features in the pyra-

FIG. 33. Lintel of Amenemhat I from his pyramid temple at el-Lisht, with the representation of the enthroned king at the *Sed*-festival. Drawing by Barry Girsh.

mid and cult complex. For example, in the pyramid, a vertical shaft seems to connect the sloping entrance passage to the burial chamber, now under water. The eastern temple is not built against the casing of the pyramid but stands on a lower level and leans against the platform of the pyramid. Compared to Old Kingdom examples, the structure is tiny, and it has a complicated building history. Building blocks from a dismantled older structure of Amenemhat I and Senwosret I, which emphasize the *Sed*-festival, have been found in the foundations of the final temple (fig. 33).

Enough traces remain of the cult complex of the successor of Amenemhat I, Senwosret I, to reconstruct its ground plan and offer some generalizations about the program of wall relief (fig. 34). Several large fragments of the offering hall preserve the king's funerary banquet and courtiers bringing offerings. From the square antechamber we have fragments of large figures of the king, who is represented standing before gods and goddesses and receiving the homage of his courtiers. Several extant fragments of the transverse corridor show ritual scenes. Many pieces of the court's limestone pillars remain, with high and narrow panels showing the king being embraced by various deities, confirming that the court was still seen as a meeting point for the gods and the king. Also belonging to the court, or possibly to the causeway, are numerous fragments featuring the smiting of enemies and the taking of booty, perhaps a last reflection of the royal cult complex's aspect as a collection point for tribute and taxes.

The inner court of the pyramid was enclosed by a limestone wall deco-

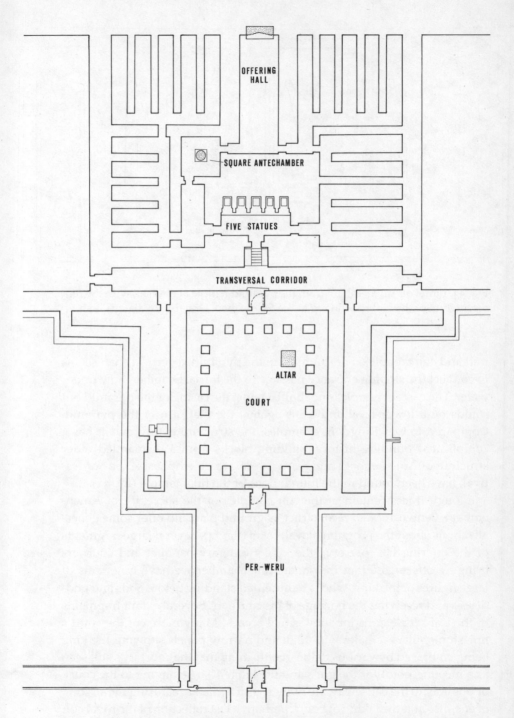

OFFERING
HALL

SQUARE ANTECHAMBER

FIVE STATUES

TRANSVERSAL CORRIDOR

ALTAR

COURT

PER-WERU

FIG. 34. Plan of the pyramid temple of Senwosret I at el-Lisht. Drawing by Dieter Arnold.

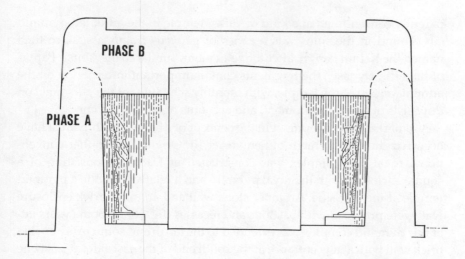

PHASE B

PHASE A

FIG. 35. Section through the causeway of Senwosret I at el-Lisht. Drawing by Dieter Arnold.

rated on both sides with one hundred colossal royal-name panels spaced at about 5 m intervals.[134] The panels rest on the heads of fecundity figures, who carry offerings toward the entrance of the temple. The huge falcon figures above the name panels emphasize that the center of the pyramid complex was a palace for the Horus-king (fig. 4b). This almost unique type of decoration was repeated only by Hatshepsut in her New Kingdom temple at Deir el-Bahri.

One interesting detail confirms the continuity in function of the royal cult complexes from the Old Kingdom to Mentuhotep Nebhepetre and Senwosret I and finally to the Mansions of Millions of Years of the New Kingdom. Senwosret I lined his causeway with life-size royal Osiride statues, set up in niches in the inner wall surfaces of the passage (fig. 35), probably for the *Sed*-festival in year 31 of his reign. The oldest examples of such statues were found in the *Sed*-festival court of Djoser (fig. 9); the latest adorn the front, courts, and hypostyle halls of the Mansions of Millions of Years of the New Kingdom.[135]

The mortuary complex of Amenemhat II at Dahshur is completely destroyed.[136] The space available between the upper end of its 20 m wide causeway and the ruined pyramid suggests that a huge building originally stood there, perhaps 105 m long and 100 m wide.

The short reign of Senwosret II, the following king, was probably the reason why his cult complex at Illahun remained insignificant and unfinished. A small 15 × 20 m mortuary chapel, which seems to have housed a granite shrine, was attached to the royal pyramid.[137] The royal cultus was apparently concentrated at a kind of valley temple in the affiliated pyramid city. Found in the ruins was a series of papyrus fragments, since then named the Kahun Papyri, after the settlement. Similar to the Abusir Papyri of the Fifth Dynasty, the fragments contain important information on the administration of the temple, with monthly schedules of the personnel on duty, lists of temple equipment, and accounts of temple income.[138]

A remarkable development in the concept of divine kingship must have occurred during the reign of Senwosret III. Originally, a rather conventional royal cult complex was constructed at Dahshur consisting of a square enclosure with the royal pyramid and a relatively modest pyramid temple at the east side. An inner stone wall and an outer brick enclosure wall were provided with bastions and recesses (fig. 18).[139] Some years later this pyramid complex was extended to the north and south by a paneled brick wall with a new entrance at the south end of the east side; at least one secondary entrance was placed in the new south wall. The new south court contained a huge stone temple. The purpose of the south temple is not yet quite understood, but one may assume that the structure supplemented the original sanctuary at the east side of the pyramid with important new cultic elements.[140] Some of the new aspects may have been those of the *Sed*-festival and of the later Mansion of Millions of Years.

Present evidence indicates that Senwosret III was also the first king since the Second Dynasty to build a large cult complex at Abydos; it consisted of a valley temple and a desert funerary enclosure with an enormous underground rock tomb.[141] There are indications that the king was buried here rather than under his pyramid at Dahshur, which seems to have remained unused.[142]

The cult complex of Amenemhat III at Dahshur was apparently unfinished when structural failures in the underground apartments of the pyramid caused the builders to abandon it. Nevertheless, the pyramid complex was surrounded by a paneled brick wall with an entrance at the south end of the east side. The wall enclosed a relatively small cult temple at the east side of the pyramid.[143] Three extensive royal burial systems were incorporated into the pyramid: the primary one containing the granite sarcophagus for the king, a secondary one probably intended to house his *ka*-statue, and burial chambers accommodating two queens. Altogether the pyramid contains an astounding twenty-four chambers and chapels.

A huge cult complex corresponding to the south temple of Senwosret III was built at Hawara in the Faiyum, the famous Labyrinth. In consequence of the building disaster at Dahshur, a second pyramid was later added to the Labyrinth by Amenemhat III. Both structures, the Labyrinth and the mortuary complex, are hopelessly destroyed, but we have descriptions by six ancient authors, including Herodotus and Strabo, both of whom saw these unique buildings while they still stood.[144] Despite their detailed descriptions, we are unable to reconstruct an accurate ground plan, but can only make general statements about certain aspects of the complex. One important feature is mentioned in the ancient sources: an unusual number of small temples or chapels. According to Pliny, "The ground plan . . . is divided among the regions or administrative districts known as nomes, of which there are 21, each having a vast hall allotted to it by name. Besides these halls, it contains temples of all the Egyptian gods; . . . Inside are columns of imperial porphyry, images of gods, statues of kings and figures of monsters."[145] Strabo also reports that

a great palace composed of many palaces—as many in number as there were Nomes in earlier times; for this is the number of courts, surrounded by colonnades, continuous with one another, all in a single row and along one wall, the structure being as it were a long wall with the courts in front of it; and the roads leading into them are exactly opposite the wall. In front of the entrances are crypts, as it were, which are long and numerous and have winding passages communicating with one another. . . . It is said that this number of courts was built because it was the custom for all the Nomes to assemble there in accordance with their rank, together with their own priests and priestesses, for the sake of sacrifice and of offering gifts to the gods and of administering justice in matters of the greatest importance.[146]

These authors placed great emphasis on the chapels of the nome gods and the assembly of all the gods, each reflective of a two-thousand-year-old tradition. Such rites and ceremonies had shaped basic features of the fortresses of the gods and the royal funerary enclosures down to the *Sed*-festival chapels in the Djoser complex (fig. 9) and were still reflected in the square antechambers of Fifth and Sixth Dynasty pyramid temples; and the idea that the royal cult complex should serve as an assembly place for the gods continued in the plans of the royal mortuary temples of the New Kingdom and later periods.[147]

A few fragments discovered by Flinders Petrie in the ruins of the Labyrinth at Hawara confirm the accuracy of some of the ancient authors' observations.[148] For example, he found parts of engaged, channeled (half-)columns that are exact duplicates of the north- and south-building columns of the Djoser complex.[149] He also recovered several fragments of unusual, animal-headed statues, some of them depicting crocodiles, which could well have been called monsters. These statues probably represented nome gods, many of them the crocodile deities of the nearby Faiyum. Finally, Petrie found remains of sculpture groups showing the king standing between two gods—late successors to the triads of Menkaure—and even a foot from an 8 m high granite colossus.

A comparison of the three pyramid complexes built by Senwosret III and Amenemhat III suggests a close relationship between the later-added south temple of Senwosret III and the Labyrinth at Hawara. One might even assume that the Labyrinth was originally built as the "south temple" of the first pyramid complex of Amenemhat III at Dahshur and was only later combined with the king's second royal cult complex.

In the Middle Kingdom, a decorative motif, the gods of Upper and Lower Egypt standing in front of their chapels, entered both the royal mortuary complexes and other temples that were connected to the cultus of the king but without specific relationship to his burial. This can be seen, for example, in the decorative program of Twelfth and Thirteenth Dynasty temple gates (fig. 36). Their architraves include a scene whose prototype appears in the Mentuhotep Temple: the enthroned king wearing the *Sed*-festival costume while receiving bundles of palm branches, the symbol representing millions of years. On both door frames the gods, arranged in two groups, are shown standing before their chapels: the gods of the north, placed with the *per-nu* chapel of Lower Egypt; the gods of the south, standing next to the *per-wer* chapel of Upper Egypt.

This type of decoration, ultimately derived from the relief program of the pyramid temple's square antechamber (fig. 29), closely connects the royal temples of the Middle Kingdom to those of the New Kingdom. Precisely the same decorative program appears on the main gates of the Ramesseum (fig. 37)[150] and at Medinet Habu, structures that were the Mansions of Millions of Years of Ramesses II and Ramesses III. The last known example of this decoration in pharaonic Egypt appears on the *Sed*-festival gate of Osorkon II at Bubastis.[151] The long history of the motif of the gods' chapels (for the development, see fig. 3) indicates that the desire to perpetuate the king's life and power remained a basic and unchanging element of buildings connected with divine kingship from the earliest dynasties to the Late Period and the end of pharaonic rule in Egypt.

List of Funerary Complexes of the Eleventh and Twelfth Dynasties (2065–2014 and 1994–1794 B.C.E.)[152]

Eleventh Dynasty:	Mentuhotep Nebhepetre	Complex at Deir el-Bahri
Twelfth Dynasty:	Amenemhat I	First tomb at Qurna
		Pyramid at el-Lisht
	Senwosret I	Pyramid at el-Lisht
	Amenemhat II	Pyramid at Dahshur
	Senwosret II	Pyramid at Illahun
	Senwosret III	Pyramid at Dahshur
		Tomb at Abydos
	Amenemhat III	First pyramid at Dahshur
		Second pyramid at Hawara ("Labyrinth")

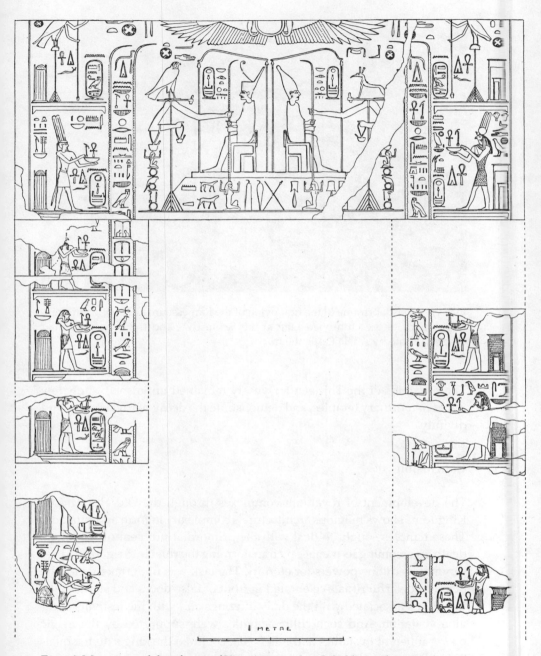

Fig. 36. Monumental doorframe of King Amenemhat-Sobekhotep from Medamud (Thirteenth Dynasty), showing the enthroned king at the *Sed*-festival receiving "millions of years" from the gods of Lower and Upper Egypt. From Rémy Cottevieille-Giraudet, *Rapport sur les fouilles de Médamoud (1931). Les monuments du Moyen Empire*, FIFAO 9/1 (Cairo: IFAO, 1933), pl. 5. The left side of the doorframe displays the *per-nu* chapel of Lower Egypt, and the right side, the *per-wer* chapel of Upper Egypt.

FIG. 37. Inner doorframe of the first pylon of the Ramesseum at Thebes, with representations of the enthroned king at the *Sed*-festival and the gods with their chapels. Photo by Adela Oppenheim.

The pyramids of the Thirteenth Dynasty remained unfinished, show few traces of mortuary temples, and demonstrate the decay of royal power and divinity.

Conclusion

The development of royal cult complexes through the Old and Middle Kingdoms shows religious architecture's complexity in form and function. These temples sought to deal with the primordial problem of the king's death, overcoming its menace by transforming the ruler into a god and preserving his divine powers for eternity. The task was undertaken with the help of powerful rituals celebrated in front of false doors and statues, like the rituals associated with the daily offerings and with the festivals of divine visitation. And such cultic activities were supported by the magic power inherent in statues and reliefs that conjured the king's divine qualities, his victories over enemies, and the eternal duration of his rule.

The architectural environment for these rituals, statues, and reliefs was of utmost importance. The buildings offered a functional shelter for the ceremonies and living images, but beyond that their form created the king's simulated otherworldly residence. This-worldly buildings were transformed into everlasting stone capable of functioning through eternity without the agency of priests. Amazing examples of "functional" dummy buildings are found in the Djoser complex. They testify to Egyptians' belief that life could be infused into anything they created, however inanimate it might seem. The architectural environment's power was intensified by symbolic elements that both memorialized and reactivated mythic episodes from the dawn of Egypt's formation.

The most essential part of Old and Middle Kingdom royal cult complexes was the pyramid, with the so-called tomb of the pharaoh. I say "so-called" because it was intended to be a transitory station for the descent, transformation, and rebirth of the ruler rather than the eternal resting place of the royal mummy. The pyramid's function as a site for magical activity assimilated it to the temples of the royal complex.

To the deification of the Egyptian ruler and the perpetuation of his divine powers religious architecture contributed its overpowering monumentality—an attribute of buildings in many other civilizations, including the America of the 1930s. Overpowering monumentality demonstrated the Egyptian ruler's capacity to create everlastingly secure bastions against the eternal threat of disorder, rebellion, and decay.

3

NEW KINGDOM «MORTUARY TEMPLES» AND «MANSIONS OF MILLIONS OF YEARS»

GERHARD HAENY

Introduction

The term "mortuary temple" as currently used in Egyptology is too much influenced by modern Western attitudes. Today the rites performed for a dead person center chiefly on burial, deposition in a tomb, but Egyptian mortuary temples were built to sustain the life of the deceased in the hereafter. In Egypt's earliest times, the dead were believed to need a material supply of food and drink, the victuals called *k3*. Such provisions gradually changed into merely symbolic offerings to the *k3*-spirit thought to be embodied in the *k3*-statue that at first was set up in the tomb and later in the vicinity of divine temples as well. Such statues were frequently sheltered in *k3*-houses. The term "*k3*-house" was still occasionally used for the huge establishments created by New Kingdom pharaohs in the domain of a god, their "royal mansions," where they expected to spend "millions of years" in a mystic union with the deity.

The arguments I present have been outlined in other contexts. Here I aim to develop them through a chronologically arranged survey of the main sources. Space does not permit me to discuss all the aspects involved.

The New Kingdom royal cult complexes in the necropolis of Western Thebes are usually called "mortuary temples." However, the term's prevalent use conceals a widespread disagreement among scholars about the meaning of the word, the criteria for assigning it to particular structures, the ritual functions of buildings so designated, and the types of cultus performed there. The term could be useful if scholars agreed on a clear definition. But we have each held our slightly differing concept, and the result has been misunderstanding and confusion.

"Mortuary temple" corresponds to no ancient Egyptian word or phrase. The designation was invented by nineteenth-century Egyptologists. Adolf Erman, the founder of the great Berlin dictionary of the Egyptian language, acknowledged as much when he wrote in 1936, "In front of each [Old Kingdom] pyramid there was placed an especially large building, which *we nowadays call the mortuary temple.*"[1] I do not know the first author to use the term "mortuary temple," but the first cult complexes to be identified as funerary were the temple of Sety I at Qurna, the temple of Ramesses II called the Ramesseum, and the temple of Ramesses III at Medinet Habu—the best-preserved ancient structures of the Theban necropolis. Writing in 1877, the British novelist and traveler Amelia B. Edwards described the three cult complexes in considerable detail and told her readers:[2] "Mariette was of [the] opinion that the Temple of Medinet Habu, erected as it is on the side of the great Theban necropolis, is, like the Ramesseum, a funerary monument erected by Rameses III in his own lifetime to his own memory.[3] [Its] battered colossi represent the king in the character of Osiris, and are in fact on a huge scale precisely what the ordinary funerary statuettes are upon a small scale . . . and they alone suffice to determine the character of the building." Concerning the temple of Sety I, Edwards said:[4] "As for the Temple of Gournah, it is, at least in part, as distinctly a memorial edifice as the Medici Chapel at Florence or the Superga at Turin." However, Edwards ended her description of the Qurna temple by admitting:[5] "Adjoining what may be called the monumental part of the building, we find a number of halls and chambers, the uses of which are unknown. Most writers assume that they were the private apartments of the king. Some [of them] go so far as to give the name of Temple-Palaces to all these great funerary structures. It is, however, far more probable that these Western Temples were erected in connection, though not in direct communication, with the royal tombs in the adjacent valley of Bab [Biban]-el-Molûk."[6]

Edwards described briefly the extant remains of other buildings in Western Thebes. She assumed, somewhat too hastily, that the same funerary character was true "of almost every important structure erected upon this side of the river."[7] For her and for many others, a building's location on the west bank, in the necropolis of Thebes, proved that its function was mortuary, a conclusion they believed confirmed by the presence there of Osiride statues sculpted at the front of pillars.

The Ramesseum and the temples of Qurna and Medinet Habu were all built during the Ramesside Period (Dynasties 19–20). They were the subject of a detailed study by Harold H. Nelson, who was from 1924 to 1947 the Director of the University of Chicago's Epigraphic Survey at Luxor.[8] Nelson compared the formulas used to designate the three cult complexes in monumental inscriptions and administrative documents. The formulas were, to use his translations: (1) "The Temple (called) 'Seti-Merenptah-is-Glorious' in the estate of Amon on the West of Thebes" [Qurna]; (2) "The Temple of Usermare-Setepenre (called) 'United-with-Thebes' in the estate of Amon on the West of Thebes" [the Ramesseum]; and (3) "The Temple of Usermare-Meriamon (called) 'United-with-Eternity' in the estate of Amon on the West of Thebes" [Medinet Habu]. According to Nelson's analysis, the formulas were composed of four elements common to all and a fifth element distinctive to each: (1) a word designating a type of building; (2) the name of the king who founded the temple: "Seti-Merenptah"—Sety I; "Usermare-Setepenre"—Ramesses II; "Usermare-Meriamon"—Ramesses III; (3) the building's status as being incorporated "in the domain of Amun"; (4) its topographic location "on the West of Thebes"; and (5) the changing element giving a distinctive name to each temple: "Seti-Merenptah-is-Glorious" in the case of Qurna; "United-with-Thebes" in the case of the Ramesseum; and "United-with-Eternity" in the case of Medinet Habu.

In order to present a concise argument, however, Nelson passed silently over some minor details in the sources he had collected:[9]

- Sety I called his cult complex not simply *ḥwt* ("temple") but frequently also *ḥwt nṯr* ("temple of god"), a term normally associated with so-called divine temples.[10]
- The formulas for the Ramesseum and Medinet Habu followed the usual custom and used the king's prenomen, or throne name (Usermaʿatre-Setepenre and Usermaʿatre-Meryamun).[11] Atypically, the formula for the temple of Qurna was composed with the king's nomen, or personal name (Sety-Merneptah).[12]
- The special name of the Qurna temple included the king's nomen, and Nelson had to translate it "Seti-Merenptah-is-Glorious" because the verb *3ḫ* ("is glorious") needed a subject. The verbal forms in the formulas for the Ramesseum and Medinet Habu have a feminine ending, and Nelson saw them linked with the feminine noun *ḥwt*, "the Temple" or "the Mansion." But his generally accepted translations do not make much sense: "the Temple united with Thebes" or "the Mansion united with eternity." It would seem more natural to introduce the names of the kings as the subjects of the verbs. Ramesses II, in being buried in the Valley of the Kings, became "united with Thebes," and Ramesses III, in dying at Thebes, "joined eternity." But I do not know how such an interpretation can be reconciled with the presently accepted rules of grammar.[13]

- Nelson did not comment on an additional formula associated with the temple of Sety I: *n ḥḥ m rnpwt*, "of millions of years," though the passage occurs twice in Nelson's reproductions of the temple's hieroglyphic inscriptions.[14] It appears first in a writing that dedicates the southern part of the temple to Ramesses I: Sety "made as his monument for his father, the Osiris King Ramesses, the making for him of [a chapel] of millions of years [within] the divine temple 'Glorious-is-Sety-Merneptah' in the estate of Amun on the West of Thebes."[15] The phrase occurs a second time in a description of the temple's processional barque. The passage reads: *sšm-ḫw n nb t3wj mn-mˁ3t-rˁ nb ḫˁw stj-mr-n-ptḥ m ḥwt.f nt ḥḥw m rnpwt n ḏt*, "the Processional Barque of the Lord of the Two Lands Menmaˁatre, the Lord of Crowns Sety-Merneptah in his Divine Temple of Millions of Years, of Eternity."[16] Elsewhere in New Kingdom inscriptions, "of millions of years" so frequently describes structures now thought to have been mortuary temples that some scholars regard the phrase as a clear indicator of a building's funerary function.[17] This interpretation meets with difficulties, as we shall see.

Nelson's investigation did not extend beyond the three Ramesside temples, but we should examine earlier evidence as well.[18] The oldest known reference to a "Mansion of Millions of Years" occurs in two lines of text inscribed on the back pillar of a statue from Dynasty 13 found at Karnak by Auguste Mariette.[19] The statue was given to the vizier *ʾIj-mr* as a favor from his royal master, who gave him permission to set it up *m pr nb.f m t3 ḥwt nt ḥḥ n rnpt ḥtp-k3-sbkḥtp*, "in the House of his Lord in the Mansion of Millions of Years (named) 'Satisfied-Is-the-*ka*-of-Sobekhotep.'"[20] Here the name of the building, like that of the temple of Sety I, uses the king's personal name rather than his prenomen (throne name).

The next reference to a "Mansion of Millions of Years" is engraved in the quarries of Tura about ten miles south of Cairo and dates to the beginning of the New Kingdom, about two hundred years after Sobekhotep. King Ahmose, the founder of Dynasty 18, writes of reopening the quarries in order to extract beautiful white limestone *r ḥwwt.f nt ḥḥw m*————"for his Mansions of Millions of————."[21] The line ends with a lacuna, but the word *rnpwt*, "years," may be supplied on the basis of an inscription that offers a rather close parallel; it was found nearby and dates to Amenhotep III.[22] If a Mansion of Millions of Years was always a mortuary temple, why does Ahmose's inscription speak of "Mansions" in the plural? We would expect a king to have only one mortuary temple somewhere near his Theban tomb. But the next line of Ahmose's inscription lists a puzzling set of buildings: "the temple of Ptah," "the temple of a god" (who has no specific name, unless the next signs—*nṯr nfr*, "the perfect god"—have to be accepted as his attribute), "Amun of *ʾIpt*," "*ḥwt nswt*, the king's mansion," ending with the summary "for all the monuments that his Majesty made." None of the buildings mentioned in that line was definitely a funerary monument. Either (1) Ahmose had stones cut for several mortuary temples "of millions of years" *and* for a number of divine cult complexes that were not "of millions of years" or (2) Ahmose's Mansions of Millions of Years included temples that are presently not identified as serving a mortuary purpose.

Assuming explanation 2 to be correct, the phrase "of millions of years" would indicate nothing more than that a structure was meant to endure for eternity. Such a possibility is not easily dismissed. It was important to the Egyptians that a structure was solid and firm, and most building texts mention the quality of the stone and the perfect work. Furthermore, the Erman-Grapow dictionary of the Egyptian language lists a number of passages that speak of a building as made *m k3t mnḫt*, "in excellent work(manship)," or *m k3t nḥḥ* (*m k3t ḏt*), "in work of eternity."[23] In no inscription that refers to the merely material qualities of a building has the phrase "of millions of years" been observed. All texts speaking of millions of years belong to the realm of religion. Countless pictorial representations and inscriptions in practically every temple portray the gods presenting the king "millions of years" in return for the offerings heaped on the altars.[24] The places where this mutual exchange was supposed to happen were not the "divine temples" in the first line, but the specific buildings each king built for himself, the "mansions" known by the king's name, where he expected to be represented by his image and to meet the gods "for millions of years" when the gods were carried past in the processions repeated at regular intervals. As every mansion was built for an individual king, we should not expect to find much uniformity in their plan and the inner organization of the rooms, in the selection of scenes carved on their walls, or in the ritual equipment with which they were furnished (of which unfortunately very little has survived). These arrangements were influenced by political and regional circumstances and quite as much by theological ideas that, although tied to a number of basic concepts, changed and developed almost imperceptibly from reign to reign. On the following pages, we shall trace this evolution, as far as it can be perceived in the monuments and documents that have resisted the agents of time.

Royal Cult Complexes of the Eighteenth Dynasty

During Dynasty 18, the rites for a deceased member of the royal family could be celebrated in more than one place, places not necessarily near the tomb. An inscription of Ahmose relates a conversation between the king and his wife-sister Ahmose-Nefertari about preparations for the cultus of their grandmother, Queen Tetisheri.[25] The king says: *wnn jsj.s mr-ʿḥʿt.s m tj 3t ḥr s3tw wst t3-wr jw 3b n ḥm dj.t irt.n.s mr st m t3 ḏsr m s3ḫt mnw nw ḥm,* "There exists her tomb (and) her *mr-ʿḥʿt* [cenotaph] at this moment on the grounds of Thebes (and) of Abydos. It is the wish of Majesty to have made for her a pyramid temple on the holy land in the vicinity of the monuments of Majesty." We learn here that funerary rites were to be celebrated for Tetisheri at three structures (tomb, cenotaph, and pyramid temple) located in two places (Thebes, the family's traditional residence, and Abydos, the sacred ground of Osiris).[26] Each of the three structures is identified by a specific Egyptian term. Tetisheri's tomb (*jsj*) was probably located in the Theban necropolis, although it has not yet been discovered.[27] Her cenotaph (here written *mr-ʿḥʿt*; elsewhere *mʿḥʿt*) stood at Abydos, possibly at the site where Tetisheri's stela was found.[28] But the place was so poorly excavated and recorded that nothing is known about the structure's layout. We can only guess that it would have been the type characteristic of Abydos— a memorial chapel located (as related texts inform us) *r rdw n nṯr ʿ3 nb 3bḏw,* "by the terrace of the great god, the lord of Abydos" (that is, in the vicinity of the temple of Osiris), and containing the royal person's stela or statue and, in front of that, an altar for offerings.[29] Nor can we reach a clear understanding of the pyramid temple (*mr st*) mentioned in Ahmose's text, even though the Abydene monuments of the king and queen-grandmother have been found and excavated.[30] The king's own buildings are referred to on the stela by the generic word *mnw,* "monuments," which conveys no specific meaning. Excavators have found the ruins of four structures extending two-thirds of a mile up a gravel terrace: a pyramid at the edge of the cultivated land, Tetisheri's temple about halfway up the terrace, a subterranean tomblike structure farther up, and an artificial temple-platform at the end of the terrace. All these constructions followed local tradition, as is proved by their proximity to a similar installation belonging to Senwosret III (Dynasty 12).[31] Evidently both complexes were, on a king's scale, a *mʿḥʿt* for reviving the monarchs' names in the presence of Osiris.

After Ahmose, the custom of erecting a royal cenotaph at Abydos, perhaps a tradition originating in the Old Kingdom, was discontinued for more than 250 years.[32] It was revived in the first three reigns of Dynasty 19, although in quite different architectural form.

The mummy of Ahmose was found in the Theban cache of reburied New Kingdom royalty discovered in 1881 near Deir el-Bahri.[33] Yet there is not a trace, architectural or inscriptional, of a Theban structure prepared for Ahmose's funeral and his memorial service, even though a commemorative cultus is amply attested there for his half-sister and wife Ahmose-Nefertari and for their son Amenhotep I. Amenhotep I (Djeserkare Amenhotep) and

Ahmose-Nefertari were venerated as local deities in grand processions conducted until the end of the New Kingdom.

The temple of Amenhotep was supposedly situated at the foot of the hill of Dra-Abu'l-Nagʿa in the northern part of the Theban necropolis, although nothing of it remains there.[34] Representations of the procession are found in the tombs of priests attached to Amenhotep's temple.[35] They cite the priests' title as ḥm-nṯr n imn-ḥtp n p3 wb3, "Priest of Amenhotep of the Forecourt"; wb3, "forecourt," is a toponym for the gravel plain in front of the entrance of the Valley of the Kings, the presumed location of this temple. In other tombs, we find titles linked to the king's prenomen (throne name): imj-rʾ pr m ḥwt ḏsr-k3-rʿ ḥr imntt w3st, "Overseer of the House in the Mansion of Djeserkare on the West of Thebes," and imj-rʾ pr ḏsr-k3-rʿ, "Overseer of the House of Djeserkare." Whether these men served the principal temple—the temple of the forecourt—or some other cult complex is difficult to determine, for the cultus of the king and his mother spread to other localities in the Theban necropolis, particularly the workmen's village of Deir el-Medina.[36] Other titles associate priests and administrators with imn m mn-st, "Amun in mn-st." Mn-st, according to some scholars, was the name of Ahmose-Nefertari's principal temple.[37] If so, the reference to Amun's presence there is puzzling and, in light of observations to be made later, should be kept in mind.

Thutmose I (Aakheperkare Thutmose) expanded the frontiers of Egypt far to the south and toward the northeast. He was the first person to prepare a rock tomb in the Valley of the Kings. The name of the building erected to serve his mortuary cultus was ḥnmt-ʿnḫ, a term whose meaning is difficult to grasp. The usual translation, "United-with-Life," does not make much sense to me, and I hesitate to use the alternative translation suggested by the dictionary, "Entering Life."[38] Did the ancient Egyptians really believe that true and eternal life began only with death? If so, the word ʿnḫ must have had a double sense, for the plural form ʿnḫw, "the living ones," is used of those alive on earth as well as of those living in the hereafter. In any case, texts with ʿnḫ must be translated with caution. Do they speak of physical life here on earth or of eternal life hereafter? The priestly titles connected with the cultus of Aakheperkare Thutmose are also difficult to interpret.[39] What differences, if any, existed between the ḥm-nṯr tpj m ḥnmt-ʿnḫ, "First Priest at ḥnmt-ʿnḫ," the ḥm-nṯr tpj n ʿ3-ḫpr-k3-rʿ, "First Priest of Aakheperkare," and the ḥm-nṯr tpj n nswt k3 n ʿ3-ḫpr-k3-rʿ, "First Priest of the Royal ka of Aakheperkare"? At this point, it may be useful to note that a Ramesside administrative document calls the temple of Thutmose I ḥwt-k3 n ʿ3-ḫpr-k3-[rʿ], "the Mansion of the ka of Aakheperkare," a term we shall have to discuss at a later stage.[40] Do these various titles denote the same or different priestly offices? And what is meant when we find—as we do under Amenhotep I—officials associated with *imn m ḥwt ḥnmt-ʿnḫ*, "Amun in the Mansion (called) *ḥnmt-ʿnḫ*"? It is too soon to attempt to answer such questions, but it is important to note that such ambiguities existed from early in the New Kingdom.

When we come to Thutmose II (Aakheperenre Thutmose), our data are on somewhat firmer ground, for his temple in Western Thebes has been excavated. Hardly a stone that stood above floor level is left in place, but a fragment of an inscription discloses the name of the building by referring to *ʿ3-ḫpr-n-rʿ m ḥwt šspt-ʿnḫ*, "Aakheperenre in the Mansion (called) 'Seizing-Life.'"[41] Reliefs on loose wall blocks depict rites relating to a royal statue in a shrine on a barque that was dragged about on a sledge by a group of minor priests.[42] These fragmentary ritual scenes have no parallel in other temples, and their details are therefore difficult to interpret. But they offer the first proof that a royal statue was central to such a temple's cultus.[43]

After the death of Thutmose II, his sister and wife Hatshepsut was entrusted with the regency for young Thutmose III, his son by a secondary wife. Within a few years, Hatshepsut herself assumed pharaonic power and privilege, and for the construction of a temple for her cultus she selected a very special site—a majestic half-circle of cliffs bounding the western end of the desert plain of Asasif. There stood the tomb and temple of Nebhepetre Mentuhotep, the Eleventh-Dynasty king who had reunited Egypt after the strife of the First Intermediate Period (fig. 38).[44] Each year, for five centuries, the image of Amun of Karnak had been brought to that temple in festal procession. Therefore Hatshepsut wanted her cult complex to stand beside Mentuhotep's and to create at least as grand an impression as his. But the only space left between Mentuhotep's enclosure wall and the cliffs was the sloping mass of chips piled up at the foot of the rocks. Hatshepsut's clever architects admirably surmounted the difficulty by designing a temple on three levels, whose upper steps covered the underlying gravel slope.[45] The three levels were linked by straight ramps along the temple's central axis.

Participants in processions arrived at the temple by way of an avenue of sphinxes and entered a wide courtyard on ground level with flower beds and ponds. At its far end, in front of the step rising to the next level, was an open hall of square pillars that was divided in the center by the ramp to the first terrace. A similar hall, its roof sustained by fluted columns, stood at the rear of the first terrace's flat open space. Today this hall is renowned for the reliefs on its back wall, which represent two major themes of Hatshepsut's life—in the southern part the chief phases of an expedition sent to countries of the East to obtain incense trees for the gardens of Amun and in the northern part the imaginary scenes by which she tried to establish her descent from Amun and thus her divine right to rule. The hall was ex-

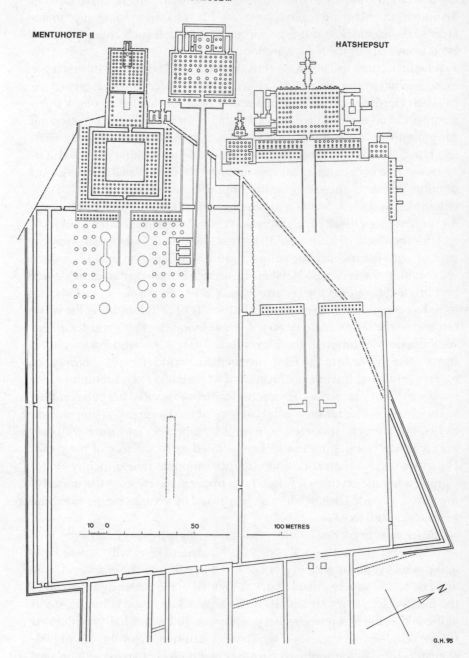

10 0   50   100 METRES

G.H. 95

FIG. 38. A plan of the temples of Deir el-Bahri, which shows that Hatshepsut had her temple squeezed in at the side of the original building of Nebhepetre Mentuhotep. Redrawing by Gerhard Haeny, combining drawings in *LÄ* 1:1013–14, 1018, and several others.

tended at both ends later in Hatshepsut's reign by adding a small sanctuary, the southern for Hathor and the northern for Anubis.

Above the hall of the first terrace and slightly behind it rose the facade of the second terrace. The front part of the second terrace was an open hall with square pillars, the outer face of each sculpted into a figure of Hatshepsut in the attitude of mummified Osiris.[46] Behind the hall were the essential rooms of the temple grouped around a wide peristyle court.[47] To the north was a second open-air court with an altar to the sun god Re. To the south were two rooms roofed over with corbel vaults. False doors occupied the center of their west walls, one inscribed for Hatshepsut and the other for her father Thutmose I; offerings were deposited there in their favor.[48] The other rooms in this section are without wall reliefs, and their purpose remains uncertain.[49] The procession of the barque of Amun reached the upper terrace by the central ramp and moved straight across the peristyle courtyard to the main sanctuary on its west side, a cavern dug into the mountain that offered temporary shelter to the image of Amun on its journey from Karnak to the Valley in the West. For five centuries the ultimate destination of the procession had been the temple of Nebhepetre Mentuhotep. We do not know whether prior to Hatshepsut's reign the barque halted at other west-bank temples of the pharaohs. It certainly did after her time, when Amun's itinerary included every royal cult complex whose cultus was still maintained.[50] In any event, Hatshepsut might have intended to oust Mentuhotep from his dominant position in the procession; perhaps for the duration of her reign she even succeeded.

The clever design of the temple of Hatshepsut was never repeated, but its elements included nearly all the essentials met in the later New Kingdom temples of Western Thebes: an axial sanctuary for the barque of Amun; a space open to the sky—either a courtyard or an unroofed part of a room—with an altar for the sun god; a room with a false door for presenting offerings to the temple's founder; and a place for commemorating a royal predecessor or predecessors.[51]

The early years of Thutmose III (Menkheperre Thutmose) were overshadowed by the regency of his aunt Hatshepsut; nonetheless, a temple in Western Thebes was built in his name. When it was excavated in the early twentieth century, not much was found in place.[52] A later reinvestigation added little.[53] Of the chief elements in Hatshepsut's temple, a sanctuary of Hathor is well attested here. Thutmose's temple also had a false door dedicated in his name, and a few fragments suggest that the room in which it stood had a vaulted ceiling whose decorations represented the hours of the night. That the cult complex also had a court with an altar to the sun god has been conjectured on the basis of many later examples. The name of this temple was ḥnkt-ʿnḫ (Henket-Ankh, "Offering-Life"). Long before the site of the temple was discovered the name had been known from a number of stamped bricks and from the titles of priests who served there. This helped to identify the building when it was excavated. In the titles of the priests, the king is always referred to by his prenomen Menkheperre, "Enduring-Is-the-Form-of-Re," and the name of the temple, rather than being inscribed in the sign *ḥwt* ("temple, mansion"), is frequently followed by the determinative *pr* ("house"). The same man may give his title as *ḥm-nṯr tpj n mn-ḫpr-rˁ*, "First Priest of Menkheperre," or as *ḥm-nṯr tpj n ỉmn m ḥnkt-ˁnḥ*, "First Priest of Amun in [the temple] 'Offering-Life.'" In one fragmentary inscription, an *ỉmj-rʾ pr n———* "Steward of the House of [a king, or a divinity]," inscribes in the sign *ḥwt* both the cartouche of Menkheperre and the name of Amun.[54] Were the king and the god so intimately linked that their names could be interchanged? Or was the man a priest of Amun only when Amun's image visited the temple?

One reference to the temple "Offering-Life" calls it a Mansion of Millions of Years, and some scholars take that to indicate its mortuary function.[55] Two other buildings of Thutmose III were, however, also called Mansions of Millions of Years: the *3ḫ-mnw* (*Akh-menu*) built at Karnak to the rear (east) of the main sanctuary of Amun in the early years after Hatshepsut's death or disappearance; and the *ḏsr-3ḫt* (*Djeser-Akhet*, "The Sacred Horizon"), erected late in Thutmose's reign above and between the temples of Nebhepetre Mentuhotep and Hatshepsut at Deir el-Bahri, evidently with the intention of attracting the procession of Amun to his own new foundation as the ultimate destination of the pilgrimage (fig. 38).

In some inscriptions, the name of Thutmose's building at the back of the great sanctuary of Amun of Karnak explicitly includes the king's name, being written *mn-ḫpr-rˁ 3ḫ mnw*, which Alan Gardiner translates "Menkheperre is Beneficent of Monuments."[56] I prefer to translate it "Splendid-Is-the-Memorial-of-Menkheperre." In a good number of other texts, the name of the king is not linked with the predicate, and the name appears simply as *3ḫ-mnw*. To quote from one of the most standard and easily translated building texts: *mn-ḫpr-rˁ stp-n-rˁ ỉr.n.f m mnw.f n jt.f ỉmn-rˁ mrwtj sˁḥˁ n.f 3ḫ-mnw m m3wt m ỉnr rwḏt*, "Menkheperre, the-Chosen-of-Re, made as his memorial for his father Amun-Re, the well-beloved, the erecting for him of the *3ḫ-mnw* (*Akh-menu*) as something new in solid sandstone." In this inscription one finds no term for the class of building to which the *Akh-menu* belonged. In other inscriptions relating to this temple, the unmodified term *ḥwt* ("temple, mansion") occurs rarely, but *ḥwt nṯr* ("temple of god") and *ḥwt ˁ3t* ("great temple, palace"), and even the combination *ḥwt nṯr ˁ3t* ("great temple of god"), are attested instead. All these formulas may be followed by the phrase "of millions of years."[57] Because *ḥwt* alone is rarely used to describe the *Akh-menu*, some scholars believe that this temple, closely linked with the abode of Amun, had a function quite different from mortuary temples. However, Egyptians did not use building terms very consistently. Evidently they liked to express their ideas in phrases repeated with small variations. Attributing too much importance to the Egyptian word used in a particular text could be misleading, and depending on its modern translation could be even more so.[58]

The axis of the *Akh-menu* was perfectly aligned with the west-east axis of the temple of Amun at Karnak, extending the cult complex to the east. But no doorway led directly from the innermost sanctuary of the main temple to the *Akh-menu*. So the *Akh-menu*, unlike most temples, could not be entered along its axis. A path between the inner and outer enclosure walls on the south side of Amun's temple led to a lateral gate in the west wall of the *Akh-menu*.

Inside that portal was a vestibule, from where a long corridor led east along a series of storerooms and a short passageway led north into the main hall. This hall was placed symmetrically across the *Akh-menu*'s west-east axis and occupied about a third of its ground plan. From here most of the building's other rooms were directly accessible. In its architectural concept, the hall was basically an open-air courtyard surrounded by a peristyle of square pillars, the open space then being covered by a high roof supported by columns shaped like tent poles, as if the roof were nothing but a light piece of cloth spread over the court to protect it from the heat of the sun.

A door in the center of the hall's east side led to a succession of three small rooms on the axis. The last of the three was a sanctuary of Amun's ithyphallic form. A doorway in the second room's south wall communicated with two small rooms arranged in parallel with the second and third axial rooms. Their walls were restored in the fourth century B.C.E. by Alexander the Great, but traces of the original reliefs prove that the second small room, parallel with the sanctuary of Amun's ithyphallic form, was dedicated to Thutmose III.[59]

An opening in the main sanctuary's north wall provided access to a secluded part of the temple. The first chamber was a kind of entrance hall, now called "the botanical garden" because the reliefs on its walls depict foreign animals and plants. The central part of its north wall was shaped like the facade of an archaic shrine with four columns in high relief and a door in their midst. This door opened into a narrow room, oriented south-north, that was about four times longer than it was wide. On a raised platform at the room's north end, a shrine made of ebony or other costly materials stood enclosed in a niche that was almost as wide as the room itself. Eight much smaller recesses were carved into the masonry of the long side walls, four on each side. An altar stood in front of the main niche, and there was also a stand for libations.[60] Paul Barguet assumed that the main shrine once housed an image of Amun, but nothing clearly indicates who the dedicatee of this part of the temple was. Puzzlingly, many of the later fairly well preserved Mansions of Millions of Years also have a room with nine wall recesses.[61]

Outside the north wall of the *Akh-menu*, an upper room reached by stairs from the main hall was erected in the Nineteenth Dynasty, but its altar, dedicated to the sun god, dates back to Thutmose III. Thutmose's sun sanctuary was probably arranged on the temple's roof. Traces of earlier flights of stairs can be seen.

The hall with eight fluted columns to the east of the southern half of the *Akh-menu*'s main hall communicates with three chapels on its south side and with two storerooms to the east. Barguet concluded from traces of wall reliefs and inscriptions in this southeastern section of the temple that these rooms had been dedicated to the funerary deity Sokar. The walls in a small chamber next to the southwest corner of the main hall were decorated with rows of seated kings, a selection of the predecessors of Thutmose III. Similar king lists have been found in some of the Mansions of Millions of Years we shall meet later.

Menkheperre Thutmose's second temple in Western Thebes was situated at Deir el-Bahri, between the cult complexes of Nebhepetre Mentuhotep and Hatshepsut (fig. 38). Sometime after the New Kingdom a mass of rocks fell from the sheer cliffs above the temple and destroyed it. The Polish expedition to Deir el-Bahri rediscovered its location only in the winter of 1961–62, but objects in museums disclosed its name long before the site was known. The objects' inscriptions designate it by *ḏsr ꜣḫt* preceded, surprisingly, by the mention of "Amun," not "Menkheperre." Eberhard Otto translated this name "Amun is sacred on the Horizon."[62] I prefer to understand that the temple was to be "Amun's Sacred Horizon" when he came to rest in the Theban West.[63] An inscription found on a fragmentary architrave of the temple itself says of the king: *sꜥḥꜥ.n.f ḥwt nṯr n ḥḥw m*———, "He erected a divine temple of millions of [years]."[64]

A scene painted in a Ramesside tomb provides more information about the rituals connected with a temple of Thutmose III in Western Thebes. In the center of the scene is a roofed structure, a type of light building that Egyptologists usually call a "kiosk."[65] The roof was sustained by square pillars, of which only those in two corners are depicted. Showing the intermediate supports would have disturbed the representation of the divine barque inside the kiosk. The portable boat, with its carrying poles and its deck-shrine, rests on a pedestal. The sides of the shrine are partially hidden by a veil, the usual practice since the time of Hatshepsut.[66] Attached to the prow and stern of the boat are royal busts wearing the complex *atef-*

crown with plumes, solar disk, and horizontal twisted horns, characteristic of the king's barque.[67] Thutmose III is represented behind the barque, undoubtedly by a statue, and we are to understand that another image of the divine king stands hidden inside the deck-shrine. The inscription above the kiosk reads: "The divine way station of the royal procession of King Menkheperre, [living] in eternity."

The simplified outlines of a temple are painted to the right of the kiosk suggesting both that the latter stands a considerable distance in front of the temple and that the royal barque was brought forward from the temple and set up in the way station to meet Amun of Karnak when the god's image crossed the Nile in the Theban Festival of the Valley.[68] The temple is called "The Mansion of King Menkheperre, justified before the great god, which is on the West of Thebes." As the specific name of this temple is not disclosed in the inscription, we have no information about which of the king's two western temples is shown. Barque processions were usually accompanied by troops of soldiers, musicians, dancers, and acrobats. However, this tomb scene depicts a retinue of only a few soldiers, and they are wrestling with each other or fencing with sticks.[69]

Each of the three temples here briefly described—the *Akh-menu* on the east bank of the Nile at Karnak and the two in the Theban necropolis on the west bank, *Djeser-Akhet* and *Henket-Ankh*—are called "Mansion of Millions of Years." Should they for that reason be considered mortuary temples? Scholars are divided on the matter, particularly concerning the *Akh-menu*. When Alan Gardiner studied the long dedicatory inscription on the outer wall of the temple and encountered the designation "Mansion of Millions of Years," he declared that the passage must concern some other building. He believed the term could be applied only to mortuary temples and cenotaphs and could therefore not be used of the *Akh-menu*, a structure closely connected with Amun's main temple at Karnak. Gardiner thought that Thutmose III built the *Akh-menu* in gratitude for Amun's support in the battle the king fought at Megiddo against the forces of the western Asiatic cities. The temple was also to store Amun's share of the booty taken there.[70]

Other scholars have taken the tent-pole columns of the *Akh-menu*'s central hall and some of its reliefs and inscriptions as pointing to the *Sed*-festival, and they regard the structure as the festival temple of Thutmose III, believing it was closely associated with the royal jubilee.[71] Barguet saw the rooms of the *Akh-menu* as attributed to several divinities—those of the center to Amun-Re and the king, those in the southeastern group to the funerary deity Sokar, those to the north to Horus and Re-Harakhti, and a sanctuary on the temple's roof to the sun god. Barguet seems to believe that by a mysterious interaction of these divinities a rejuvenation of the king was achieved.[72]

In coming to Amenhotep II (Aakheperure Amenhotep), we meet a singular problem that, as far as I can see, cannot be presently solved.[73] The inscription on a beaker in the possession of the Louvre refers to the ceremony of stretching the cord for a building of Amenhotep that is designated ḥwt.f nt imntt šspt-ꜥnḫ, "His Mansion of the West (called) 'Receiving-Life.'" We have already met this name, for it had previously been given to the western temple of Thutmose II. It seems strange that the name of a building most probably still used should be repeated only two generations later for another temple in the same area, the more so because a scholar has recorded in private tombs of Amenhotep's contemporaries a different name for the king's temple: iꜥb-3ḫt, "Joining-the-Horizon."[74] In 1896, Flinders Petrie excavated in Western Thebes the scanty remains of a temple further disturbed by later occupation. On the basis of recovered foundation deposits, the temple could be attributed to Amenhotep II.[75] The inscriptions on the objects do not, however, disclose the temple's name, nor do the titles of persons attached to the cultus of the king contribute toward a solution. The persons are briefly called First and Second Priest, Lector Priest, or Wꜥb-priest of Aakheperure. One man of superior rank stated that he was heading the wꜥbw n imn m ḥwt ꜥ3-ḫprw-rꜥ m w3st, "the Wꜥb-priests of Amun in the Mansion of Aakheperure in Thebes."[76]

The temple of Thutmose IV (Menkheperure Thutmose), situated in the southern part of the Theban necropolis, was excavated for the first time in 1896 by Petrie. His work produced only a few objects and a rather sketchy plan.[77] Constructed on the sloping fringe of the desert, the temple was laid out in several steps, the two lower ones marked by brick pylons. The facade of the temple proper, built in stone, was shaped as a wide entrance hall with a double row of columns. Next came a wide open courtyard with colonnades on all four sides. Of the roofed portions of the inner temple only parts of the foundations were left.[78]

Tomb inscriptions of priests employed in this temple are rare, and their usual titles—either "Priest of Menkheperure" or "Priest of Amun of Menkheperure"—are no more informative than those of the priests of Amenhotep II. Two rather exceptional titles are imj-rꜥ dpwt imn n t3 ḥwt mn-ḫprw-rꜥ, "Overseer of the Boats of Amun in the Mansion of Menkheperure," and w3ḥ mww n p3 ḳnj n nswt mn-ḫprw-rꜥ, "Distributor of Water for the Palanquin of King Menkheperure."[79]

Inscriptions from the time of Amenhotep III (Nebmaꜥatre Amenhotep) are considerably more informative. In the second year of his reign, he had the quarries at Tura reopened to obtain their fine stone, for throughout his reign he enlarged and embellished his buildings, sometimes entirely changing their plans. His inscription at Tura closely parallels that of Ahmose: "Order of his Majesty to open the quarries anew to cut the beautiful white stone of Tura to build his Mansions of Millions of Years, after his Majesty had found buildings in a state of falling into ruin since the time of their beginning."[80] The rapid decay that was observed apparently did not induce the king to show concern for better craftsmanship. Of all the buildings he founded and greatly enlarged later on, only one has survived nearly intact—the temple of Luxor.[81] Some of his temples are impressive in their ruin, but others have disappeared completely.

The temple that Amenhotep III built in Western Thebes was larger than the temple of Amun of Karnak in its most expanded form. Yet of the western temple there remain only the two colossal statues of the king that once guarded its entrance.[82] In the field behind these, the modern visitor finds only a few column bases and some other fragments marking the site, and a huge stela reerected where it had fallen.

In an inscription on a stela found reused in the temple of Merneptah, Amenhotep describes some of his buildings in pompous terms that do not convey a clear image of them. Concerning his temple of the west, the king says that "he made it as his monument for his father Amun, the Lord of thrones, making for him a splendid divine temple on the west side of Thebes, a fortress of eternity, everlasting, of beautiful white sandstone adorned all over with gold; its floors are inlaid with silver, all its doors with electrum. Widened and much enlarged, made lasting for eternity and festive, this very great monument was made to number a mass of statues of the Lord, (made) of granite from Elephantine, of quartzite and many (other) precious stones finished in work of eternity. Their height rises to the sky; their sight blinds (the peoples') faces like the sun disk when it glistens in the early morning."[83] The inscription goes on to describe the height of the temple's pylons, the number of its storerooms, the volume of its supplies, and the great size of its work force of foreign slaves. The text then says: "Its beautiful name, which his Majesty has given, is 'Receiving Amun (and) exalting his beauty.' (It is) a resting-place of the Lord of the Gods at his Festival of the Valley in Amun's procession to the West to visit the gods of the West when he will reward his Majesty with life and dominion."[84]

This inscription leaves the impression that the temple was built exclusively to receive Amun during his procession to the west bank in the Festival of the Valley. But a different view is imposed by the inscriptions on the stelae and statuary fragments from the temple site itself. In these, almost every reference to Amun is counterbalanced by one to Ptah-Sokar-Osiris, as if the god of Karnak and the divinity of Memphis had equal shares in the temple—Amun owning the half south of the east-west axis and Ptah-Sokar-Osiris owning the half north of it.[85] Herbert Ricke, the most recent investigator of the site, even suggested that a special limestone temple had been built for Ptah-Sokar-Osiris within the temple enclosure.[86]

The titles of the people employed at the cult complex confirm the presence of two owners. Some persons were attached only to the *ḥwt nb-m3ˁt-rˁ* (temple of Nebmaˁatre Amenhotep), and others, only to the *ḥwt skr* (temple of Sokar), the latter being rarely, but more completely, designated *ḥwt ptḥ-skr* (temple of Ptah-Sokar) or *ḥwt ptḥ-skr-wsîr* (temple of Ptah-Sokar-Osiris).[87] But the inscriptions and titles, as numerous as they are, do not enable us to determine whether the temples of Amenhotep and Ptah-Sokar-Osiris were two separate units in a common precinct or two halves of a single temple divided along its central axis.

As mentioned above, a huge stela from Amenhotep's immense western temple has been reerected. Its text has the form of a conversation. First the king invites Amun to take possession of the building prepared for him. Then Amun expresses his gratitude for the temple and his satisfaction with its beauty and perfection. Finally the ennead of minor gods in Amun's retinue chime in, telling the god to come *r ḥwt-nṭr.k nt ḏt*, "to your Divine Temple of Eternity." They are grateful that the king had also prepared chapels and statues for them, saying: *dj.n.f ḥtp.n m ḥwt-ˁ3t, m ḥwt.f nt ḥḥw m rnpwt*, "he made us rest in the palace, in his Mansion of Millions of Years."[88] The text of this stela demonstrates once again Egyptians' penchant for designating a single cult complex by a variety of terms: "Divine Temple of Eternity," "palace", and "Mansion of Millions of Years." The first speaks of the temple as Amun's while the other two speak of it as the king's.

As we saw when considering the temples of Ahmose and Thutmose III, the view that "Mansion of Millions of Years" was used exclusively for mortuary temples and cenotaphs is rather weak. So it will not surprise us to find the phrase applied to a structure that Amenhotep III built on the east bank, about two miles south of Karnak at Luxor.[89] On the basis of long known and well-studied relief scenes carved on the wall of its entrance colonnade, scholars have generally regarded the temple of Luxor to have been devoted exclusively to the service of Amun.[90] The scenes illustrate the main phases of Amun's festive procession from Karnak to Luxor and back again. Hieroglyphic inscriptions refer to this annual event as *ḥb.f nfr n ʾIpt*, "His beautiful feast of *Opet*."[91] The reliefs on the long walls of the colonnade provide no definite clue as to the reasons for Amun's visit to his "southern sanctuary" at Luxor. Yet, because the word *ipt* was also used for the quarters housing the king's women, scholars have long interpreted the temple's designation to mean "the Southern Harem" and have concluded therefrom that Amun went to Luxor to participate in a kind of "Sacred Marriage." They have even seen confirmation for this idea in frequent representations of Amun's ithyphallic form on the temple's walls, particularly prominent in late graffiti. Recent investigations, including the one by Lanny Bell in this volume, show that this understanding of Luxor's function and purpose must be abandoned.[92]

The reliefs of the Luxor colonnade were carved late in Dynasty 18, in the time of Tutankhamun and Ay, successors of Amenhotep III after the heretical period of Amarna.[93] We do not know, however, when Amun's festive procession from Karnak to Luxor was inaugurated. It is first attested in the reign of Hatshepsut. She had its episodes represented on the walls of the shrine for the barque of Amun that she built at Karnak. This shrine, the so-called Chapelle Rouge, was dismantled soon after her death, and its blocks were reused in other buildings. A good number of them have been recovered, and a photographic reconstruction has been presented.[94] The scenes on the shrine were arranged systematically, each course of blocks representing a definite subject. For that reason, one may draw conclusions although many blocks are still missing. The procession to Luxor was depicted on the third course of the shrine's exterior south side, and the return journey was shown on its fifth course. On the opposing north side of the shrine, the third course depicted Amun's procession to the western necropolis during the Festival of the Valley. Only two blocks of the course are preserved; the first shows priests carrying the barque of Amun from Karnak to the river station, and the second portrays the barque arriving at Hatshepsut's Deir el-Bahri temple. The fifth course of the north wall showed Amun's return from Deir el-Bahri to Karnak.[95] By chance, the river scenes of traveling northward from Luxor along the east bank and of crossing eastward from Deir el-Bahri are preserved in reliefs where one cannot distinguish between the journeys. Even the scenes of events taking place after the two landings present exactly the same sequence and have but few variations in composition. It is tempting to conclude that the ritual aims of Amun's two processions—to Luxor and to Deir el-Bahri—were essentially the same.

Remarkable differences can be noticed, however, between the representation of the *Opet*-festival on Hatshepsut's Chapelle Rouge and the one from a later time in the Luxor colonnade. In the former, the barque of Amun was transported from Karnak to Luxor over land, resting along its course at a number of way stations. Only on the barque's return to Karnak was it transported by a great barge on the Nile. Furthermore, in both of Hatshepsut's processions, to Luxor and to Deir el-Bahri, Amun's barque was accompanied only by Hatshepsut, Thutmose III, and the necessary porters, although on the way back these were joined by numbers of joyful attendants. In the later representations in the Luxor colonnade, Amun traveled by river barge both to and from Luxor, and he was now accompanied by special boats for his consort Mut and their son Khonsu. The king's presence as chief ritualist is self-evident. No representation of a Festival of the Valley comparable to Hatshepsut's exists for the later Eighteenth Dynasty.

The plan of Luxor Temple shows no similarity to earlier Mansions of Millions of Years. The former disposition of their rooms, asymmetrical and clustered, was reorganized into an orderly symmetrical sequence along a central axis oriented north-south, and all the minor shrines were given equal size and lined up along the temple's side walls (see Chap. 4, fig. 56, from no. 24 southward). We do not know the extent to which traditional demands and ritual regulations had to be overruled for such a clear plan to be devised and executed.[96] Here we are concerned only with the innermost group of rooms—the secluded chambers of the Amun of Luxor—which could not be entered along the axis, but could be reached only by lateral corridors along the rows of chapels (south of no. 15). The innermost group consisted of three rooms built against the back wall of the temple and of a large wide hall extending in front of them across the building's axis.

Of the three rooms, the one in the center (no. 18) once contained, between the southernmost pair of columns, an elevated platform on which the sacred shrine of Amun stood. We would expect the rooms' relief scenes to disclose the essence of the rites celebrated there, but, insofar as they are not destroyed, they only portray the king extending a variety of gifts to Amun, who is represented in both his normal and ithyphallic forms.[97]

In the wide hall, at the top of the small side walls, exceptionally large windows open east and west. Beneath the windows are representations of the solar barque, which on the east wall is called $m^c n\underline{d}t$, "barque of the morning," and on the west, $msktt$ "barque of the setting." Both representations are accompanied by the text of hymns to the sun god in his daily course and nighttime passage. Composed for the adoration of Amun in his aspect as Re-Harakhti, the hymns sought to assure the king using them that he was well equipped to accompany Re on his eternal orbit.[98] Similar representations of sun barques and copies of the hymns are found almost exclusively in funerary contexts, but they also occur in temples that may be considered Mansions of Millions of Years.[99] This wide hall preceding the innermost sanctuary of the Luxor temple was doubtless intended as a place for adoring Amun in his aspect as Re. Although the hall is quite exceptional in its architectural disposition, it had the same functions as the solar courts in Hatshepsut's temple at Deir el-Bahri and Thutmose III's *Akh-menu* at Karnak. Did Amenhotep III replace the Luxor temple existing in Hatshepsut's time with his own structure in order to assure himself of continuing his life in the never-ending company of Amun-Re?

The temple Amenhotep III dedicated to Amun at Soleb—far in the South, between the second and third cataracts of the Nile—was also a Mansion of

Millions of Years. The king addressed the god, saying: "I built for you your house (*pr*) of millions of years in the region (of) Amun-Re, the Lord of the Two Lands (called) 'Kha-em-Maʿat,' rich of electrum, a resting-place of my father at all his feasts."[100] Another inscription describes the place as *mnnw*, "fortress," a stronghold for the king's rule. Three scenes engraved one above the other on the gate posts of the first pylon show that Amun had to share his temple with a deified Amenhotep III. Both gods are posed as if stepping from the temple to meet the king; Amun is represented in the lowest scene, and deified Amenhotep, in the higher ones. The latter's name is inscribed "Nebmaʿatre, Lord of Nubia," and his image displays the chief marks of deity: the slender beard with curving end, the *w3s*-scepter in one hand, and the *ankh*-sign of life in the other. And he wears additional divine insignia. His royal *nms*-headcloth is topped by a low cylindrical cap surmounted by the full-moon disk combined with an upward-curved crescent—the head ornament normally attributed to moon gods Thoth and especially Khonsu, who in Thebes was considered son of Amun.[101] In countless inscriptions, Amenhotep presented himself as son of Amun. Why should he not also adopt his "brother" Khonsu?[102]

The headcloth of the king is adorned with another distinctive feature, ram's horns curving downward around the ears.[103] The species having such horns was, according to zoologists, indigenous not to Egypt but to the mountainous regions of Kush (i.e., the Sudan). By accident, Egyptology first became familiar with this feature through some two-dimensional representations of Amenhotep III at Soleb and through the granite rams with downward curving horns that were sculpted for Soleb and later removed by Kushite kings to their chief sanctuary of Amun at Gebel Barkal. Also long known had been the avenues at Karnak lined with rows of criosphinxes—sandstone images of Amun having lion's bodies and ram's heads with horns curving downward around the ears—figures dating mostly to the very end of the Eighteenth Dynasty and the earlier part of the Nineteenth. These observations led nineteenth-century scholars to advance the idea that the image of ram-headed Amun had been devised in the Kushite Sudan and was then introduced into Egypt from Soleb in the time of Amenhotep III. This idea is still held today by a majority of scholars, but I believe downward curving horns were adopted into three-dimensional art because by representing rams' horns in that way the sculptor could avoid serious technical problems.[104]

All the Mansions of Millions of Years so far considered belonged to the domain of Amun, the god of Thebes. But the long inscription on a statue of an official of Amenhotep III, also named Amenhotep, speaks of a mansion in the domain of Ptah, the god of Memphis.[105] The statue was "given as a favor" from the king and was placed "in the Mansion of Nebmaʿatre (called) 'United-with-Ptah,' which his Majesty newly made for his father [Ptah-South-of-His-Wall in the] cultivated land west of Memphis."[106] Amenhotep, the official, had been promoted by his king "to direct the work in his Mansion of Millions of Years, which he newly made in his cultivated land west of Memphis, in the district of Ankh-Tawy."[107] "After the work had been well completed, his Majesty instituted new divine offerings as presents for every day for his father Ptah-South-of-His-Wall and the divinities of his mansion (granting) supplies of goods for ever. He appointed W^cb-priests and prophets . . . (and) he gave fields and cattle, farm-laborers and herdsmen from the spoils his Majesty brought from all foreign lands. All the offices of this temple his Majesty filled in the best way."[108] Then comes a comparison of the role of this Mansion at Memphis to the role of the Mansions at Thebes: "His Majesty made this temple to be provisioning the temple of Ptah according to all its written deeds (just) like the mansions of the kings ($bjtjw$) that are beside his father Amun in the southern city."[109] Ptah's relationship to this mansion was clearly the same as Amun's at Thebes, and we may assume that the function of all mansions was essentially the same regardless of the deity to which they were attached.

Three rather short reigns mark the end of the Eighteenth Dynasty. Tutankhamun returned from Amarna to Thebes and was buried in the Valley of the Kings. A single inscription refers to a temple for his mortuary cultus, but its site is not known.[110] It may well be that Ay, his successor, built for him a commemorative chapel. Blocks inscribed with both kings' names were found reused in the Second Pylon at Karnak. In an exceptional painting of Tutankhamun's sarcophagus chamber, Ay also portrayed himself performing the Opening of the Mouth ritual for his predecessor (see Chap. 4, fig. 78).[111]

Ay built his own temple named "The Mansion of Kheperkheperure-ʾIrma ͨat (called) 'Enduring-Is-the-Memorial-in-the-Place-of-Eternity.'" Excavation has shown that Ay's successor, Haremhab, usurped it and renamed it for himself; for jar sealings are inscribed "The Mansion of Djeserkheperure-Setepenre," and a note on an ostracon states that grain was delivered from there to the village of the necropolis workmen.[112] On a relief fragment apparently coming from Saqqara, a person named $Injwj3$ claims to have been $n\underline{t}r$ $\d{h}m$ tpj n $t3$ $\d{h}wt$ $\underline{d}sr$-$\d{h}prw$-r^c stp-n-r^c $s3$ $pt\d{h}$ mrj, "Chief Priest in the Mansion of Djeserkheperure Setepenre, the beloved son of Ptah."[113] Did Haremhab found an additional temple in Memphis near the temple of Ptah, following the example of Amenhotep III, or was $Injwj3$ Chief Priest at the tomb Haremhab had prepared at Saqqara when he was still chief commander of the army? The latter monument could have been renamed after Haremhab's coronation.

Royal Cult Complexes of the Ramesside Period

In the introduction to this chapter, we considered aspects of the temples of Sety I, Ramesses II, and Ramesses III, and we analyzed part of Nelson's study of them. We take up Nelson's argument again, turning to his interpretation of their reliefs. In a scene of the enthroned Ramesses III at Medinet Habu, the king wears the *atef*-crown, with its two horizontal twisted horns and vertical plumes above a *nms*-headcloth, and he holds the *w3s*-scepter of dominion in his right hand and the *ankh*-sign of life in his left. Behind him stands a female figure who extends her arms protectively around his shoulders (fig. 39). On her head is a tablet shaped like the *ḥwt*-sign ("temple") and inscribed with Medinet Habu's distinctive name, *ḥnmt-nḥḥ* ("United-with-Eternity"). She symbolizes the temple embracing the dead king.[114]

A similar scene occurs twice in the temple of Sety I at Qurna.[115] In Room III, the *ḥwt*-sign giving the temple's name is held between the upraised arms of the *k3*-sign, producing the reading *ḥwt-k3*, "The Mansion of the *ka*."[116] Inscribed around the figures are both the personified temple's words to the king: "Behold, I am behind you. I am your temple, your mother, for ever and ever"; and the king's address to Amun: "I am your son, O Lord of Gods, Amun-Re, the primeval one of the Two Lands. Make divine my image (*sšmw*). Protect (*ḥw*) my temple. Make it festive with your *k3* every day."[117]

The Qurna figure of the personified temple is found at the north end of the west wall of Room V (fig. 40). The reliefs of this chapel have been described and fully studied by Louis-A. Christophe.[118] The scene on its west wall shows a *Iunmutef*-priest offering incense to "Osiris King Menmaʿatre, Son of Re Sety-Merneptah," who sits in a chapel under the protection of the personified temple. The priest addresses the king: "Pure shall be your *k3*, censed your head with incense, the fragrance of the god to your members; the two great ones purify you like Re."[119] The purification by the great ones is illustrated on the chapel's north wall. Amun-Re and Sety stand back to back in the center. Horus and Thoth approach them from opposite sides, and each pours a wide jet of water on the two central figures. Horus says to Menmaʿatre, "Your purification is the purification of Amun-Re, and vice versa," and Thoth addresses similar words to the king.[120] So the scene signifies a formal union of king and god.

The scene on the east wall of the chapel parallels the one on the west wall. Here the king himself acts in the place of the *Iunmutef*-priest, offering incense and libation to ithyphallic Min-Amun-Re and celebrating the ritual of the Opening of the Mouth that should enable the image to partake of the pile of offerings heaped in front of him.[121]

FIG. 39. Female figure who symbolizes the temple "United-with-Eternity" embracing the deceased Ramesses III. Reprinted from *Medinet Habu* 6, *the Temple Proper* 2, OIP 84 (1964), pl. 447 (right-hand page), courtesy of The Oriental Institute of The University of Chicago.

Nelson found further evidence of belief in a close connection between god and king. At Medinet Habu, one of Amun's specific forms is "Amun-United-with-Eternity"—that is, Amun of the western temple of Ramesses III. A relief shows Amun-United-with-Eternity back to back with the standard form of Amun, identified as "Amun-Re, King of the Gods, Lord of the Sky" on the lintel of the main entrance of the temple.[122] Each form receives offerings from Ramesses III. A meeting of the barque of Amun-United-with-Eternity with the visiting barque of Amun of Karnak is shown in a large scene on the north wall of the temple's first court.[123] The barque of Amun of Medinet Habu is also shown in the temple of Ramesses III in the

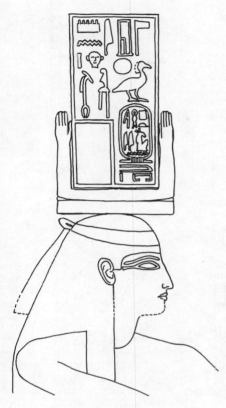

FIG. 40. The head of the female figure representing the temple of Sety I at Qurna, from Room V. Redrawing by Gerhard Haeny, based on W. M. Flinders Petrie, *Qurneh*, BSAE 16 (1909), pl. 45, and Champollion-le-Jeune, *Monuments de l'Égypte et de la Nubie* (Paris: F. Didot Frères, 1835–45), vol. 2, pl. 151, 3.

great forecourt of Karnak, where it follows the barque of Amun of Karnak at the *Opet*-festival.[124] On the prow and stern of the barque we find not the expected head of a ram but the bust of the king wearing the elaborate *ḥnw*-crown. In addition, the barque's deck-shrine is topped by a frieze of royal cartouches.[125] All this clearly indicates that Amun-United-with-Eternity and the king were seen as one (cf. fig. 41).

A processional boat of Ramesses II is portrayed at Medinet Habu, where Ramesses III offers it incense. It is "the barque of Userma῾atre- Setepenre United-with-Thebes" that was brought over from the temple of Ramesses II to receive honors from Ramesses III. Above the boat is a long inscription in which the image in the barque shrine says to the censing king: "Utterance of Amun-Re residing in United-with-Thebes (the Ramesseum) to his son Userma῾atre-Meryamun (Ramesses III): Beautiful is the monument that you have made. . . . Your Mansion shall be firmly established like the sky, for ever."[126] We have here at Medinet Habu clear evidence of a Mansion of Millions of Years that includes a chapel for commemorating an honored predecessor, Ramesses II.[127]

FIG. 41. The barque of Ramesses III, from a large scene on the north wall of Unit-ed-with-Eternity's first court. Reprinted from *Medinet Habu 4, Festival Scenes of Ramses III,* OIP 51 (1940), pl. 231 (right-hand page), courtesy of The Oriental Institute of The University of Chicago.

Beginning a chronological survey of Dynasty 19, we must mention what was possibly the greatest enterprise of Sety I, his creation of the Great Hypostyle Hall at Karnak. He accomplished this by covering the open courtyard between the Third Pylon of Amenhotep III and the Second Pylon of Haremhab with a roof supported by 134 columns, the ones along the central aisle rising to a height of over 22 meters (72 feet).[128] Here the barques of Amun, Mut, and Khonsu were to assemble before leaving Karnak in festive procession. Sety named the hall "Glorious Is Sety-Merneptah." He gave that same name to his temple across the Nile at Qurna, almost exactly opposite Karnak. The Qurna temple's name was differentiated from the Hall's only by added phrases that specified its location—*ḥr ỉmj-wrt w3st* or *ḥr ỉmntt w3st,* both meaning "on the West of Thebes." [129] Two other phrases occasionally accompanied the name "Glorious Is Sety-Merneptah": *m ḥft-*

ḥr n ipt-swt, "in front of Karnak," and *m wb3 n ipt-swt,* "in the forecourt of Karnak." A scholarly discussion arose about which building was designated by these formulas, the temple at Qurna or the Great Hall at Karnak. If such topographical indications had any specific meaning then in my opinion the latter phrases refer to the Great Hall of Karnak.[130] But adopting the solution proposed here leads immediately to another problem, for one text states that Sety I "executed the work in his Mansion of Millions of Years in the forecourt of Karnak." Could the Great Hypostyle Hall in the front part of the temple of Amun at Karnak have been built as a Mansion of Millions of Years for Sety I? Those who limit Mansions of Millions of Years to the so-called mortuary temples would be opposed to the idea. But a closer study of the reliefs and inscriptions of the Great Hypostyle Hall of Karnak could eventually lead to a positive answer.[131]

Space permits me to describe only a few of Qurna's architectural features.[132] Beyond the portico and facade, the core temple has at its center a large hall whose high roof is supported by six columns. On each side of the hall, doors open into three chapels.[133] Five doors in the hall's rear wall communicate with three long chambers that received divine barques (Amun's in the center, Khonsu's to the right, and Mut's to the left) and two chambers of unknown function. Enough survives of the temple's back wall to prove that the sanctuary had an element not met so far: a false door with two simulated openings separated by a central pillar, surmounted by an imitation of elaborate tracery work, and set up where the east-west axis of the temple met the back wall.[134] A symbolic door of this type is often found in buildings of Sety I and his son Ramesses II, usually at the center rear of barque chambers, where no niche or shrine other than the deck-shrine of the barque itself was provided for divine images.

To the north of the large hall and barque chambers is an open courtyard, at whose center is an altar for the sun god.[135] To the south of the large main hall is a small group of rooms that Sety prepared to commemorate his father Ramesses I. At Sety's death, the decoration of its entrance hall was not complete, so Ramesses II seized the opportunity to depict himself being introduced by Montu to Amun-Re and Ramesses I and presenting an offering to Amun-Re, Khonsu, and Ramesses I. In another scene, the young Ramesses II kneels on the sign for lordship and is crowned between Mut and Amun-Re. Behind the divine couple stand Khonsu and Sety, each holding the crook and flagellum, the symbols of the office of Osiris in the hereafter. Note that the deceased king, whether Ramesses I or Sety I, is here represented in the company of the gods as if, although posed behind the deities, he has attained the same standing. This observation may contribute an answer to the question of deification. West of this entrance hall are three parallel chambers. At the rear (west end) of the one in the middle is a false door of the type described in the previous paragraph. Reliefs on both side walls represent Sety offering incense to the barque of Amun, proof that Amun sojourned here during the Festival of the Valley. In another scene, Sety anoints a statue of Ramesses I.

The name given to both the Hypostyle Hall of Karnak and the temple of Qurna was bestowed a third time—on a temple at Memphis called "Glorious Is Sety-Merneptah in the domain of Ptah." No material trace of the building has survived, but its existence is proved by its mention in two ancient geographical dictionaries and by inscriptions from the Memphite tomb of a certain Saj-em-peteref indicating that he was "head of the goldsmiths in the Mansion of Menma'atre (Sety I)."[136] This mansion, like the Memphite temple of Amenhotep III, might have been a Mansion of Millions of Years linked with the cult complex of Ptah, but that is a guess based only on the form of its name.

The temple that Sety built at Abydos, in the domain of Osiris, was without doubt a Mansion of Millions of Years. He died before it was finished, but Ramesses II completed the work. The building was dedicated to Osiris and a number of gods who were mythologically or theologically related to him, and its main part comprises their barque chambers lined up side by side. The chamber in the center, on the main axis, is Amun's; the three chambers ranging to the north belong to Osiris, Isis, and Horus; the three to the south belong to Harakhti (the god of Heliopolis), Ptah, and Sety I. The back wall of each barque chamber has the shape of the double false door, except in the chamber of Osiris, where a regular doorway permits entry to a wide hall communicating with further rooms and chapels. A lateral annex to the core temple afforded space for the cultus of Ptah-Sokar, the Memphite god of death, and for such menial functions as storing the goods and utensils used in the temple service and in butchering cattle for meat offerings. The service rooms of the annex are connected to the temple's inner hall by a long gallery whose west wall depicts Sety and Ramesses II offering incense before a list of seventy-eight kings, an abridged history of Egypt from Menes to his own time. A stairway branching off the gallery led westward toward a tree-shaded mound covering an underground cenotaph of exceptional design. Ten stout granite pillars set on a platform supported its heavy roof construction. A deep channel filled with subsoil water surrounded the platform, which was accessible by stairs at its two ends. On this "island," the two goddesses Isis and Nephthys were thought to bewail the corpse of Osiris lying on its bier, a scene illustrated in many temples and private tombs. The central part of the cenotaph was accessible from outside the temple enclosure through a long vaulted corridor and two antechambers linked by a passage.

At Abydos, as at Thebes, Sety commemorated his father Ramesses I by building a small shrine in his name. Perhaps the shrine comprised additional rooms in mud brick, but only the innermost stone chamber is preserved. Its fine reliefs and inscriptions, unfortunately damaged in many parts, can be admired in New York City's Metropolitan Museum of Art; they make an important contribution to our understanding of Mansions of Millions of Years.[137] One of the perpendicular lines inscribed on both door posts declares that Sety "made as his memorial for his father, the king of Upper and Lower Egypt Menpehtyre, the son of Re Ramesses, making for him a Mansion of Millions of Years on the side of the lords of eternity" (for this and the other details from the scene that follow, see fig. 42). On the small wall surfaces right and left of the door, the two kings face each other. On the left, Sety wears the ḥmw-crown and greets his father with an extended hand, saying: "Welcome, perfect god. May you occupy the place I have made for you and look at your 'Mansion of Justification' at the side of the one who is perfect (Wenennefer). I fixed for you offerings in it and libations as daily presents." On the right, the figure of Ramesses I is damaged and incomplete, but his right hand holds either the flagellum or the crook of Osiris, and his left, the sign of life. His reply to Sety is also somewhat damaged: "[I am the one who] obeys the whole Ennead. I listen to their decision attributing to you the throne of Atum and the years of Horus as defender of those who gave this land to you by bequest and who subdued for you the Nine Bows (all foreign countries)." The dialogue continues below the figures. Sety says: "I am your son. I have done beneficial things for you. I built for you a mansion for your *ka* to the north of my great temple; I dig its watering-pond planted with trees and adorned with flowers; I make your statue rest in its interior, supplying it with offerings for every day like [those of all gods]. I am your true son of your heart. . . . I exalt your name to the sky; I elevate your crown like the one of Re; I maintain your name alive on earth as Horus did for his father Osiris." Of Ramesses' reply, a few of the final words can confidently be translated: "[Rejoicing are] the gods for your deeds. They increase your years on earth and double for you the jubilees as you have done beneficent things for me. I am your true father."[138]

By chance, the statue that had been sculpted for the sanctuary of Ramesses I was discovered in the hands of dealers, so the somewhat damaged inscription on its back pillar has been copied. It reads: "The Lord of the Universe has created his perfection. His very son protected him as Horus protected the one who begot him, the King of Upper and Lower Egypt Menpehtyre. . . . [The King Sety I] made his name live on in the nome of Abydos. He let him take [his] place in his memorial (mꜥḥꜥt) that he made as his monument for his father, the son of Re Ramesses I . . . that the name of his father will remain firmly established in the nome of Abydos for ever

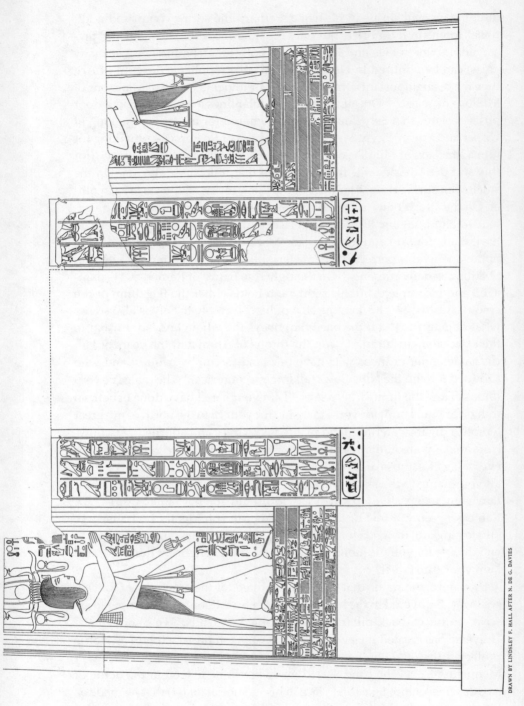

FIG. 42. Decoration of the facade of the Central Chapel of the temple of Ramesses I at Abydos. Reprinted by permission of The Met-

and ever. Yet his Majesty made this for his father Menpehtyre. . . ."[139] We met the term *m'ḥ't* early in our investigation. It designated the memorials built by kings and private persons in the Abydene necropolis near the temple of Osiris to protect their image carved on stelae or sculpted in the round and the offering table that usually stood in front of it. The lower part of a stela found in the vicinity of the chapel of Ramesses I is inscribed with a long text in which Sety surveys the short reign of his father and relates what he has done for him. I quote only two short passages: "He (Ramesses) entered heaven. I (Sety) stood in his place. I am the one who keeps his name alive. I am like Re in the early morning since I received the vestments of my father"; and "He began to become a god. Look, I was guarding the one from whom I issued, letting appear his likeness as a god. I made for him a mansion on the site of Abydos, to the north of my august mansion. I made his statue rest in it, provided like [those of other] kings."[140]

Ramesses II built more Mansions of Millions of Years than any other pharaoh. "The Temple of Userma'atre-Setepenre (called) 'United-with-Thebes' in the estate of Amun on the West of Thebes"—the Ramesseum—has already been mentioned. On architraves, inscriptions designate its hypostyle hall "a resting place of the Lord of the Gods in his Beautiful Festival of the Valley." That the temple was also considered a Mansion of Millions of Years is attested in inscriptions on vine jars and, rarely, in titles of officials charged with the temple's administration.[141] We can be certain that an official was employed at the Ramesseum only if the mansion referred to in his title is designated by the name "United-with-Thebes" or the location "on the West of Thebes."

Most scholars agree that Ramesses II was deified in his temple at Abu Simbel, but—contrary to my expectation—I have found only one text calling it a Mansion of Millions of Years.[142] The lack of any further confirmation does not, however, preclude the temple's having been such a mansion. Labib Habachi observes that the exterior parts of the Great Temple at Abu Simbel seem to be divided into a southern half dedicated to Amun-Re and a northern half dedicated to Re-Harakhti.[143] He further observes that inside, from the first hall inward to the sanctuary, Re-Harakhti is replaced by a human figure labeled "Ramesses." In most cases the name is not inscribed in a cartouche, in order to distinguish the figure from Ramesses the king, who is shown opposite it presenting various offerings. An exception to the replacement occurs on the back wall of the sanctuary, where the four figures sculpted out of live rock include both "Userma'atre-Setepenre Ramesses-Meryamun" and "Harakhti, residing in the domain (*pr*) of Ramesses in this town." They sit to the right side, and to the left, "Amun-Re, Lord of the Sky" and "Ptah, Lord of Truth."[144]

On the south wall of the second hall, Ramesses II offers incense to the

barque of Amun-Re. On the north wall, he burns incense and pours a libation to another barque on whose prow and stern are heads of falcons surmounted by sun disks. These symbols clearly mark the boat as Harakhti's,
but the inscription names the owner "Ramesses-Meryamun, resident in the
domain of Ramesses." Ramesses has either replaced Harakhti or become
Harakhti, probably the latter; for such a union of identities is clearly expressed on the temple's facade, where a figure of Harakhti, carved in a
niche above the door and holding *ankh*-signs in both hands, is symbolically designated Userma῾atre, Ramesses' throne name. Below the figure's
right hand is the sign "*user*," under its left hand is an image of Ma῾at, and
the figure itself can be read "Re"—"Userma῾atre."[145]

Above the door leading into the second hall, to the north and south of
this central axis, a figure of Ramesses II with a sun disk above his head has
been inserted into the original representations of divine couples, between
Amun-Re and Mut on the south side and between Min-Amun-Kamutef
and Mut on the north.[146] The figure of Ramesses on the south has the
downward-curving ram's horn at the side of the head, as does a figure of
him in an offering scene in one of the lateral chambers. In another scene,
the figure Ramesses-Meryamun (without the cartouche) has a hawk head
surmounted by the crescent and disk. Both exceptional marks, the downward-curving ram's horn and the crescent and disk, are also connected
with Amenhotep III at Soleb, and many scholars believe them to be clear
signs of these kings' deification. It seems somewhat odd, however, that
only Amenhotep III and Ramesses II bear these marks, since deification
must be admitted as a possibility for all pharaohs.

In front of the facade of the temple at Abu Simbel sit four colossal statues carved out of the live rock. The four were apparently sculpted exactly
alike, but each is distinguished by a particular phrase added to the king's
name. Little attention has been paid to the Egyptian custom of expanding
the names of kings represented in statues. It certainly existed in the times
of Amenhotep III and Ramesses II, but its origin and meaning are largely
unknown.[147] Labib Habachi has found cases where such statues were the
objects of worship, as proved either by stelae with representations of men,
even kings, adoring such statues or by copies of documents regulating the
funds and personnel for their continued worship.[148] At Abu Simbel, the
particular name of each of the four statues is not linked exclusively to it,
for the names also turn up on the statues sculpted with the pillars of the
first inner hall, the so-called Osiride pillars.[149] The distinguishing phrases
were simply additions to the name of the pharaoh represented in the statues, like the flowery epithets that expanded the five names of his official
protocol. Why some of these statues were considered worthy of special attention, even worship, remains entirely unknown.

Abu Simbel is but the largest and best known of a series of temples that Ramesses II built in Nubia: from north to south, Beit el-Wali, Gerf Hussein, Wadi el-Sebuʿa, el-Derr, Abu Simbel, Aksha, and perhaps places south of the Second Cataract. Most are now drowned in the lake waters behind the Aswan High Dam, but existing records show they had features similar to Abu Simbel's, albeit more modest. In one scene at Aksha, Ramesses offers *maʿat* to "Amun-Re resident in the domain of Usermaʿatre, the Great God, the Lord of Nubia." In another, Ramesses faces his own effigy, which wears the complex *ḥnw*-crown and is labeled "The Lord of the Two Lands, User-maʿatre-Setepenre, the Great God, Lord of Nubia."[150]

At el-Derr, on both side walls of the sanctuary, Ramesses offers incense and libation before a sacred barque with hawk heads on its prow and stern, like the barque of Ramesses-Harakhti at Abu Simbel. On the south wall, the action of the king is described by a longer text: "Making (the gift) of incense, libation, *irp-* and *j3rr*-wine, of all things perfect and pure to the *k3* of the king," identified as Ramesses II by both cartouches of his nomen and prenomen. We would have to expect that the king's *ka* resided in the deck-shrine on the sacred barque. Behind it comes a scene in which Ramesses anoints a statue of "Harakhti, the Great God, Lord of the Sky."[151] On the opposite wall, a royal person stands behind the barque. It is Ramesses II, identified both by the pair of cartouches and by the *user*-sign in his right hand, the *maʿat*-feather in his left, and the sun disk of Re on his head—an emblematic repetition of the king's throne name, as in the niche of the facade at Abu Simbel.[152] In a following scene, Ramesses offers cloth to "Ptah, Lord of *Maʿat*, King of the Two Lands, resident in his divine temple (*ḥwt.f ntr*)." El-Derr was clearly Ptah's, just as Gerf Hussein and Wadi el-Sebuʿa were Amun's. Yet on an architrave at el-Derr, an inscription designates the temple a Mansion of Millions of Years.[153] So far I have found only this second use of the term for the Ramesside temples in Nubia, despite the fact that the theme of them all is essentially the same—the elevation of the pharaoh among the gods.

At Wadi el-Sebuʿa, the divine images in the sanctuary's niche have been destroyed and replaced by a painting of Christian saints. So Ramesses II is depicted on both sides of the niche presenting flowers to Saint Peter! On the lintel of the niche is the engraved picture of the sun barque with a ram-headed Re-Harakhti on board in a pavilion; the boat is adored by the king on one side and three baboons on the other. The theme is somewhat similar to one we met at Luxor and will meet again at Medinet Habu.[154] On the two side walls, the king brings offerings and flowers to the barque of Amun-Re and to the hawk-headed barque called "the barque of Ramesses-Meryamun in the domain of Amun."[155] The offering of flowers, written *rn-pwt*, could have a symbolic second sense, for the root *rnp* means "young, fresh" and is sometimes rendered "become young again, rejuvenate." But how can we decide whether the regeneration or rebirth of the deceased was a concept in the minds of the ancient Egyptians or is one that we have superimposed on them?

The group of deities among whom Ramesses II is portrayed varies from temple to temple. In the oblong hall that precedes the sanctuary at Wadi el-Sebuʿa, Ramesses wears the crescent-and-disk insignia and sits under a canopy with "Ptah of Ramesses-Meryamun in the domain of Ptah" and "Ptah-Tatenen, of high plumes and a pair of pointed horns" (a reference to the god's head ornament).[156] "Hathor, Mistress of . . . " is seated behind the image of the king. In the sanctuary of el-Derr, the statue group is badly destroyed, and the figure of Ptah has even been completely obliterated and replaced by three lines of inscription. But otherwise the group resembles the one at Abu Simbel, the king being seated between Amun and Harakhti. At Gerf Hussein, niches are carved into the walls of the hall having the Osiride pillars, and in the high relief of each niche Ramesses sits between two gods, usually a god and a goddess—for example, Amun-Re and Mut, Ptah and Sekhmet, Harakhti and Jusaʿas. In the sanctuary, Ramesses is accompanied by Ptah, Ptah-Tatenen, and Hathor, as in the relief at Wadi el-Sebuʿa described above.[157]

The Nubian temples of Ramesses II are clearly interrelated, with the possible exception of Beit el-Wali, the northernmost.[158] We may assume that they shared a common function, so perhaps it is only by chance that their role as Mansions of Millions of Years is mentioned in only two extant inscriptions.

Ramesses II, like his father Sety I, built a Mansion of Millions of Years at Abydos. He designated it "the Mansion of Usermaʿatre-Setepenre (called) 'United-with-the-Wide-Land (ḥnmt t3-wr).'"[159] Fragments of a sculpture that grouped five approximately life-sized figures on a common seat were found in or near its sanctuary and reassembled there. Some of the inscriptions and attributes identifying the figures are missing, but the central figure with the atef-crown, flagellum, and crook is Osiris. Isis sits on his left, with the crown of the queens of the period. On her left is a figure labeled "Osiris Menmaʿatre," that is, Sety I as Osiris. He wears the crown of Tatenen, a sun disk surmounted by two plumes and horizontal ram's horns. To the right of the central Osiris is the much damaged "Horus, Son of Isis, (beloved of?) Ramesses-Meryamun." To his right is only part of a figure's head. It wears the royal nms-headcloth, topped, we may guess, with the double crown of Upper and Lower Egypt—perhaps representing Ramesses II.[160]

Despite the large number of rooms, the temple of Ramesses II at Abydos has an almost perfect simplicity of plan along an east-west axis.[161] The first central hall is flanked to the south and north by two chapels entered from the raised portico on the west side of the temple's peristyle courtyard. The southernmost of the chapels received the barque of Ramesses' father, Sety I, which is represented on a wall inside. An inscription at the door calls this chapel "a ḥwt-k3, a chapel of the ka, for his (Sety's) sšm-ḥw barque in the procession of his father Osiris in my (Ramesses') Mansion of Millions of Years." The other southern chapel is also a ḥwt-k3; it apparently served the cultus of an older group of Ramesses' forefathers.[162] In the middle of the west end of the temple, beyond a second centered hall, are three large chapels for receiving the images of the triad of Abydos—Osiris, in the center; Isis, to the north; and Horus, to the south. In the corners north and south of these chapels but entered from antechambers to their east, off the second hall, are rooms with nine niches cut into their walls, presumably for images of the Ennead in the company of Osiris.

Perhaps Ramesses II followed the example of Amenhotep III and Sety I and founded a Mansion of Millions of Years at Memphis, in the domain of Ptah, and perhaps at Heliopolis or Per-Ramesses, the new capital he created in the eastern Delta. Definite evidence is lacking. However, literary papyri inform us that Per-Ramesses was provided with temples, including a "House of Amun" to the west that might have housed the statue of the "Amun of Userma῾atre-Setepenre" mentioned on a fragmentary stela from a later reign in the Nineteenth Dynasty.[163]

The son and successor of Ramesses II was Merneptah. His temple in Western Thebes was found to be largely destroyed when Sir Flinders Petrie excavated it at the end of the nineteenth century.[164] According to the Swiss Institute in Cairo, which currently is reinvestigating it, the layout appears closely related to the west-bank temple of Sety I. So far the name of the temple, "the Mansion of Baenre-Meryamun in the domain of Amun on the west of Thebes," and its designation as a Mansion of Millions of Years are found only in inscriptions of officials employed there.[165]

Sety II had no known temple in Western Thebes, but in the forecourt of the temple of Amun at Karnak he built a Mansion of Millions of Years that was reduced to its most modest form.[166] The building comprised three parallel rooms for receiving the barques of Amun, Mut, and Khonsu on processional occasions. In principle, it resembled the triple barque shrine that Ramesses II fashioned at Luxor, in the courtyard at the back of the west tower of his pylon, when he rebuilt the way station of Hatshepsut.[167] The reliefs and, in particular, the inscriptions have suffered considerable damage, so it cannot be proved that the term st wrt, "sanctuary," used of Khonsu's barque chamber was applied also to the chambers of Amun and Mut.[168] Also partly obliterated are the term "[Mansion of] Millions of Years" and the structure's distinctive name (rn.s nfr) "[the Mansion of] Sety-Merneptah (Sety II) in the domain of Amun."[169] In three surviving niches located in the rear wall of Amun's chamber, *Iunmutef*-priests on the sides present offerings to the king at the back. One of the better-preserved addresses by the priest to the king is: "The (things) going forth on the altar in front of Amun-Re, King of the Gods, at Karnak as daily supplies shall be for the royal *ka* of my master, the perfect king."[170] In two niches in the rear wall of Khonsu's chamber and three in the east side wall, the cast of characters in the relief scene differs from Amun's chamber. Here the king takes the role of the *Iunmutef*-priest, and his offerings are presented to pairs of deities standing back to back. In the rear-wall niches, we find a pair of Khonsu figures. In two side-wall niches Khonsu stands with Thoth, and in the third Mut stands with an unidentifiable male, possibly Amun-Re. In Nubia, Amenhotep III and Ramesses II were sometimes portrayed with the attributes of Khonsu. It is possible that one of the doubled Khonsu-figures in each rear-wall niche and one or both of those in the side-wall niches represent the king. The reliefs and inscriptions are badly broken and do not permit a conclusion.[171]

The second of the two known queens of Sety II, Tausert, survived her husband and acted as regent for his young successor Siptah. After Siptah's death, she ruled Egypt in her own name for some years.[172] Petrie discovered the sites of Siptah's and Tausert's temples in the Theban necropolis to the north and south of the Ramesseum. On the bare ground of both temples only the foundation trenches remained visible, but Petrie identified the owners through the offerings deposited in the clean sand used to fill the trenches.[173] Two stone tablets in the shape of bricks were almost certainly part of the foundation gifts in Tausert's temple. They are inscribed with the cartouches of the queen preceded by "Mansion of Millions of Years in the domain of Amun."[174]

A stela from the Delta that possibly also belongs to the reign of Tausert was published by Gardiner.[175] Its long inscription had suffered considerably, and the names of both royal persons concerned with the text had been obliterated. Missing is even the title of the royal lady who ordered the construction of "a sanctuary (*ip.t*) for the statue of 'Amun of Userma͗atre-Setepenre' (Ramesses II)." This divine image was normally stationed in a temple whose location is unknown (Tanis is a possible guess); it was carried in procession to the sanctuary only for certain feasts.[176] The commander of "the fortress of the Sea" that was possibly nearby seems to have been charged with administering the foundation, but, surprisingly, its general oversight was entrusted to two Theban officials—the royal scribe and steward of the Mansion of Millions of Years of a king whose cartouche has been erased; and the steward of the House (*pr*) of Sety-Merneptah, a man named Paibasa. Unfortunately the inscription's many defects prevent a better understanding of the organization of sanctuaries of this type.

The temple built by Ramesses III in the southern part of the Theban necropolis, the "Mansion of Userma'atre-Meryamun (called) 'United-with-Eternity,'" has already been referred to several times. As the best preserved of the so-called mortuary temples, it was the focus of Nelson's investigations. At his instigation, its still impressive remains were thoroughly studied and recorded by the University of Chicago's Epigraphic Survey. All its reliefs and inscriptions were accurately reproduced and made accessible to scholars in a number of splendid volumes.[177] This wealth of collected information has, however, not yet been fully exploited.[178]

To build his temple in Western Thebes, Ramesses III selected a site close to a sanctuary whose origins lay in the early Middle Kingdom.[179] The sanctuary, rebuilt by Hatshepsut and again by Thutmose III, was destined to house its own image of Amun of $dsr-st$, the "sacred place," as well as to receive the visiting image of Amun of Luxor every tenth day. Ramesses III enclosed this venerable sanctuary within the stout walls delimiting his sacred precinct.

The organizational system of the area surrounding the temple proper, with its storerooms and dwellings for the priests, reminds one of the plans of Ramesside frontier fortresses.[180] A huge pylon formed the center of the east side of an inner enclosure, and the gateway between its two towers led into a first courtyard. A colonnade protected the courtyard's south wall, in the center of which was the Window of Appearance, by which the "Palace" to the south communicated with the courtyard.[181] A similar portico on the north side of the courtyard was sustained by square pillars fronted by royal statues carved out of the same masonry blocks. Another, smaller pylon delimited a second courtyard, whose peristyle comprised Osiride pillars east and west and ordinary columns north and south. From the west portico, the gate of the temple proper opened into a first hypostyle hall whose three central aisles were higher than the lateral ones. The rooms accessible on the hall's south side have been designated, on the basis of their preserved reliefs and inscriptions, the "Treasury" and a chapel for the barque of Ramesses II. The rooms aligned on the hall's north side housed minor deities difficult to identify because of the heavier destruction in these parts. Gates farther west on the temple's axis led into a second and a third hall, each with eight columns, and then into a nearly square room with four pillars that received the barque of Amun of Karnak. Narrower chapels flanking the square room accommodated the barques of Mut and Khonsu, Amun's companions, while the room to its west, at the back of the temple proper, featured a double false door of the type described above in connection with buildings of Sety I.

Since the time of Hatshepsut, all the temples of the Theban west had been prepared to receive the barque of Amun of Karnak in their central axis during the Beautiful Feast of the Valley. Compared with the earlier temples, the plan of Medinet Habu appears reduced, even congested in its layout.[182] The side chambers of the second and third halls and the barque chambers are extremely small, and access to them is tortuous and narrow. They are grouped according to their functions. The group to the north of the divine triad's barque chambers was destined for the gods of the northern Heliopolis; Room 31, in particular, had nine wall niches, recalling the Ennead of Heliopolis. On the opposite side of the barque chambers, Room 35 was dedicated to Montu of the southern Heliopolis (originally Armant, later Thebes). Accessible from the second hypostyle hall were three rooms to the north, the largest partly open to the sky and containing the remains of an altar for the sun god Re and wall reliefs of Ramesses III and baboons adoring Re's heavenly barques. The corresponding group of rooms to the south (20–27) is remarkable for both a chapel for Osiris (22) and a chapel with a vaulted ceiling and a double false door in its west wall where Ramesses III was to receive offerings. An attempt to describe the function of all forty-eight rooms grouped around the axial halls of Amun would be gratuitous, the more so because their state of preservation leaves many questions unanswered.

An exceptional document—Papyrus Harris I—lists all the donations Ramesses III made to Egyptian temples during his reign.[183] Its seventy-nine pages mention a large number of constructions, and it describes several in moderate detail, indicating, for example, some of the statues made for particular rooms. Yet its descriptions are too short to permit us to visualize the buildings or to determine why some were designated by *ḥwt* and others by *pr* and why the building term was in some cases linked with the king's prenomen or nomen and in some cases, with a god's name. Surprisingly the phrase *m ḥḥ n rnpwt*, "of millions of years," is but twice connected with buildings, once with the temple of Medinet Habu and once with a temple of Re to the north of Heliopolis that is named by the king's nomen.[184] Nevertheless at least some of the temples not designated by the phrase had the same function as the two that are.[185] Despite the wealth of data, it remains difficult to work out the criteria that determined the use of specific Egyptian terms.

Ramesses III was followed by a series of eight pharaohs also named Ramesses but with distinguishing additions and with differing throne names. Traces of temple constructions in the Theban necropolis are known only for Ramesses IV and Ramesses V.[186] The temple *ḥwt nb-m3ˁt-rˁ*, "Mansion of Nebmaˁatre," is named in several priestly titles and administrative documents from Dynasty 20. Whether it designates a building of Ramesses VI is still undecided, for he adopted the same prenomen as Amenhotep

III.[187] It is, however, rather unlikely that a commemorative cultus for Amenhotep III was continued beyond the end of Dynasty 18 and even less likely that it was resumed toward the end of Dynasty 20. Similar doubts persist concerning the few subsequent instances where ḥwt is followed by the prenomen of a later king.[188]

Conclusion

Confronted with the need to bring the disparate evidence of the preceding pages to a reasonable conclusion, I am reminded of the preface to Henri Frankfort's *Kingship and the Gods,* from which I quote, with slight modification, the first two sentences: "The creations of the Egyptian mind are elusive. Its concepts seem ill defined, defying clear limitations."[189]

Scholars of the natural sciences have become aware that the results they attain are influenced and modified by the tools they use. Scholars of the humanities rarely reflect on the intellectual tools they use—the words and concepts of modern languages—nor do they question their tools' adequacy for treating the objects of their studies. As I stated at the beginning, the ancient Egyptians had no word for our concept "mortuary temple." Yet scholars have accepted the meaning of this modern term as so obvious that they have felt no need to define it closely, being satisfied with something so vague as "a royal temple in the Theban necropolis, near the royal tombs and visited by Amun's procession during the Festival of the Valley." Everyone has been aware, of course, that ancient Egyptians' attitudes toward life and death were different from ours.[190] Otto introduced the term "memorial temple" in place of "mortuary temple" and "funerary temple."[191] But this change does not solve the problem. In a recent article, Luc Gabolde proposes a distinction between "funerary" and "memorial" temples, again without defining their distinguishing traits.[192] In his opinion, the western temple of Thutmose II, which so far has been called his "mortuary temple," was built by Thutmose III and should be termed a "memorial temple." Gabolde also uses "memorial temple" for the building whose blocks—inscribed with the names of Tutankhamun and his successor Ay and with fragments of a representation of the same statue ritual depicted at the temple of Thutmose II—were found reused in the Second Pylon at Karnak. Gabolde does not clarify whether his basis for calling these two structures "memorial temple" is the presence of the same rare ritual in both monuments or the apparent founding of both by a king's successor. If the latter, then the term would apply as well to the temple built by Sety I for Ramesses I at Abydos and to the rooms of Ramesses I included in the temple of Sety I at Qurna. Why should we distinguish in this way between temples

built to commemorate a venerated predecessor and others built to perpetuate the founder's own name? Temples of both types are, in truth, "memorials."

Understandably, scholars try to determine the specific purpose of individual rooms in a royal temple, but we should never forget that all the
rooms contributed to a single aim achieved in multiple ways: the com-
memoration of the founder's name in front of the gods.

Rejecting the term "mortuary temple," I pointed to an expression that is
frequent, though not regular, in texts referring to temples of the Theban
necropolis—the phrase "Mansion of Millions of Years." This phrase was
not limited, however, to these buildings but was applied to a substantial
number of other constructions raised in the vicinity of temples where a deity was supposed to reside. Our modern, methodical mind would demand
that buildings called by a common term should present a cluster of common features. With Mansions of Millions of Years, however, we find an
amazing variety of plans, of dispositions of rooms, and of reliefs and texts
on their walls.[193] If certain features are repeated in several buildings, they
are missing in others. Such variety makes it difficult to discover general
rules.

Part of our difficulty in tracing the rules that governed the planning of
Mansions of Millions of Years comes from their defective state of preservation; in many cases investigators cannot compare one building with another because essential parts are missing. Another part of our difficulty
comes from limited access to data; many mansions are only partially published. But the chief part of our difficulty comes from the Egyptian mind's
broad and marked difference from our own.

Ancient Egyptians could express their ideas in many different ways—
ritual action, pictorial representation, emblematic rendering, and oral and
written expression.[194] Of these various modes, writing so dominates our
own civilization that we have almost lost the ability to understand other
modes. Not surprisingly, Egyptology has focused on philology, on copying and translating texts, on lexicography and linguistics. Rare are the
studies of wall reliefs that seek to determine the *meaning* of the attitudes,
attributes, dress, and headgear of kings and gods.

Even in writing, ancient Egyptians could express essentially the same
meaning in rather different forms. On the one hand, they seem to have been
averse to fundamental changes, preferring to repeat the same models in-
definitely; yet on the other hand they frequently employed a large variety
of sign combinations to write the same word. If one were to attend to phras-
ing, one would be surprised to see in how many different ways the same
idea could be formulated in the Egyptian language.

In the figurative arts, too, essentially the same meaning could be expressed in rather different forms. Barbara Switalski Lesko's study of the royal mortuary suites attributes particular importance to Room 25 at Medinet Habu.[195] Its vaulted ceiling is engraved with an astronomical chart, and its rear wall is shaped as a double false door. Lesko points out that a room in Hatshepsut's temple at Deir el-Bahri also has a vaulted ceiling, in this case decorated with stars accompanied by a representation of the hours of the day and the night, and that a false door—albeit of the earlier and much simpler form—is inserted into the room's rear wall. Fragments in the temples of Thutmose III and Amenhotep II prove that these same elements were used there. We may readily accept Lesko's conclusion that the vaulted rooms served a common cultic purpose: the depositing of offerings for the deceased pharaoh. Nevertheless, the changes in the elements that have to transmit the same idea should not be overlooked. The ceiling decoration was radically changed from the representation of the hours to the star charts; and at some indeterminate moment between the reigns of Hatshepsut and Sety I, the traditional simple false door was replaced by a double false door with rather complicated tracery on top. Again, essentially the same meaning could be expressed in rather different forms.[196]

I have difficulty accepting Lesko's idea that the offerings in these vaulted rooms were presented to the royal mummy. We know practically nothing about the procedures at royal funerals; it is not at all certain that the burial procession ever entered the "mortuary temples." I fear the temptation to attribute great importance to the funeral is influenced by modern attitudes toward death. Our thinking tends to be categorical, reducing our choices to yes or no, alive or dead; and the prospect of a continued life, which religion offers, has little influence on our daily practices. Thus we have difficulty understanding the ancient Egyptians, who, while accepting life on earth, also looked forward, beyond death, to a continued life in eternity, for which they made in their time all possible preparations.

Despite the highly spiritual background of these preparations for continued life, they had a definite material side. It was not sufficient to deposit the offerings at the false door where the spirit of the deceased was supposed to receive them; his presence needed to be substantiated through the person's image carved on the false door or through a statue inscribed with his name, lest the wrong spirit profit from the goods. For the statue of stone or wood to partake of the gifts laid before it, it had to be made alive, fictively, through the performance of the complicated Opening of the Mouth ritual. The spirit's life was to last for eternity, so care had to be taken for continued supplies, either by depicting files of offering bearers on the walls beside the false door or by establishing a foundation producing income with its own lands and personnel.

From early in the Old Kingdom, the Egyptian mortuary cultus in general was practiced both at the false door in the tomb and in front of the deceased's statue, which at first was enclosed in a "serdab," a separate chamber within the tomb's superstructure. Experience soon proved that this method of assuring a constant supply for the spirit was unreliable. First, the defect was repaired by carrying the statue to the temple of a god, where it could receive a share in the offerings presented to the deity. Then, to avoid cumbersome transportation, the statue was set up in the vicinity of a temple. Such a statue could not be left unprotected, so a shelter—called ḥwt-k3 or, as at Abydos, mˁḥˁt—was built.[197] These were, in my opinion, the precursors of the "Mansions of Millions of Years," the name given to the constructions for royal statues from the Second Intermediate Period onward.

Scholars widely disagree about the aim the priests hoped (or pretended) to achieve through the rituals performed in these temples. Many, mainly those writing in English and French, speak of "deification"; indeed the French even speak of the "regeneration" or "rejuvenation of the god king."[198] But a number of scholars, mostly German, emphatically oppose the idea that the ancient Egyptians attributed godlike qualities to their kings.[199] These, however, still readily admit the existence of something like a concept of divine nature in the cultuses of Ahmose-Nefertari and her son Amenhotep I at Thebes, and also of Amenhotep III in his temple at Soleb.[200]

This scholarly disagreement exists because the criteria for "deification" have not been worked out. An answer satisfying to everyone will probably never be given. Yet one cannot deny that pharaohs made tremendous efforts to pose as gods. They had themselves portrayed receiving life from the hands of the gods and even sitting among the gods. Whether they themselves, or the multitude of their subjects, believed the pose, who can tell?

4

THE NEW KINGDOM «DIVINE» TEMPLE: THE EXAMPLE OF LUXOR

LANNY BELL

Introduction

This discussion of the role of the New Kingdom "divine" temple in Egyptian society is based on Luxor Temple, a rich mine of information heretofore largely unexploited.[1] Luxor Temple is a particularly good subject with which to begin a study of the "divine" cultic temple of the New Kingdom because it is architecturally compact and coherent, even deceptively simple, particularly in comparison with Karnak, the most elaborate God's House still standing in Egypt. Because Luxor Temple is representative in so many ways, detailed knowledge of it teaches something about all related temples.

The attempt to unravel the secrets of Luxor Temple leads along many paths, each of which has a number of offshoots. These include the history of the temple's construction and decoration, its relationships to other temples, and several important historical implications. New evidence also permits us to glimpse the temple's prehistory. Throughout, the various functions of the temple are set in the context of ancient Egyptian culture as a whole, and the temple's relevance to ordinary Egyptians is addressed. The *Opet*-festival and the cultus of the royal *ka* will serve as starting points for exploring how temple rituals promoted social cohesion by validating the king's preeminent role in society.[2] We shall see that public access into certain areas of Luxor Temple was permitted, especially during annual festivals, when the gods, the priests, the king, and representatives of the people of Egypt all came together there.

Before turning to the temple, however, it will be helpful to summarize several features of ancient Egyptian thought and culture.

Ma'at: Order

The fundamental principle of Egyptian culture was expressed in the term *ma'at*: "truth," "justice," "cosmic order," the "well-ordered state"—handed down from the gods, perfect and intact. *Ma'at* codified the cultural status quo, the Egyptian way of life and way of doing things projected back into the timelessness before time. *Ma'at* was the concept that gave meaning to life by structuring both the human and divine worlds.

Ma'at was custom, or tradition, or traditional values, or even culture itself. *Ma'at* was what made the Egyptians *Egyptian,* distinguishing them from all other beings. They alone had been given *ma'at*; therefore they were the gods' chosen people.[3] *Ma'at* regulated behavior; it was common law; it was orthodoxy admitting of no variance; it was the *only* way. Abstractly, that which stood outside *ma'at* was unreality or falsehood; in practical terms, anyone, Egyptian or other, who operated beyond its bounds was regarded as a criminal or savage.

Ma'at was the food of the gods, and the king alone was righteous enough to offer it as sacrifice. The living king was a special person; he possessed a dual nature. He was simultaneously mortal and divine, human and superhuman. He was the living incarnation of deity, the divinely chosen intermediary, unique in his ability to cross freely the boundaries separating heaven, earth, and netherworld and to function effectively, for the sake of humanity, in all three realms. Godhood was revealed through the king's life, deeds, and very being. At the king's initiation (coronation), he was hailed as *m3'* or *m3'-ḥrw,* "justified."[4] In artistic representations of the *ma'at*-offering, his royal name was equated with *ma'at*.[5] The king performed the cultic mysteries; he handled the ritual instruments, dedicated the sacrifices, recited the sacrosanct texts, and ministered to, responded to, impersonated, and even became god, thereby fulfilling his obligation to renew and perpetuate the creation by maintaining the divinely ordained cosmic order—*ma'at*.[6]

Chaos: Disorder

The Egyptians had an abiding, deeply rooted fear of *ma'at's* opposite: disorder, by which they meant any change or alteration in the system, not just its breakdown. Progress—involving divergence or digression from an existing path—was viewed as decline, for Egyptians believed the world ought essentially to stay always the same. They interpreted history from a mythological perspective; that is, they understood most events as particularizations of cosmic principles, tendencies, or movements established at the beginning of time. Occurrences consistent with primordial prototypes were reality. Occurrences inconsistent with them—that is, random, unique, or unparalleled—were nonreality.

The Egyptians must have sensed the precariousness of existence on their "island oasis," situated as it was between the twin terrors of flood and desert. The very waters that granted life could also deal death; for when the Nile was too high it brought destructive flood, and when it was too low it resulted in devastating famine. Thus the river could symbolize the watery abyss at the beginning of time when chaos prevailed.[7] The desert's unpredictable storms and wild animals and its nomads roaming freely in an incoherent wilderness could also symbolize forces of chaos outside the Egyptians' system and beyond their control.

Chaos was personified by the trickster-god Seth, who ruled thunder and lightning and the violent storms of wind, sand, and rain that originated in the desert, and also by Apophis, the dragon (serpent monster) who, in the never-ending struggle between light and darkness, tried to swallow the sun, particularly when it was most vulnerable during the subterranean west-east journey that followed its daily death and burial (sunset). During night's complete darkness, one object was visually indistinguishable from another; they merged together or blended, as in the Void. At the first light of dawn, objects again became visually distinct; they once more came into existence. Thus luminosity, brilliance, and radiance possessed creative power and signaled deity's presence.[8] The king's accession to the throne and mounting of his chariot were likened to the sun's rising; and the king's public manifestation at the Window of Appearance was compared to the sun's appearance on the eastern horizon.[9]

Secular and Sacred Time

Egyptians were aware of time's passage for the same reason that we are: persons pass through consecutive phases of life—birth, puberty, aging, death—that can neither be avoided nor repeated. But this linear time, or, as we call it, "real" or concrete time, belonged to the purely secular world, the world of ordinary human affairs. The time connected with the sacred was the abstract, cyclical time associated with perpetual recurrences and repetitions.[10] Egyptians experienced sacred, cyclical time in the succession of day and night, the phases of the moon, the rotation of the seasons, the mating behavior of animals, and the migrations of fish and birds; especially striking to them was the annual flooding of the Nile, regularly followed by the reemergence of dry land, the reappearance of vegetation, and the flowering and dying of annual plants. Egyptians marked the recurrence of these phenomena by weekly, monthly, and annual holy days.[11] Every annual festive occasion concluded with a New Year's celebration, and each New Year's day represented beginning all over again. The usual word for "year," *rnpit*, literally means "renewal" or "a new beginning." (Re)birth-symbolism permeated Egyptian religion. For example, the epithet *wḥm msiwt* (literally, "repeating birth," used to characterize a few kings' reigns as well as a whole era at the troubled end of Dynasty 20) signifies "rebirth (or renaissance)," in the sense of the restoration of the originally perfect state—the immaculate world of the time of creation—and the beginning of a new age of salvation.[12]

The life cycle of some beings was construed to occur within sacred time rather than secular time. The divine King and the other gods participated in an eternal cycle of death and rebirth in which they maintained their personal identity—a characteristic that set them apart from the world of mortals.[13] During the *Sed*-festival, the living king, as part of his eternal cycle, underwent a ritual death and rejuvenation.[14] In the rite's critical climax, the king experienced the nadir of his strength; during his moment of almost simultaneous death and rebirth, he returned fleetingly to the chaotic state. This was Egypt's time of greatest danger, when the success or failure of the rite—indeed, the very fate of the world—hung in the balance. An almost unbearable tension gripped the priests at the service and the people who waited outside, and when the king reappeared, successfully rejuvenated, their high excitement and enormous relief quickly turned to jubilation.

Components of Personhood

Egyptian ideas about the nature of the person, individuality, and self-identity were complicated. In discussing the subject, we need to keep in mind our tendency to underestimate the importance of private ancestor cultuses, a fundamental phenomenon of ancient Egyptian culture.[15]

The components of Egyptian personhood were: the corpse or body (*ḥ3wt*), the heart (*ib* or *ḥ3ty*), the name (*rn*), the shade or shadow (*šwyt*), and three entities that are for us the most difficult and abstract of all—the *akh* (*3ḫ*), the *ba* (*b3*), and the *ka* (*k3*) (fig. 43).

The body's importance was expressed in the practice of mummification.[16] The heart was the center of both thought or intellect and emotions or feelings. The name expressed or revealed a person's true nature or essence. The shade was both an emanation from a deity and a reflection of divine power (light); it was drawn as a silhouette of the body, and it symbolized divinity's indwelling of an object or being (roughly speaking, incarnation).[17]

The *ba* was depicted as a human-headed bird. *Ba*'s root shows that the

FIG. 43. The Sons of Horus present four aspects of the personality—*ka*, heart, *ba*, and shade, from right to left—before the deceased Petosiris (out of the picture on the far right) in his tomb at Tuna el-Gebel (reign of Philip Arrhidaeus). Drawing by Carol Meyer, after G. Lefebvre.

word pertained to power.[18] In the realm of the supernatural, *ba* refers to a god's manifestation. *Ba* generally occurs in contexts related to mobility and physical functioning (the appetites, for instance, including continued sexual activity in the afterlife). The *ba* was tied to a particular body, with which it needed to maintain close contact so that they could periodically unite. In a sense, the *ba* was the "spiritual body."

Akh's root shows that it had to do with "effective" action or speech and with physical integrity, expressed concretely through the reintegration of the dead body during mummification.[19] The *akh*-spirits were worshiped in domestic ancestor shrines and seem to have been the ghosts of the recently dead, whose physical presence continued to be felt by loved ones. In a liminal state between this world and the next, the *akh*-spirits might intercede on a person's behalf or interfere in his or her affairs.[20] An *3ḫ iḳr* (excellent, virtuous, or worthy *akh*) was a beneficent or well-disposed spirit, but an angry *akh*-spirit—for instance, that of an improperly buried person—could become a demon.

The *ka*, unlike the *ba*, was only temporarily associated with a particular body. It was itself noncorporeal and was separated from a body by death, subsequently entering a new life-form. Just as a god's *ka* took up transitory residence in a statue-body, endowing it with life, so an ancestor *ka* temporarily occupied and animated the body of an ordinary person, and the royal *ka* transiently inhabited and empowered the body of an individual king.[21] The *ka* was not individual-specific. It was generic to a family and was infinitely replicated within it; it personified inherited life force (fig. 44). Every Egyptian could claim direct descent from a mythic divine ancestor who stood at the head of the lineage and guaranteed that each descendent

FIG. 44. A man carrying four children shows the pose of the *ka*-arms. Dynasty 11; Theban Tomb 386. The logical way to carry this many children would be to embrace them with arms held against the chest. I suggest the scene represents an artistic convention that elucidates my interpretation of the function of the *ka*. Restored drawing by Carol Meyer, after B. Jaroš-Deckert.

infant's body would be shaped by the imprint of its father's *ka*-spirit.[22] Through that mythic divine progenitor, every Egyptian could also claim a connection to the life force of the creator god himself. The *ka* carried the force of the miraculous moment of First Creation across countless consecutive generations, obviating the necessity for repeating the creative act at the passing of each generation. The procreative *ka* generated, animated, nourished, sustained, and maintained a family, lineage, or clan and identified the individual as a member of it. The living were the current representatives of their mythic ancestor's *ka*-spirit, but the totality of each *ka* was all members of the lineage, both living and dead.[23]

The Temple and the People

Temples were microcosms, realizations in miniature of the landscape of world order. There the visible met the invisible, the human touched the divine, and earth joined sky and netherworld. Obelisks pierced the heavens, and flag masts supported the canopy of the sky; pylons mimicked the horizon, and columns held starry ceilings aloft; sacred lakes teemed with life, like the abyss or primeval swamp, and wells tapped the regenerative power of creation's waters.[24]

But there was danger in relinking heaven, earth, and netherworld, realms that had been separated and distinguished at the First Creation. Through the blurring of distinctive differences, world order might collapse in the very place designed to maintain it. The attendant danger contributed importantly to the aura of sanctity and mystery that enveloped the temple.

At first glance, the great New Kingdom temple might seem to have been the domain of gods, kings, and priests exclusively. After all, the temple circumscribed and architecturally delimited a site whose sacredness distinguished it from the mundane populated space around it. The temple was set apart—both ritually, by consecrating the ground on which it was erected and out of which it seemed organically to grow, and architecturally, by building an imposing series of progressively more restrictive walls to surround and protect it. The temple's ritual and architectural barriers repulsed the chaotic forces that continually threatened the ordered world within.[25]

Situated in sacred space and time, the temple was a divine domain on earth. Patterned on the mansion and estate of a nobleman or king, it was an abode for gods. Entrance was gained through a fortified gateway or soaring pylon (fig. 45).[26] From that point, typically, a long, straight axial way led inward through a series of open courts. Along it, the rooms became ever smaller and darker, an effect achieved partly through raised floors and lowered ceilings. The route's portals were punctuated by magnificently adorned wooden doors that swung open and shut on pivots; most major entranceways had double doors. Doors had both practical utility and intrinsic symbolic power: closed, they excluded intruders; open, they admitted the chosen. The axial way through portals, courts, and chamber complexes led ultimately to the somewhat cramped private apartment of the god—the sanctuary itself. Typically constructed over a hillock or symbolic mound, this elevated room was the mythological center of the universe, where the primordial event of creation had occurred.[27]

Egyptian temples were equipped at cultic focal points with miraculous portals. Into the solid masonry of offering chapels a fine stone slab (stela) could be set, often in a niche specifically prepared for it.[28] Alternatively, a part of the chapel wall itself could be carved in the shape of a stela. The forms of the stelae varied considerably, yet all depicted elements associated with doorways—lintel, jamb, torus molding, central recess, upper and lower pivots, bolt, door leaves. However, the stelae had no moving parts, no aperture, and no room or hollow behind. Many scholars have called them "false doors."[29] To the extent that this designation suggests the portals were mock or sham, it misleads. The portals were not meant to function in palpable space. Rather they worked in divine dimension. They were

FIG. 45. Pylon of Luxor Temple, showing present condition. Photo by Lanny Bell.

gateways permitting direct, *magical* communication between earth, sky, and netherworld. Ordinary mortals could not cross their thresholds, but the blessed dead and the living king, as well as priests and other initiates, could pass through them to the kingdom of heaven. Nor were these stelae the temple's only portals of otherworldly transport. The wooden doors of the sanctuary shrine, which enclosed the divine image, were called the "doors of heaven." At their opening, ritual participants were projected into the realm of the divine.

The cultic images housed in the sanctuaries were made of precious materials, most commonly gilded wood inlaid with colored glass and semi-precious stones. They were sometimes life-sized (at least by human standards!). There were also much smaller images, some made of solid gold. Cultic images were often taken from their cloistered sanctuaries and carried in procession outside the temple on portable barques.[30] Sometimes divine processions linked temples. Within New Kingdom Thebes, festival connections existed between the temples and gods of Karnak and Deir el-Bahri, Karnak and Luxor, and Luxor and Medinet Habu. Even temples distant from each other could be linked in this way. Hathor of Dendera traveled over one hundred miles each way to visit Horus of Edfu for the annual consummation of their sacred marriage. It should be noted that whenever gods processed through the mundane world, they were hidden from profane eyes. They rode inside a closed, veiled shrine or naos on a barque's deck and were identified to onlookers only by symbols placed on the boat's prow and stern.[31]

For all these reasons, one finds it hard to imagine that ordinary humanity had a significant role to play in the cosmic setting of the temple; and for all these reasons, one finds it easy to imagine that temples were the domain of gods, kings, and priests alone. But just as the king was both apart from humanity (as an intimate of the gods) and a part of it, so too the temple was both apart from the world and a part of it. This can be seen, for example, in the temple's arcane kingship rituals, which for full effectiveness needed a public component as well as a private one. Had the rituals been performed in complete obscurity, without public participation, they could not have elicited the popular support necessary to maintain, over three millennia, kingship's power and position.[32] The great state temples of the New Kingdom—despite their forbidding exteriors, massive enclosure walls, restrictive pylon barriers, and fortified gateways—were accessible to Egypt's populace and were relevant to the surrounding communities' daily life.[33]

True, access to the stone platform of the temple's most sacred part was strictly limited, but other parts of the temple were open to pilgrims, at least on special occasions. These were formally designated "places of making supplication and of hearing the petitions of gods and men," and they were located not only at gateways but also in open courtyards. Also, during annual festivals representatives of the populace were ushered into the less restricted outer courtyards and ceremonial halls of the temple. There, in the role of a congregation or community of adoration, they worshiped the gods, marveled at the temple's splendor, participated in internal processions, and bore witness to the miraculous effect of the secret rites performed within the dark and distant holy of holies, rites that piloted the world through various cosmological crises. Ancient texts specify that the people's function was to "adore (the king or god), that they might live (thereby)."

Temple decorations were intended primarily for gods' eyes, but those in public areas were meant for people's as well. The estimated 1–5 percent who were literate could read some of the texts, and everyone could "read" portions of the art work.[34] Although ancient Egyptians' understanding of esoteric theological matters would hardly have been more sophisticated than modern worshipers', the celebrant's lofty words and staged actions (as interpreted to the people by the priests), the god's response (as reported back from the temple platform through the priests), and the art work's stories and messages (as understood through the people's own eyes) must have made satisfactory sense to them. The spectacular endurance of pharaonic civilization attests eloquently to the success of kings and priests in engaging people in the ritual process that maintained and renewed the established religious, political, and social system.

During the extravagant public displays associated with periodic festivals, deities could choose to intervene in human affairs by making oracular pronouncements, including judgments in disputes. When processions reached their prescribed halting places, people were sometimes allowed to approach the boat shrine (naos) to address yes-or-no-type questions to the god within. The deity's answering nod was read in the swaying of the barque—forward or back, right or left—as it rested on the priests' shoulders.[35] Egyptian society was a close-knit community of shared assumptions and values, and a form of mass psychology doubtless influenced both the movement of the naos (caused by shifts in the priests' posture) and its interpretation. The unconsciously directed barque probably expressed what everyone already thought, and fair judgment was usually rendered.

Portable divine images and barques also played a role in transmitting people's prayers to the gods. Other media for such prayers were the divine images engraved on a temple's doors and exterior walls, sacred animals, statues of kings and of blessed deceased private individuals, and the living king himself.

Popular veneration made use of a variety of other portable objects that had acquired direct connection to god through contact with a divine being.[36] Perhaps they had been worn, touched, or used by a god or had been in some other way present to god. Such utensils were thought to possess a divine spark or charge and to bear a lasting impression of the deity.[37] They were seen as images (or, hypostases) of god, reflections of god's power, media for god's communication, and/or instruments for transmitting god's life-giving force. The particular device used to cross the boundary between sacred and profane could change from time to time, place to place, and god to god, but the concept underlying the practice and the basic pattern of cultic manipulation remained the same.

One of my favorite ancient Egyptian celebrations illustrates many of the phenomena discussed to this point. It is the Theban Festival of the Valley, or *Talfest*, attested from Dynasty 11 onward.[38] The new moon in the second month of summer (*šmw*) signaled the beginning of the festival. It was a sort of annual family reunion during which ancestors were reintegrated into the family and bonds between the living and dead were strengthened. The festival and its rituals helped to confirm the priority of the family over the individual within Egypt's social and political organization.[39] The distinctive offering of the Valley Festival was the holocaust, a burnt sacrifice consumed entirely by flames. Priests poured a heavy, myrrh-scented oil over the holocaust, and thick, sweet-smelling smoke rose heavenward, establishing a link from earth.

The Valley Festival was the Theban version of a popular Hathor festival celebrated throughout Egypt from at least the Old Kingdom. In the Theban necropolis Hathor, in her cow form, is often depicted emerging from the surrounding hills to receive the dead as Mistress of the West(ern Mountain). But in keeping with the theological system developed at Thebes, the major role in the Valley Festival was played not by Hathor but by Amun-Re, the national god. During the festival performance, his portable barque was transported aboard his splendidly decorated, gilded riverine barge from Karnak to the west bank of the Nile. There, in his chapel, near Hathor's in the spectacular limestone bay of the sacred mountain at Deir el-Bahri, Amun-Re took up residence. From there, he visited the royal cult complexes of the west bank, especially the temple of the reigning king.

The citizenry of ancient Luxor participated in the Valley Festival with great enthusiasm. Their most characteristic adornment (besides fine white garments and the perfumed unguent cone that perched atop their head) was the beautiful $w3h$-collar or garland, composed of fragrant petals of fresh flowers. This accessory of dress, symbolizing regeneration, was distributed to all guests, both living and dead.[40] The living prepared for encountering their deceased loved ones by observing an all-night vigil at the tombs. Then, in an induced, ecstatic state, they crossed into the realm of the divine ancestors, with alcohol as their drug of choice.[41] The hypnotic rhythms of music and dance added to people's ecstasy and also summoned the ancestors' spirits. Feasting sealed the communion of the living with the dead, as is typical in rites of incorporation.[42]

The kas of both immediate family and more distant ancestors were revived by bringing near them highly scented floral collars, garlands, and sprays that mediated the life force of Amun-Re. While the god's cultic image rested overnight in the holy grotto of Deir el-Bahri, elaborately worked $ankh$-bouquets were stacked around it to receive his regenerative power (see also Appendix II).[43] At the dawn of the New Year, a lighted torch was extinguished in a bowl of cow's milk (itself a symbol of rebirth) to signify the successful return of the dead to Hathor. Then the large $ankh$-bouquets, pungent with Amun-Re's regenerative power, were purchased from priests and distributed to the dead in the offering chapels of their Theban tombs (fig. 46). The presentation of the bouquets, and of the other offerings of the Valley Festival, was typically introduced by the phrase n $k3.k$, "To your ka!"

Divine Kingship and the Royal Ka

The doctrine of divine kingship was the central, dynamic principle underlying Egypt's social, political, and economic structures.[44] First, according to the doctrine, kingship was ordained by the gods at the beginning of time

FIG. 46. Presentation of ʿnḥ-bouquets to the ancestors during the Festival of the Valley. Theban Tomb 217. Photo by Lanny Bell.

in accordance with *maʿat*. The integration of politics and religion had been divinely prescribed, and the sovereign wielded both temporal and spiritual power.[45] Second, the reigning pharaoh was the physical son of the universal sun god, the Creator.[46] In a miraculous divine birth, the king had been begotten by Amun-Re, in the guise of a mortal (typically, the previous king), and born of a blessed woman chosen to conceive him and become mother of god (typically, a queen) (fig. 47). Third, the living king was an incarnation of the dynastic god Horus, and the deceased king was identified with Horus' divine father, Osiris.[47] Theban theologians, in an attempt to systematize the theoretical framework of divine kingship, combined various motifs to create a version in which the solar king of the gods, Amun-Re, was substituted for Osiris, and Horus was recast in his ancient solar guise.

Since kings died, how could they be considered divine? In the Egyptian worldview, death did not disprove divinity. Gods died *and* they were immortal, for they experienced a practically infinite series of rebirths—as did the divine King. Kings as *individuals* came and went, but kingship as an *office* never died. In ascending the throne, a mortal came to embody kingship and became immortal. Elevated above the mass of humanity in a partly secret, partly public coronation ceremony, the heir was transformed into a new being and initiated into a new, mysterious existence. He was changed

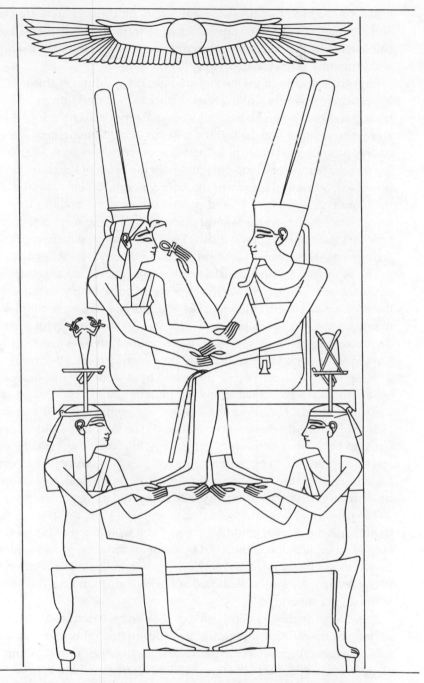

FIG. 47. Divine conception of Amenhotep III by Amun-Re and Queen Mutemwiya, supported by the goddesses Selket (left) and Neith (right). The Birth Room at Luxor Temple. Restored drawing by Carol Meyer, after R. Schwaller de Lubicz.

into a king, a mixed being—simultaneously mortal and immortal, human and divine (fig. 48). Enthronements were miraculous moments of kingship's rebirth, as again and again a mortal entered into the divine domain, and humanity united with divinity.

Egyptians' theory of divine kingship has many ethnographic parallels.[48] In particular, it bears a striking resemblance to medieval Europe's legal doctrine of the king's two bodies.[49] Europeans grappled with the problems of absolute monarchy and the legitimate status of individual rulers. Their elaborately promulgated doctrine helped to smooth transitions in reign by holding that the demise of a king did not signify the death of kingship. Each king possessed, at one and the same time, both a mortal, fallible natural body and the immortal, incorruptible, and perfect supernatural body or *corpus mysticum*—the noncorporeal, mystical office or *persona* (the corporate body) that survived the natural body's death. The *persona mystica* of European monarchs perpetuated immortal kingship, as did the royal *ka* of Egyptian kings.

The royal *ka* was the immortal creative spirit of divine kingship, a form of the Creator's collective *ka*. The *ka* of a particular king was but a specific instance, or fragment, of the royal *ka*. Individual kings were fundamentally interchangeable, even identical. Reliefs depicting the divine birth of individual kings actually represent the rebirth of divine kingship (fig. 49). Carved for reigning monarchs, what they portray is an anachronism. Possessing the royal *ka* and being possessed by it were *potential* at a person's birth, but they were *actualized* only at his coronation, when his legitimacy upon the Horus Throne of the Living was confirmed and publicly acclaimed.[50] Only at a person's coronation did he take on a divine aspect and cease to be solely human (fig. 50).[51] Only in retrospect could he be portrayed as predestined by the Creator to rule Egypt as truly perfect from the beginning, as divine seed, son of the Creator, the very flesh of god, one with the Father, god's incarnation on earth, his sacred image.[52]

The royal *ka* was the divine aspect of a mortal king, the divine principle in humankind. A ruler could legitimately be worshiped in his own cultus only as an incarnation of the royal *ka,* as a manifestation of divine kingship. Even though the *ka* imparted some portion of holiness to the physical beings it occupied, a king was adored not in his human, mortal form but only in his divine aspect.[53]

Possessing the royal *ka* and being possessed by it demonstrated a king's divine origins, proved the legitimacy of his divine inheritance, and established his membership in the fictive royal clan—the "family" comprising all previous occupants of the throne, however distant in time, however different in lineage (fig. 51). The royal *ka* resided in an individual king; but when he died, it continued on, without end or limit, taking fresh body in each new reign.[54]

FIG. 48. Amenhotep III kneels before Amun-Re (defaced under Akhenaten and subsequently restored), who lays his hand on the king's solar *atef*-crown to confirm that this aspect of the coronation ritual has been correctly performed. The divine king also wears the ram's horn of Amun-Re. Chamber of the Divine King at Luxor Temple. Photo by Lanny Bell.

Fig. 49. Creation of Amenhotep III as an incarnation of the royal *ka*. The body of the young king is shaped on a potter's wheel by the god Khnum of Elephantine, as the *ka* assumes the shape of the new body it will inhabit. Amenhotep holds a *rekhyet*-bird, indicating that he was born to rule. Birth Room at Luxor Temple. Restored drawing by Carol Meyer, after H. Brunner and Al. Gayet and a photo by Lanny Bell.

Royal temples and tombs at Thebes frequently show the *ka* accompanying the king. The king's *ka* could be represented either abstractly as a pair of upraised arms (often on a divine standard, which might itself exhibit human arms) or anthropomorphically as a figure with *ka*-arms perched hieroglyphically on its head (fig. 52).[55] In either case, a banner displaying a royal Horus- or *ka*-name is usually supported between the arms. The *ka* usually carries a standard topped by a human head.[56] The *ka* may be shown following the king as a kind of double or twin (fig. 53). But the doubling was merely visual, an optical illusion. Conceptually, the *ka* and the king were understood to be united. The two were, in fact, one.

In Theban royal art, the *ka* accompanies the king from birth to death. The *ka* first appears at the king's conception, in conjunction with his newly formed body (fig. 49). In some scenes, the adult king is portrayed as an in-

Fig. 50. Amun-Re (defaced under Akhenaten and subsequently restored) lays his hands in a *ka*-like gesture on the *ḫprš*-crown worn by Hatshepsut, who kneels before him. Obelisk lying near the Sacred Lake at Karnak. Photo by Lanny Bell.

FIG. 51. Thutmose III had defaced on this rebus frieze the *ka*-element in Hatshepsut's prenomen (Maˁat-Ka-Re) in an attempt to deprive her of the royal *ka* and, consequently, of her legitimacy as king. Fragment lying on a column base in the Hypostyle Hall at Karnak. Photo by Lanny Bell.

fant or young child, sometimes suckled by a goddess (fig. 54). Nursing both incorporated him into the inner circle of the gods and rejuvenated his *ka*.[57] Ritual suckling played a role in the *Opet*-festival's ceremonies of rebirth for divine kingship. In death scenes, the king's *ka* introduces him to Osiris, the god of both dying and regenerated vegetation (fig. 55). Osiris was lord of the netherworld and as such the alter ego of the king's Father, the sun god. "To go to (one's) *ka*" was "to die." When the king died, his body was buried with Osiris, his eternal physical existence was assured by means of his effigy—that is, his transfigured, enabled (*sȝḫ*), ritually reintegrated body— and his *ka* returned to heaven.[58] There the *ka* continued to be worshiped as a form of the sun god, whose essence it shared and into whom it now again merged.

A Brief Description of Luxor Temple

Luxor Temple stands as a major New Kingdom cult complex (fig. 56).[59] It was located in ancient Thebes along the east bank of the Nile, between the river and the ancient town of Luxor to its east.[60] The temple reached vir-

FIG. 52. *Ka*-figures of Amenhotep III at Luxor Temple: *(a)* abstract; and *(b)* anthropomorphic. Restored drawings by Carol Meyer, after H. Brunner.

Fig. 53. *Ka*-statue of the divine Amenhotep III—the king followed by the anthropomorphic *ka*-figure—defaced under Akhenaten and subsequently restored. Offering Vestibule at Luxor Temple. Photo by Lanny Bell.

FIG. 54. In this double scene, Amun-Re lays his hands on the white crown worn by Philip Arrhidaeus, who kneels before him, and the newly reborn king suckles at his divine mother's breast (here, Amunet). The southern exterior wall of the red granite Barque Shrine at Karnak was surely copied from the Barque Shrine of Thutmose III, which it replaced. Drawing by Carol Meyer, after a drawing by C. R. Lepsius and a photo by R. Schwaller de Lubicz.

tually its complete form within a period of about 150 years, between the reigns of Amenhotep III (Dynasty 18) and Ramesses II (Dynasty 19). Traditional Egyptian rituals were practiced there into Roman times.

Was there a Luxor Temple before the reign of Amenhotep III? Very little is known, but the existing evidence suggests that a structure for celebrating the cultus of the divine king existed at Luxor from at least the time of Hatshepsut and Thutmose III (early Dynasty 18).[61] For example, sandstone drums from polygonal columns that are typical of the period of Hatshepsut and Thutmose III were reused in walls erected by Amenhotep III from

FIG. 55. The royal *ka* embraces Tutankhamun from behind as he unites with Osiris. The burial chamber of Tutankhamun's tomb in the Valley of the Kings. Photo by Lanny Bell.

approximately the area of the Offering Vestibule (fig. 56, no. 25) southward.[62] The drums were probably remains from a Thutmoside structure that once stood in Luxor's sanctuary area. Also, materials originally decorated for Hatshepsut, Thutmose III, and Amenhotep II were reused in the triple barque shrine of Ramesses II (figs. 56, no. 4; 57); and, in 1989, statues from the reign of Thutmose III were found buried in the western half of the sun court (fig. 56, no. 11) in the Luxor Cachette.[63] Finally, Hatshepsut erected a series of six way stations for the *Opet*-festival land procession from Karnak to Luxor (fig. 58).[64] She obviously built this road to lead somewhere![65]

The axis of the Luxor Temple ran approximately north-south, roughly paralleling the course of the Nile. Typical of Egyptian temples, it was constructed from the inside out. The sanctuary was built first; next the entrance way leading to it was elaborated; then subsidiary structures were added to magnify the grandeur of the structure as a whole. Thus the platform at the south end was the first component; to that was added the courtyard of Amenhotep III (figs. 56, no. 11; 59); next came the colonnade (figs. 56, no. 10; 60); finally, Ramesses II constructed his pylon and courtyard at the north end (figs. 56, nos. 8, 3; 45; 57).

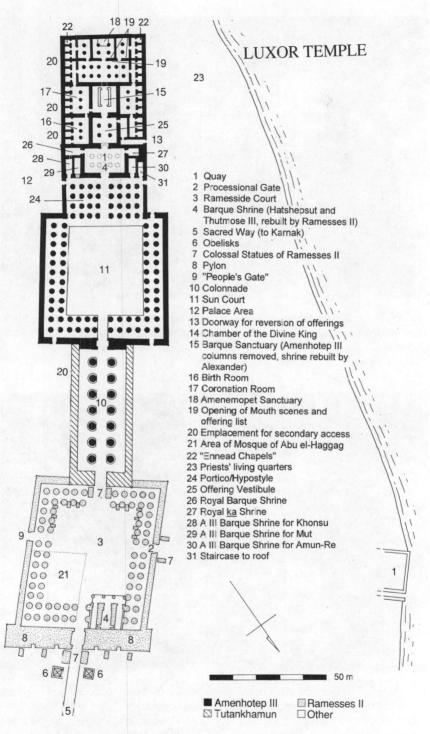

LUXOR TEMPLE

1 Quay
2 Processional Gate
3 Ramesside Court
4 Barque Shrine (Hatshepsut and
   Thutmose III, rebuilt by Ramesses II)
5 Sacred Way (to Karnak)
6 Obelisks
7 Colossal Statues of Ramesses II
8 Pylon
9 "People's Gate"
10 Colonnade
11 Sun Court
12 Palace Area
13 Doorway for reversion of offerings
14 Chamber of the Divine King
15 Barque Sanctuary (Amenhotep III
   columns removed, shrine rebuilt by
   Alexander)
16 Birth Room
17 Coronation Room
18 Amenemopet Sanctuary
19 Opening of Mouth scenes and
   offering list
20 Emplacement for secondary access
21 Area of Mosque of Abu el-Haggag
22 "Ennead Chapels"
23 Priests' living quarters
24 Portico/Hypostyle
25 Offering Vestibule
26 Royal Barque Shrine
27 Royal ka Shrine
28 A III Barque Shrine for Khonsu
29 A III Barque Shrine for Mut
30 A III Barque Shrine for Amun-Re
31 Staircase to roof

50 m

■ Amenhotep III   ▨ Ramesses II
▧ Tutankhamun   ☐ Other

FIG. 56. Plan of Luxor Temple. Drawing by Carol Meyer.

FIG. 57. Triple Barque Shrine of Ramesses II, which reuses material from the Sixth Way Station of Hatshepsut. The First Courtyard at Luxor Temple. Photo by Lanny Bell.

FIG. 58. Adoring *paʿet*-people in a rebus inscription (defaced under Akhenaten and subsequently restored). Fragment with original decoration from the Sixth Way Station of Hatshepsut on the processional route to Luxor Temple, lying on the floor of the central Chapel of Amun-Re in the Triple Barque Shrine. Photo by Lanny Bell.

FIG. 59. Southern end of the Second Courtyard at Luxor Temple, showing the north face of the socle that marks the temple platform and the apse for the cult of the Roman emperors. Photo by Lanny Bell.

Visitors approaching Luxor Temple can travel a short way along an ancient road that originally extended about 1.5 miles from the north (figs. 56, no. 5; 61). Paved with stone and flanked by human-headed sphinxes, this ceremonial avenue linked Karnak and Luxor temples and now leads to the huge double towers of the pylon of Ramesses II.[66] The towers once supported four enormous cedar-of-Lebanon flag masts from which pennants streamed. In front of the pylon stood a pair of towering obelisks and six colossal statues of the deified king (figs. 56, nos. 6, 7; 62).[67]

Passing through the pylon of Ramesses II, visitors gain access to the king's large open peristyle court, framed by a double rank of columns (fig. 63).[68] To the right, in the court's northwest quadrant, is a porticoed triple barque shrine built against the back of the pylon's west wing (fig. 57).[69] In the middle of the court, along the sides, both the eastern and western walls have a doorway (fig. 56, nos. 9, 2).[70] In the court's southern half, eleven colossal statues of the king stand between the columns in the first rank (the five on the east nearly balancing the six on the west), and two more colossal statues flank the entranceway to the Eighteenth Dynasty colonnade that lies beyond (fig. 64).[71]

Before Ramesses II added his obelisks, statues, pylon, and peristyle court to the front of Luxor Temple, this imposing colonnade was the first stone

FIG. 60. Colonnade of the Luxor Temple, built for the most part under Tutankhamun. Photo by Lanny Bell.

FIG. 61. Southern end of the Avenue of Sphinxes between Karnak and Luxor Temples, as seen from atop the Luxor Pylon. The Mosque of Maqeshqesh stands center rear. Photo by Lanny Bell.

FIG. 62. Representation, dating to the First Jubilee of Ramesses II, of the Pylon of Luxor Temple. First Courtyard at Luxor Temple. Restored drawing by Carol Meyer, after a photo by E. Otto.

structure entered.[72] Fully roofed, with fourteen gigantic columns supporting the stone slabs, the colonnade was almost completely darkened (fig. 60). The only illumination came from shafts of light admitted by high clerestory windows. Defacements made on the facade of the colonnade by agents of Akhenaten prove that Amenhotep III had laid its foundations and built its walls high enough to outline some of its decoration before his death.[73] However, the colonnade was primarily decorated by Tutankhamun and Ay, whose cartouches were subsequently erased by Haremhab and recarved with his own name. The side walls depict in great detail many episodes of the *Opet*-festival procession that linked Karnak and Luxor temples in the time of Tutankhamun.[74] The colonnade's southernmost reliefs were executed early in Dynasty 19 by Sety I, the father of Ramesses II.

Exiting the colonnade through the gateway at its southern end, visitors

FIG. 63. Southeast corner of the First Courtyard at Luxor Temple, showing the location of the People's Gate (far left). In modern times, a barque stand has been set up near the middle of the court. Photo by Lanny Bell.

enter the large peristyle sun court of Amenhotep III (fig. 59). Subsidiary doorways located near three of its corners offer alternative access. The sun court was not part of the core temple originally planned and executed by Amenhotep III, which stood on the stone platform or base immediately to the south.[75] Rather, the sun court was the core temple's first northward extension.

As visitors move southward onto the stone platform, the open sun court gives way to a cluster of relatively small, tightly packed rooms. Here, beyond the view of other people, the king and selected priests carried out the temple's most mysterious rites. Because the core temple underwent extensive alteration and renovation during the eighteen hundred years of its continuous cultic usage, the original form and function of some chambers can be deduced only architectonically.

First, visitors pass through a portico, the so-called hypostyle (fig. 56, no. 24). In its eastern and western walls are subsidiary doorways. The eastern doorway probably led to a small mud-brick palace where, during the *Opet*-festival, the king garbed, rested, and ate (no. 12). The western doorway probably led to the priests' living quarters (no. 23). Opening off the back, or southern end, of the portico were individual barque shrines for the The-

Fig. 64. Colossus of Ramesses II beside the entrance to the Colonnade in the First Courtyard at Luxor Temple. Photo by Lanny Bell.

ban triad (opening off the west side, Amun-Re; off the east side, Mut and Khonsu).[76]

Next, walking straight along the axial way, visitors enter a once columned hall, the Chamber of the Divine King (fig. 56, no. 14). Off this room open two small peripheral chapels, now in ruinous condition. At the beginning of the fourth century C.E., the Romans removed the hall's columns, raised its floor level (using drums from the columns of the Kushite kiosk that once stood before the Ramesside pylon), and converted it into a place for worshiping the divine emperor (fig. 59).[77]

Stooping through a small doorway at the rear of the hall, visitors come to the Offering Vestibule (fig. 56, no. 25).[78] Near its southwest corner another doorway opens into a jogged passageway leading outside the temple, used for the reversion of offerings (fig. 56, no. 13).

From the vestibule, visitors pass into the central barque sanctuary, where the portable image of Amun-Re of Karnak resided when he visited Luxor Temple for the *Opet*-festival (fig. 56, no. 15). The sanctuary's inner shrine was reconstructed in the name of the Macedonian conqueror Alexander the Great (fourth century B.C.E.) and bears his decoration.[79] But this late version rests on the foundations of the barque shrine built by Amenhotep III, some of whose original decorations are preserved on the sanctuary walls that surround the inner shrine.[80] A doorway in the northeast corner of the sanctuary leads to a suite of two rooms (nos. 16, 17) on whose walls are portrayed episodes from the divine birth cycle of Amenhotep III (figs. 47, 49); his apotheosis as the sun god, his coronation, and one of his jubilees. Flanking the barque sanctuary and set into the eastern and western walls of the core temple was a series of tiny chapels—now almost completely ruined (fig. 56, no. 22). At least some of these apparently received statues of gods associated with Amun-Re, members of the Theban Ennead.[81]

During pharaonic times, the axial way of Luxor Temple ended at the solid back wall of the barque sanctuary. Today visitors can pass through an open doorway in that wall to enter what was originally an essentially separate temple immediately to the south (fig. 56, no. 18).[82] This was the Southern *Opet*, the sanctuary of the distinctive form of the Amun of Luxor Temple: Amenemopet. There the god's cult image resided on a large stand built directly over the mythic mound of creation.[83] In antiquity, the only access to the sanctuary was off-axis, through a doorway at the southern end of the two-room suite containing the birth and coronation scenes.[84] In a sense, Luxor Temple originally had two axes: a north-south axis leading to the barque sanctuary and an east-west (solar) axis through the *Opet*-temple.[85] The barque sanctuary of Amun-Re of Karnak and the hidden sanctuary of Amenemopet of Luxor were separated physically but were related both conceptually and ritually.[86]

Luxor Temple and the *Opet*-Festival

From at least the New Kingdom onward, Luxor Temple was the mytho-logic power base of the living divine king and the foremost national shrine for his cultus. Completed under Ramesses II, it served the needs of all later rulers without substantive modification. One temple fit all, for the king's individual identity was to a very great extent subsumed under the royal *ka*—the unique divine spirit handed down from ruler to ruler from before the dawn of history and shared by all Egyptian kings. The royal *ka* was given extraordinary prominence at Luxor Temple.[87] The profusion there of references and representations has no parallel elsewhere.[88] During the temple's annual *Opet*-festival, the reigning monarch was identified with the royal *ka*, divine kingship was reborn, and the individual king's right to rule was reconfirmed.[89] At the climax, Amun-Re's powers were transferred to the king, and he then came into appearance before the representatives of the populace who waited anxiously in the public areas of the temple for their first glimpse of the transfigured monarch.[90]

The cosmic significance of the *Opet*-festival was tremendous. Beyond its role in the cultus of the king, it secured the regeneration of the Creator, Amun of Luxor, the rebirth of Amun-Re of Karnak, and the re-creation of the cosmos.[91] Gods became weary by the end of each year, when the agricultural cycle had run its course. They and their creation needed a recharge, a fresh input of energy. The dying gods needed to step outside the created world to tap the pure, uncontrolled power of the boundless chaos surrounding the cosmos, the seething miasma whence the cosmos had originated. Opening the door to the uncreated was no simple operation and was fraught with danger. Improperly done, it could unleash the full destructive potential of disorder. But properly done, through the prescribed rituals of the *Opet*-festival presided over by the divine king, the opening could produce rebirth and re-creation.

From at least as early as the Old Kingdom, the ancient Egyptians employed three separate calendars—lunar, solar/sidereal, and civil.[92] In prehistoric times, the lunar calendar had twelve months and 354 days, unsynchronized with the cycle of solar seasons, which repeats approximately every $365\frac{1}{4}$ days.[93] In historic times, the lunar calendar was modified to allow the first new moon of the lunar year to occur near the heliacal rising of Sirius (the dog star, called Sothis by the Egyptians) and roughly within the season of the Nile's annual flooding. This was accomplished by adding a thirteenth (intercalary) lunar month once every three years or so.[94] The "solilunar" calendar of twelve- and thirteen-month years stayed roughly synchronous with the solar/sidereal year and the natural rhythms of the inundation, the seasons, and the agricultural cycle, and it was this calendar that the ancient Egyptians used to determine the dates for religious festivals.[95]

The *Opet*-festival was the longest celebration in the Theban festival calendar and was apparently considered the most important. In accordance with the solilunar calendar, it began on the fifteenth or nineteenth day of the second month of the first season, called Inundation (*i3ḥit*). Its celebration grew from eleven days in length to twenty-four or even twenty-seven days as the festival was developed and elaborated through the years.[96] Despite minor fluctuations, the date of the *Opet*-festival always fell somewhere near the beginning of the Nile's three-month flood season.

Key elements in the public celebration of the *Opet*-festival were the procession of the king from Karnak to Luxor, his fateful, face-to-face meeting there with his divine father, Amun-Re, and his procession back to Karnak. The extant record of the procession is rather sketchy, but a fair amount of early pictorial and textual material survives from the reigns of Hatshepsut, Amenhotep III, and Tutankhamun.[97] From this and the available architectural evidence (particularly from the reign of Ramesses II), we can deduce the course of the procession and some of its events.[98]

The procession linked the cult complexes of Karnak and Luxor (fig. 65). The Temple of Amun-Re at Karnak had two main axes: the primary one oriented east-west, parallel to the daily course of the sun, and the secondary one oriented generally north-south, parallel to the Nile.[99] The solar axis symbolized Amun-Re. The river axis led to Luxor Temple and must have been constructed with the *Opet*-festival in mind, for from the beginning of Luxor's architectural history (so far as we know it), its primary axis was reciprocally oriented.[100]

The area at Karnak whose function corresponded most closely to Luxor Temple's was the Festival Hall (*Akhmenu*) of Thutmose III (fig. 65, no. 2).[101] Located behind the main sanctuary of Amun-Re, it was a separate cult complex where the theme of regeneration was expressed especially strongly and the barque of the divine living king probably resided. The Festival Hall was a Great Mansion of Millions of Years, a focus for the union of king and god. Its architecture and decoration symbolized the whole domain of Amun-Re. With the extension of the Egyptian empire into Western Asia during the New Kingdom, Amun-Re came to be seen as a universal god, the ruler of all. In the *Akhmenu*, the king is portrayed as Amun-Re's earthly manifestation, and a fragmentary series of scenes depicts festival processions that seem to pertain, in part, to the *Opet*-festival.[102]

Major episodes of the *Opet*-festival procession are represented schematically in the reliefs of the colonnade at Luxor Temple.[103] But data gleaned from elsewhere, including the architectural record, suggest that the actual course of events was a bit different. In the colonnade's first scenes, the king,

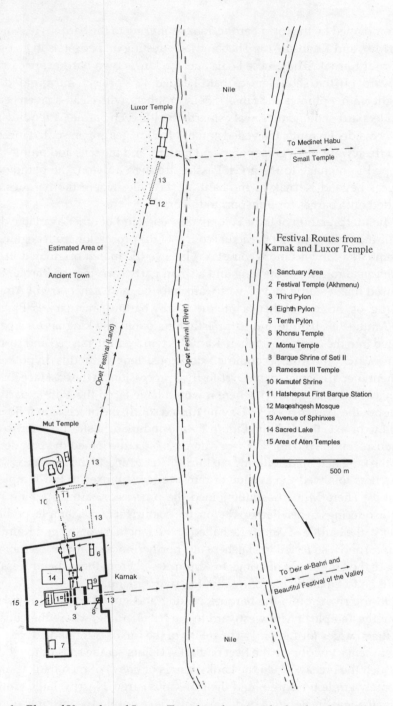

Nile

Luxor Temple

To Medinet Habu

Small Temple

13

12

Estimated Area of

Ancient Town

Festival Routes from Karnak and Luxor Temple

1 Sanctuary Area
2 Festival Temple (Akhmenu)
3 Third Pylon
4 Eighth Pylon
5 Tenth Pylon
6 Khonsu Temple
7 Montu Temple
8 Barque Shrine of Seti II
9 Ramesses III Temple
10 Kamutef Shrine
11 Hatshepsut First Barque Station
12 Maqeshqesh Mosque
13 Avenue of Sphinxes
14 Sacred Lake
15 Area of Aten Temples

Opet Festival (Land)

Opet Festival (River)

500 m

Mut Temple

13

4

11

10

13

5

6

14

4

9

Karnak

To Deir al-Bahri and

Beautiful Festival of the Valley

15

2

13

3

8

7

Nile

FIG. 65. Plan of Karnak and Luxor Temples, showing the land and river routes of the *Opet*-festival procession and indicating festival interconnections with other temples in the area. Drawing by Carol Meyer.

THE NEW KINGDOM «DIVINE» TEMPLE   159

accompanied by the royal barque, makes offering to the barques of Amun-Re, Mut, and Khonsu—the Theban triad—resting on pedestals in an open court at Karnak. Then these boats and the king's own barque are carried forward on the shoulders of bald-headed W^cb-priests, surrounded by bright feather plumes and fans.[104] Four prophets, with clean-shaven heads and leopard-skin mantles, walk smartly beside each barque, attending the deity inside. En route, the veiled and hidden images are presented incense and fresh water with great pomp and fanfare, and the fans and plumes are dipped in homage to the gods. Passing through a pylon, the parade advances beyond Karnak to the bank of the Nile, where the barques are loaded onto barges for transport to Luxor.

My interpretation of these colonnade scenes and of other available data leads me to suggest that the actual course of the procession from beginning to embarkation was more complex. I believe the march originated in the *Akhmenu*. From there the king and a small party carrying the barque that housed his *ka*-statue moved westward into the main sanctuary of Amun-Re (fig. 65, no. 1) and thence into the nearby barque sanctuary.[105] Picking up Amun-Re's barque and its priestly attendants, the king and his party exited into the open court where Karnak's two axes intersected and turned southward onto the secondary axis. Consistent with this hypothesis, Amenhotep III depicted the *Opet*-festival procession on the east face (back) of his Third Pylon (no. 3), where it would have faced the exiting party at the spot the axes crossed.[106] Having turned south, the procession followed the Luxor axis through the Eighth Pylon, and made a short detour to the Khonsu Temple (no. 6).[107] There Khonsu's *ka*-statue joined the parade, after the king had made offerings to him.[108] Returning to the Luxor axis, the marchers followed the avenue of ram-headed sphinxes to the Temple of Mut.[109] There Mut's *ka*-statue joined the procession, after the king had made offerings to her. Perhaps before the sojourn at Mut's temple, perhaps after it, the barque of Amun-Re halted at the sanctuary of the god Kamutef (no. 10) and also rested in Hatshepsut's northernmost way station (no. 11), where the king made offerings to Amun-Re.[110] From there the procession went on to Luxor by one of two routes, river or land.[111]

On the river route, the barques of king and god(s) traveled overland from the Temple of Mut westward to the Nile landing, where they boarded their barges for Luxor.[112] The reliefs of the Luxor colonnade depict the river scenes vividly. As the fleet embarks, sailors set the sails of tow boats to catch the breeze.[113] On the banks, gangs or crews of men haul at ropes to safely guide the barges and their precious cargo. Nearby, large crowds mass to view the flotilla. Loud roars must have erupted as the king, queen, and gods sailed past. On land, paralleling and keeping pace with the flotilla, Egyptian and foreign detachments of the army—some with hair feathers, all in full battle array (carrying battle axes, bows, spears, clubs, and shields)—march behind standards adorned with colorful plumes and streamers. Horses and chariots appear, similarly decorated. People chant and clap; musicians pluck lutes and shake sistrums and beat drums. Acrobatic dancers perform in time with the intoxicating rhythms.[114] What a profusion of people and animals, sounds and movements, costumes and ornaments! What a babble of tongues! And over the din, trumpeters signal the various movements of the drama. Finally, the water procession arrives at Luxor's landing, where it is met by the lines of princes, princesses, and high officials who are now at the head of the overland group, carrying bouquets and other offerings and leading fattened, festooned cattle that are destined for sacrifice. The barques are carried off the barges and through a gateway into the temple. There they are set down, with offerings heaped before them.

In reality, however, the procession from the Temple of Mut to Luxor sometimes followed the land route. On these occasions, the barques of king and god(s) were carried right through to Luxor Temple on the sphinx-lined road (figs. 56, no. 5; 65, no. 13; 61).[115] They rested en route at Hatshepsut's way stations; these, numbered I through VI from north to south, are depicted schematically on red quartzite blocks from her dismantled Karnak barque sanctuary (the Chapelle Rouge) (fig. 66).[116] Hatshepsut was a prolific builder. Besides the *Opet* way stations, she added significantly to Karnak, enhanced the Temple of Mut with the grandeur of stone construction, erected the core of the stone Temple of Amun at Medinet Habu, and constructed her great royal cult complex at Deir el-Bahri.[117] At each of these conceptually interrelated sites, she gave prominence to the cultus of the divine ruler, which may have been the driving force behind her building activity. Ostensibly her promotion to the throne had been sanctioned by an oracular pronouncement of Amun-Re himself. But she had seized effective control from the hands of the young Thutmose III, and she continued to share power with him, as coregent, until she disappeared and presumably died. Hatshepsut may have become obsessed with demonstrating her legitimacy and may therefore have come to advance the development of Theban divine-ruler theology dramatically. Hatshepsut was demonstrably the first king to depict himself (herself) being begotten by Amun-Re as ruler-designate, the first to give prominence in the Theban triad to the divine feminine principle (in the form of Mut), and the first to portray the *Opet*-festival. It is indeed not absolutely certain that the *Opet*-festival was celebrated before her reign, although it is logical to assume that it was. In any case, Hatshepsut seems to have actively developed, or at least elaborated, the *Opet*-festival to her own benefit, perhaps grafting it onto a preexisting cultus at Luxor.

Fig. 66. Sixth Way Station of Hatshepsut, as represented on a block from her Barque Shrine at Karnak. Photo by Lanny Bell.

The evidence from Hatshepsut's reign shows that in celebrating the *Opet*-festival she used the land route from Karnak to Luxor but took the river route back from Luxor to Karnak.[118] Amun-Re, having been rejuvenated at Luxor, returned to Karnak in triumph, his glistening barge riding the crest of the fresh, fertilizing flood waters of the Nile, which he, as Creator, brought to the whole of Egypt.[119] By the time of Tutankhamun, the river route apparently was used for both legs of the journey. Thutmose III and Amenhotep III had already taken the river route to Luxor, perhaps exclusively, as attested by evidence from Karnak.[120] The factors that determined whether a pharaoh followed the land route or water route to Luxor are difficult, if not impossible, to fathom. Perhaps particular kings favored one form of pageantry over the other. Perhaps Amenhotep III wanted to display to maximum effect the new barge that he had commissioned for Amun-Re, an argument that could apply to Tutankhamun as well.[121] Perhaps the height of the Nile influenced the choice, the land route being used when the flood was late or too low to permit convenient navigation. We simply cannot say.

From Ramesses II onward, when the splendid procession reached Luxor Temple the barques entered the peristyle courtyard (fig. 56, no. 3) by one of two ceremonial entrances.[122] When the barques moved overland, the great pylon was employed (no. 8). When they moved by river, they used

FIG. 67. Procession of offerings and sacrifices presented during the *Opet*-festival. A scene in the First Courtyard at Luxor Temple. Photo by Lanny Bell.

the much smaller gateway (no. 2) opposite the quay (no. 1) in the court's western wall. The decoration of the peristyle court was appropriate to entry through either gateway. However, Ramesses II must have used the river entry much more frequently than the land entry, for his triple barque shrine (no. 4) is oriented to the south (at a right angle to the river route) rather than to the east (at a right angle to the land route).[123]

Upon entering the peristyle court, the procession turned toward the triple shrine for the offerings, sacrifices, and other rituals that hailed the gods' arrival (fig. 67). Then, after an appropriate rest, the procession resumed its journey toward the inner barque sanctuary (fig. 56, no. 15), disappearing into the darkened colonnade (no. 10). This routine is confirmed by the wall reliefs in the western half of the court. Conventionally in Egyptian art, a deity is represented as looking out from the shrine in which he resides for the ritual being depicted, and the king is shown facing the deity and, therefore, that shrine.[124] The large reliefs in the upper register of panels north of the western gateway pose the god in association with the triple barque shrine, while those south of the gateway reverse the orientation and associate the god with the inner barque sanctuary at the south end of the temple.[125]

Were representatives of the populace already present in the peristyle court when the divine barques entered in procession? I believe so. Ramesses II constructed his courtyard in a transitional space that previously had stood outside the temple precinct and had had a tradition of public access—the precinct of *Opet* Way Station VI, which Hatshepsut had established outside Luxor Temple. Ramesses II probably dismantled the way station, which had a single chapel for Amun-Re, in order to build a triple shrine that could accommodate all the Theban triad (figs. 58, 57).[126] But in so doing, he had to provide for admitting the populace to the court so they could continue to experience the oracles and other manifestations of royal and divine power that had attended the station. The decorative motifs visible on the fragments of Hatshepsut's way station that were reused in the triple shrine prove that people had been able to approach the station.[127] Both *rekhyet-* and *paʿet-*people are depicted adoring Amun-Re.[128] For our purposes, the word *rekhyet* may be translated "common people." The *paʿet* were evidently a more elite mythological component of the population, originally perhaps members of the royal clan.[129] Hatshepsut's decorations include at least three series of kneeling humans (the *paʿet-*folk, fig. 58) and standing birds (the *rekhyet-*folk), both depicted over baskets, worshiping Amun-Re.[130] The figures, with texts before and after them, constitute part of the rebus which reads, "Adoring Amun-Re [with various epithets] by all the *rekhyet* (or *paʿet*), that they might live."[131]

We know that Ramesses II gave representatives of the people access to the peristyle court during the *Opet-*festival because we find small *rekhyet-*figures carved on the large sandstone columns erected around his court (fig. 68). Here the figures are drawn as small lapwing birds with human arms and hands upraised in adoration. They sit on small hemispherical baskets. This rendering of the *rekhyet*—partly theriomorphic, partly anthropomorphic—bestows mythological significance on the king's subjects. The figures occur in a rebus-writing of the phrase "all the *rekhyet* adore." A cartouche of Ramesses II placed before each bird yields the reading "(It is) Ramesses II whom all the *rekhyet* adore."[132] This highly decorative device, found often on temple columns, pillars, and walls, might be considered one of the banalities of ancient Egyptian art, hardly more than "filler." But their distribution is significant here and provides a key for visualizing the court in use, alive with the excited activity of the *Opet-*festival. The *rekhyet* are found in a frieze at about face-level, but *only* on the columns of the eastern half of the court, where they are oriented toward the north-south axis.[133] This asymmetry was deliberate and not accidental, as is proven by the reliefs and inscriptions associated with the eastern doorway of the court (fig. 56, no. 9). There, on the exterior of the court's eastern wall, both *rekhyet-*people (fig. 69) and *paʿet-*people (fig. 70) kneel with arms upraised in adoration. Their figures are completely anthropomorphic, and they are not perched on baskets. The full name of this doorway was "The Great Gateway of the King of Upper and Lower Egypt Ramesses II, Whom

FIG. 68. Adoring *rekhyet*-figure with the cartouche of Ramesses II. Column on the southeast side of the First Courtyard at Luxor Temple. Photo by Lanny Bell.

Fig. 69. Adoring *rekhyet*-figures depicted on the south exterior side of the People's Gate at Luxor Temple. Photo by Lanny Bell.

Fig. 70. Adoring *paʿet*-people depicted on the north exterior side of the People's Gate at Luxor Temple. The view across the First Courtyard—with *rekhyet*-figures on the nearest column—toward the site of the ancient riverine processional gate shows modern visitors. Photo by Lanny Bell.

FIG. 71. Inscription naming the gateway, on the north interior side of the People's Gate in the First Courtyard at Luxor Temple. The name of Amun-Re can be seen to have been replaced by that of Ramesses II. Photo by Lanny Bell.

All the *Rekhyet* Adore That They Might Live" (fig. 71). Opening from the presumed site of the New Kingdom town of Luxor, this doorway was effectively the "people's gate," and through it select townsfolk and officials were admitted to stand in the eastern half of the courtyard in order to observe the stately *Opet*-festival procession.[134] Police or troops surely cordoned off the people's area to restrain the enthusiastic crowd and keep the western half clear so the procession could move through it freely and in a dignified, orderly fashion.

Several further pieces of evidence attest the people's presence in the peristyle court on more occasions, at least for other festivals. First, the colossi of the deified Ramesses II flanking the entrance to the Eighteenth Dynasty colonnade south of his court were, like those standing outside his pylon, *ka*-statues—cultic images of the king as an incarnation of the royal *ka* (fig. 72). The *ka*-statues outside the pylon were accessible to ordinary people, and they mediated suppliants' pleas to the great, hidden god whose sanctuary lay beyond. The colossi of the king outside the colonnade (in the peristyle court) probably functioned similarly.[135]

Second, a relief depiction of Khonsu on the exterior, eastern wall of the moon god's chapel (the easternmost element of Ramesses II's triple barque shrine) was enclosed and configured as a shrine for the people.[136]

FIG. 72. Base inscription naming the statue of the deified Ramesses II (fig. 64) as the royal *ka* "Re of the Rulers." To the right and left are officiating *Iunmutef*-priests. Photo by Lanny Bell.

Third, common persons were admitted to the Amun-Re chapel (the central element of the triple shrine), although presumably not when it was in use for festival processions. In the chapel's rear wall there was a double "false door," whose special configuration emphasized the identity between god and king (fig. 73).[137] Two pairs of figures—powerful representations of the divine—framed the ritual portal and were the focus of people's adoration and veneration:

First, carved in relief to the immediate right and left of the double doorway was a symmetrical pair of colossal ram-headed staffs.[138] This distinctive artistic treatment was probably patterned on the similar design, dating to Amenhotep III, in Amun-Re's inner barque sanctuary (fig. 56, no. 15).[139] The repetition alerts us to the two spots' essential unity of function; both were facilities for the exchange of messages between worlds. But whereas no one except the king and his most important priests could approach god in his inner barque sanctuary, common people, too, could forward prayers to god through the outer barque shrine, a kind of divinely appointed "telephone booth."[140]

Second, recessed into the side walls to the right and left of the double door was a symmetrical pair of covered niches containing life-sized standing images of the divine Ramesses II. The two *ka*-statues originally housed

FIG. 73. Double false door flanked by *mdw-špsy* standards of Amun-Re, at the back of his chapel in the Triple Barque Shrine at Luxor Temple. The Hatshepsut block (fig. 58) lies on the ground at the lower left. Photo by Lanny Bell.

there have long since disappeared, but depictions in relief record their forms. The statues actually faced outward from the side walls, toward each other, parallel to the plane of the double door. But in conformity with the conventions of Egyptian art, reliefs show them with their backs to the double door, a pose that connected them closely to the ritual portal and emphasized their cultic status.[141] Each statue was attended by the god Thoth (the Egyptian spiritual guide or divine mediator) and a *Iunmutef*-priest.[142] The latter, garbed in the skin of a leopard or panther, was associated with affairs of the *ka,* especially transitions in status (cf. fig. 72).[143] Reliefs on the back wall of each niche portray clearly its *ka*-statue's special attributes, which were intended to validate the king's union with Amun-Re. The western statue displayed the ram's horn of Amun-Re sprouting from the king's temple and curving across his cheek. The ram was a favorite representation of the power of Amun-Re, and the Theban iconography of divine kingship fairly commonly used the ram's horns to symbolize a ruler's sonship to Amun-Re and his union, through the royal *ka,* with the Creator (fig. 48).[144] The eastern statue featured in the king's right hand, resting on his shoulder, the ram-headed *mdw-špsy* standard, a symbol for the *ka* of Amun-Re.[145] To all who beheld either *ka*-statue, it said: "The king possesses god's *ka.*" Thus each symbolized the unity of king and god.

Both pairs of figures—the symmetrical colossal ram-headed staffs and the royal *ka*-statues in the symmetrical covered niches—were objects for popular adoration and veneration, and they evidence common people's access to the peristyle court.

But let us rejoin the *Opet*-festival procession itself. Observed excitedly by the exuberant representatives of the people, the king had completed the welcoming offerings for the gods at the triple barque shrine and, together with the other marchers, had left the court of Ramesses II, disappearing from sight into the darkened colonnade (figs. 56, no. 10; 60). In due time, the procession emerged from the colonnade into the bright sunlight of the court of Amenhotep III (figs. 56, no. 11; 59). There, I believe, it once again received the acclamation of common people specially chosen and assembled to witness further episodes in their divine king's miraculous transformation (fig. 74). Before a peristyle court or colonnade had ever existed, before Amenhotep III had enclosed the open area outside the core temple with this courtyard, select members of the populace had congregated here to watch the king and the priests carrying the sacred barques as they mounted the temple platform and disappeared inside. Duplicate inscriptions on the pilasters at the east and west corners of the core temple's portico proclaim, "All low-lying lands and all highlands are at the feet of this vigorous god [*ntr nfr,* the king] whom all the gods love and all the *rekhyet* adore, that they might live" (fig. 75).[146] The *rekhyet* are represented here, as

FIG. 74. Second Courtyard at Luxor Temple, filled with participants and onlookers at the modern Festival of the Oars. Photo by Lanny Bell.

FIG. 75. *Rekhyet*-inscription on the north face of the eastern pilaster of the Second Courtyard at Luxor Temple, on the facade of the original stone temple of Amenhotep III. Photo by Lanny Bell.

on the sandstone columns of the court of Ramesses II, as lapwing birds with human arms and hands upraised in adoration. After Amenhotep III built his courtyard and laid the foundations for the colonnade, the main temple area open to the public must have shifted northward from the portico to the space between the colonnade and Hatshepsut's sixth barque station, the area that Ramesses II later enclosed. But even after the construction of the sun court of Amenhotep III, tradition must have demanded the fulfillment of the portico's inscription; during the *Opet*-festival procession, common people needed to be present in front of the core temple to adore the king.[147] Representatives of the populace could gain access to the court without passing through the colonnade by using the small doorway near the court's northeast corner. Perhaps at the conclusion of the rites in the colonnade, some or all of the people exited through the east gate of the Ramesside court, hurried past the colonnade, and funneled through the northeast door of the sun court. There they readied themselves to reverence the king anew when he emerged from the colonnade. Or perhaps a totally different group of people were assigned the sun-court role of adoration.

After the king, gods, and priests passed through the sun court, they entered the secluded core temple and disappeared from the view of the throng, who remained in place to await their eventual return. Doors enclosed the procession, and further rites took place in secret. But the architecture, decorations, and inscriptions in the various rooms of the temple platform provide a guide to the procession's course and actions.[148]

The disposition of the barques was changed somewhat between the reigns of Amenhotep III and Ramesses II, but from Ramesses II onward it happened this way.[149] The barques of Mut and Khonsu were installed in their respective chapels (fig. 56, nos. 29, 30) before the Chamber of the Divine King (no. 14) and immediately south of the hypostyle portico (no. 24).[150] The barques of Amun-Re and the divine king proceeded farther.[151] Amun-Re's would complete the course to the barque sanctuary at the terminus of the processional way (cf. fig. 76). The king's came to rest in the chapel opening off the southeast corner of the Chamber of the Divine King. Later, apparently, his portable *ka*-statue was removed from the barque and accompanied the king on his journey with Amun-Re to the barque sanctuary. The Chamber of the Divine King, the room in which the divinity of the king was most prominently portrayed, was a real power point in Luxor Temple (fig. 56, no. 14).[152] There, after the king's purification by water and ritual introduction to Amun-Re, the coronation rites were repeated.[153] The god (or rather, the priest playing the role of god) placed the various forms of crown, one by one, on the king's head, verifying that they fit and that the pharaoh was ready to assume the many duties of kingship on earth. During each separate crowning, the king knelt before Amun-Re *with his back toward the god*, and the deity placed his hands on the king's head or crown from behind in the protective gesture characteristic of the royal *ka* (figs. 50, 54; cf. fig. 48).[154] Through this laying on of hands, the royal *ka* was transmitted metaphysically from Father to Son.[155] The rite rejuvenated the king, as is signified by a small suckling scene nearby (cf. fig. 54). Once more divine kingship was being reborn.[156]

Throughout the *Opet*-festival, the *ka*-attributes and -energy of the king had grown steadily, through a series of transformations, as he advanced toward the barque sanctuary of his divine Father, Amun-Re, the source of the royal *ka*.[157] Of these transformations, the rites in the Chamber of the Divine King had been, to this point, the most powerful. But the climactic episode of the king's *Opet*-transfiguration was yet to come. So on he went, together with the barque of Amun-Re, his own *ka*-statue, and high ranking priests, to the end point of the *Opet*-axis, the inner sanctuary of Amun-Re (fig. 56, no. 15).

There, as priests recited sacred texts, the king presented a series of highly significant offerings to Amun-Re, who remained hidden in his barque. An efficacious royal offering gave rise to a reciprocal divine blessing.[158] When the king performed a sacrifice properly and it had a re-creative effect on god, the deity responded in kind, re-creating the king. The more sig-

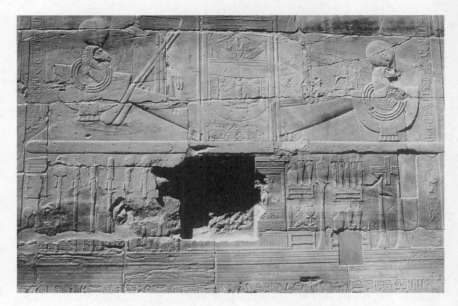

Fig. 76. Representation of the barque of Amun-Re resting on a barque stand. Various forms of *mdw-špsy* standards are portrayed beneath the carrying poles. Barque Chapel at the Qurna Temple of Sety I. Photo by Lanny Bell.

nificant the king's offering, the greater the risk of failure *but* the greater the potential for renewal. Wordplay signaled each offering's possible benefit to the king. Presenting god "pure water" (*wꜥb*)—that is, New Year's water, the first fresh, invigorating waters collected from the recent inundation—could make the king "pure" (*wꜥb*); offering god "fresh flowers" (*rnpyt*) could make the king "young" (*rnpi.ti*); and burning "incense" (*snṯr*) for god could "deify" (*snṯri*) the king. After the presentation of the offerings and the accomplishment of their aim, the king approached the naos of the barque, opened its doors, and came into the presence of his divine father, standing directly before him. Instantly, Amun-Re's glory reflected back onto the king, and the pharaoh became a renascent god, with a renewed persona and additional names. The king then knelt before Amun-Re, this time facing the god, and the deity crowned him—definitively (fig. 77).

Both dramatically and architectonically, the *Opet* celebration reached its consummation in the barque sanctuary when, after offerings, the kneeling king faced Amun-Re and received the crown. I am convinced, however, that in preparation for the offerings and climactic coronation the king had acted to reawaken and put to decisive use the creative powers of Amenemopet. Amenemopet was the autochthonous god of Luxor, the Amun of Luxor Temple, the local manifestation of the self-begotten primordial god

Fig. 77. Amenhotep III kneels facing Amun-Re in order to be crowned by the god (defaced under Akhenaten and subsequently restored). Barque Sanctuary at Luxor Temple. Photo by Lanny Bell.

Kamutef, the First Principle and Creator of the world, and a form of the royal *ka*—all in one.[159] I can easily imagine that after the king had accompanied the barque of Amun-Re to its sanctuary (fig. 56, no. 15) he immediately went through the Coronation Room (no. 17) and into the *Opet*-sanctuary, the divine residence of Amenemopet (no. 18). There the king would have set in motion the new creation cycle that the *Opet*-festival and the rebirth of divine kingship were to energize. He probably did this by performing an Opening of the Mouth ceremony on Amenemopet the Creator, touching an adze-like implement to the lips of his cultic statue, thereby reawakening and recharging him (cf. fig. 78).[160] The symbolic blade of this tool was a small bit of meteoric iron—a magical metal, associated with the heavens, that had provided the "spark" or "lightning strike" that brought the first generation of beings into existence. Following the opening of Amenemopet's mouth, the king would have returned to the barque sanctuary carrying the life force of the regenerated god to the still moribund Amun-Re of Karnak. There the life force would have been passed from Amenemopet to Amun-Re by a ritual merging of the gods.[161] Both gods having been rejuvenated, the institution of divine kingship and the creation of the world could once more occur.

When the king, priests, and gods had completed their secret rites within the dark, mysterious chambers of the core temple, they presented themselves again in the sun court. The assembled throng had been anxiously awaiting evidence of the rituals' efficacy, and they must have roared at the sight of the regenerated divine king, splendidly arrayed and glorious in triumph, and the barques of the revitalized triad, as they reemerged into the bright sunlight. For days to come, common people throughout the land would celebrate the rebirth of the world, abandoning themselves to unrestrained jubilation—and its excesses.

After the king, gods, and priests had taken a brief rest from their strenuous labors, they set forth on the trip back to Karnak. Although the return procession of the rejuvenated king and gods must have had many thrilling moments, further peaks of excitement must have been difficult to achieve and sustain in this period following the liturgical climax. The ritual point having been made so dramatically, I imagine the mood of the homeward-bound passengers was somewhat muted, and their rituals, somewhat abridged, however grand the flotilla's display and however fervid the people's response. Reentering Karnak through the monumental Third Pylon (fig. 65, no. 3), the divine beings disappeared quickly into the restricted parts of the temple. The barque of Amun-Re was probably the first to be reinstalled in its shrine, followed by those of the king, Mut, and Khonsu as the king reported to Amun-Re in Karnak's main sanctuary (no. 1), bringing the festival to an end.

Fig. 78. King Ay performing the Opening of the Mouth ritual for his deceased predecessor, Tutankhamun. The burial chamber of Tutankhamun's tomb in the Valley of the Kings. Photo by Lanny Bell.

Other Important Functions of Luxor Temple

The *Opet*-sanctuary was no doubt built over the mythological creation mound that Egyptians believed to have arisen there, and the decoration of its walls symbolized the east-west course of the sun. However, very little is known about the special cultus of the god of the sanctuary—Amenemopet, the Amun of Luxor Temple. It has been proposed that his original cultic form was the ram, a powerful fertility symbol, and I have also theorized a revitalizing role for him in the *Opet*-festival.[162] In any case, the worship of Amenemopet continued in the sanctuary as long as there was a Luxor Temple. After Roman modifications to the Chamber of the Divine King blocked the north-south axis, the southern end of the cult complex remained accessible. Small secondary doorways (fig. 56, no. 20) were cut through the core temple's east wall to permit entrance to the barque sanctuary, the *Opet*-sanctuary, and the rooms ancillary to them.[163]

Some first-millennium B.C.E. religious materials from the Theban region contain important clues to the cultus of Amenemopet during the New Kingdom.[164] In the speculative theology underlying the Theban cosmogony, the primal being contained within himself—complete and perfect—the seeds of the whole cosmos. But the act of creation was assisted by the Ogdoad, a group of eight shadowy demiurges engendered and born at Luxor and referred to in the texts as "the Progenitors and the Mothers." They were the elemental gods, symbolizing the potential of the energy latent within the semichaotic state of the mysterious, predawn world. Apparently the Ogdoad's vital forces were expended in creation, and their burial place was the mythological mound called *Djeme*. In the reign of Hatshepsut, the small temple of Medinet Habu was built over *Djeme*, on Thebes' west bank. During the Decade Festival, Amenemopet the Creator left his residence in Luxor Temple and crossed the Nile to visit Medinet Habu (at least symbolically, if not actually).[165] There he was regenerated by merging with his own primordial form—the chthonic Amun manifest in a wondrous serpent (Kematef).[166] Amenemopet subsequently reenacted funerary services for the Ogdoad, who were construed as his own ancestors. He revivified their *ka*s, thereby renewing the world that evolved from them. Interestingly, a prototype of the first-millennium Decade Festival is attested as early as Ramesses II. By that time, it seems, Luxor was already considered a primary creation site and the birthplace of Amun-Re of Karnak.

During another Theban festival known as the Appearance of Amun-Min-Kamutef, Amenemopet was mysteriously reunited with the national creator god Min, or the self-begotten Theban fertility god Kamutef. During the New Kingdom, this was Luxor Temple's second most important annual celebration, after the *Opet*-festival.[167] Its procession probably followed the avenue of sphinxes from the Kamutef sanctuary (fig. 65, no. 10), where it originated, to Luxor Temple, which it entered through the pylon of Ramesses II.[168] In this procession, the cultic figure of Min was carried on the shoulders of the *W῾b*-priests fully exposed to public view, not hidden in the naos of a barque. A small portable screen or blind was apparently erected around the god when privacy was required.

Conclusion

I have presented a new theory of the history and functions of Luxor Temple. The temple's importance has long been acknowledged, but its uniqueness has heretofore remained undefinable. Most scholars have understood the temple as an appendage of the Karnak complex but have left open the precise relationship between the two. Most have described Luxor architecturally, not functionally, portraying it as a sanctuary dedicated to the Theban triad but saying little about its special cultus. Studies of the temple's most renowned feast, the *Opet*-festival, have focused primarily on the procession; the purpose of the celebration has been unexplained.

Luxor Temple remains, more than a century after its architectural excavation, largely unpublished. This is the principal reason for the difficulty in interpreting it. Libraries do not have the documentation needed to understand it. Scholars must know the temple firsthand, from bottom to top.

Furthermore, because religion and politics overlapped in ancient Egypt, Luxor Temple was embedded in the whole fabric of New Kingdom society, and it united fundamental aspects of social and political life as well as religion. So scholars must start from a perspective broad enough and detailed enough to fit the temple into the totality of the culture.

I was fortunate to acquire firsthand knowledge of Luxor Temple during my five seasons of fieldwork in the Theban necropolis and my twelve years of residence in modern Luxor. I also gained insights by trying to explain the temple to the relentlessly inquisitive members of numerous academic study tours. These circumstances have prepared me to come to grips with the temple's secrets.

I have attempted to connect the most significant architectural and decorative features of Luxor Temple to relevant textual materials and to relate my interpretation of these features to ancient Egyptian temples' overall roles. In so doing, I have used the raw data, or "facts," of the culture plus conceptual models developed by anthropologists and historians of religion to uncover the meanings that sophisticated cultural constructs have for the people who believe in them.

To summarize my theory, Luxor Temple, the Southern Residence of Amun, was actually two temples in one, serving two different manifestations of the god.[169] The small *Opet* Temple proper was the dwelling place of the mysterious Amenemopet of Luxor, and the much larger *Opet*-festival Annex—all of Luxor Temple north of the Hidden Sanctuary—was, in essence, an elaborate barque shrine for accommodating Amun-Re of Karnak and his full entourage during his annual visit to Luxor. Amenemopet's closed sanctuary was presumably the site where priests performed for him a standard daily offering ritual. The First Courtyard of the larger temple was most likely open much of the year for ordinary people to pray in. The two temples at Luxor and the two forms of Amun were physically united once a year during the *Opet*-festival, when the annual ritual rebirth of the royal *ka*, the immortal creative spirit of divine kingship, miraculously restored the worlds of the gods and of humankind.

The pharaoh was a god-king. During the *Opet*-festival at Luxor he was worshiped as the living royal *ka*, the chief earthly manifestation of the Creator. As the son of god, he was himself, both in spirit and in flesh, god. His visible activities in the human world had invisible counterparts in the divine world, and his ritual actions had important consequences for these two parallel, interconnected realms. The rites confirming and reinforcing his special status assumed understandable prominence in the religious calendars of the great national temples.

I have led the reader step by step through the *Opet*-festival, pointing out where the pharaoh walked, what the priests did, where the people stood, and how the participants interacted; and a picture has begun to emerge of the liturgy—the recitations, offerings, and other cultic activities carried out at the ritual focal points. The display of royal splendor in the presence of ordinary people doubtless impressed on them the king's power and the elite's privileged position. But their participation in the liturgy probably also convinced them that they too played an important role in society. As with all people, the Egyptians seem to have hoped for salvation, longed for the eternal, and trusted that the divinely appointed institutions and rituals would gain for them their aspirations.

In considering the social relationships reflected in Luxor's religious ceremonies, I have raised the question of Egypt's kinship system. The ancestral *ka* was a component of personhood that enfolded multiple cultural roles: genetic—governing social structure and family organization, obligations, and inheritance; legal and political—determining legitimacy (including the king's); psychological—shaping personal identity and individuality; and, of course, religious and funerary.[170] Every birth—and every coronation—was the rebirth of a *ka* and therefore a renewal of life rather than its inception. The steady replacement of each human, divine, and cosmological generation by an essentially identical one assured the order and stability of the world.

The inequality in Egypt's hierarchical social structure was rooted in and perpetuated by hereditary classes who were assigned differing social and political behaviors. In the all-pervasive ancestor cultus, the rank of a person's family *ka* legitimized class distinctions. The royal *ka* was ranked highest of all, and the worship of the royal *ka*—associating the fictive royal clan directly with Amun-Re, the all-powerful Creator and King of the Gods—validated the king's superior position over the rest of humanity. Thus the rites performed at Luxor Temple supported the social structure of New Kingdom Egypt by assigning the various classes roles that anchored their place in the hierarchy and by linking order in the human realm to that in the divine realm.

Appendix I: Luxor Temple in the Reign of Akhenaten

The boy who became Amenhotep IV, and then Akhenaten, lived during the construction of the new Luxor Temple and the development of its theology.[171] As his father's designated successor, he doubtless learned the cultus of the royal *ka* and the liturgy of the *Opet*-festival. As king, he chose to pursue a special vision of divinity, divine kingship, and the relationship between the king and the solar Creator, his celestial Father. Whether he did so under the influence of Amenhotep III or on his own initiative is not clear. In any case, at Thebes Akhenaten began a major religious reform that, however short-lived, shook conservative Egypt to its political and intellectual foundations.

At Luxor Temple Akhenaten undertook no new building activity, but on the east side of Karnak he quickly erected an enormous complex (fig. 65, no. 15). Located behind Karnak, outside the Amun precinct proper, this complex was oriented toward the eastern horizon rather than toward the western horizon as was the main axis of Karnak. In choosing this spot, the king symbolically turned his back on Amun. Since the time of Thutmose III, East Karnak had been the site of the contra-temple where the god of the rising sun, Re-Horakhty, was adored as the morning form of Amun-Re.[172] Here was also a chapel for popular veneration of the king deified as Amun-Re-Who-Hears-Prayers. In attaching his new construction to this contra-temple, with its associated chapel devoted to the king, Akhenaten combined popular worship of the king as the Aten with worship of the god previously manifest in Re-Harakhti, now understood to be the Aten.

The king's early Aten temples at Karnak celebrated a fundamental identity between king and god. The rich repertoire of forms that other temples had used to depict manifestations of the divine was drastically reduced. No concept of god other than the Aten was permitted; and the Aten's singular artistic representation was the solar disk.[173] The rays of this celestial disk extended to earth, often ending in human hands presenting the $^c n \underline{h}$ (the hieroglyph for life) to the king's nostril. Gone from the Aten temples was the closed central sanctuary containing the god's naos and statue; gone, the divine barque and cultic paraphernalia. In the strictest form of the new religion, the sole earthly image of the Aten was the king, and depictions of the daily attendance on the king can be compared to the daily service for the gods. The king in his palace took the place of the divine statues in their sanctuaries. Furthermore, the king was adored in domestic shrines, where stelae and statuettes dedicated to him served as surrogates for the Aten. The living king was the conduit by which ordinary worshipers could approach the godhead.[174] God and king became virtually indistinguishable; they were envisioned as a dyad, god-and-king. It could have seemed to some people that the Aten had no existence independent of the king, for the god was explicitly depicted as a king. The sun disk bore the royal uraeus, and the divine names, expanded by epithets, were encircled by the royal cartouches.

What Akhenaten sought to achieve when he began his religious revolution in Thebes is disputed, but he certainly did not seek to diminish people's belief in his divinity. And crucial to that belief was the myth of the Creator's begetting of the king and bestowing of the royal *ka*. Ritual performances associated with the drama of divine kingship—specifically, those of the *Opet*-festival at Luxor Temple—would certainly have served his purposes and were probably continued in some form. But Akhenaten found it necessary to purify the temple of images and references inconsistent with, or offensive to, worship of the Aten (cf. figs. 48, 53, 58, 77, 50), and very likely the sanctuary of Amenemopet was either ignored or blocked off. Among the decorative elements associated with Akhenaten's temples in East Karnak are colossal statues of the deified king as a form of the Aten and numerous representations of *Sed*-festival ceremonies celebrated jointly by the king and god. I have mentioned a connection between the *Sed*-festival and the *Opet*-festival.[175] If in the early years of the new regime some form of the *Opet*-festival was celebrated and some sort of link was maintained between Karnak and Luxor, the precinct of the Aten in East Karnak probably served as the new northern terminus of the festival's procession.[176] At the Aten temples, god in all his glory was visible to the public every day in the open courtyards, where all rites were performed. As Akhenaten's revolution proceeded and the mysteries of traditional Theban theology became more and more irrelevant—along with the architectural style that situated the residence of the god deep inside the temple, in a darkened sanctuary inaccessible to nearly everyone—most of the offerings and other important rituals at Luxor Temple, including those of any *Opet*-festival, would increasingly have been conducted in the open courtyards, to emphasize the new cultus' public aspects.

Then Akhenaten removed himself, his god, his court, and his patronage from Thebes to a new city of god, Akhetaten, "The Horizon of the Aten" (modern Amarna); and the old religion, with all its temples and rites, was declared officially dead. Akhetaten was a remote, virgin site in Middle Egypt, far from any major population center and 270 miles from Thebes— a royal retreat indeed. The city was built around a new temple complex, the only shrines in the whole of Egypt that continued to function, the new center of the world. For the universal god to have had on earth only one, isolated residence seems paradoxical. In Akhetaten, temple ritual was minimized. Like the omnipresent sun itself, and in its company, the king daily moved across his domain, receiving the adulation of the pilgrims and other privileged few who managed to be, or had to be, in the city.

We do not know what arrangements, if any, the king made for the succession of kingship and regeneration of the royal *ka*. In the New Age, the god who was manifest in the whole world seems nevertheless to have become more unapproachable than ever. Had it not been for Egypt's rejection of Akhenaten and all he stood for, the story of Luxor Temple would have ended here.

Appendix II: The *Ankh*-Bouquet and Other Life-Bestowing Sacred Objects

Certain objects thought to be infused with a divine charge were media for transferring a god's restorative, life-giving force from the sacred realm to the profane.[177] Many of these were called ʿnḫ (*ankh*; "life," "life force," or "life-form"). They were presented during renewal festivals, often while reciting some variant of the formula ḥsỉ.f tw mrỉ.f tw sw3ḏ.f tw sḥr.f ḥftyw.k, "May he be gracious unto you, may he extend (his) love to you, may he grant you prosperity, and may he overthrow your enemies."

The following were some of the life-bestowing devices operative in the New Kingdom:[178]

1. The well-known, often extremely elaborate ʿnḫ-bouquets (fig. 46). Sometimes constructed in the shape of an ʿnḫ-sign, these floral arrangements could assume a variety of individual forms.[179] Best known from the Theban Valley Festival, they were also associated with related festivals celebrated, for example, at Elkab, Gebel el-Silsila, Saqqara, and even Amarna (Akhenaten's capital). The bouquets were featured in the New Kingdom Ritual of Amenhotep I, persisted into Saite times in the Theban necropolis, and continued to have special significance in the Ptolemaic Period at the temple of Edfu. ʿnḫ-bouquets came from the altars of the Theban holy family—Amun-Re, Mut, and Khonsu—plus (Re-)Harakhti, Hathor, Ptah, Herishef, and the Aten.[180]

2. The clothing of the god that was removed and replaced each New Year during The W3g-festival, when divine cult statues were refurbished in the sfḫ-ritual.[181] The cast-off vestments remained sacred and reverted to the priests for distribution to the deceased. The floral w3ḥ-collar or garland, worn during the Theban Valley Festival by all guests, both living and dead, was such an item of apparel. At Abydos, the king assumed the god Osiris's w3ḥ ny m3ʿ-ḫrw ("floral collar [or garland] of justification"), specifically associated with the successful transfer of royal power from Osiris to his son Horus.[182] By Ptolemaic and Roman times the w3ḥ-garland had become the triumphal fillet or wreath offered to a variety of gods.[183]

3. The tall mdw-špsy pole or standard ("splendid or august staff") (figs. 79, 76, 73).[184] Particularly important at Luxor Temple, it was also called ʿnḫ and regarded as a manifestation of the royal or divine *ka*. In paintings, reliefs, and sculptures, the mdw-špsy standard was frequently shown both accompanying portable divine barques and held upright, either singly or in pairs, in the arms of kings and private individuals. It was also portrayed as an independent object of veneration.

4. The snw-offerings. These were the temple breads that reverted from the altar of god to the care of the priests. The offerings are attested in the role of

Fig. 79. *Mdw-špsy* standard of Amun-Re carried before the enshrined king. Theban Tomb 55. Restored drawing by Carol Meyer, after Norman Davies.

ꜥnḫ ("life force") during the Middle Kingdom, in the Hathoric rites celebrated at Meir.[185]

5. The sistrum and *mnἰt*-necklace. The life-bestowing role of these objects, like that of the *snw*-bread, is attested at Meir. In Theban tombs their use in this role persisted into Saite times.

All of these items are shown in the decoration of royal monuments, where they are exchanged between god and king. But they also appear in the tombs of private citizens, where they convey god's blessing to the person directly and immediately, without the king as priest-intermediary. The objects' appearances in private tombs may help us reconstruct the development of personal piety in ancient Egypt; that is, they may help us discern the evolutionary process by which ordinary men and women came to make direct, personal approaches to god unmediated by priests.

5

TEMPLES OF THE PTOLEMAIC AND ROMAN PERIODS: ANCIENT TRADITIONS IN NEW CONTEXTS

RAGNHILD BJERRE FINNESTAD

Introduction

Scholarly appraisal of the Egyptian temples built under the Ptolemies and Romans has varied between disparagement and encomium. The temples date from a period when foreign intervention and influence brought great transformations to Egyptian society and culture, and scholars have not always regarded them as "genuinely" or "authentically" Egyptian. To many these buildings have seemed little more than uninspired imitations of their glorious predecessors, pastiches exhibiting clear signs of decadence and degeneration.

Growing recognition of how deeply immersed in pharaonic traditions the late temples are has brought a reevaluation of both their historical significance and their aesthetic merit. It is no longer unusual to see a "true striving for perfection" in their exuberant decoration, classical economy of structure, and high quality of execution.[1] A steadily expanding literature convinces us that these temples are worthy of our appreciation and important for understanding Egyptian temples in general.

Temples of the Ptolemaic and Roman periods are the products of a temple-building program of large scale, probably initiated by the Egyptian

I extend my sincere thanks to Richard H. Pierce and Paul J. Frandsen for helpful comments on this essay.

FIG. 80. The pronaos of the temple at Dendera, built in the first century B.C.E., under Tiberius, Caligula, and Nero. Its columns are shaped like a collection of sistrums—the sacred instrument of Hathor. Photo by R. Bjerre Finnestad.

clergy.[2] All over Egypt numbers of temples were built, rebuilt, or expanded.[3] While the majority have been destroyed, a handful remain in a state that gives us some indication of their former grandeur and quality. These are the temples of Hathor at Dendera (fig. 80), Khnum at Esna (fig. 81), Horus at Edfu (figs. 82, 83), Sobek and Horus at Kom Ombo, and Isis at Philae (recently moved to the neighboring island of Agilkia because of the lake newly formed behind the Aswan High Dam; figs. 84–86). Built during the rule of the Ptolemies, their decorations were augmented during Roman times.

Among the smaller edifices are temples like the one consecrated to Hathor and Maʿat at Deir el-Medina (fig. 87), on the west bank of Thebes (where the Old Kingdom sage Imhotep and the New Kingdom sage Amenhotep were venerated), and that of Montu at Medamud, northeast of Luxor. Mention should also be made of the temples of Isis at Aswan, of Amun at Dabod (rededicated to Isis during the reign of the Ptolemies), of Mandulis, Isis, and Osiris at Kalabsha (fig. 88), and of the deified Peteese and Pihor at Dendur.[4]

Greco-Roman building activities spanned almost six hundred years, no less than one-sixth of all the temple-building time in Egypt. The last cartouches contain the names of Roman emperors and were inscribed during

FIG. 81. The facade of the temple of Esna, typical of the Ptolemaic and Roman periods. The hall of Esna was built in the first century C.E., during the reigns of Claudius and Vespasian; decoration work ended under Decius, in the third century. This hall is the only part of the temple that is left intact; its numerous texts and reliefs are, nevertheless, an invaluable source of information. Photo: Bildarchiv Foto Marburg 86.360; reprinted by permission.

FIG. 82. Facade of the temple of Edfu. Construction of the pronaos of Edfu was begun in 140 B.C.E. and completed with decorations in 116 B.C.E. Photo: Bildarchiv Foto Marburg 93.046; reprinted by permission.

FIG. 83. The temple of Horus at Edfu, built between 237 and 57 B.C.E. On its majestic pylon can be seen the long grooves into which the wooden flagstaffs were set. Photo: Bildarchiv Foto Marburg 93.045; reprinted by permission.

the third century C.E. (the very last was Decius, 249–251, at Esna)[5]. Evidence suggests that the temples' general pattern was developed within a relatively short span of time early in the period. They reflect a certain architectural and decorative concordance. Builders and decorators must have been clear about what they wanted. However, both architects and decorators appear to have drawn from a wide repertoire of traditions, for the temples, though carrying a common stamp, possess individuality—the result of both different selections from the rich store of traditions and distinctive combinations. The conventional options served as starting points for new developments, whose inventiveness has been detailed by many scholars. These developments refute the view that Greco-Roman temples were little more than empty forms copied from a not entirely comprehended past.[6] The temples conformed to convention and showed almost no foreign influence; nevertheless, it is also obvious that their makers took tradition into their own competent hands and, with purpose and understanding, carried them further.[7] The temples were certainly not dead relics.

FIG. 84. On the island of Philae was a large collection of Ptolemaic and Roman buildings. Among them the temple of Isis was the main edifice. The major part of this temple was built in the third century B.C.E., during the reigns of Ptolemy II Philadelphus and Ptolemy III Euergetes. The beautiful island of Philae was beloved by artists—among them David Roberts, who made this drawing of it published in 1846. The scenery could be enjoyed until the first Aswan dam was built in 1902. When the artificial lake south of Aswan was formed by the modern High Dam, Philae was partly submerged, but the buildings were saved by removing them to Agilkia. Photo by Byron E. Shafer, from *Egypt and Nubia*, vol. 1, pl. 26, The Brooklyn Museum Library Collection Wilbour Library of Egyptology.

Temples built under the Ptolemies and the Romans have a characteristic flavor; they are not just collections of ancient elements put together mechanically, if cleverly. Rather, they have their own vibrant personality. Even so, the Greco-Roman temples are products of a long development. How much of their style had matured in the Late Period, before the Ptolemies, can be only partially discerned from fleeting glimpses.

Greco-Roman temples continued basic traditions of construction and room arrangement (fig. 89). They had a big entrance gate (which the Greeks called *pylon*) (fig. 89, nos. 20–21), a courtyard (no. 19), columnar halls (no. 16), a hall for food offerings (no. 11), and smaller rooms serving as sanctuaries (no. 2) and storerooms for cultic equipment (nos. 22–23). They had chapels on the roof (preserved only in the temple of Hathor at Dendera) and subterranean crypts.[8] Some elements were taken from the traditional

FIG. 85. The plight of the buildings on Philae before they were removed to Agilkia. In the foreground is a small Hathor-temple; behind, the kiosk of Trajan. Photo: Bildarchiv Foto Marburg 93.113; reprinted by permission.

mansion and were tied to the idea that temples were dwellings of gods. As in earlier periods, the temples were not houses for a congregation of believers but divine residences.

The late temples also had special features, such as the screen wall of the pronaos: a columnar entrance or fore-hall (*ḫntj*) fronting the naos.[9] Another feature of Greco-Roman temples was the central sanctuary, a separate structure with its own roof surrounded by a corridor.[10] It was dark, having only one or two small apertures in the roof or at the top of the walls (Dendera, Philae) or none at all (Edfu). Yet for even these new architectural features precursors can be found.[11]

Birth houses were standard buildings in the temple precincts (fig. 90).[12] They were small temples annexed to the main temple, erected for celebrating the birth of the young child in the divine family triad. The celebration also had reference to the king's divine descent (fig. 91).[13]

In addition to the main temple and the smaller sanctuaries for various deities and ritual purposes, the temple precincts contained a rich variety of buildings for carrying out the institution's numerous activities: magazines, kitchens, animal shelters, workshops, scribes' studies, administrative buildings, and dwellings for the priests, other personnel, and visitors.

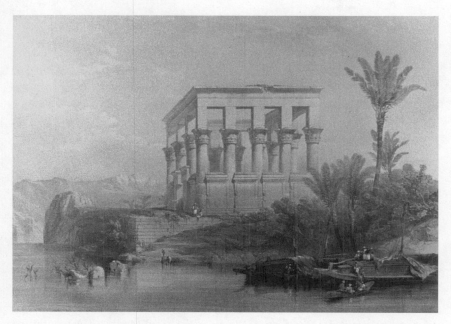

Fig. 86. The kiosk of Trajan on Philae, as David Roberts saw it. Photo by Byron E. Shafer, from *Egypt and Nubia*, vol. 2, pl. 22, The Brooklyn Museum Library Collection Wilbour Library of Egyptology.

Like earlier Egyptian temples, Greco-Roman temples were more than religious institutions in the narrow sense; they were also important centers for cultural, agricultural, and manufacturing activities. Furthermore, temple savants occupied themselves with a wide range of scholarly disciplines, an activity that acquired special significance in Ptolemaic and Roman times, when the temples became the chief official repositories of Egyptian learning.

Greco-Roman temples are better preserved than earlier temples. Their architectural structures and decorative layouts are visible. They also are more richly decorated with reliefs and texts. The texts claim that the decoration was made according to ancient models or rules (*sšm*), but the historical implications of this claim are difficult to fathom. Given the great variation in composition, the rules must have been quite general. That the claim was made is significant for understanding Egyptian self-conception and identity, however.

The style of the decoration is unmistakably Egyptian—and unmistakably Egyptian of the Ptolemaic and Roman periods. A widespread opinion maintains that the reliefs lack the vigor and vitality of earlier examples, that they are endless, unimaginatively arranged rows of almost plump figures,

FIG. 87. The simple facade of the small temple at Deir el-Medina. The temple was built during the third and second centuries B.C.E. Photo by R. Bjerre Finnestad.

FIG. 88. The temple at Kalabsha, as David Roberts saw it. Photo by Byron E. Shafer, from *Egypt and Nubia*, vol. 2, pl. 39, The Brooklyn Museum Library Collection Wilbour Library of Egyptology.

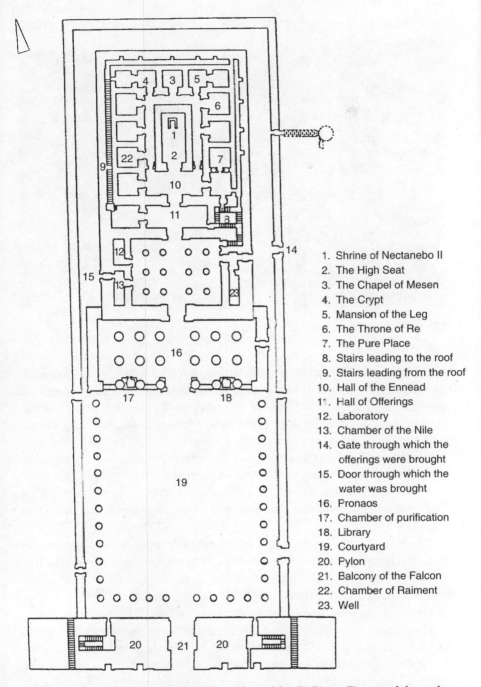

1. Shrine of Nectanebo II
2. The High Seat
3. The Chapel of Mesen
4. The Crypt
5. Mansion of the Leg
6. The Throne of Re
7. The Pure Place
8. Stairs leading to the roof
9. Stairs leading from the roof
10. Hall of the Ennead
11. Hall of Offerings
12. Laboratory
13. Chamber of the Nile
14. Gate through which the
    offerings were brought
15. Door through which the
    water was brought
16. Pronaos
17. Chamber of purification
18. Library
19. Courtyard
20. Pylon
21. Balcony of the Falcon
22. Chamber of Raiment
23. Well

FIG. 89. A plan of the temple at Edfu. Adapted by R. Bjerre Finnestad from the adaptation of Chassinat's plan in Bertha Porter and Rosalind L. B. Moss, *Topographical Bibliography of Ancient Egyptian Hieroglyphic Texts, Reliefs, and Paintings VI* (Oxford: Clarendon Press, 1939), p. 120.

FIG. 90. The birth house at Edfu. Photo by R. Bjerre Finnestad.

"shuffling along" with "their smug smiles, dimpled knees, and doughnut-like navels," "taking part in a solemn religious ritual, carefully marked off into panels by regimented lines of hieroglyphs."[14] This representative description is biased, but it does point to a stylistic feature that deserves attention: the figures are hieratic, highly formal, *and* sensuous—a rare combination (fig. 92). The decorative style varied somewhat according to the period and according to the kind of scene depicted; compare the style of the fecundity figures or of Isis and Hathor, with that of the warrior-king Horus smiting his enemies. The artists of these late temples matched style to theme.

The texts carved on the walls are apparently extracts and summaries from the heterogeneous collection of books in the temple archives (fig. 93). Awed scholars have measured their prodigious quantity in miles; it is equally significant, however, that the texts are representative of the entire spectrum of ancient Egyptian religion and scholarly learning.

The subject matter of some of the images and inscriptions can be found in earlier temples; that of others is encountered only in these late temples. The themes include ritual scenes that record daily and festival rites—hymnic invocations, offerings, processions, foundation scenes, inauguration scenes. There are also mythological motifs, such as the creation of the world and the fights and victories of deities (fig. 94).[15] Astronomical texts and images are carved on the ceilings, and inscriptions running along the walls

Fig. 91. A scene in the birth house of Edfu, at the entrance to the inner vestibule. The birth house was dedicated to Horus, Hathor, and Harsomtus (Horus-Uniter-of-the-Two-Lands). Photo by R. Bjerre Finnestad.

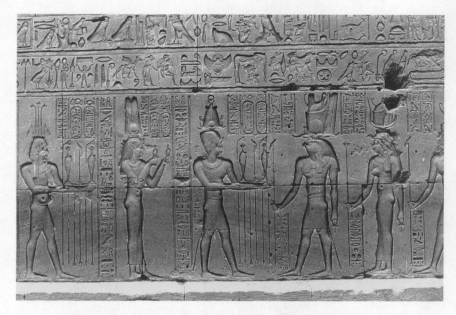

FIG. 92. On the base of the temple at Edfu are scenes depicting a procession of the fertility powers of Egypt, who, headed by the king, carry forth their rich produce to the god of Edfu. Photo by R. Bjerre Finnestad.

describe the edifice, its measurements, and its rooms—their names, decorations, contents, purposes, and locations.[16] Even the doors are named and their purposes stated.

Descriptions and measurements are also given for the primeval sanctuaries of gods. How to interpret these texts is arguable. Because "primeval" refers to a concept stressing ancestral authority rather than time, the texts cannot be used straightforwardly—that is, literally—for historical reconstruction.[17] Further complicating our assessment of these descriptions and measurements is the fact that Egyptians of the Ptolemaic and Roman periods had a lively interest in symbolic numbers.[18]

Unique to Ptolemaic decoration are scenes depicting the cultic role of the queen and the dynastic cultus of the Ptolemies. Ptolemaic queens are shown together with the king offering to the gods (fig. 95), and the queens are found relatively often in scenes of the dynastic cultus.[19] Of course, representations of queens are not without precursors in earlier pharaonic traditions. The iconographic vocabulary is marked by a certain continuity, but the cultic context is characterized by innovation.[20]

Also among the temple texts are geographical-topographical descriptions of Egypt. Lists of the forty-two nomes contain the names of cultic sites, their relics, their priests and priestesses, sacred canals, sacred trees

FIG. 93. The wall surrounding the temple of Edfu, unique in its preservation, is covered with texts and reliefs, a rich source of information about mythical and ritual traditions of the temple. Photo: Bildarchiv Foto Marburg 86.298; reprinted by permission.

and mounds, festivals, taboos, arable land, and marsh land.[21] Adolf Erman sees in such decorations a kind of central archive for cosmological learning, but he adds sarcastically: "what a delight to discover and compile all these things, and what useful knowledge!"[22]

The distribution of the scenes and texts throughout the temple was premeditated and reflected various bipartite schemes.[23] Complementary relationships are found between facing walls, higher and lower parts of the building, the inside and the outside of the building, and the symmetrical halves created by the axial road bifurcating the halls (figs. 96, 97).[24]

Many scholars have understood the decorative profusion characteristic of Greco-Roman temples as an indication of decline and weakness. The decorators, they claim, did not know how to set limits or to recognize what was essential. "The late period . . . becomes loquacious" is Hermann Kees's comment.[25] The question of why all these texts were carved has been answered variously. Kees talks about a "fear of forgetting."[26] Erman points to changing cultural contexts that created a reflective distance from the ancient traditions; the traditions were no longer taken for granted and could be preserved for posterity only with effort.[27] Jan Assmann expands Er-

FIG. 94. Texts and reliefs pertaining to the Victory of Horus are carved into the western inside face of the wall surrounding the temple at Edfu. On the base, Nile divinities are depicted carrying forth their produce. Photo by R. Bjerre Finnestad.

man's perspective to include not just temple epigraphy but the entire temple: epigraphy, architecture, cultus, and ethics. He sees these temples as a comprehensive codification of cultural identity, a "monumentalized memory" (*gebaute Erinnerung*) of an Egyptian culture felt to be waning, a bulwark against Greek-Hellenistic forms.[28] It is unnecessary, indeed hardly pertinent, to regard the temples as defensive castles against Greek-Hellenistic traditions—even the existence of the implied self-conception requires discussion—but the temple's role as codification of cultural identity and memory seems highly important. Such a role appears to have been ancient, even though its extensive reflection on the walls was a late phenomenon.

These explanations of the abundance of texts and reliefs do not, however, address their religious function. To do this we must take into account the Egyptians' conceptions of temple and of sacred script and image. Viewing the texts and reliefs from this perspective, two important functions are discovered: they defined the space and the actions that took place there, and they made what they represented cultically present.[29]

The long and arduous task of describing the temples and making their reliefs and texts accessible to the wider scholarly community has been accompanied by never ending problems in deciphering, translating, and in-

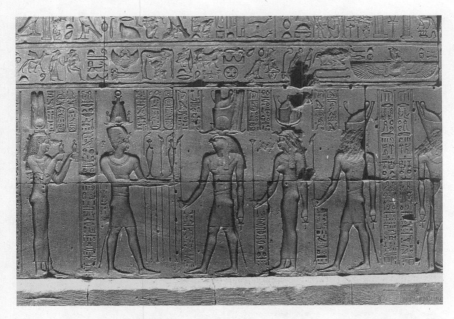

FIG. 95. At Edfu, the king and queen (left), in their most typical ritual act: carrying forth the offerings to the gods (right). Photo by R. Bjerre Finnestad.

terpreting them.[30] The script poses difficulties for us. The inscriptions used a greatly expanded repertoire of signs, the result of considerable increase through the ages.[31] In the Roman Period the number surpassed seven thousand. Then, too, the writing of words followed norms of orthography that varied idiosyncratically from temple to temple. Also, an inventive, subtle utilization of the pictographic and phonographic functions of the hieroglyphs expanded their expressive capacity. Translators' ability to unravel the expressive possibilities of the script has come a long way but is still short of the mark.[32] Finally, the scribes drew upon centuries of semantic accumulation. It is not always possible today to distinguish a word or phrase's denotative meaning from all of its connotative meanings, and frequently it has more than one denotative meaning.[33] The translator's task of abstracting intention is not easy. Of course, the connotative meanings are also important. They derive from a long history of semantic development and provide the words with a resonance echoing ancient times. For all of these reasons, the finding of equivalent words or phrases in a modern target language is often a frustrating task. To make things harder, quite a few of the ideas articulated by the ancients are not found in our modern conceptual universe—among them, some concepts central to the world of the temple.

FIG. 96. The sun disk carved into the outer face of the northern wall of the temple naos at Edfu. It is placed on the axis of the structure, along which the processional route ran. Photo by R. Bjerre Finnestad.

FIG. 97. The winged sun disk carved into the middle of the inside face of
the northern surrounding wall at Edfu, opposite the sun disk on the naos
wall (fig. 96). The winged sun disk is the image of the god of Behdet, to
whom are attributed the functions of both Re and Horus. He is Creator and
protecting ruler of the world. Photo by R. Bjerre Finnestad.

Other kinds of problems are raised by the mythological statements found in temple texts. Mythology is a symbolic mode of discourse. Symbols can be read on various levels of meaning and with reference to various existential contexts. They can be continuously reapplied to new historical situations and reinterpreted in new conceptual contexts. This open-endedness explains how the ancient symbols could still be used in Ptolemaic and Roman times. As a vehicle of thought, the symbol is particularly well suited for articulating the ambivalent and paradoxical sides of human existence—for example, the interdependent relationship of such opposites as birth and death or cosmos and chaos, to which the symbol of the sun's course points in Egyptian mythology. Religious language, which aims at formulating comprehensive views on human existence, is characterized by extensive use of symbols. But problems also attend the deciphering and interpreting of pictorial language—reliefs, statues, and architecture—for the symbols used in this mode of representing thought carry a multitude of meanings too.

The relationship between the forms of expression and their conceptual content is not a simple one. A form can have several and changing meanings, but there are limits to its possibilities for meaning. There are also limits to the kinds of question we can ask of the source material. For example, temple documents are communal, and inasmuch as they conveyed traditions of the community, they are not primary sources for understanding private attitudes and beliefs. Often that which is collectively stated and that which is privately held do not coincide.

The profusion of reliefs and inscriptions found in Greco-Roman temples makes them a unique source of general knowledge about Egyptian temple cultus. The temples offer us not only myriads of details but also the conceptual frameworks and substructures that define or lend meaning to the details. They communicate much more explicitly than earlier temples the religious meanings they carried, and because they are well preserved we can discern the interplay between the reliefs, texts, architectural features, and ritual enactments. A Greco-Roman temple had in its totality a powerful expressive capacity.

The study of later temples yields insights into earlier ones; it sharpens our gaze, focuses our attention on otherwise overlooked features, and stimulates hypotheses. In fact, what scholarship has to say about the conceptual framework of Egyptian temples has in large part been deduced from the late temples' lavish source material and its extensive reflection of earlier traditions.[34]

We should not, however, overlook the new developments represented by Greco-Roman temples or refrain from asking to what extent the traditional forms had acquired new content in the Ptolemaic and Roman periods. Continuity presupposes change; change is, paradoxically, the sine qua non for the transfer of tradition. To pass to new generations, the forms must accommodate to new sociocultural contexts through reinterpretations and remotivations.

So the late temples are indispensable for assessing the meaning of Egyptian temple cultus. The wider source material pertinent to the Ptolemaic and Roman periods allows us to sketch some of the temples' functions within society; temples had never been an isolated sector of society, and they continued to be important cultural and social institutions under the Ptolemies and Romans.

Here I concentrate on two topics: the religious meaning of the temple and of its cultus and the integration of the temples into Egyptian society. The relationship between meaning and context is complex. Put simply, the temples' religious meaning involved their sociocultural contexts and vice versa. Many sectors of society and culture changed during the Ptolemaic and Roman periods, and the interactions between meaning and contexts must be given special attention.

Much can be said about the difficulty of interpreting a culture that existed seventeen to twenty-two hundred years ago. The difficulty begins with the thorny problems that challenge all scholars working across cultural boundaries and continues with the problems peculiar to interpreting a society that cannot be experienced firsthand. All understandings of ancient Egyptian religion will inevitably be the products of two cultures—the Egyptians' and the interpreter's. The interpreter's own culture predisposes him or her to particular ways of apprehending the source material and rendering its meaning. A final, definite exposition will therefore never be put on the table.

Although we cannot bring back the Egyptian temple and its cultus just as they were, we can nevertheless recapture some of the basic concepts—expressed in architecture, imagery, texts, and actions—that structured the Egyptians' distinctive vision of the world.

The Cultic Vision of the World

An interpretive perspective widely shared by students of the late temples is that the temples—their architecture and decoration—were metaphors for Egypt's world. The bipartite distribution of reliefs and texts not only served an aesthetic preference for order but also referred to such ancient cosmological bipartitions as east/west in the solar ideology and Upper Egypt/Lower Egypt or Valley/Delta in the Two Lands ideology. The bipartitions within the single, unified temple corresponded to the cosmic dichotomies whose parts together constituted the world in its wholeness.[35] A vertical scheme of cosmological partition can also be discerned in late temple architecture and decoration. On temple bases are incised the emblematic plants of Egypt—the papyrus and the lily (fig. 98)—and processions of fecundity figures carrying the produce of Egypt's fertility (figs. 92, far left; 94).[36] Columns are compounded of palms, papyrus, lotus, and reeds, vegetation growing from the inundated earth (fig. 99). On the ceilings are carved the sun, the moon, and the stars, the last two lending a nocturnal aspect to the temple landscape.

Simultaneously, the temples depicted the world of the gods. The walls and columns teem with gods who are standing, marching, sitting, communing with the king; the ceilings abound with divinities who are flying, sailing, and moving in their courses.

The coinciding of these two levels of meaning signifies that Egypt's world was a sacred world. This visual cosmographic exposition was drawn into temple ritual so that the cultic performances interacted with the architectural features and the carved texts and reliefs. Architecture and decoration were integral to the cultic proceedings. Thus, for scholars seeking to understand the "message" of the cultus, the temple's metaphoric values are like the lines of a navigator's chart.

Temple ceremonies are customarily divided into two groups: daily and festival. Certain characteristics differentiated the two, but they were joined by central theological concepts, to which we shall pay particular attention. They also shared an emphasis on what is conceived and perceived through the eye. Both were clearly the products of people who expressed their religious beliefs in images, and both displayed an unusual correspondence between the mental images of words and the concrete images of architecture, decoration, and ritual form. The ceremonies of the Ptolemaic and Roman temples mastered fully exhibited the Egyptian faculty for visual articulation.

The daily rituals carried out inside the temple comprised three main services, performed at sunrise, midday, and sunset. The timing followed the solar circuit, and a solar mythology exerted decisive influence on the cultus. The most important of the three was the morning service, during which the theological meaning of the sunrise was ritually displayed as an appearance of the Creator, whose light then brought the world into appearance. During the night, the movements of the stars were observed by the priests who kept watch over the great cosmic progression toward morning.

We shall look more closely at the morning ceremonies, using examples from Edfu, the best preserved of the temples, but focusing on features with parallels at other temples. Edfu is well suited for demonstrating the coherence and interplay of its components.[37]

FIG. 98. On the facade of the temple at Esna, the king stands between the goddesses of Upper and Lower Egypt, who lead him before Khnum. On the base are carved the plant emblems of Egypt. Photo by R. Bjerre Finnestad.

The temple of Horus at Edfu (fig. 100) was built on the site of an earlier temple. Its relationship with the temple of Hathor at Dendera can be taken as an example of the kind of close connection that could exist between temples. Theology and cultus of the two were coordinated.[38] Horus of Edfu received attention in the cultus at Dendera, and the pantheon of Edfu was included in the Dendera cultus.[39] A list of all the gods of Edfu is inscribed in the hypostyle hall at Dendera, and in the Edfu temple we find the festival calendar of Dendera.[40] The two temples cooperated in celebrating the famous festival of the Reunion of Hathor and Horus.

The acts of the morning ritual at Edfu consisted of hymnic addresses, the presentation of myrrh and cloth to the statues of god, anointings, libations, and censings.[41] The central place in the morning service was the sanctuary of the High Seat (*st wrt*) (fig. 89, no. 2), which lay at the core of the temple naos.[42] This sanctuary was also central to the image of the world presented in the morning cultus.[43] Its name connected it with the mythic high

FIG. 99. Capitals of columns in the hall of the temple at Esna. Photo by R. Bjerre Finnestad.

mound (*st wrt*) which arises out of the waters of Nun and on which the Creator begins his creation of the world by dispelling darkness. Contained within a smaller shrine in the sanctuary (figs. 89, no. 1; 101) was a statue of the god of Edfu as the solar Creator, the god of "the beginning."[44] Also in the sanctuary, resting on a pedestal, was the cultic boat of the god (fig. 102).

At sunrise, the officiating priest opened the sealed doors of the High Seat. The priest proceeded to the smaller shrine of the god's statue, opened its doors, and revealed the statue. Texts and reliefs on the inside east wall of the sanctuary represent the act of uncovering the face (*wn ḥr*) and the priest's recitation: "You arise as Khepri as you come out of Nenet, and your rays spread over the world!"[45] Texts and reliefs on the west wall represent the act of seeing god (*m33-nṯr*) and the priest's recitation: "I have seen the god. . . . I have gazed upon the statue of Khepri, the sacred image of the Falcon of Gold."[46] The face seen by the priest at sunrise was the sun god's. On the frieze of the sanctuary the sun god is carved in the form of the Winged Beetle, the icon of the god as he comes into being in his first, matinal manifestation.

The act of seeing god was a most significant rite of the morning ritual; but other acts were important.[47] Fumigations were indispensable to the statue ritual. Incense and perfumes were brought from the lateral sacristy

FIG. 100. The pylon of the temple at Edfu. At the flagstaffs, Horus and Hathor are depicted as rulers of Egypt, the divine royal couple. Before them, the Ptolemaic king (Neos Dionysos Auletes) slays his enemies. Between the pylon's towers is the Balcony of the Falcon. Photo: Bildarchiv Foto Marburg 86.299; reprinted by permission.

called the Laboratory (fig. 89, no. 12). Food and drink were presented in the Hall of Offerings (no. 11) to all the gods of the temple.

The morning ritual revolved around three key concepts: seeing god, the appearance ($ḫ^cw$) of god, and the coming out (*prt*) of god. Partly overlapping, partly complementary, these concepts belonged to a religious cosmology in which sunlight was the divine, vital, creative element in the world. Each day the sun god appeared anew, and at that moment the world took form in his light, appearing with him. The coming of light out of darkness ended the formlessness of night and initiated a dynamic coming into being. Being seen is the criterion of this creation. The horizon, the topos of first light and, consequently, of transition into existence, was given a cultic counterpart in the temple.[48] A hymn inscribed in the hall outside the sanctuary of the High Seat reads, "Praise to you, god of Behdet, splendid *ᶜpj* who shines in the horizon!" and, "Horus of Behdet, great god, lord of the sky . . . who comes out of the horizon in the Two-Temples-of-the-South-and-the-North!"[49] "Come out" is an inadequate translation for *prj*, whose meaning includes "emerge from darkness," "become visible," "take shape," and "come into being." Here we are confronted with the basic problem of

FIG. 101. At the rear, in the dark core of the temple of Edfu, at the end of the processional road running through the temple, stands the monolithic shrine of black granite that contained the statue of Horus. The shrine dates from Nectanebo II and represented the cosmic beginning in the ritual creation of Egypt. In front of the shrine can be discerned the pedestal that supported the processional barque of the god. Photo: Bildarchiv Foto Marburg 86.312; reprinted by permission.

FIG. 102. Replica in wood and stucco of the processional barque of Horus. The god is represented with a falcon head. On his chest he wears the winged scarab—the image of the god in his first form, as he appears from darkness. Photo by R. Bjerre Finnestad.

translation mentioned initially. The difficulties we have in finding equivalents to *prj* stem from the fact that its semantic field is determined by conceptual categories alien to our conception of the world.

The opening of the doors along the temple's processional path from the High Seat (the boat sanctuary of the solar Creator) through the halls and out the pylon gates derived a special significance from these three concepts and their cosmological frame of reference. Gates and doors were dominant features of the temple architecture. They had an important function in the liturgical staging of the coming of god. A gate or door enables one to traverse a barrier or cross a boundary. The barriers/boundaries in temples signified those between day and night, life and death, and cosmos and chaos (chaos being the state of not having taken form in the Creator's light).[50] The prodigious size of the entrance pylon far exceeded the requirement for its pragmatic function but fit its function of representing the gate of cosmos—the horizon.[51] The pylon heralded that the temple was a place of existential transition, and its decoration showed that the coming of the Creator and ruler of the world confronted and overcame chaos and expanded the territory of cosmos. Paralleling the mythic images of the Creator-god's dispelling of Apophis, the power of darkness and chaos, reliefs on the pylon portrayed the god-king victoriously slaying his enemies (fig. 100).[52]

The gate aspect of the temple was repetitive. A series of doors crossed the axial processional path. The small monolithic sanctuary inside the sanctuary of the High Seat was dominated by doors. So was the facade of the pronaos. As one moved outward, the size of the portals increased gradually from the small doors of the innermost sanctuary to the big ones of the pronaos, as if room were being made for an expanding deity.

The gate aspect of the temple became particularly prominent during festivals, when the appearance of god was ritually choreographed in processions coming out from the naos into the forecourt. The forecourt could be named Court of Appearance, a designation underlining the importance of that coming out in the temple cultus.[53]

But the gate aspect of the temple was prominent also in daily rituals. Each morning, the doors that crossed the axial road swung open to allow light and the god of light to enter: "When the two doors of Mesen are opened the sun rises like Re shining in the horizon."[54] The opening of the doors was accompanied by adoration and hymnic invocations, praise giving, and recitals of names and epithets uttered to evoke the divine presence.[55] The words of such compositions were inscribed near the doorways through which the Creator made his epiphany. Carved on the lintels of the doors and on the ceilings over the axial road were images of the god of Behdet, the coming Creator, as the winged sun (fig. 101; cf. fig. 103). The axial road represented the course of the sun god. The sanctuary of the High Seat

FIG. 103. The temple of Philae, as drawn by David Roberts. Photo by Byron E. Shafer, from *Egypt and Nubia* 1, pl. 40, The Brooklyn Museum Library Collection Wilbour Library of Egyptology. Note the winged disk on the ceilings and cornice over the axial road.

and the inner halls were dark places which were illuminated artificially.[56] It was only when the main doors were opened that the High Seat and inner halls received daylight, entering along the path of the axial road (fig. 101). When those doors swung open, light traveled inward along the axial road and "united with" the Falcon-of-Gold image in the sanctuary and with images on the ceiling. According to the morning hymn, Horus, as *ᶜpj* "comes from the night sky (Nenet) every day to see his image (*bs*) in the High Seat. He descends to his image (*sḫm*); he joins (*snsn*) his images (*ᶜḥmw*)."[57] The passage refers to the creative power of the sun god: in his light the images take form; they are seen to come into being.

The sanctuary was situated where the temple space was narrowest, the ceiling lowest, and the floor highest. As one proceeded along the road from the High Seat (fig. 89, no. 2) through the pillared halls toward the Court of Appearance (no. 19), the space gradually expanded, the walls receded, the floor was lowered, and the ceiling rose, upheld by tall columns—symbolic of the sky uplifted by Shu.[58] Thus architecture shaped the vision of the expanding cosmic world.

The coming out of god was mythologically conceived in two images, both of which made clear that coming out was a coming into being. One was the birth of the solar child from his mother, the night sky goddess. The other image was the emergence of the sun god from the dark regions of the universe where nothing could be seen—the realm of death, Duat. In temple texts, the interior of the mother goddess and the realm of death were sometimes identified.[59] There were two traditions about the location of Duat: the nocturnal sky and the underworld.[60] Both traditions are found on the walls of the late temples, although the ritual texts and reliefs discussed here seem to prefer the nocturnal celestial location.[61] The identification of Duat with the mother of the Creator is a clue to the paradoxical relationship between life and death formulated by the temple cultus. Life and death were seen as reciprocal states constituting an ongoing cycle.

The ancient mythology of the night sky as the mother of the solar Creator is reflected extensively in temple reliefs and texts. Indeed, the dark inner room of the temple was itself a symbol of the mother of the Creator.[62] The morning hymn engraved around the door of the sanctuary of the High Seat alludes both to the cosmos and to the temple when it says that the god of Edfu flies "through Nenet," the dark night sky, his mother through whom he moves to be born in the morning.[63] A hymn inscribed in the hall outside the sanctuary refers to the appearing sun god as the coming of the "splendid child who illumines the earth," the "young child in the morning."[64] The same hymn calls the sun god "old man at night." So, within this birth-and-aging imagery, when the sanctuary texts say that the god goes to sleep in the temple, they mean that his place of death, as well as birth, is here. Indeed, one of the names of the temple was "Duat" (*d3t-n-b3*).[65] The temple, as image of the world, encompassed Duat; the realm of death, according to temple cosmology, was not outside the world.

Temple texts call the rising sun the *ba* of the sun god.[66] *Ba* is difficult to translate, for it denotes a concept that is not found in Western classifications of the forms of existence. But the word refers to the dynamic aspect of the god that daily makes the transition from Duat.

Behind the temple rites lies a theology or natural philosophy about how the universe regenerates. We can reconstruct parts of it with the help of source material like the Book of the Dead, which was still used in the Ptolemaic Period and was even included in temple liturgy.[67] When in the morning ritual the solar god came, the world seen by his light simultaneously came into being. This combined theology and natural philosophy, which developed over generations, found various formulations in mythology.[68] The theology of Akhenaten explicated the ontological basis inherent in solar mythology in nonmythic language: to be-come is to enter into visibility.[69] The cosmogonic power attributed to sunlight helps us understand the emphasis placed on vision in the cultus.

In the major late temples we see how influential this solar cosmology had become, for it is found in all of them. In Esna, Khnum is praised as the solar god (fig. 98).[70] In the cultuses of Hathor of Dendera and Isis of Philae, these great mother-goddesses give birth to the solar god, but they also function as active solar deities in their own rights, both creating and vanquishing.

Hathor of Dendera is called "daughter of Re."[71] The appellation alludes to the hypostasized protective sun-aspect of Re, the mythic uraeus, depicted as a snake encircling the sun.[72] However, Hathor is also presented as an independent solar ruler, a female version of the sun as sovereign power.[73] Like the sun god, she sails in her boat "together with her Ennead."[74] Her solar aspect is given an illustrious decorative expression on the outside of the temple naos: in the middle of the rear wall the face of Hathor resting on the sign for gold and with the sun on her head brilliantly marks the axis of the naos (fig. 104).

A similar cosmology centers around Isis at Philae. In a hymnic address inscribed in the sanctuary, she is invoked as "the one who rises and dispels darkness."[75] She is the "Mistress of flame who assaults the rebels, Who slays Apopis in an instant, Uraeus of Re," but she is also invoked as a female solar ruler, "the female Horus (ḥrt)" who "took possession of the Two Lands," who "smites millions (by) cutting off (their) heads, Great of massacre against her Enemy."[76] In an inscription on the first pylon, Isis is said to be "the Golden One," "who illumines the Two Lands with her radiance, and fills the earth with gold-dust."[77] Gold-dust is a metaphor for sunlight. Gold was used extensively in the decoration of the late temples.[78] At Philae, Dendera, Edfu, and other temples as well, images on the walls of the sanctuary were probably covered, wholly or in part, with gold.[79] In another invocation, inscribed in the sanctuary at Philae, Isis is called upon to come to her house and "join her Image (ḥnm sšmw.s), Her radiance inundating the faces, Like (the radiance of) Re when he shows himself in the morning."[80] We do not have an ancient Egyptian exposition of the relationship between the light and the image, but the texts quoted seem to presuppose that the light participates in the image that thus becomes visible.

The coming of the solar Creator and of the world that exists in his light was a principal theme of the temple cultus. The various architectonic, pictorial, textual, and ritual statements convey a religious evaluation of sunlight. That this grand theological tradition in Egyptian thought is so extensively, consistently, and creatively represented is a sign of the vitality of these late temples.[81]

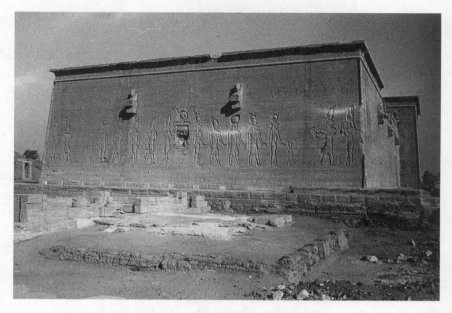

FIG. 104. The rear south wall of the temple at Dendera. The face of Hathor, "the Golden One," marks the axis of the naos, along which the ritual route of the solar deity was constructed inside the building. On the walls can also be observed the lion-headed spouts that permit the rainwater accumulated on the roof to escape while being directed away from the decorations on the walls. Photo by R. Bjerre Finnestad.

Seeing god in the temples was an experience sensed through the eyes, not an inner, mental, metaphysical contemplation. The manifestation of god was an actual coming into visibility from a hidden state in darkness— a literal, liturgical vision. In Egypt during this late age, there were foreign cultuses that stressed mental visions of god, and scholars have long discussed whether the cultus of Egyptian temples underwent similar "spiritualization." A description of Egyptian clergy by a priest named Chaeremon has been taken to indicate such a transformation in the temple cultus of the pharaonic tradition. Apparently, Chaeremon was a temple scholar of the first century C.E. His writings are now lost, but in a passage mediated to us by Porphyry,[82] a third-century Neoplatonist, Chaeremon says of the priests that they "devoted their whole life to contemplation and vision of the divine. Through this vision they procured for themselves honour, security, and piety; through contemplation they procured knowledge; and through both a certain esoteric and venerable way of life."[83]

Chaeremon's description seems to speak of inner visions of god. But in evaluating his report, certain circumstances need to be considered. The report was addressed to non-Egyptians, and in attempting to explain Egyptian traditions to a Hellenistic public, some adaptation would have been necessary.[84] This granted, it is a significant fact that Porphyry thought of Chaeremon as a Stoic, which might suggest that the contemplation of which he spoke was not an inner, mental vision.[85] According to Stoics, theology was also physics, and Stoic interpretations of myth referred to the physical universe. On this point, an Egyptian priest-scholar and a Stoic would not stand far apart; Porphyry's classification of Chaeremon might be congruous with an Egyptian priest's philosophical position.

Egyptian temples articulated god's presence in the cultus as a *physical* presence. This conception of god was transmitted in a variety of concordant formulations. The temple was god's habitation, where he dwelt together with his family. There he slept during the night, was awakened in the morning, and was regularly offered food and drink. At the same time, this house of god was an image of the world created by the solar god as a place where Egypt's many gods appeared. When one beheld the temple, this representation of Egypt, one beheld divinities: the building was covered, inside and out, with reliefs of the gods. On the base, the divinities of the fertile earth brought forth their produce. On the wall registers above them and on the stems of the plant-shaped columns, the architraves, the lintels, and the ceilings, a myriad of deities stood, sat, or in some way acted—a compilation of Egypt's profuse pantheon. They must have been even more conspicuous when they were painted in striking colors or covered with gold, their vivid figures annulling the impression of the heavy, solid building. The "excessive" reliefs of gods should not be understood in isolation; they belonged to the temple as an image of the world, and seen thus they formulated an important statement about it: the "endless rows of gods" are the bearers of a grandiose conception of the world as a living, divine, multiplex organism. The temple, with its interplay of architecture and reliefs, offered a visual exposition of the essential, substantial relationship between the world and the divine. When the morning light united with the divine images, the cosmos unfolded as a pantheon—a gorgeous, forceful display of the divine nature of the world, cast in the dramatis personae of myth.

In the symbolism of the temple, the world of Egypt acquired ultimate meaning. The gods were not just temporary visitors in the world. They belonged to the world and in some sense *were* the world. Concealed during the night, they appeared in the morning along with the world.

Intrinsic to this vision of a divine world reborn each morning were the concepts of nonbeing and death. A mortuary aspect was implicit in temple cultus, and it was made explicit through the use of various mortuary traditions. Among the most important were those associated with the cultus of Osiris and Sokar, whose chapels were located in rear rooms or subter-ranean crypts.[86] All late temples possessed an Osiris reliquary (Edfu kept a leg of Osiris). In temple theology, the god of death and the god of creation were interdependent. They represented the two poles of the all-encom-passing cyclical movement of divine being through time and space. The God of All contained them both. This thought had had a long development. It had been succinctly formulated in a New Kingdom hymn to Amun: "his *ba* (the sun) is in the sky; his body (*ḏt.f*) is in the West [i.e., his dead body]."[87] Myth and ritual centering on the gods' ancestors was another mortuary feature in temple cultuses, as was worship of the king's ances-tors. Features like these blur our distinction between "mortuary temples" and "divine temples." On the conceptual level, our problem in categoriz-ing temples arises from the implicit and explicit integration of life and death in all temple cultuses.[88]

The mortuary aspect of the late Egyptian temples was, it seems, reflect-ed in their architecture. François Daumas has, for example, pointed to the sepulchral semblance of the rectangular series of walls that enclosed the boat sanctuary. He compares the way god was "hidden" in the innermost core of the temple with the dead king in his nested set of coffins and shrines.[89] The star-studded ceiling over the ambulatory around the sanc-tuary represented the dark night enveloping the place, thus qualifying it as a place of death. Daumas's observation is keen, and it is consistent with the ontology that encompassed the cultuses of both temple and tomb: life emerges from death, and death resides in the innermost recesses of divine being. Against this background, the inclusion of funerary literature among the inscriptions in the late temples becomes understandable.[90]

The Greco-Roman temples allow us to apprehend their imaging of the world as a dynamic cycle. The interplay and alternation of light and dark-ness and of inside and outside presented a world of complementary states of being, a world in process, a world of repeating transformations—cos-mos⇔chaos, life⇔death. As a structure, the temple was a dark box, but in ritual the temple came alive with light and color and became the stage for performing the transformations of the world.[91]

The buildings that once presented the world as a living, divine organism now stand as gray and static stone, defying our faculties of imagination. Ironically, our fascination with their architecture and artistry tends to di-vert our attention from their operative side—the sights, sounds, smells, and movements of ritual enactment. These components, once so vibrant but now long gone, interacted with the sculpted stone and paint to convey the god's physical presence and power through the eyes, the nose, the ears. The god was seen in the entering sunlight and golden luminescence of stat-ues and images. The god was smelled in the pervasive fragrance of myrrh and incense. So important was the odor of divine presence to temple cultus that the walls of the Laboratory (fig. 89, no. 12) were inscribed with recipes for perfumes and incense.[92] When gods moved in processions, their scent attended them; they moved amid censers billowing clouds of aromatic smoke. Then, too, the god was heard in the words and music reverberating through the temple halls. Hathor was the goddess of music, and the sound of the sistrum, her instrument, was an epiphany. At Dendera, the columns supporting the roof of the halls were shaped like sistrums, as if the sky were uplifted by their music (fig. 105; cf. fig. 80). Here is another challenge to our imagination—what was it like, this all-pervading yet elusive sound of the sistrums?

The god's presence in the temple was not an exclusively solemn affair. Hathor was the goddess of joy, and her presence filled Egypt with gladness. Hymns to Hathor inscribed in birth houses (fig. 106) and in her temple on Philae (fig. 85) refer to rhythmic music, dancing, and intoxication (still another way of sensing the goddess!).[93]

Temples thus used many means to represent the omnipresence of deity in the world. An expressive verbal formulation is given by the morning hymn inscribed around the door of the central sanctuary of the temple at Edfu. The hymn calls upon the Creator and the gods residing with him in the temple to arise. From the invocations it appears that the pantheon constitutes the world. More precisely, the world is defined as the living body of the Creator, and the various parts of this cosmic body are equated with the gods: his teeth are the Ennead; his collar bones are Isis and Nephthys; his two arms are Shu and Tefnut.[94] All the organs of the divine cosmic being are invoked, even his interior, his belly, which is equated with the night sky: "Thy belly and what are in it, heaven furnished with its stars, awake in peace."[95] The equation situates the Creator's place of origin within his own dark, inner, hidden parts. This is the god "who comes into being by himself," a concept expressed often and variously in late Egyptian religion. The morning hymn goes on to address the temple and its parts: the sanctuary, chapels, halls, courtyard, and doors. It invokes the temple as the living form of the Creator, called into being as a cultic body.[96] When, in rituals, the statue of the god emerged from the place "of the beginning," at the dark center of the temple where the hymn is engraved, the event acquired meaning from this comprehensive conception of the temple: it symbolized the Creator emerging from his own innermost being (fig. 101).

In this theology the world is understood to be the manifestation of its Creator. Phenomena that are categorized in modern Western cultures as inanimate material objects—like the sun, the moon, and the sky—were drawn by Egyptians into the Creator's divine living body. By imaging that divine body the temple rendered the Creator ritually accessible.[97]

FIG. 105. Columns in the shape of Hathor-faced sistrums supporting the star-studded ceiling of the temple at Dendera. Photo by R. Bjerre Finnestad.

FIG. 106. The two birth houses at Dendera. In the foreground is the one built under Nectanebo I; in the background, the Roman birth house decorated during the
reign of Trajan. Between them lie the remains of a Christian basilica. Photo by
Solveig Greve.

Thus the temple was not only a statement of human belief, it also had
sacramental functions. It embodied the Creator's cultic presence and enabled ritual communication. In Egyptian religion, the approach to god was
predominantly sacramental and sensory. The cognitive approach, so important in Western religion, was not stressed.

Western ideas about god influence what we expect to find in Egypt's
temple cultus. The West thinks of God as a world-transcending, supernatural being whose substance is spiritual and metaphysical. An image can
represent God, but God exists above it or behind it, not as it. The inner eye
of the mind can perceive God through the image, but only imperfectly. God
belongs to a sphere of being different from this world and cannot be di-

rectly sensed, perceived, or experienced by beings in this world. Therefore, God's "true being" is hidden from humankind. Western observers have difficulty understanding and explaining the sensuous theophanies of Egypt's immanent gods. The West also thinks of God as eternal and unchanging. But Egypt's sensuously perceived gods constituted a changing world. They took form recurrently; they were born repeatedly.[98] And their Creator was not eternal. He had a beginning, and his life was bound up in an essential way with the existence of the world.[99]

Special theophanies of Egypt's gods occurred during the various festivals that were observed throughout the year. Lists of the festivals appear in long series of texts inscribed on temple walls.[100] These occasions plus the days that marked phases of the lunar month resulted in numerous celebrations.[101] Those connected with the seasons lasted several days.

The festival calendars from late temples describe the ceremonies more fully than earlier calendars. A rite typical of an annual festival was the appearance of god in procession. Some processions took place within the temple walls and led to the courtyard or roof; others marched out through the pylon but remained within the temple precincts; still others left the precincts and visited other sacred sites. From five to ten processions occurred each month, depending on the season.

Many scholars have focused on the processional rite as the decisive difference between the festival celebrations and daily observances.[102] In festivals, the statue of god came out from the inner parts of the temple, whereas in the daily observances it did not. Nevertheless, some basic theological concepts are found in both the daily morning ritual and the festival procession. The usual terms for the processional appearance of god are *ḫꜥw* and *prt*, words that connect the rite with the cosmological image of sunrise.[103] Thus, the theo-cosmological concepts of appearance and coming out are integral not only to daily cultus but also to festival cultus. The procession of god from the pronaos of the dark temple interior into the open courtyard acquired meaning from the solar symbolism and connoted the coming of the victor and the vanquishing of darkness—night, death, chaos. The procession defined god as both Creator and conqueror. So, in conceptual treatment, the daily and festival theophanies can be regarded as variations on the same theme. On the other hand, ordinary persons would have experienced a great difference between the daily and festival theophanies, in that processions out of the temple enclosure were accessible to them. The larger festivals also involved merry feasting, which meant abundant food and drink for the people.

Some of the annual festivals were observed in all temples, although the specific ritual performances differed from place to place. Examples of celebrations held universally were the Festival of Opening the Year, the Birth of God ceremonies in the birth houses, and the Osiris festivals of the fourth month.[104] Other festivals were not celebrated in all temples. The Coronation of the Sacred Falcon at Edfu, the Festival of Victory at Edfu, and the Festival of Intoxication at Dendera are examples of festivals that had strong local color.[105] Festivals could also be joint undertakings—for example, the Festival of the Reunion celebrated cooperatively by Edfu and Dendera. The most important festivals in the life of a given temple were represented in the texts and images on the walls. Some festivals were ancient, but only late temples allow much insight into their observance.

Opening the Year was the first of the annual festivals. Its purpose was to renew the powers that regenerated Egypt (fig. 107). Ideally, the festival accompanied the rising of the Nile, whose religious relevance, exhibited in the temple cultus, was a function of its existential significance as the precondition for agricultural life in Egypt.[106]

A central event of Opening the Year was the union of the sun with the statue of god. The fullest descriptions are found in the temples at Edfu and Dendera, where the ceremonies, apparently the most important in the festival, were performed on the roof (fig. 108). At Edfu, a statue of Horus as falcon was taken from the chapel called Mesen, which lay axially north of the sanctuary of the High Seat, along the rearmost wall. Also along this wall were chapels and crypts belonging to the mortuary cultus of Osiris and Sokar. The statue, after a sojourn in the chapel called the Pure Place, was carried in its portable shrine to the roof of the temple. It was accompanied by ancestor gods.[107] The procession is depicted on the walls of the stairs to the roof. The corresponding procession of Hathor at Dendera is also portrayed on the stairway walls. Hathor's statue, in the form of a falcon with a human head, was taken from one of the subterranean crypts.[108]

On the roof, the statue of the god was placed in a kiosk. The climax of the ceremony was removing the kiosk's awning so that the statue's face was revealed and its "uniting with" (ḥnm) the sun took place.[109] The statue was of gold, the sun's own substance.[110] According to the solar theology underlying not only this ceremony but also the daily temple cultus and the mortuary cultus, by "uniting with" the image of god sunlight had the power to regenerate it.[111] The image was obviously considered a form of divine being.

After the ḥnm-jtn, the statue descended into the dark temple by a sloping flight of stairs resembling those descending into tombs.[112] The tomblike aspect of the dark temple naos might have been prominent during the ceremony, especially at Dendera, where the statue of Hathor was first taken from a subterranean crypt and then brought back after it had "seen the sun."[113] The event is strongly suggestive of presentations in mortuary texts and imagery of the departure of the ba from the tomb to "see the sun."

FIG. 107. The procession of Opening the Year, headed by the king (far left), as depicted on the staircase leading to the roof of the temple at Dendera. Photo by R. Bjerre Finnestad.

FIG. 108. The kiosk on the roof of the temple at Dendera received the procession from below during the celebrations of Opening the Year. Here the statue of Hathor was revealed, so that it could "unite with" the sun. Photo by R. Bjerre Finnestad.

The annual Festival of the Coronation of the Sacred Falcon at Edfu had strong local features but universal relevance.[114] It is represented in texts and images on the inner face of the temple's enclosure wall. In late temples, sacred animals were venerated as forms of the god. At Edfu, the falcon was the sacred animal of Horus in his divine-ruler aspect (fig. 109), and falcons were reared in a grove within the temple precincts.[115] During the festival, which took place in the fifth month, a new falcon was selected from the falcons in the sacred grove and was crowned as king. A falconine statue of Horus and statues of the mythical ancestor kings were carried in procession from the temple, through the great pylon, and out to the separate temple of the Sacred Falcon. There the falcon to be crowned was chosen.[116] At some point during the festival proceedings it was displayed on the roof over the main doors between the two wings of the pylon. This place was called the Balcony of the Falcon (fig. 100) or Window of Appearance, and it set the new falcon within the mythology of the solar ruler's victorious appearance on the horizon.[117] The Sacred Falcon represented both Horus, divine ruler of all Egypt, and the reigning pharaoh, fusing the two ritually and linking the festival with the religious ideology of the state. The festival is one of many indications that the ancient ideal integration of kingship into temple cultus was still important under the Ptolemies and Romans.

FIG. 109. One of the two great granite statues of Horus fronting the pylon of his temple at Edfu. Photo by R. Bjerre Finnestad.

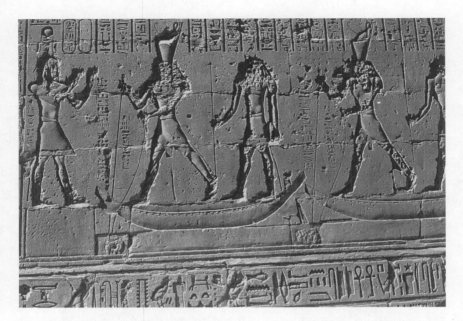

FIG. 110. Scene from the reliefs and texts pertaining to the Victory of Horus. The god vanquishes his enemy, who is depicted as a hippopotamus beneath the ship's bow. Photo by R. Bjerre Finnestad.

Another festival of special significance for Edfu was the Festival of Victory (fig. 110).[118] Observed in the sixth month of the year, it celebrated the myth of Horus' victory over his enemies. Reliefs depicting the festival's mythology occupy a great amount of space on the inner surface of the temple's enclosure wall. They portray Horus harpooning his enemies, depicted as hippopotamuses and crocodiles.[119] The accompanying texts again show that Horus and the reigning king were ritually merged. The territorial compass of the myth was the whole of Egypt. The motif of the victorious Horus occurs frequently in other texts and reliefs at Edfu, a sign that the festival was an important one.[120]

The Festival of the Reunion (*ḥb n sḫn*) of Hathor and Horus was one of the most famous religious events in Upper Egypt.[121] It took place in the eleventh month of the year, when the goddess left her temple at Dendera and sailed upstream to meet Horus at Edfu.[122] The flotilla from Dendera is portrayed at Edfu on the base of the courtyard walls. The festival was extremely popular and was celebrated not only by the people of the two towns but also by the people living between and beyond. En route, the goddess went ashore at several places, including Thebes, to visit the resident gods and goddesses. Throngs of pilgrims streamed to one of these towns or to Edfu, and official deputies were sent from Elephantine, Hierakonpolis, and Kom Mer, and perhaps from other places as well.

Hathor spent the nights of the following two weeks with Horus in the sanctuary of the High Seat. Her boat is depicted on the sanctuary wall. The daytime celebrations included processions to the necropolis of the dead gods and to neighboring sanctuaries. There were also numerous food offerings, including those of the harvest.[123] The festival was a rich mixture of mythical and ritual traditions, but it had a focus on the theme of cyclical regeneration of life. The spouse of Horus came as a goddess of life and vitality.

In the portrait of Egypt drawn by the temple cultus, the land was represented as home and provider. In both roles the land was held sacred. Home for the gods, it was the ultimate habitation of the Egyptian community. The role of the land as provider was prominently reflected in the cultus. Every day the land's produce of bread, meat, vegetables, fruit, water, wine, beer, and milk was presented to the gods in the Hall of Offerings, and during the festivals lavish offerings from the land were given. The festivals were connected with the seasons, with the movements of the sun and the flood stages of the Nile, and with the effect of these phenomena on germination, growth, and harvest. Offerings from the land are the most frequent theme in temple decoration. All over the building, the king, representative of the Egyptian community, is depicted carrying forth the sustenance provided by the divinities of the land's fertility (figs. 92, 95). Such decoration demonstrates that an important function of the cultus was to celebrate and sanctify the cycle of sustenance. The daily and festival cultuses abounded in mythologies and rituals related to the reciprocal circulation of produce bestowed by the gods and offerings given to the gods. The cultus formed a ritual relationship with the utilization of Egypt's inundated soil and, by hallowing the agricultural use of the land, conferred the highest value on that use.

The mythical symbolism of the cultus did not abstract it from the concrete reality of agricultural subsistence. The imagery of gods and divine acts did not represent some other world; it represented the world of Egypt, conceived as divine. The cultus combined symbolic meanings with concrete, pragmatic references. To lay bare the existential implications of temple mythology, one must consider the late temples' role within the agricultural economy of Ptolemaic and Roman Egypt. Doing so clarifies the this-worldly referents of the temples' mythical symbolism and indicates whether the referents belonged to an older socioeconomic order that had ceased to exist or agreed with the order of the Ptolemaic and Roman periods.

The Temples' Integration into Society

The late temples were thoroughly integrated into Egypt's society and economy, and three functions can be singled out as especially important. First, the temple cultus ascribed value. As already discussed, it ascribed to Egypt and to life in Egypt the highest value by conceiving it as sacred. Second, the clergy of the temple transmitted a comprehensive and normative body of knowledge about the ways to perceive, experience, and understand the world and to conduct communal life. Third, the temples played active roles in land utilization. The last two functions require further discussion.

The temples were comprehensive institutions involving great numbers of people and numerous categories of personnel. The daily cultus was in the hands of several kinds of priests.[124] The highest were the servants of god (*ḥmw nṯr*); they were called *prophētai* by the Greeks.[125] Some of the prophets were female; they were so in the cultus of Hathor, for example.[126] The rules for the recruitment of prophets required that they belong to a sacerdotal family.[127] Some of these families gained great social influence.[128] Prophets also had to be able to read the sacred documents, which meant that those who conducted the ancient cultus in the late period knew what they were doing.[129]

The daily rites of attending and robing the statues were performed in the late temples by priests whom the Greeks called *hierostolistai*.[130] The stolists were deputies to the prophets and, when necessary, could also take over their work.

The prophets and stolists were assisted by various specialized priests, such as those who carried the sacred boat and other sacred objects (called by the Greeks *pastophoroi*), those who slaughtered the sacrificial animals, the wardens and their assistants, and the singers and musicians.[131] Some of the singers were female—once again in the cultus of Hathor, for example—where their role as representatives of the goddess of music was especially important.

During the priests' periods of service, they had to observe a set of taboos, such as abstaining from certain kinds of food and drink.[132] The list of taboos varied from temple to temple. The behavior demanded of those who entered was specified by cultic and ethical rules and admonitions inscribed on doors through which the priests entered the temple.[133] Cultic purity was a precondition: "Do not enter unclean." During the periods of priestly service, sexual abstinence was demanded. Priests were enjoined to be serious and conscientious in their work. They were not to neglect their cultic duties and were not to steal from the offerings. They were not to tell lies in the temple, to accept bribes, or to tamper with scales and measures.[134] The general aspect of these ethical rules suggests that they were not merely a canon for priests but represented a universal model for Egyptian moral life.[135]

Attached to the temples were groups of auxiliary laymen who assisted the officiating priest by guarding the doors, lighting the lamps, "erasing the priest's footprints" as he left the sanctuary, and bringing food to the altars. They also assisted the personnel engaged in the practical work of the temples (such as the bakers, butchers, and decorators) and helped tend the animals.

Then there were the scribes and scholars of the House of Life, called by the Greeks *hierogrammateis*.[136] Some were priests; all were guardians of liturgical and other kinds of texts, copying and commenting on them. They also participated in the construction and decoration of temples.[137] They were indispensable to temple administration, managing for example, the lands registered to the temples, a task that required scribes competent in keeping accounts.

The immense transfer of Egyptian tradition from one age to another depended on these scholar-scribes; it is both their work and the result of their work that we study. They worked in temple annexes that housed the libraries and served as places of study and writing.[138] Naturally, the temple archives were comprehensive, and the libraries were large.[139] In these centers of learning, a variety of disciplines were pursued: mythology, liturgy, iconography, arithmetic, geometry, law, medicine, astronomy, the interpretation of dreams, the study of the Nile and its inundation, and all other sciences pertaining to Egypt: geography, topography, history, and philology (the language of the hieroglyphic texts was dead). This broad spectrum of disciplines necessitated scholarly specialization. For example, some important members of the community of priest-scholars made astronomical observations.[140] They kept the time, found the right moments for cultic and noncultic acts, and worked out lists of lucky and unlucky days.

Some of the priests knew Greek and maintained contact with Greek scholars. Ptolemaic Egyptian thought, far from being a relic of a dying pagan system, was vital and in correspondence with much of Hellenistic thought.[141]

Notwithstanding differentiations among the various categories of priests, they acted in many respects as a socioreligious group. They cooperated in cultic, administrative, and economic matters, and they met in synods. During a long period under the Ptolemies, they were expected to meet in annual conventions to discuss with representatives of the state matters pertaining to politics and cultus.[142]

Laypeople did not have access to the daily cultic ceremonies performed in the temple sanctuary; only priests were allowed to "see god." This was not true of all temples in Ptolemaic Egypt. In those of the nonindigenous Greek or Oriental cultuses, the officiants could be laypeople. A priest in a large Egyptian temple had a representational function that a priest in a Greek or Oriental temple in Egypt lacked; he dealt with the gods as an official representative of the Egyptian community. His right to represent the Egyptian people derived from his being the vicar of their supreme representative, the king. This understanding of the representational relationship between priest, king, and community was ancient, and it continued in the late periods. For example, the cultic-ritual scenes in late temples still depicted kings, rather than priests, as the officiants. In reality, the relationship between the Egyptian priest and the Ptolemaic king varied with time, place, and person, as it had when priest and king were both Egyptian.[143] But since cultic ideology required the priests to represent the king, Ptolemaic kingship was integral to temple cultus.[144]

Thus, in continuity with pharaonic custom, the Ptolemaic king was the prototypical high priest, the highest representative of the gods to the people and of the people to the gods. Texts and reliefs presented the ruler as Horus, king of the universe and son of Re, the solar Creator. He was depicted building the temple—the image of Egypt—with the help of the gods, and he was depicted offering to the gods the produce of the land. Such scenes accorded with conventional iconography, and both Ptolemaic and Roman rulers were drawn to look like Egyptian pharaohs (e.g., fig. 111).

The Ptolemies not only followed the tradition that ascribed to the king the central role in temple cultus, they even strengthened their cultic position by introducing a dynastic cultus that incorporated the Ptolemaic house into the temple.[145] The dynastic cultus was a Hellenistic innovation, but it was assimilated to Egyptian forms of royal cult.[146] The deified ancestors of the Ptolemies were incorporated into Egyptian temples as "gods who share the sanctuary" with the god.[147] The dynastic cultus was observed as part of the daily cultus and in festivals as well.[148] Its religious purpose is indicated in a scene at Edfu, where the reigning king, Ptolemy IV Philopator, is shown together with his queen, Arsinoe III, and his parents and grandparents accepting the fruits of the earth from the god of the Nile, Hapy, who commissions the king to give the fruits to both the gods and the people.[149]

In another Ptolemaic development, temple reliefs frequently depicted the queen at the king's side as royal spouse or coregent.[150] Those of Cleopatra VII in the temple of Hathor at Dendera are well known (fig. 112).[151] Such scenes signal the Ptolemaic queen's inclusion in the concept of monarchy as it related to these cultic situations. It is difficult to say whether the queen's salient iconographic role was connected with developments in

Fig. 111. The king depicted on the throne uniting Upper and Lower Egypt between figures representing fertile Egypt. Note their respective plant emblems, the lily (left) and the papyrus (right). This motif belongs to old iconographic traditions. Photo by R. Bjerre Finnestad.

Fig. 112. Far right, Cleopatra VII Philopator and her son Ptolemy Cæsarion before the pantheon of Dendera. Photo by R. Bjerre Finnestad.

political reality. The relationship between theory and practice is complex and often surprising, and the source material available is not sufficient to reach a firm conclusion. The inclusion of the queen in the iconography of monarchy had precursors in the New Kingdom.[152] It was rooted in ancient ideas of Egyptian monarchy, even though its use in the Ptolemaic Period may have been conditioned by the kings' focus on dynasty and dynastic cultus. In the Roman Period, the empress was not represented on the walls of Egyptian temples, even though the deified emperor was.[153]

The kingship traditions of temple ideology and Ptolemaic governmental policy differed at points and were not identical.[154] The discrepancy between the Egyptian kingship ideology and Roman imperial rule was even greater. Nonetheless, philosophical discussion of the royal office had gone on in the Hellenistic world, and there were areas of agreement between Egyptian and Hellenistic kingship ideologies.[155] For example, the concept of the king as both the state and the state's link with world order is found in Greek-Hellenistic thought. The king's engagement in religious matters was in agreement with both Egyptian and Greek-Hellenistic kingship ideology.[156] Even Roman imperial ideas coincided on specific points with pharaonic ideas, for example on the ruler's duties in war. Under the Roman emperors, the maintenance of Egypt's borders against all foes was sanctified through traditional temple forms. So Titus (79–81 C.E.) is depicted at Esna in the conventional pharaoh-smiting-his-enemies pose.

We turn now from the ideological position of priests and rulers to their actual role in land utilization. The value ascribed to the land of Egypt by the temple cultus was not mere ideology. The temples invested great time and energy in managing the land and in developing agricultural competencies. They cooperated in exchanges of products and labor, and they shaped and took part in a network of economic and social relationships.[157] Large tracts of land were registered to the temples.[158] Priests kept cadasters and administered leases of land. They helped predict the amount of arable land that would be available each year. Every temple had a Nilometer to measure the level of the flood waters, and on that basis the area of silt cover was forecast. Temple personnel had a hand in building and repairing the canals and dikes that were so important to irrigation farming. Then they participated in sowing the land and in collecting the harvest, handling great quantities of food. The temples' role in the efficient utilization of Egypt's resources was a weighty reason for the support of these religious institutions by Ptolemaic and Roman rulers. As a sign of how important the temple estates were in temple ideology, the register of the Edfu temple's land holdings, which stretched from Gebel el-Silsila to Thebes, was inscribed on the outer face of the enclosure wall. The texts were presented in the context of Offering the Field, a ceremony associated with the *Sed*-festival and the royal ritual of taking possession of the land by circumambulating the temple grounds.[159]

The temples' pragmatic functions need to be taken into account when expounding their religious worldview. The temple cultus and mythology had greater reference to the concrete world than one might at first think. Temple texts, rituals, and imagery attached symbolic and pragmatic meanings to activities of sustenance and support, which became more than merely "materialistic" acts (to use a concept current in our system of values). The abundant food offerings can be explained within this pragmatic, religious context. They were not an extravagant waste of resources for the sake of an unreal mythic world. After the food was presented to the gods, it reverted to the priests and was shared among them according to their rank in the hierarchy.[160] The sanctified food of the gods nourished and sustained the temple personnel and, in accordance with the mythical and ritual vision of the temple cult, endowed that pragmatic function with the highest religious meaning and value. The offering rite should be viewed together with this sequel. Thus seen, they constituted a consecration of the recycling and redistribution of the fruits of the earth.

The traditional correspondence between the king's administrative role in actualizing the land's fertile potential and his cultic role was still the basis for the ideology of kingship reflected in the rites, texts, and decorations of the late temples. The cultus and images of the major temples continued to center on the divine ruler, Creator, and defender of the world of Egypt, whose "son," the king, carried out his divine functions; and this continuity corresponded with political realities. When Ptolemaic kings and Roman emperors were shown carrying offerings and communing with the powers of sustenance, thereby hallowing the agricultural use of the land, the scenes accorded with the pragmatic engagement of these rulers.[161] The fact that these late rulers were not of Egyptian descent did not affect the temples' presentation of kingship's meaning. Neither did the fact that the people represented by these kings (and priests) included many more non-Egyptians than had earlier been the case. Yet in reality these circumstances must have given the traditions of kingship different significance.

Old Cultuses in New Contexts

All sectors of Egyptian sociocultural life underwent change during the Ptolemaic and Roman periods: economy, government, demography, religion. Granted, the social and cultural contexts had always been changing, and the temples had continually adapted. Yet the period we are describing deserves to be called a "period of transition," even though the continuity was great and the change was gradual, unfolding over hundreds of years.

The Ptolemies followed a dual policy toward the great Egyptian temples. On the one hand, the temples' political and economic power was decisively curtailed. The Ptolemies, and the Roman rulers, took control of temple revenues.[162] (Indeed, during Roman rule the temples were subject to the central secular authority.)[163] On the other hand, the Ptolemies supported the extensive program of building and rebuilding Egyptian temples, and they endowed the temples with gifts and cultic foundations.[164] They also extended many of the temple estates, for to feed the priests and others employed in temple service required large areas of land and large numbers of peasant workers. So although the political and economic autonomy of the temples was in various ways limited under Ptolemaic rule, the Ptolemies nonetheless supported them both as agricultural and religious institutions.

It has been said that the Ptolemaic rulers supported the temples for purely economic reasons—that they were interested in stability and prosperity and catered to Egypt's religious traditions for that purpose only.[165] True, the temples were a center of agricultural power, and agriculture was the single most important component in Egypt's economic structure. Ptolemaic and Roman rulers were intent on exploiting the natural resources of land and water more effectively than ever by reclaiming uncultivated land, experimenting with scientific agriculture, and improving irrigation and drainage. They did see the economic vitality of the temples as crucial to the overall vitality of Egypt. However, it would be a mistake to concentrate solely on the economic component of the interconnecting motivations and comprehensive worldview that underlay their temple policies. The ridicule of Egyptian religion by Roman authors is well known, especially the ridicule of the animal cultuses.[166] Yet, for Greeks, Romans, and Egyptians alike, religion was rooted in place. Greek and Roman rulers simply would not ignore local religious reality. Furthermore, these peoples had many religious ideas in common, even if they were expressed in different languages.[167] Finally, and perhaps most decisively for our argument, they shared a type of society that did not compartmentalize religious values and institutions. Just as the pragmatic and the religious intertwined in all aspects of Egyptian life, including the temples, so too a mixture of the pragmatic and the religious doubtless motivated the Ptolemaic and Roman support for these temples. In any event, from the time of the very first Ptolemy, these kings supported the Egyptian national religion.[168]

The religious scene during the Ptolemaic and Roman periods was diverse and complex. Egyptian traditions existed side by side with non-Egyptian traditions, or mingled with them to produce new gods, new cultuses, and new cultic communities.[169] Important Ptolemaic and Roman institutions, like the temples of Serapis, existed in all major towns.[170] Cultuses existed for traditional Greek and Roman deities and for deities from other countries. In addition, Jewish religion had been practiced in Egypt since the sixth century B.C.E., and in the Roman Period many Christian churches were established. The patterns of interaction and relationship between the various religions were extremely complicated, and they largely elude us. The Egyptian traditions, both inside and outside the temple walls, were vital and far from drained of strength, and even in the heavily Hellenized syncretistic milieus there were obvious Egyptian influences on the Greeks.[171] Before the time of expanding universal religions, the concept that religion belonged to a particular region was deeply rooted in people's thought, and Greeks and Romans living in Egypt felt a need to "acclimatize" their gods and religious practices to the place.

Against this background of religious pluralism and interacting influences, it is truly remarkable that the great Egyptian temples reflect so very few Hellenistic features. The zodiacal ceilings (with their suggestion of a multispheric sky) are, however, one example.[172] Then, too, some aspects of ancient Egyptian tradition probably received renewed or heightened attention because they resonated with important Hellenistic concepts or developments. The stress on the sky in the Greco-Roman temples may have been influenced by the strong Hellenistic interest in astrology.[173] Some decorative features of the ceilings may indicate assimilations between ancient Egyptian and Hellenistic traditions; for instance, the reliefs of double and triple figures of Nut in Dendera and Philae may have represented the idea of several spheres.[174] It is, however, difficult to say whether this feature was new or old, for the roofs of earlier temples no longer exist.

Some of the non-Egyptian conceptions of the world present in Egypt during these late periods diametrically opposed the conception celebrated by traditional Egyptian temples and their cultuses, for instance, by maintaining that god was not present in the created world. Did such alien conceptions of the world influence the interpretation of ancient Egyptian traditions made by temple priests? This question has been much debated and cannot be given extensive treatment here. Suffice it to note how difficult it would have been to reinterpret the temple's conception of the world drastically enough to accommodate the idea of a god transcending the world. The traditional temple was a tight weave of world-as-divine symbols. The plait of its particular visual forms, ritual behaviors, and conceptual contents virtually excluded an intrusive interpretation that god was transcendental to the world. During the long history of Egyptian religion, the mythological traditions had been variously actualized, but the ontological premises had remained firmly fixed.

It seems, then, that the immanentist worldview of the traditional temple was not reinterpreted to assimilate it to transcendental Hellenistic worldviews. That Egyptian priests communicated with Hellenistic milieus and translated their traditions into languages and frames of reference understandable to Hellenistic audiences does not change this fact. The "spiritualizing" interpretations of temple texts and rites sometimes presented today are unfounded.

Egyptian temples were the temples of the majority population, and their traditions had the full support of Egyptians. All the same, these traditions constituted just one component, albeit a major one, in a motley assembly of religious traditions, and individual Egyptians could participate in religious activities that did show Hellenistic influences. Syncretistic developments can be seen in certain nonliturgical religious temple activities and in the religious praxis at the burial grounds.[175]

It has been said that the official cultuses, maintained by a body of priests and utilized by the rulers, were probably detached from the functional worldview of ordinary men and women, but there are reasons to hold a different opinion. Ordinary people did not, of course, follow the theological subtleties of the temple scholars, and they were scarcely interested in doing so. They did not have access to the inner temple, and they did not participate in the liturgy. Nonetheless, evidence suggests that on vital points the temple-formulated worldview was shared by the common people. It is difficult to uncover what individuals believed. Temple texts cannot serve as sources, for they present the officially valid community beliefs. The sources for what individuals believed come from sites where individuals performed religious activities. Some of these throw light on the connections between individuals' beliefs and temple traditions.[176]

The temples were important socioreligious forums for exchanging religious beliefs among large numbers of people, and of course the frequent temple festivals became lively meeting places for the populations of neighboring towns. Popular devotional activities took place around the temple and even within the temple enclosure, often assisted by priests.[177] Many people came specifically for dream interpretations or oracles. Others visited, often from great distances, to seek medical help at those temples reputed to be centers of healing. Within the precincts of Hathor's temple at Dendera there was a sanatorium with baths and probably also facilities for healing incubation.[178] Temple gates were traditional places for ordinary persons to pray and for their legal disputes to be settled.[179] Reliefs of gods on the external walls could mediate between the god and persons standing outside the walls. Pious people wishing to lead an ascetic life could lodge within the temple precincts, and wrongdoers could find asylum there.

Since priests were involved in all these activities and took part in the multifaceted, heterogeneous religious life of the people, it is reasonable to assume that the fundamentals of life set forth in the temple cultus were shared by popular religion and were understood by most Egyptians to be grounded in nature. Places and objects filled with divine power, gods omnipresent and immanent, creative force released by sacred words, life and death as phases of the divine rhythm of regeneration—all were concepts that structured Egyptian thought, and they were reflected in temple cultus and popular religion alike.

One could perhaps argue that had the temples not conformed to the average Egyptian's way of perceiving and knowing the world, the cultuses would hardly have been given such monumental expression. Worship so costly could have continued only if its religious meaning was vital and valid for large numbers of people. The opinion that traditional Egyptian culture receded behind temple walls as its last resort, while transitions to completely different cultures and religions went on outside, is simplistic and hardly correct.[180]

Broader study of continuity and change in Egyptian religion supports the view that the late temples were not isolated from the rest of life. After the temples had finally closed, when the great masses of Egyptians had converted to Coptic Christianity, some of the rites and ideas belonging to ancient Egyptian temples reemerged in that religion.[181] Manifestly, temple traditions had lived on to be modified and reinterpreted, and to be integrated into the new conceptual and institutional contexts of Christianity. Saints' cultuses, pilgrimages, magical papyri, mortuary traditions, dreams, healings, oracles, and other practices show various kinds of continuity.[182] The religion that became dominant after the closing of the temples can be fully explained only by referring to traditions that emanated from those very temples.[183]

With the exception of the temple of Isis on Philae, the temples were officially closed in 392 C.E. under Emperor Theodosius I. Philae marked the southern frontier of Roman Egypt, and its temple continued to serve the Nubian tribes in the region and pilgrims from afar. After the mid-fifth century, Christian churches coexisted with it on the island.[184] Then between 535 and 537 C.E., by order of Justinian, this last Egyptian temple was closed.[185]

NOTES

Abbreviations

AAWLM	Abhandlungen der geistes- und sozialwissenschaftlichen Klasse, Akademie der Wissenschaften und der Literatur in Mainz (Wiesbaden: Steiner).
ADAIK	Abhandlungen des Deutschen Archäologischen Instituts, Abteilung Kairo, Ägyptologische Reihe (Glückstadt: Augustin).
ÄgAbh	Ägyptologische Abhandlungen (Wiesbaden: Harrassowitz).
AH	Aegyptiaca Helvetica (Basel: Ägyptologisches Seminar der Universität Basel; and Geneva: Centre d'études orientales de l'Université de Genève).
AJA	*American Journal of Archaeology.*
ASAE	*Annales du Service des Antiquités de l'Égypte.*
Ausgrabungen	Ausgrabungen der Deutschen Orient-Gesellschaft in Abusir 1902–1908 (Leipzig: Hinrichs).
AVDAIK	Archäologische Veröffentlichungen des Deutschen Archäologischen Instituts, Abteilung Kairo (Mainz: von Zabern).
BdÉ	Bibliothèque d'Étude (Cairo: L'Institut Français d'Archéologie Orientale).
BeiträgeBf	Beiträge zur Ägyptischen Bauforschung und Altertumskunde (Zurich: Borchardt-Institut für ägyptische Bauforschung und Altertumskunde; or Cairo: Schweizerisches Institut für ägyptische Bauforschung und Altertumskunde in Kairo; or Wiesbaden: Franz Steiner).
BeitrSudanF	*Beiträge zur Sudanforschung.*

BES	Brown Egyptological Studies (Providence: Brown University Press; London: Lund Humphries).
BiAe	Bibliotheca Aegyptiaca (Brussels: Fondation Égyptologique Reine Élisabeth).
BIFAO	*Bulletin de l'Institut Français d'Archéologie Orientale.*
BiOr	*Bibliotheca Orientalis.*
BOREAS	Acta Universitatis Upsaliensis: BOREAS (Uppsala: [Uppsala Universitet]).
BRL	*Bulletin of the John Rylands Library.*
BSAE	British School of Archaeology in Egypt and Egyptian Research Account (London: Bernard Quaritch).
CdÉ	*Chronique d'Égypte.*
CEDAE	Centre d'Étude et Documentation sur l'ancienne Égypte.
DHA	*Histoire et archéologie: Les Dossiers* (Dijon: Archéologia) 101 (1986) = "Égypte. Louqsor: Temple du *Kâ* royal"; 136 (1989) = "Thèbes: Les temples de millions d'années."
DÖAW	Denkschriften, Österreichische Akademie der Wissenschaften, Philosophisch-historische Klasse.
EEF	Egyptian Exploration Fund.
Egypt and Nubia	Croly, George. *The Holy Land, Syria, Idumea, Arabia, Egypt and Nubia*, 4–5 [= *Egypt and Nubia* 1–2]. London: F. G. Moon, 1846 and 1849.
ÉPRO	Études préliminaires aux religions orientales dans l'Empire Romain (Leiden: Brill).
ERA	Egyptian Research Account (London: Bernard Quaritch).
FIFAO	Fouilles de l'Institut Français d'Archéologie Orientale du Caire (Cairo: L'Institut Français d'Archéologie Orientale).
GM	*Göttinger Miszellen.*
GOF	Göttinger Orientforschungen: Reihe 4, Ägypten (Wiesbaden: Harrassowitz).
IFAO	L'Institut Français d'Archéologie Orientale du Caire.
JARCE	*Journal of the American Research Center in Egypt.*
JEA	*Journal of Egyptian Archaeology.*
JNES	*Journal of Near Eastern Studies.*
LÄ	*Lexikon der Ägyptologie,* ed. Wolfgang Helck, Eberhard Otto, and Wolfhart Westendorf, 7 vols. (Wiesbaden: Harrassowitz, 1972–).
MÄS	Münchner Ägyptologische Studien.
MDAIK	*Mitteilungen des Deutschen Archäologischen Instituts, Abteilung Kairo.*
MIFAO	Mémoires publiés par les Membres de l'Institut Français d'Archéologie Orientale du Caire (Cairo: L'Institut Français d'Archéologie Orientale).
MMA	Metropolitan Museum of Art, New York City.
MMAF	Mémoires publiés par les Membres de la Mission Archéologique Française au Caire (unless otherwise indicated, Cairo: L'Institut Français d'Archéologie Orientale).
OBO	Orbis biblicus et orientalis (Freiburg, Switzerland: Universitätsverlag; Göttingen: Vandenhoeck & Ruprecht).

OIP	Oriental Institute Publications (Chicago: The Oriental Institute, University of Chicago Press).
OLA	Orientalia Lovaniensia Analecta (Louvain: Katholieke Universiteit Leuven, Departement Oriëntalistiek).
OMRO	*Oudheidekundige Mededelingen uit het Rijksmuseum van Oudheden te Leiden.*
RAPH	Recherches d'Archéologie, de Philologie, et d'Histoire (Cairo: L'Institut Français d'Archéologie Orientale).
RdÉ	*Revue d'Égyptologie.*
SAE	Service des Antiquités de l'Égypte, Cairo.
SAK	*Studien zur Altägyptischen Kultur.*
SAOC	Studies in Ancient Oriental Civilization (Chicago: The Oriental Institute, University of Chicago Press).
SDAIK	Sonderschriften des Deutschen Archäologischen Instituts, Abteilung Kairo (Mainz: von Zabern).
TIN	Les temples immergés de la Nubie (Cairo: IFAO).
VA	*Varia Aegyptiaca.*
WZKM	*Wiener Zeitschrift für die Kunde des Morgenlandes.*
YES	Yale Egyptological Studies (New Haven: Yale Egyptological Seminar, Department of Near Eastern Languages and Civilizations, Yale University).
ZÄS	*Zeitschrift für Ägyptische Sprache und Altertumskunde.*

Chapter 1: Temples, Priests, and Rituals: An Overview

1. See John Baines, "Society, Morality, and Religious Practice," in *Religion in Ancient Egypt: Gods, Myths, and Personal Practice*, ed. Byron E. Shafer (Ithaca: Cornell University Press; London: Routledge, 1991), pp. 127–29.

2. On the nonexistent, see Erik Hornung, *Conceptions of God in Ancient Egypt: The One and the Many*, trans. John Baines (Ithaca: Cornell University Press, 1982), pp. 172–84; first published as *Der Eine und die Vielen: Ägyptische Gottesvorstellungen* (Darmstadt: Wissenschaftliche Buchgesellschaft, 1971), pp. 166–79.

3. Hornung, *Conceptions of God*, pp. 213–16 [*Eine und Vielen*, pp. 209–12].

4. Hornung, *Conceptions of God*, pp. 179–82 [*Eine und Vielen*, pp. 174–77]; and Baines, in *Religion in Ancient Egypt*, ed. Shafer, pp. 124–25.

5. Jonathan Z. Smith, *Map Is Not Territory: Studies in the History of Religions*, Studies in Judaism in Late Antiquity 23 (Leiden: Brill, 1978), p. 97.

6. Jonathan Z. Smith, *Imagining Religion: From Babylon to Jonestown* (Chicago: University of Chicago Press, 1982), p. 54.

7. Smith, *Map Is Not Territory*, p. 94.

8. Cf. the discussion of the views of Mircea Eliade by Robert L. Moore, "Space and Transformation in Human Experience," in *Anthropology and the Study of Religion*, ed. Moore and Frank E. Reynolds (Chicago: Center for the Scientific Study of Religion, 1984), pp. 129–33.

9. Maurice Halbwachs, as quoted in Jonathan Z. Smith, *To Take Place: Toward Theory in Ritual* (Chicago: University of Chicago Press, 1987), p. 1.

10. Egyptians could use the hieroglyphic determinative for space when writing

words for time, which suggests that they did associate space-type qualities with time. See Lászlo Kákosy, "Zeit," *LÄ* 6:1363.

11. Cf. ibid., 1362.

12. Ibid. In the 354-day "uncorrected" lunar calendar used in the Islamic world, the backward rotation of festival days through the seasons becomes obvious within a person's lifespan. In ancient Egypt, the variance between the solar year—the interval between heliacal risings of the star Sirius at the time of the inundation—and the 365-day calendar was but one day every four years. So rotation through the seasons would scarcely have been noticeable during an average lifespan (about thirty years). However, the rotation and irregularity were known to Egyptians who tracked both the solar calendar and the 365-day calendar.

13. Scholars often list three other temple types: solar shrines or temples; barque chapels or stations; and *mammisis* (divine-birth houses). None of the three is a focus of study here. They were, however, sometimes associated with "divine" or "mortuary" temples, so the reader will find several references to them in the Index.

14. Scholars often suggest that Theban "mortuary" temples were built exclusively on the west bank of the Nile, the direction of the dying (i.e., setting) sun, and that Theban "divine" temples were built exclusively on the east bank of the Nile, the direction of the newly born (i.e., rising) sun. In Chapter 3, Haeny shows that this is not correct.

15. See Chapter 3. See also Rainer Stadelmann, "Totentempel III," *LÄ* 6:706, 708–9; and Wolfgang Helck, "Tempelbenennungen," *LÄ* 6:363–64.

16. The temple of Hatshepsut at Deir el-Bahri, with its terraced or staircase architecture, was the end station for the procession.

17. See Chapter 4; also Stadelmann, "Totentempel III," *LÄ* 6:708–10.

18. As a rule, each temple was dedicated to more than one god, although each had a principal deity. The main god was accompanied by what Erik Hornung terms "a whole divine community"; *Idea into Image: Essays on Ancient Egyptian Thought,* trans. Elizabeth Bredeck ([New York]: Timken, 1992), p. 128; first published as *Geist der Pharaonenzeit* (Zurich: Artemis, 1989), p. 129. Of particular popularity in the New Kingdom were "trinities," divine families composed of father, mother, and child.

19. Cf. Dieter Kessler, "Tempelbesitz," *LÄ* 6:365; and Jac. J. Janssen, "The Role of the Temple in the Egyptian Economy during the New Kingdom," in *State and Temple Economy in the Ancient Near East,* 2 vols., ed. Edward Lipinski, OLA 5–6 (1979), 2:508–9.

20. Jan Assmann, "State and Religion in the New Kingdom," in *Religion and Philosophy in Ancient Egypt,* ed. William Kelly Simpson, YES 3 (1989), p. 56.

21. Ibid., p. 65.

22. Lord of the Rituals, *nb jrjt jḥt,* was a title in use from Dynasty 11. See Winfried Barta, "Kult," *LÄ* 3:839.

23. Alfred Adler, "The Ritual Doubling of the Person of the King," in *Between Belief and Transgression: Structuralist Essays in Religion, History, and Myth,* ed. Michel Izard and Pierre Smith, trans. John Leavitt (Chicago: University of Chicago Press, 1982), p. 181.

24. See Wolfgang Helck, "Tempelbestattung," *LÄ* 6:376; and Malte Roemer, "Tanis," *LÄ* 6:203–4. Helck refers to Dynasties 21 and 22 as Dynasties 22 and 23.

25. Jan Assmann, "Totenkult, Totenglauben," *LÄ* 6:662–63.

26. Ibid., 674, n. 41. Throughout this chapter, the word "god" is meant to include the divine king whenever appropriate.

27. See Chapter 5.

28. The word "complex" is central to the usefulness of these terms. It denotes not only the multiplicity of structures associated with a cultic assemblage but also the multiplicity of functions, subjects, and symbols associated with it.

29. Remains of Middle Kingdom divine cult complexes with stone architecture have been found at Tod, Medinet Madi, and Medamud. For information on pre–New Kingdom temples and discussion of their significance, see Barry J. Kemp, *Ancient Egypt: Anatomy of a Civilization* (London and New York: Routledge, 1989), pp. 65–83; and David O'Connor, "The Status of Early Egyptian Temples: An Alternative Theory," in *The Followers of Horus: Studies Dedicated to Michael Allen Hoffman, 1944–1990,* ed. Renée Friedman and Barbara Adams, Egyptian Studies Association Publication 2, Oxbow Monographs 20 (Oxford: Oxbow; Bloomington, Ind.: David Brown, 1992), pp. 83–98.

30. A. Rosalie David, *The Ancient Egyptians: Religious Beliefs and Practices* (London and New York: Routledge & Kegan Paul, 1982), p. 32.

31. Hornung, *Idea into Image* [n. 18], p. 116 [*Geist,* pp. 115–16]; Kemp, *Ancient Egypt,* pp. 65–83; and O'Connor in *Followers of Horus,* ed. Friedman and Adams, pp. 83–98. The solar temples at Abu Ghurab (Dynasty 5), usually associated with the cultus of the god Re, are excluded from this description. Although built separately from the kings' pyramid complexes, they were, in all probability, closely linked with the royal cultus.

32. Assmann, "Totenkult, Totenglauben," *LÄ* 6:665.

33. The architecture of royal cult complexes will not be discussed here. A detailed summary of the Early Dynastic Period and Old and Middle Kingdoms will be found in Chapter 2; the New Kingdom is discussed in Chapter 3.

34. See A. Rosalie David, *Religious Ritual at Abydos (c. 1300 BC)* (Warminster: Aris & Phillips, 1973), p. 3; Frank Teichmann, *Der Mensch und Sein Tempel: Ägypten* (Stuttgart: Urachhaus, 1978), pp. 171, 180; and Hornung, *Idea into Image,* pp. 118–19 [*Geist,* p. 118].

35. The complex symbolism of lustrations doubtless included allusion to the first moment of creation, when the existent emerged from the dark, unbounded waters of the nonexistent. Mircea Eliade has observed: "Ritual lustrations and purifications with water are performed with the purpose of bringing into the present for a fleeting instant 'that time', that *illud tempus,* when the creation took place"; *Patterns in Comparative Religion,* trans. Rosemary Sheed (Cleveland: World, 1963), p. 212.

36. Concerning commoners' access to the temple's inner courts, see Chapter 4 and Carolyn Routledge, "Constructing Religious Practice: Ritual and Space in Egyptian Architecture," a paper presented at the November 1991 meeting of the American Academy of Religion. Routledge argues that the temple proper was divided into two zones of increasing sacredness: (1) the front courts ("large, unroofed, undivided . . . free-standing pillars and statues"); and (2) the rear rooms and sanctuary ("roofed . . . small . . . very limited lighting, small corridors and sometimes subterranean rooms") (p. 5). Routledge applies the gamma-analysis technique described by Bill Hillier and Julienne Hanson, *The Social Logic of Space* (Cambridge: Cambridge University Press, 1984), pp. 147–49, 179–83. She describes the front courts as "asymmetric" ("rooms tend to be arranged in an hierarchical pattern . . . to pass to room C from room A you must go through room B. . . . strong control over mobility of visitors") and the rear rooms as "symmetric" ("rooms tend to be equally accessible from a common point," less control over people's mobility) (p. 6).

37. I owe this description to L. Bell.

38. Gateways symbolize the vagina in many cultures. See, for example, the statement by Victor Turner, "Death and the Dead in the Pilgrimage Process," in *Religious Encounters with Death: Insights from the History and Anthropology of Religions*, ed. Frank E. Reynolds and Earle H. Waugh (University Park: Pennsylvania State University Press, 1977), pp. 26–27. Such symbolism seems likely for the pylon and other gateways in the Egyptian temple. The daily rebirth of the sun from the vagina of the night-sky goddess is a frequent image in temple art. See Finnestad's discussions in Chapter 5 of the gate-aspect of the temple, the temple as image of the divine body, and the Creator's coming forth and emerging from his own innermost being.

39. For further discussion of this symbolism, see Chapter 5.

40. Assmann, "State and Religion," in *Religion and Philosophy in Ancient Egypt* [n. 20], ed. Simpson, pp. 63–64.

41. Hourig Stadelmann-Sourouzian, "Tempelstatuen," *LÄ* 6:412–13. As time went on and temple statues multiplied in the courts and spilled over to congest passageways, many statues were placed in caches; archeologists found deposited in the Seventh Pylon at Karnak over 2,000 images of private persons, kings, and gods, representing all periods from Dynasty 11 to the Ptolemies. A few nonroyal persons became so famous for their temple statue's ability to intercede with the gods that they were divinized—e.g., Amenhotep, son of Hapu, a high official during the reign of Amenhotep III (Dynasty 18).

42. See L. Bell's detailed discussion in Chapter 4.

43. I thank L. Bell for this description.

44. "Liminal," meaning "at the threshold" (Latin: *limen*) or "marginal," is a term made prominent in ritual studies by Arnold van Gennep and Victor Turner. It describes the time and space of "betwixt and between" that characterize rites of passage, wherein the subject moves from an old time, place, state, or condition to a new one. See, for example, van Gennep, *The Rites of Passage*, trans. Monika B. Vizedom and Gabrielle L. Caffee (Chicago: University of Chicago Press, 1960), pp. 10–11, 19–21 [first published as *Les rites de passage* (Paris: E. Nourry, 1909)]; Turner, *The Forest of Symbols: Aspects of Ndembu Ritual* (Ithaca: Cornell University Press, 1967), pp. 93–111; and Moore, in *Anthropology and the Study of Religion* [n. 8], ed. Moore and Reynolds, pp. 136–37.

45. For additional information on the architecture and symbolism of the divine cult complex, see Chapters 4 and 5.

46. Hornung, *Idea into Image* [n. 18], p. 84 [*Geist*, p. 88].

47. Hornung, *Idea into Image*, p. 91 [*Geist*, p. 93].

48. That the Egyptians viewed the temple's outermost enclosure wall, usually made of mud brick, as a fluid boundary between the cosmos and the primeval unbounded waters of the nonexistent is suggested by the walls' construction and decoration.

49. Hornung, *Idea into Image*, p. 116 [*Geist*, p. 116].

50. For these and other details, see such summaries as: Jaroslav Černý, *Ancient Egyptian Religion* (London: Hutchinson, 1952; reprint, Westport, Conn.: Green-

wood, 1979), pp. 114–15; David, *Religious Ritual* [n. 34], pp. 70–72; Bernadette Letellier, "Gründungszeremonien," *LÄ* 2:912–13; and Karola Zibelius-Chen, "Tempelgründung," *LÄ* 6:385–86.

51. The ritual's focus on mud bricks and wood is a sign of its antiquity. When stone became the principal building material, the ritual and its implements went largely unchanged. Representations of the ritual are found on monuments from the Early Dynastic through Roman periods.

52. The turning over of the temple to god was renewed each New Year's Day. For the dedication rites, see the summaries by Černý, David, and Zibelius-Chen cited in note 50.

53. Opening of the Mouth rituals were performed on a number of other objects and occasions, notably on mummified corpses in mortuary rites and on the statues of gods, living kings, and deceased persons in a variety of cultic ceremonies. See such studies as: R. Bjerre Finnestad, "The Meaning and Purpose of *Opening the Mouth* in Mortuary Contexts," *Numen* 25 (1978): 118–34; and Ann Macy Roth, "The *psš-kf* and the 'Opening of the Mouth' Ceremony: A Ritual of Birth and Rebirth," *JEA* 78 (1992): 113–47. Finnestad hypothesizes that the general purpose of the rite, in all its contexts, was to make the object operative as a medium for communicating with the beyond. Consistent with her hypothesis, in Chapter 5 of this book she discusses the temple as an embodiment of the Creator's cultic presence that rendered the Creator ritually accessible and enabled communication between god and humankind. Roth suggests that the *psš-kf* implement employed in Opening of the Mouth was used in ordinary life to cut a newborn infant's umbilical cord, preparing it to live and be nourished independently.

54. Additional details about the symbolism of divine cult complexes are found in Chapters 4 and 5.

55. The image of the island of creation is found at the temple of Edfu in cosmogonical texts dating to the Greco-Roman Period. See E. A. E. Reymond, *The Mythical Origin of the Egyptian Temple* (Manchester: Manchester University Press; New York: Barnes & Noble, 1969). Reymond thinks that the mythological tradition underlying these texts is Memphite and archaic (see especially pp. 273–85, 327). Relevant to theses developed in this volume, Reymond believes that in Memphite tradition the first primeval temple—the temple of the Falcon—originated on land having multiple symbolic correlations: the Creator and creation, mortuary themes and cultuses, and worship of the ancestors (see especially pp. 276–77).

56. During the annual flooding of the Nile, some of the floors in many temples would have been covered by water, and there the inclined path to the sanctuary would literally have risen up out of the waters; Hornung, *Idea into Image* [n. 18], pp. 123–24 [*Geist*, p. 123].

57. Hellmut Brunner, "Die Sonnenbahn in ägyptischen Tempeln," in *Archäologie und Altes Testament: Festschrift für Kurt Galling*, ed. Arnulf Kuschke and Ernst Kutsch (Tübingen: J. C. B. Mohr [Paul Siebeck], 1970), pp. 31–33; Teichmann, *Mensch und Sein Tempel: Ägypten* [n. 34], p. 161; and Jan Assmann, "Death and Initiation in the Funerary Religion of Ancient Egypt," trans. M. Grauer and R. Meyer, in *Religion and Philosophy in Ancient Egypt* [n. 20], ed. Simpson, pp. 136–37 [first published in German, in *Sehnsucht nach dem Ursprung: Zu Mircea Eliade*, ed. H. P. Duerr (Frankfurt: Syndikat, 1983), pp. 336–59].

58. Hornung, *Idea into Image*, pp. 127–28 [*Geist*, p. 128].

59. For summaries of the temple's economic role, see Wolfgang Helck, "Tempel-wirtschaft," *LÄ* 6:414–20, and Kemp, *Ancient Egypt* [n. 29], pp. 190–97.
60. Kemp, *Ancient Egypt*, pp. 232–60.
61. On barter and trade, see ibid., pp. 248–60. As for agriculture, the average New Kingdom farm was five arouras (about 3 acres) and would have provided emmer and barley for a family of eight or so; David O'Connor, "New Kingdom and Third Intermediate Period, 1552–664 BC," in *Ancient Egypt: A Social History,* by B. G. Trigger et al. (Cambridge: Cambridge University Press, 1983), p. 227. In the Ptolemaic Period, middle-class farms were from 10 to 100 arouras (about 6 to 60 acres, enough to feed 15–150), and farms of the rich were more than 100 arouras (over 60 acres, enough to feed more than 150); Janet H. Johnson, "The Role of the Egyptian Priesthood in Ptolemaic Egypt," in *Egyptological Studies in Honor of Richard A. Parker,* ed. Leonard H. Lesko (Hanover, N.H.: University Press of New England, 1986), p. 76.
62. See, for example, Janssen, in *State and Temple Economy* [n. 19], ed. Lipinski, 2:507–9.
63. Temple lands were not necessarily located adjacent to the temple or even in the same region. For example, most Old Kingdom royal cult complexes were concentrated within a fifteen-mile radius of Memphis, but their lands were scattered throughout Egypt; Ann Macy Roth, "The Organization and Functioning of the Royal Mortuary Cults of the Old Kingdom in Egypt," in *The Organization of Power: Aspects of Bureaucracy in the Ancient Near East,* 2d ed., ed. McGuire Gibson and Robert D. Biggs, SAOC 46 (1991), p. 116. The percentage of arable land controlled by temples is disputed. It doubtless varied from age to age. According to the Harris Papyrus (which O'Connor assigns to the reign of Ramesses IV, Dynasty 20) at least one-third and perhaps more was owned by temples; O'Connor, in *Ancient Egypt,* by Trigger et al., p. 227. Helck states that during the Ramesside Period (Dynasties 19–20) a majority was held by temples; "Tempelwirtschaft," *LÄ* 6:418. In the Ptolemaic Period, according to Diodorus Siculus (first century B.C.E.), priests, warriors, and king controlled most of the land; *Diodorus of Sicily,* with trans. by C. H. Oldfather, Loeb Classical Library (New York: G. P. Putnam's Sons; London: Heinemann, 1933), 1:250–55 (Book 1, 73).
64. From royal decrees of Dynasty 6 we learn that workers for the temple of Min at Coptos were exempt from forced state labor. The exemption for temple workers may have been granted more widely. See Edward Brovarski, "Tempelpersonal. I. AR," *LÄ* 6:392.
65. Helck, "Tempelwirtschaft," *LÄ* 6:419.
66. Statistics given by Janssen, in *State and Temple Economy* [n. 19], ed. Lipinski, 2:511–13, suggest that the redistributed daily food offerings from Medinet Habu, the royal cult complex of Ramesses III, could have fed approximately 3,600–4,000 persons. On special high festival days, the food offerings could have provided daily rations for an *additional* 1,500–5,000 people, depending on the festival.
67. Anthony J. Spalinger, "A Redistributive Pattern at Assiut," *Journal of the American Oriental Society* 105 (1985): 7–20; Barry J. Kemp, "Old Kingdom, Middle Kingdom and Second Intermediate Period c. 2686–1552 BC," in *Ancient Egypt* [n. 61], by Trigger et al., pp. 106–7.
68. This is the thesis of Louis Dumont, *Homo Hierarchicus,* as described in Smith, *To Take Place* [n. 9], pp. 54–55. Smith uses the word "power," but I have replaced it with "dominance." See the discussion of "power" in note 162 below.

69. Černý, *Ancient Egyptian Religion* [n. 50], pp. 99, 102.

70. Kemp, in *Ancient Egypt,* by Trigger et al., p. 109; Helck, "Tempelwirtschaft," *LÄ* 6:417.

71. In royal cult complexes, according to Brovarski, "Tempelpersonal. I. AR," *LÄ* 6:393, some of the king's tenants (*ḥntjw-š*) doubled as priests. See also the paragraph containing note 103 and the note itself.

72. Some priests held office in more than one temple.

73. Most high-level priests had scribal training, however, so they probably had some proficiency in reading religious texts.

74. Wolfgang Helck, "Priester, Priesterorganisation, Priestertitel," *LÄ* 4:1091.

75. Ibid., 1092.

76. Assmann, "Death and Initiation," in *Religion and Philosophy in Ancient Egypt* [n. 57], ed. Simpson, p. 151. Assmann cites Reinhard Grieshammer's article "Zum 'Sitz im Leben' des negativen Sündenbekenntnisses," *Zeitschrift der Deutschen Morgenländischen Gesellschaft,* Supp. 2 (1974): 19–25.

77. *The Ancient Egyptian Book of the Dead,* rev. ed., trans. Raymond O. Faulkner, ed. Carol Andrews (London: British Museum; New York: Macmillan, 1985), p. 31. Translations of Book of the Dead, chap. 125, are found in many other editions and anthologies.

78. Serge Sauneron, *The Priests of Ancient Egypt,* trans. Ann Morrissett, Evergreen Profile Book 12 (London: Evergreen Books; New York: Grove, 1960), pp. 47–49; available in a revised French ed. as *Les prêtres de l'ancienne Égypte,* 2d ed. (Paris: Persea, 1988), pp. 54–55. Also, Helck, "Priester," *LÄ* 4:1091.

79. For an important anthropological discussion of the cultural role of purity regulations, see Mary Douglas, *Purity and Danger: An Analysis of the Concepts of Pollution and Taboo* (London: Routledge & Kegan Paul, 1966); and Douglas, *Implicit Meanings: Essays in Anthropology* (London: Routledge & Kegan Paul, 1975), pp. 47–59.

80. See Reinhard Grieshammer, "Reinheit, kultische," *LÄ* 5:213; Christa Müller, "Kahlköpfigkeit," *LÄ* 3:291; Alan B. Lloyd, "The Late Period, 664–323 BC," in *Ancient Egypt* [n. 61], by Trigger et al., p. 308; and Sauneron, *Priests of Ancient Egypt,* pp. 38–39 [*Prêtres,* 2d ed., pp. 45–46]. Priests were only seasonally celibate; the prohibition of sexual intercourse pertained only during their term of duty in the temples. Some of the proscribed foods were beans, fish, beef, pork, mutton, pigeon, garlic, and vegetables.

81. Helck, "Priester," *LÄ* 4:1085.

82. Ibid., 1087.

83. Dieter Jankuhn, "Hoherpriester," *LÄ* 2:1239–40.

84. Dietrich Wildung suggests that the title *wr ḥrp(w) ḥmwt* was at first purely secular and that it was not given to the High Priest until Dynasty 6; "Hoherpriester von Memphis," *LÄ* 2:1256–57.

85. We do not know whether there were phyles at divine cult complexes before the end of the Old Kingdom.

86. One could be Servant of God in several royal cult complexes.

87. Roth, in *Organization of Power,* 2d ed. [n. 63], ed. Gibson and Biggs, pp. 117–18.

88. Henry G. Fischer, "Priesterin," *LÄ* 4:1100–1101; and Gay Robins, *Women in Ancient Egypt* ([London]: British Museum, 1993), p. 142.

89. Fischer, "Priesterin," *LÄ* 4:1101; Brovarski, "Tempelpersonal. I. AR," *LÄ* 6:394.

90. Robins, *Women in Ancient Egypt,* p. 144.

91. Ibid.; and Fischer, "Priesterin," *LÄ* 4:1101.

92. Dieter Müller, "Gottesharim," *LÄ* 2:815; and Robins, *Women in Ancient Egypt*, p. 148.

93. Robins, *Women in Ancient Egypt*, pp. 148–49.

94. Ibid., p. 149.

95. The word w^cb means "one who is pure (or clean)."

96. Helck, "Priester," *LÄ* 4:1086.

97. Robins, *Women in Ancient Egypt*, pp. 142, 144; Fischer, "Priesterin," *LÄ* 4:1101.

98. This is the view of Frédérique von Känel, *Les prêtres-ouâb de Sekhmet et les conjurateurs de Serket*, Bibliothèque de l'École des Hautes Études: Sciences Religieuses 87 (Paris: Presses Universitaires de France, 1984), pp. 235–39, 254–55, 277.

99. Eberhard Otto, "Cheriheb," *LÄ* 1:940.

100. Robins, *Women in Ancient Egypt*, p. 144.

101. Brovarski, "Tempelpersonal. I. AR," *LÄ* 6:389.

102. Ibid.

103. Ann Macy Roth, "The Distribution of the Old Kingdom Title *ḫntj-š*," in *Akten des vierten internationalen Ägyptologen-Kongresses, München 1985*, ed. Sylvia Schoske, SAK, Beiheft 4 (Hamburg: Helmut Buske, 1991), pp. 177–86 (esp. 183–84).

104. Jan Assmann notes that a few Old Kingdom mastabas took as an architectural model not only the offering room of the royal cult complex but also, in simplified form, elements of the divine cult complex. This practice became general in the rock tombs of the Middle Kingdom, where the statue shrine was the axial plan's principal goal. Assmann suggests that the grave had become a veritable temple of the deceased. See "Totenkult, Totenglauben," *LÄ* 6:666–67.

105. Bettina Schmitz, "Sem(priester)," *LÄ* 5:833–34.

106. Participation by the Lector Priest apparently began during Dynasty 5. It was probably borrowed from the royal mortuary cultus when the belief developed that private persons, like the king, ascended to heaven and needed the Lector Priest's recitation of transfiguration rites. See Assmann, "Totenkult, Totenglauben," *LÄ* 6:666.

107. Kemp, in *Ancient Egypt* [n. 67], by Trigger et al., pp. 110–11.

108. Helck, "Tempelwirtschaft," *LÄ* 6:417–18, and "Priester," *LÄ* 4:1088. Above, I omit two categories of priest whose titles are not easily translated: the month's *sWt*-priest, two portions; and the month's *jmy-jst-ᶜ*, two portions. The papyrus also lists several categories of nonpriestly temple personnel: the policeman or constable, one portion; four doorkeepers, one-third portion each; two night watchmen, one-third each; and a temple worker, one-third. Phyle priests entitled to a ration for their ninety days on duty were often paid a quarter-ration 360 days a year rather than a full ration ninety days a year; Kemp, in *Ancient Egypt*, by Trigger et al., p. 106. From the Middle Kingdom onward, phyles clearly existed in both divine and royal cult complexes. Their number was reduced (until the Ptolemaic Period) from five to four, each serving three months a year. Local variations in the number of phyles probably existed.

109. Fischer, "Priesterin," *LÄ* 4:1100–1101; Robins, *Women in Ancient Egypt*, pp. 142, 144, 148.

110. Jankuhn, "Hoherpriester," *LÄ* 2:1240.

111. Sauneron, *Priests of Ancient Egypt* [n. 78], pp. 103–4 [*Prêtres*, 2d ed., pp. 112–13].

112. Helck, "Priester," *LÄ* 4:1090.

113. Royal cult complexes were organized in much the same way as divine cult complexes, with High Priests, Second Servants of God, Lector Priests, Fathers of God, and *W^{c}b*-priests; ibid.

114. Fischer, "Priesterin," *LÄ* 4:1102.

115. Ibid., 1101; and Gay Robins, "The God's Wife of Amun in the 18th Dynasty in Egypt," in *Images of Women in Antiquity*, ed. Averil Cameron and Amélie Kuhrt (London: Croom Helm, 1983), p. 70.

116. For these and other details, see Robins, in *Images of Women*, ed. Cameron and Kuhrt, pp. 70–78; Robins, *Women in Ancient Egypt* [n. 88], pp. 153–54, 156; and Lana Troy, *Patterns of Queenship in Ancient Egyptian Myth and History*, BOREAS 14 (1986), pp. 97–99.

117. Robins, in *Images of Women*, ed. Cameron and Kuhrt, pp. 71, 75.

118. Fischer, "Priesterin," *LÄ* 4:1102–3.

119. Robins, *Women in Ancient Egypt*, p. 156; also, Robins, in *Images of Women*, ed. Cameron and Kuhrt, p. 71.

120. Robins, *Women in Ancient Egypt*, pp. 153, 156; see also Troy, *Patterns of Queenship*, pp. 97–99.

121. The title *jt-ntr* first occurs in the Old Kingdom, where it is held by three High Priests of Heliopolis and a Great *W^{c}b*-priest of Memphis; Brovarski, "Tempelpersonal. I. AR." *LÄ* 6:389.

122. Helck, "Priester," *LÄ* 4:1089.

123. Elizabeth Riefstahl, *Thebes in the Time of Amunhotep III* (Norman: University of Oklahoma Press, 1964), p. 155.

124. Helck, "Priester," *LÄ* 4:1089.

125. Ibid., 1091; and Riefstahl, *Thebes*, p. 155.

126. Wolfgang Helck, "Priestertracht," *LÄ* 4:1105.

127. Helck, "Priester," *LÄ* 4:1090; Jankuhn, "Hoherpriester," *LÄ* 2:1240.

128. Peter Kaplony, "Totenpriester," *LÄ* 6:680–81.

129. Sauneron, *Priests of Ancient Egypt* [n. 78], p. 56 [*Prêtres*, 2d ed., p. 60].

130. Ibid., p. 55 [p. 59].

131. On the priestly titles of queens and princesses, see Fischer, "Priesterin," *LÄ* 4:1103.

132. O'Connor, in *Ancient Egypt* [n. 61], by Trigger et al., p. 241.

133. On *ḥmt-ntr ḥtḥr*, see Fischer, "Priesterin," *LÄ* 4:1103.

134. M. L. Bierbrier, "Hoherpriester des Amun," *LÄ* 2:1248.

135. Herman de Meulenaere, "Priester(tum) (SpZt)," *LÄ* 4:1097.

136. Helck, "Priester," *LÄ* 4:1090–92; and Lloyd, in *Ancient Egypt* [n. 80], by Trigger et al., pp. 304–9.

137. Lloyd, in *Ancient Egypt*, by Trigger et al., p. 307.

138. Jan Quaegebeur, "Priester(tum) (griech.-röm.)," *LÄ* 4:1098.

139. Ibid., 1099.

140. Indeed, many Egyptians of high civil rank also seem to have added to their wealth by taking on priestly titles; Johnson, in *Egyptological Studies* [n. 61], ed. Lesko, p. 81.

141. Ibid., pp. 77–78.

142. Dorothy J. Thompson, "The High Priests of Memphis under Ptolemaic Rule," in *Pagan Priests: Religion and Power in the Ancient World*, ed. Mary Beard and John North (Ithaca: Cornell University Press, 1990), p. 101.

143. Ibid., pp. 97, 106.

144. Fischer, "Priesterin," *LÄ* 4:1103.

145. Thompson, in *Pagan Priests,* ed. Beard and North, p. 102.

146. Quaegebeur, "Priester(tum) (griech.-röm.)," *LÄ* 4:1098–99.

147. I am indebted throughout this summary to Catherine Bell. Her extraordinary book—*Ritual Theory, Ritual Practice* (New York and Oxford: Oxford University Press, 1992)—will, I believe, reframe the scholarly discussion of ritual. Those familiar with the literature will recognize that her formulations draw on and go beyond the thinking of many other scholars—notably, for issues presented here, Maurice Bloch, Pierre Bourdieu, Kenelm Burridge, David Cannadine, Philip Converse, Mary Douglas, Michel Foucault, Clifford Geertz, Antonio Gramsci, and J. G. Merquior.

148. Cf. C. Bell, *Ritual Theory, Ritual Practice,* pp. 14–23, 112, 184–93; Ronald L. Grimes, *Beginnings in Ritual Studies* (Lanham, Md.: University Press of America, 1982), p. 60; and Walter Burkert, "The Problem of Ritual Killing," in *Violent Origins: Walter Burkert, René Girard, and Jonathan Z. Smith on Ritual Killing and Cultural Formation,* ed. Robert G. Hamerton-Kelly (Stanford: Stanford University Press, 1987), p. 155. By and large, contemporary Western scholars have valued religious thought over religious action, doctrine over ritual. Many argue that Christianity (in contrast to Judaism and Islam) is primarily a religion of ortho*doxy* and only secondarily a religion of ortho*praxy*. Within Christianity, ritual has been particularly undervalued by Protestants, whose worship ordinarily centers on the thought-full sermon rather than the action-full sacrament. So far as we know, priests in ancient Egypt never preached sermons! C. Bell, drawing on Philip Converse, states (pp. 184–85) that people understand the concrete matters of ritual far better than they understand religious beliefs. The latter are relatively unstable and unsystematic and are often inconsistent.

149. C. Bell, *Ritual Theory, Ritual Practice,* pp. 134, 211.

150. Ibid., pp. 81–82, 90.

151. S. J. Tambiah, "A Performative Approach to Ritual," *Proceedings of the British Academy* 65 (1979): 115.

152. Eugene G. d'Aquili and Charles D. Laughlin, Jr., "The Neurobiology of Myth and Ritual," in d'Aquili, Laughlin, John McManus, et al., *The Spectrum of Ritual: A Biogenetic Structural Analysis* (New York: Columbia University Press, 1979), pp. 172–80; and, in the same volume, Barbara W. Lex, "The Neurobiology of Ritual Trance," p. 144. Walter Burkert—in *Violent Origins* [n. 148], ed. Hamerton-Kelly, pp. 151–52—contends that ritual probably *preceded* language in the evolution of both *Homo neanderthalensis* and *Homo sapiens*.

153. Charles D. Laughlin, "Ritual and the Symbolic Function: A Summary of Biogenetic Structural Theory," *Journal of Ritual Studies* 4 (Winter 1990): 31–32.

154. See, for example, Sigmund Freud, "Obsessive Acts and Religious Practices," in *Collected Papers,* trans. supervised by Joan Riviere (London: Hogarth Press and the Institute of Psycho-Analysis, 1957), 2:25–35; René Girard, *Violence and the Sacred,* trans. Patrick Gregory (Baltimore: Johns Hopkins University Press, 1977); first published as *La violence et le sacré* (Paris: B. Grasset, 1972); and Bronislaw Malinowski, *Magic, Science and Religion, and Other Essays* (Boston: Beacon Press, 1948).

155. C. Bell, *Ritual Theory, Ritual Practice* [n. 147], pp. 70–74, 90–93, 220. The Christian sacraments of Baptism and the Lord's Supper exemplify this proposition.

156. Victor Turner and Edith Turner, *Image and Pilgrimage in Christian Culture: Anthropological Perspectives* (New York: Columbia University Press, 1978), pp. 244–45.

157. See V. Turner, *Forest of Symbols* [n. 44], p. 19. Exemplifying analogous quality, a climbing pole was associated with the ithyphallic Egyptian god Min. Exemplifying natural association, the fruit of the persea tree was associated with the flooding of the Nile and became an Egyptian symbol for the giving and renewing of life; Philippe Derchain, "Symbols and Metaphors in Literature and Representations of Private Life," *Royal Anthropological Institute News*, no. 15 (August 1976): 9. Exemplifying mental link, in first-century Greek-speaking Christianity, the fish became a symbol for the religion because the Greek word for fish, *ichthús*, was an acronym for the religion's profession of faith *"Iēsoûs Christós Theoû Uiós Sōtér*," "Jesus Christ, Son of God, Savior." Exemplifying cultural convention, heavy wigs were worn to Egyptian nuptials and apparently took on sexual symbolism; ibid., pp. 9–10.

158. Elizabeth G. Traube, *Cosmology and Social Life: Ritual Exchange among the Mambai of East Timor* (Chicago: University of Chicago Press, 1986), pp. 178, 239; Ronald L. Grimes, "Infelicitous Performances and Ritual Criticism," *Semeia* 41 (1988): 105; Grimes, *Beginnings in Ritual Studies* [n. 148], p. 103; V. Turner, *Forest of Symbols*, p. 50; V. Turner and E. Turner, *Image and Pilgrimage*, pp. 245–46; C. Bell, *Ritual Theory, Ritual Practice*, p. 183.

159. V. Turner and E. Turner, *Image and Pilgrimage*, pp. 246–48; V. Turner, *Forest of Symbols*, pp. 20, 26, 50–51.

160. V. Turner, *Forest of Symbols*, pp. 36, 54; Clifford Geertz, *The Interpretation of Cultures: Selected Essays* (New York: Basic Books, 1973), p. 90.

161. Tambiah, *Proceedings of the British Academy* 65, pp. 153–57. Erik Hornung argues that Tutankhamun (Dynasty 18) increased the number of carrying poles for the image of Ptah from seven to eleven because "Ptah's importance now approached that of Amun," for whose image Tutankhamun ordered an increase from eleven poles to thirteen; *Idea into Image* [n. 18], p. 84 [*Geist*, p. 88]. I assume Hornung would say that the increase was both an index of the rising earthly power of Ptah's priests and an image of the rising cosmic power attributed to Ptah; and I would add that the pole-increases were probably an index and image of Tutankhamun's personal claim to significance, both earthly and cosmic.

162. C. Bell, *Ritual Theory, Ritual Practice*, pp. 193–201. The key to understanding this proposition is to understand "power." Bell (pp. 197–200) draws extensively on the thinking of Michel Foucault to argue that power is not a "thing" that sovereigns or the ruling class possess and wield; power is not the entity "control over others." Rather, power is a contingent, imprecise, local, organizational, and *relational* phenomenon. Power, as relational, does not act on persons directly; rather it influences their actions indirectly. Bell (p. 200) quotes Foucault: to govern is "to structure the possible field of action of others." Furthermore, relationships of power are established from the bottom up as well as from the top down; they grow out of "preexisting forms of behavior, socialized bodies, and local relations of power, which could not be mere projections of the central power and still effectively maintain and legitimate that power" (p. 200). A relationship of power must be built on the governed's freedom to choose, to be insubordinate, and to engage in struggle. Without freedom, what occurs in the relationship is not "power" but "the force of necessity" (p. 201).

163. C. Bell, *Ritual Theory, Ritual Practice,* pp. 109–10, 169, 191–96, 221–22; Geertz, *Interpretation of Cultures,* p. 119; V. Turner and E. Turner, *Image and Pilgrimage,* p. 244. A person who believes that ritual is *primarily* an instrument for legitimizing the ideology of the elite might agree with the third and fourth sentences of this proposition, for, as Bell states (p. 191), "ideology is *not* a coherent set of ideas, statements, or attitudes imposed on people who dutifully internalize them. . . . Any ideology is always in dialogue with, and thus shaped and constrained by, the voices it is suppressing, manipulating, echoing. . . . When they agree, they do not passively follow or obey; they appropriate, negotiate, qualify."

164. C. Bell, *Ritual Theory, Ritual Practice,* pp. 81, 83–85, 170, 196–201, 218.

165. For example, in ancient Egypt the opposition between order and chaos was never finally resolved; chaos was subdued but not annihilated. Also, the systems by which a person acceded to priesthood—royal appointment and family inheritance—set up a binary opposition between state and family that was differently negotiated in different eras and was never finally resolved.

166. C. Bell, *Ritual Theory, Ritual Practice,* pp. 101–7; she finds dyads *f, g,* and *h* in the Roman Catholic mass, with *h* being dominant (pp. 101–2).

167. Ibid., pp. 93, 98–101, 109–10, 116, 140–41, 200–204, 206–7, 214–15, 220–21. C. Bell (pp. 99–100, citing Roy A. Rappaport, *Ecology, Meaning and Religion*) offers this example of producing a ritualized body that moves between adherence and resistance: "the act of kneeling does not so much communicate a message about subordination as it generates a body identified with subordination. . . . [R]equired kneeling does not merely *communicate* subordination to the kneeler. For all intents and purposes, kneeling produces a subordinated kneeler in and through the act itself. . . . [S]uch an act may in fact set up a bifurcation between the external show of subordination and an internal act of resistance." Related to this point (and to note 166 above), Bell finds that the Roman Catholic mass generates a body identified with "an experience of a *higher* spiritual authority [dyad *g*] as an *internalized* reality [dyad *h*]" (p. 102, italics and bracketed material added). Bell later observes (p. 214) that "Catholicism is a consent to papal power and a resistance to it at the same time." Protestant Christianity has generally held that differing ritual practices result from differing theologies, but Grimes has rightly asked whether it might not be the other way round, that theological differences follow from differing ritual practices, from kneeling or not kneeling; *Beginnings in Ritual* [n. 148], p. 98.

168. C. Bell, *Ritual Theory, Ritual Practice,* pp. 123–24, 210. It is of course simpler to revise and recontextualize rituals based on oral tradition than it is to revise and recontextualize rituals based on written tradition.

169. Grimes, *Beginnings in Ritual,* p. 57; Tambiah, *Proceedings of the British Academy* 65: 165–66.

170. Perhaps the populace did not so much believe in the divinity of the king as consent to his unique, unrivaled rank within the social hierarchy. For an anthropological understanding of divine kingship and ritual, see Clifford Geertz, *Negara: The Theatre State in Nineteenth-Century Bali* (Princeton: Princeton University Press, 1980), esp. pp. 124–36; also C. Bell, *Ritual Theory, Ritual Practice,* pp. 193–95.

171. The ancient Egyptian belief that the dead were part of society was a significant reason for mortuary rituals' great importance.

172. Leaders of the ritual process had a major advantage in gaining and retaining social status and authority.

173. Akhenaten (Dynasty 18) was the king most ambitious in his effort to redirect culture and society and most spectacular in his failure to do so. He imposed his beliefs by negating people's access to traditional ritual; he did not generate their consent by encouraging their participation in traditional ritual judiciously revised.

174. Neither funeral rites nor private mortuary rituals are treated here, for they were not directly related to temples. Of the many temple rituals, only a few are discussed here. Most data come from the New Kingdom and subsequent periods. Egyptologists have long noted similarities between the royal mortuary cultus and the cultus at divine cult complexes. They have disagreed about the direction of borrowing, however. According to Hans Bonnet, the royal cultus borrowed from the divine; "Totenkult," *Reallexikon der ägyptischen Religionsgeschichte* (Berlin: de Gruyter, 1952), pp. 828–29. According to Jan Assmann, the divine cultus borrowed from the royal; "Totenkult, Totenglaube," *LÄ* 6:674 n. 42. For our purposes, the similarities are the important factor, not the direction of borrowing.

175. Barta, "Kult," *LÄ* 3:839.

176. In Chapter 2, Arnold describes the daily morning and evening offering services conducted for the king at the pyramid temples of Dynasties 5 and 6 and the royal statue rituals performed as part of those services in the Chapel of the Five Niches. The Pyramid Texts describe a daily morning sacrifice for the sun god Re. We also learn of a daily toilette for god. See Barta, "Kult," *LÄ* 3:840–41; and Brovarski, "Tempelpersonal. I. AR," *LÄ* 6:389–90.

177. The principal sources for the scenes and texts are the chapels of the temple of Sety I at Abydos (Dynasty 19), a hieratic papyrus in the Berlin museum that portrays the cultus of Amun and Mut at Karnak (Dynasty 22), and the sanctuaries of the temples of Horus at Edfu and Hathor at Dendera (Ptolemaic Period).

178. Barta, "Kult," *LÄ* 3:841–44. Finnestad interprets some of the symbols and meanings of this ritual in Chapter 5.

179. At larger temples, the king or officiating priest was probably assisted in the sanctuary by several other priests. The question of who went into the sanctuary was an issue of ritual power subject to the negotiation intrinsic to ritual power. Incense is a gummy resin. When burned, it gives off a white, intensely aromatic smoke. Incense was burned in all Egyptian offering rituals.

180. In the morning ritual, water libations were mostly purificatory, but those preparatory to the food offerings may have symbolized the renewal of life; J. F. Borghouts, "Libation," *LÄ* 3:1014–15. The fullest representation of the offering ritual is preserved in the Ritual of Amenhotep, which served the cultus of the deified Amenhotep I (Dynasty 18). The food ritual for the daily meal was observed not only in royal cult complexes but also in divine cult complexes. The principal sources for our knowledge of the food ritual are two papyri from the time of Ramesses II, the hypostyle hall of Sety I at Karnak, and the first court of the temple of Ramesses III at Medinet Habu—all from Dynasty 19.

181. Evidence from the temples of Horus at Edfu and Isis at Philae points to midday and evening rituals during the Ptolemaic Period, and the rituals probably existed long before that. They were shorter than the morning ritual; they took place outside the sanctuary in an adjacent room; and they featured libations, censings, additional purifications, and simple offerings. See Barta, "Kult." *LÄ* 3:845.

182. Offerings were part of many ceremonies other than the daily temple rituals. They were integral to festivals and to private mortuary rituals like the Opening of the Mouth.

183. Gertie Englund, "Gifts to the Gods—a Necessity for the Preservation of Cosmos and Life: Theory and Praxis," in *Gifts to the Gods: Proceedings of the Uppsala Symposium 1985*, ed. Tullia Linders and Gullög Nordquist, BOREAS 15 (1987), p. 57. One might add to the list: doves, lettuce, cucumbers, squash, melons, raisins, fresh water, flowers, clothing and adornment, and various cultic implements. The great majority of food offerings were not meat, but in meat offerings a priest tested the animal's ritual purity both before and after its slaughter by inspecting blood collected in a bowl; Arne Eggebrecht, "Schlachten," *LÄ* 5:639. During at least the New Kingdom, pigs were sacrificed, although they later became taboo; Wolfgang Helck, "Schwein," *LÄ* 5:763–64. From an early period, sheep, their milk, and wool seem to have been taboo for temple use; Lothar Störk, "Schaf," *LÄ* 5:523.

184. It was E. B. Tylor who set forth the thesis that sacrifice is universally a gift to the gods and a part of the divine/human exchange through which humankind seeks to secure gods' favor, minimize their hostility, pay them homage, and express self-abnegation; *Primitive Culture* (London: J. Murray, 1871). I disagree with many of Tylor's presuppositions and conclusions and with any attempt to explain the various types of offering and sacrifice by a single concept or device. Nonetheless, "offering a gift to god" is a conscious motivation in many types of sacrifice, and it was certainly so in ancient Egypt.

185. Erik Hornung, "Gott–Mensch–Beziehung," *LÄ* 2:788–89; Hornung, *Conceptions of God* [n. 2], pp. 203-6 [*Eine und Vielen*, pp. 198–99]. Hornung's interpretation of Egyptian offerings emphasizes the primacy of *do quia dedisti* over *do ut des*.

186. Englund, in *Gifts to the Gods*, ed. Linders and Nordquist, pp. 61, 63.

187. For a discussion of other types of *ankh*-symbols, see L. Bell's Appendix II in Chapter 4.

188. Hartwig Altenmüller, "Opfer," *LÄ* 4:580.

189. Alan B. Lloyd, "Psychology and Society in the Ancient Egyptian Cult of the Dead," in *Religion and Philosophy in Ancient Egypt* [n. 20], ed. Simpson, p. 122.

190. Paul John Frandsen, "Trade and Cult," in *The Religion of the Ancient Egyptians: Cognitive Structures and Popular Expressions*, ed. Gertie Englund, BOREAS 20 (1989), pp. 99–100.

191. Wolfgang Helck, "Rituale," *LÄ* 5:273.

192. Englund, in *Gifts to the Gods*, ed. Linders and Nordquist, p. 57; Troy, *Patterns of Queenship* [n. 116], pp. 41, 43. Troy (p. 41) says, ". . . Osiris takes on the qualities of the self–generating god."

193. Englund, in *Gifts to the Gods*, ed. Linders and Nordquist, p. 57; Hornung, *Idea into Image* [n. 18], p. 142 [*Geist*, p. 142].

194. Explicit equations of offerings with Maʿat are attested in the Berlin Service Book; see Alexandre Moret, *Le rituel du culte divin journalier en Égypte* (Paris: Ernest Leroux, 1902), pp. 141–42. Emily Teeter reminded me of this reference.

195. Hornung, *Conceptions of God* [n. 2], pp. 213–16 [*Eine und Vielen*, pp. 209–12]; Hornung, *Idea into Image*, pp. 131–32 [*Geist*, pp. 131–32]; Altenmüller, "Opfer," *LÄ* 4:581; Frandsen, in *Religion of the Ancient Egyptians*, ed. Englund, p. 104.

196. Henri Hubert and Marcel Mauss were the first to argue that the distinctive characteristic of sacrifice is the object's mediation of the relationship between donor ("sacrifier"), officiant ("sacrificer"), and god; *Sacrifice: Its Nature and Function*, trans. W. D. Halls (Chicago: University of Chicago Press, 1964), first published as "Essai sur la nature et la fonction du sacrifice," *L'Année Sociologique* 2 (1897–98): 29–138. Their thesis has been refined by many, including Valerio Valeri, *Kingship and Sacrifice: Ritual and Society in Ancient Hawaii,* trans. Paula Wissing (Chicago: University of Chicago, 1985). Valeri argues that sacrifice, rather than simply reflecting the relationship among the parties, creates it; for only in the course of ritual action do the gods acquire their full symbolic character. Each sacrifice is a function of its purpose and occasion, the god(s) to whom it is offered, its content and symbolic value, and its manipulation and apportionment (p. 38). The object offered must simultaneously evoke the god, the donor, and the donor's hoped-for results (pp. 50–51). The roles of the Hawaiian king as both the "sacrifier" of the community and the "sacrificer" for the community (p. 140) parallel the roles of the ancient Egyptian king.

197. Edmund Leach, *Culture and Communication: The Logic by Which Symbols Are Connected* (Cambridge: Cambridge University Press, 1976), pp. 83–84; J. H. M. Beattie, "On Understanding Sacrifice," in *Sacrifice,* ed. M. F. C. Bourdillon and Meyer Fortes (London and New York: Academic Press, 1980), p. 30.

198. Mauss, *The Gift: Forms and Functions of Exchange in Archaic Societies,* trans. Ian Cunnison (New York: Norton, 1967), p. 10; first published as "Essai sur le don: Forme et raison de l'échange dans les sociétés archaïques," *L'Année Sociologique,* second series 1 (1923–24): 30–186 (reprint in Mauss, *Sociologie et anthropologie,* 3d ed. [Paris: Quadrige/Presses Universitaires de France, 1989], pp. 145–279).

199. Miriam Lichtheim, *Ancient Egyptian Literature* 1: *The Old and Middle Kingdoms* (Berkeley: University of California Press, 1973), p. 106. Her translation of *bit* by "loaf" is disputed; other scholars prefer "character." Either translation supports the point made here.

200. Englund, in *Gifts to the Gods* [n. 183], ed. Linders and Nordquist, p. 64. Another factor enabling the officiant to substitute representations for material objects was the belief that form conveys essence.

201. Ibid., pp. 60–61. Besides signifying that the king offers himself, the scene, as Englund notes, may also indicate that the king and his gift will remain permanently present in the temple, transcending his death.

202. In the Memphite Theology (lines 55–58), Ptah creates the gods, humankind, and all phenomena by pronouncing their names; Lichtheim, *Ancient Egyptian Literature,* 1:54–55.

203. Frandsen, in *Religion of the Ancient Egyptians* [n. 190], ed. Englund, pp. 100–101, 104–5; Englund, in *Gifts to the Gods,* ed. Linders and Nordquist, p. 60. Emily Teeter advises me that many kings captioned the offering of the rebus of their royal name "*ḥnk m3ᶜt n——*" "presenting Maᶜat to ——." The scenes of Ramesses IV at the Khonsu Temple were a notable exception to this captioning.

204. Englund, in *Gifts to the Gods,* ed. Linders and Nordquist, p. 64; Arne Eggebrecht, "Brandopfer," *LÄ* 1:848–49.

205. Walter Burkert hypothesizes that hunting was a formative, prehistoric antecedent of ritual sacrifice and its accompanying meal; in *Violent Origins* [n. 148], ed. Hamerton-Kelly, pp. 164–68, 212; and *Homo Necans: The Anthropology of Ancient Greek Sacrificial Ritual and Myth,* trans. Peter Bing (Berkeley: University of California Press, 1983); first published as *Homo Necans: Interpretationen altgriechischer Opferriten und Mythen,* Religionengeschichtliche Versuche und Vorarbeiten 32 (Berlin: de Gruyter, 1972).

206. The provisions given to the royal and private temple statues supported the retired government officials who tended them. On private mortuary cultuses, see L. Bell's detailed description of the Theban Festival of the Valley in Chapter 4.

207. Cf. Walter Burkert, "Offerings in Perspective: Surrender, Distribution, Exchange," in *Gifts to the Gods* [n. 183], ed. Linders and Nordquist, p. 46.

208. W. Robertson Smith hypothesized that sacrifice originated in and focuses on the ritual meal of communion between humankind and god, which establishes bonds of unity among participants; *Lectures on the Religion of the Semites,* first Series: *The Fundamental Institutions* (Edinburgh: A. & C. Black, 1889). Insofar as Robertson Smith believed that all communion meals are totemic and that all sacrifices originated in a totemic meal, he is wrong. Nonetheless, many sacrificial meals are experienced as communion with god; see Meyer Fortes, "Preface," in *Sacrifice* [n. 197], ed. Bourdillon and Fortes, p. xvi. Such was the case in Egypt, I believe. The so-called "Cannibal Hymn" of Unas (Utterances 273–74 of the Pyramid Texts, Dynasty 5) may give coarse expression to the king's communion with the gods through sacrificial meals celebrated both during his lifetime and thereafter in his mortuary cultus. See Lichtheim, *Ancient Egyptian Literature* [n. 199], 1:36–38.

209. Hartwig Altenmüller, "Feste," *LÄ* 2:171–91.

210. For details on some transregional, multitemple, and local observances, see Chapter 5. C. Bell observes that many ritual systems construct central rites from local rites and local rites from simplified central rites, often for the purpose of extending the central government's influence over local areas; *Ritual Theory, Ritual Practice* [n. 147], pp. 128–29.

211. The sidereal calendar began the new year in the season of inundation at the heliacal rising of the star Sothis following a period of absence from the sky. In the modern calendar this occurs, in the locale of ancient Memphis, about July 19th. The sidereal year averaged $365\frac{1}{4}$ days. The major festival of this type was the Coming Out of Sothis (*prt spdt*). The lunar month averages $29\frac{1}{2}$ days. A famous lunar festival was the Beautiful Festival of the Valley (*ḥb nfr n jnt*) at Thebes. It began on the new moon of the tenth month; Erhart Graefe, "Talfest," *LÄ* 6:187. See Chapter 4 for details of this festival.

212. For further information on ancient Egypt's calendars, see Chapter 4.

213. On Opening the Year, see Chapter 5.

214. For details, including further discussion of *Opet*'s date, see Chapter 4. *Opet* originated as a local festival in Thebes and took on transregional importance.

215. See Chapter 2; also, Altenmüller, "Feste," *LÄ* 2:175–76, 181.

216. Emma Brunner-Traut, "Minfest," *LÄ* 4:141–43. This agricultural festival was not the ceremony of Climbing for Min mentioned in Chapter 2. The latter was a royal festival observed in royal cult complexes.

217. For details, see Chapter 5.

218. For details, see Chapter 5.

219. For details, see Chapter 4. This festival of the dead was local. Throughout Egypt, however, kin went to necropolises to provide offerings for the deceased and to feast and drink boisterously, transferring vitality to the relatively static order of the dead. They did so in conjunction with several lunar festivals (Beginning of the Month and Beginning of the Second Half of the Month) and a number of transregional festivals (e.g., Opening of the Year, *w3g*, Thoth, Sokar, First Day of the Year [*tpj rnpt*], Departure of Min, and the Five Extra Days). See Ursula Verhoeven, "Totenfeste," *LÄ* 6:645. Egyptians believed that the deceased could simultaneously be with Osiris in the Netherworld and with family in this world. Many cultures think of multilocality as a trait the dead share with the gods. See

Mircea Eliade, "Mythologies of Death: An Introduction," in *Religious Encounters with Death* [n. 38], ed. Reynolds and Waugh, pp. 18–19.

220. For details, see Chapter 5.

221. For details, see Chapter 2.

222. Festivals were also observed for divinized individuals other than kings—for example, Queen Ahmose-Nefertari (Dynasty 18) and Imhotep, the architect of King Djoser (Dynasty 3).

223. On this assembly of the gods, see Chapter 2.

224. See also Chapter 4.

225. On the statue burial, see Chapter 2; on the *ka*, see Chapter 4.

226. The sequence of events listed in this paragraph is not certain.

227. See Chapter 2.

228. See Chapter 2.

229. Wolfgang Helck, "Festleiter," *LÄ* 2:192. In the New Kingdom, the leader was called *sšm-ḥb* of the god.

230. Offering quantities were an index of festivals' importance. According to the Medinet Habu calendar of Ramesses III (Dynasty 19), the gargantuan offerings during the *Opet*-festival included 11,341 extralarge loaves of bread and 385 jugs of extrastrong beer. See Harold H. Nelson and Uvo Hölscher, *Work in Western Thebes 1931–33*, Oriental Institute Communications 18 (Chicago: University of Chicago Press, 1934), p. 58.

231. For details about festival processions, see Chapters 4 and 5.

232. From Papyrus Leiden I 350, Strophe 60, as translated by Hellmut Brunner in Walter Beyerlin (ed.), *Near Eastern Religious Texts Relating to the Old Testament*, trans. John Bowden (London: SCM Press; Philadelphia: Westminster Press, 1978), p. 23; first published in German in *Religionsgeschichtliches Textbuch zum Alten Testament* (Göttingen: Vandenhoeck & Ruprecht, 1975), pp. 49–50.

233. Readers not familiar with Egyptian religion and culture will find introductory information complementary to this chapter's in Chapter 4. Before reading Chapter 2, they may wish to consult Chapter 4's Introduction—the sections on *Maʿat*: Order; Chaos: Disorder; Secular and Sacred Time; and Components of Personhood—and Divine Kingship and the Royal *Ka*. Before reading Chapter 3, they may wish also to consult Chapter 4's The Temple and the People, from the beginning through the text at note 31 and from the text at note 38 through the end of the section.

234. Old and Middle Kingdom divine cult complexes are not well represented in the extant data.

235. The earliest example, an isolated one, dates to Dynasty 13.

Chapter 2: Royal Cult Complexes of the Old and Middle Kingdoms

1. Barry J. Kemp describes their function in the following manner: "[The pyramid temples should] be regarded first and foremost as temples for the royal statues with a royal tomb attached to each, which, acting as a huge reliquary, gave enormous authority to what was, in essence, an ancestor cult and an important factor in the stability of government." In B. G. Trigger, B. J. Kemp, D. O'Connor, and A. B. Lloyd, *Ancient Egypt: A Social History* (Cambridge: Cambridge University Press, 1983), p. 85.

2. See David P. Silverman, "Divinity and Deities in Ancient Egypt," in *Religion in Ancient Egypt,* ed. Byron E. Shafer (Ithaca: Cornell University Press, 1991), pp. 58–87.

3. By "symbolic architecture," I mean architecture that is not intended to be used for earthly, human activities, but which copies or represents an ancient, mythological prototype. Such architecture recreates the original building as well as its religious or historical environment. In German it is called *darstellende Architektur.*

4. Herbert Ricke was the first scholar to demonstrate a possible modern approach to Egyptian religious architecture when he wrote his astonishing but controversial *Bemerkungen zur ägyptischen Baukunst des Alten Reiches,* 2 vols., BeiträgeBf 4 and 5 (1944, 1950). He was also the last architectural historian daring enough to propose a comprehensive solution to the problem of meaning.

5. Paule Posener-Kriéger and Jean Louis de Cenival, *Hieratic Papyri in the British Museum,* 5th ser., *The Abu Sir Papyri* (London: British Museum, 1968); Paule Posener-Kriéger, *Les archives du temple funéraire de Néferirkarê-Kakaï* 1–2, BdÉ 65 (1976). Miroslav Verner of the Czechoslovakian expedition at Abusir has since found many more fragments, which are being studied by Paule Posener-Kriéger.

6. For a history of the buildings constructed during Dynasties 1–2, see Jean-Philippe Lauer, "Le premier temple de culte funéraire en Égypte," *BIFAO* 80 (1980): 45–67. This chapter will not address the old Egyptological question: Did the kings of the early dynasties build one or more tombs, and which were the "real" ones and which cenotaphs? In this chapter I assume that the Abydos tombs were the royal tombs and that the mastabas at Saqqara must have served another purpose.

7. Barry J. Kemp, "Abydos and the Royal Tombs of the First Dynasty," *JEA* 52 (1966): 13–22; David O'Connor, "New Funerary Enclosures (*Talbezirke*) of the Early Dynastic Period at Abydos," *JARCE* 26 (1989): 51–86.

8. In Egyptian iconography, the royal "palace" is usually depicted with a double gate.

9. Near the center of the court of the enclosure of Khasekhemwy were recently found the remains of an artificial hill covered with brick paving, suggesting that other enclosures might have had such a hill also. See O'Connor, "New Funerary Enclosures," *JARCE* 26 (1989): 54.

10. The possibility remains that a few more enclosures are hidden between enclosures E, A, and B in the south and G in the north.

11. Werner Kaiser, "Ein Kultbezirk des Königs Den in Sakkara," *MDAIK* 41 (1985): 47–60.

12. The constructions are represented as places for the performance of royal funerary ceremonies in the wall decoration of private tombs from the Old Kingdom on. See Jürgen Settgast, *Untersuchungen zu altägyptischen Bestattungsdarstellungen,* ADAIK 3 (1963). For their accommodation of royal funerary statues, see Werner Kaiser, "Zu den königlichen Talbezirken der 1. und 2. Dynastie in Abydos und zur Baugeschichte des Djoser-Grabmals," *MDAIK* 25 (1969): 1–21; Jean-Philippe Lauer, "A propos des vestiges des murs à redans encadrés par les 'tombs of the courtiers' et des 'forts' d'Abydos," *MDAIK* 25 (1969): 79–84; Wolfgang Helck, "Zu den 'Talbezirken' in Abydos," *MDAIK* 28 (1972): 95–99.

13. Peter Kaplony, "Gottespalast und Götterfestungen in der ägyptischen Frühzeit," *ZÄS* 88 (1962–63): 5–16. Heinrich Schäfer (*Ein Bruchstück altägyptischer Annalen* [Berlin: Königl. Akademie der Wissenschaften, 1902], pp. 16, 19) sug-

gested that the fortresses of the gods might be identical with the royal tombs of the early dynastic period, an idea repeated by Werner Kaiser (*MDAIK* 25 [1969]: 20 n. 4). Rainer Stadelmann ("Die ḫntjw-š, der Königsbezirk š n pr-ꜥ ꜣ und die Namen der Grabanlagen der Frühzeit," Supplement to *BIFAO* 81 [1981]: 161) instead suggests connecting the names of the fortresses of the gods only to the funerary enclosures in the desert. In addition, he carefully tries to link the names of the fortresses to another term that plays an important role from the Fourth to the Sixth Dynasties, the š (lake, basin), which he sees as the term for the whole royal funerary complex (Adolf Erman and Hermann Grapow, ed., *Wörterbuch der aegyptischen Sprache* [Leipzig: J. C. Hinrichs, 1926–31], 4:397–98). As a result, Stadelmann prefers the translation "complex" of the gods, rather than "fortress" of the gods.

14. We know from Herodotus, *History* 2.99, that Menes built such a structure, the "White Fortress," at Memphis. (For text and translation see *Herodotus*, trans. A. D. Godley, Loeb Classical Library [London: William Heinemann; New York: G. P. Putnam's Sons, 1931], 1:384–87.) The writing of *jnbw ḥḏ* with three signs for walls during the reign of Djoser (John Garstang, *Maḥâsna and Bêt Khallâf*, ERA 7 [1903], pl. 9) suggests that several such enclosures were built at Memphis after the time of Menes.

15. There is no evidence for an identification of this name with the Djoser complex. Names of more fortresses of the period of Djoser are known; see, for example, Garstang, *Maḥâsna and Bêt Khallâf*, pl. 8.

16. The development of the names of the Egyptian nomes from the predynastic standards shows the importance of the standards. The *nṯr*-hieroglyph for "god" or "divine" also depicts such a fetish. For a general discussion, see Erik Hornung, *Conceptions of God in Ancient Egypt: The One and the Many*, trans. John Baines (Ithaca: Cornell University Press, 1982).

17. Werner Kaiser, "Einige Bemerkungen zur ägyptischen Frühzeit I," *ZÄS* 84 (1959): 119–32; Peter Munro, "Bemerkungen zu einem Sedfest-Relief in der Stadtmauer von Kairo," *ZÄS* 86 (1961): 61–74.

18. David O'Connor, "The Status of Early Egyptian Temples: An Alternative Theory," in *The Followers of Horus: Studies Dedicated to Michael Allen Hoffman, 1944–1990*, ed. Renée Friedman and Barbara Adams, Egyptian Studies Association Publication 2, Oxbow Monographs 20 (Oxford: Oxbow; Bloomington, Ind.: David Brown, 1992), pp. 83–98.

19. The temple enclosure of Osiris at Abydos (not to be confused with the funerary enclosures in the desert).

20. Even Senwosret I seems to have constructed such a fortress. See Pierre Lacau and Henri Chevrier, *Une chapelle de Sésostris Iᵉʳ à Karnak* (Cairo: IFAO, 1969), pp. 67–68, 208, pls. 21–22. The names of the Mansions of Millions of Years and other temples of the New Kingdom are occasionally written within the picture of a fortified enclosure, certainly with the intention of stressing their continuity with the ancient fortresses of the gods.

21. That the "Followers of Horus" traveled in boats can be concluded from the Palermo Stone, where the word is written with a boat, and from the placement of the standards of the gods on the prows of later divine barques. For visiting gods, see also Ursula Rössler-Köhler, "Götterbesuch," *LÄ* 2:669–71.

22. David O'Connor found twelve 30-m-long wooden boats buried at the northern end of the east side of the funerary enclosure of King Khasekhemwy at Abydos. See O'Connor, in *Followers of Horus*, ed. Friedman and Adams, pp. 83–98.

23. Because of the steep slope east of the pyramid of Senwosret III, his boat burials were placed along the south side of the enclosure.

24. Apparently the principle items brought to the royal treasury were different kinds of oils. Such deliveries would explain the enormous quantities of clay and stone vessels found in the actual royal tombs of the first three dynasties.

25. The king's victory over enemies, hunts, animal combats, boats, processions of the standards of the gods, etc. are already the main subjects of such early images as the painting in a chieftain's tomb at Hierakonpolis and the Narmer Palette. These still play a prominent role in the function of the later pyramid temples and consequently in their decorative program.

26. We find this palace represented again in the southeast corner of the Djoser complex at Saqqara. The last remnants of these palaces seem to be the palaces of the mortuary temples of the New Kingdom, which are placed in a corresponding spot, namely to the left behind the entrance.

27. For Khasekhemwy, see O'Connor, "New Funerary Enclosures," *JARCE* 26 (1989): 54. For Hierakonpolis, see J. E. Quibell and F. W. Green, *Hierakonpolis II*, ERA 5 (1902), pp. 5–6. For Heliopolis, see Herbert Ricke, "Der 'Hohe Sand in Heliopolis'," *ZÄS* 71 (1935): 107–11. Abydos plays a major role in the development of the royal cult complexes of the Second and Third Dynasties.

28. The best known example is the stela of King Djet from his tomb at Abydos. Fig. 4a is based on a three-dimensional representation of this image; see Ludwig Borchardt's reconstruction of an alabaster statue base in the shape of a fortress of the gods from Mit Rahina (Egyptian Museum, Cairo). It probably bore the figure of a squatting falcon; see Borchardt, "Miscellen: Zwei Sockel," *ZÄS* 41 (1904): 85–86. For a similar combination see *Geschenk des Nils: Aegyptische Kunstwerke aus Schweizer Besitz* (Basel: Schweizerischer Bankverein, 1978), object no. 75, pp. 26–27 and pl. 75. For the Horus on his palace as a cult object, see Alan H. Gardiner, ed., *The Temple of King Sethos I at Abydos*, vol. 3, *The Osiris Complex* (London: Egypt Exploration Society; Chicago: University of Chicago Press, 1938), pl. 16.

29. Kaplony, "Gottespalast und Götterfestungen," *ZÄS* 88 (1962–63): 5–16.

30. At present it is not possible to answer questions about tax collection, revenue distribution, and the struggle for political power in early dynastic Egypt. That the absolute power of the king was contested is suggested by the replacement of the Horus-falcon with the symbol of the god Seth in the reign of Peribsen; by wars against the northerners under Khasekhem that resulted in the reunification of Egypt under Khasekhemwy; and finally by the looting and burning of royal tombs during the first dynasties.

31. For good examples of the processions of standards during the *Sed*-festival, see Hermann Kees, *Die grosse Festdarstellung*, vol. 3 of *Das Re-Heiligtum des Königs Newoser-Re (Rathures)*, ed. Friedrich Wilhelm Freiherr von Bissing (Leipzig: J. C. Hinrichs, 1928), pls. 4, 6, 13; Edouard Naville, *The Festival-Hall of Osorkon II in the Great Temple of Bubastis (1887–1889)*, EEF 10 (London: Kegan Paul, Trench, Trübner 1892), numerous pls.

32. Kees, *Die grosse Festdarstellung*, pp. 8–9; Jürgen Brinks, *Die Entwicklung der königlichen Grabanlagen des Alten Reiches*, Hildesheimer Ägyptologische Beiträge 10 (Hildesheim: Gerstenberg, 1979), p. 80.

33. Kees, *Die grosse Festdarstellung*, pp. 28, 53, pls. 9 [193], 10 [198, 201–4]; Naville, *Osorkon II*, pls. 5, 13, 25.

34. Kees, *Die grosse Festdarstellung*, pp. 27–28. For an official commanded by the

king to bring the cult images of Horus and Isis from Hierakonpolis to the residence at *Jt-t3wy*, see William C. Hayes, "Ḥoremkhaʿuef of Nekhen and his Trip to It-towe," *JEA* 33 (1947): 3–11.

35. Eric Uphill, "The Egyptian Sed-Festival Rites," *JNES* 24 (1965): 365–83 (esp. 378–79).

36. Lacau and Chevrier, *Chapelle de Sésostris Iᵉʳ* [n. 20], pp. 67–68, 208, pls. 21–22. The fortress has not been identified. For the celebration of the *Sed*-festival in the palace complex, see Ricke, *Bemerkungen AR* [n. 4], 1:148–50 n. 268.

37. Following Jean Vercoutter, *L'Égypte et la vallée du Nil* (Paris: Presses Universitaires de France, 1992), 1:200, 222.

38. Only two kings of the Second Dynasty (Peribsen and Khasekhemwy) built their tombs and funerary enclosures at Abydos. The tombs of the first four kings of the dynasty seem to be located at Saqqara. Neither of these tombs nor the matching funerary enclosures in the desert of Saqqara, west of the Djoser complex, have been thoroughly studied. See Rainer Stadelmann, *Die ägyptischen Pyramiden: Vom Ziegelbau zum Weltwunder*, Kulturgeschichte der antiken Welt 30 (Mainz: von Zabern; Darmstadt: Wissenschaftlichen Buchgesellschaft, 1985), pp. 30–31, 37 (fig. 11).

39. Cecil M. Firth and J. E. Quibell, *The Step Pyramid* (Cairo: IFAO, 1935). Jean-Philippe Lauer, *La pyramide à degrés*, vols. 1–2, *L'architecture*; 3, *Compléments* (Cairo: IFAO, 1936, 1939); P. Lacau and J.-Ph. Lauer, *La pyramide à degrés*, vol. 4, *Inscriptions gravées sur les vases*; vol. 5, *Inscriptions à l'encre sur les vases* (Cairo: IFAO, 1959–1965). Jean-Philippe Lauer, *Études complémentaires sur les monuments du roi Zoser à Saqqarah*, *ASAE* Supp. 9 (Cairo: IFAO, 1948). Étienne Drioton and Jean-Philippe Lauer, *Sakkarah: The Monuments of Zoser* (Cairo: IFAO, 1939). Jean-Philippe Lauer, *Histoire monumentale des pyramides d'Égypte*, BdÉ 39 (1962), pp. 65–176. Kaiser, *MDAIK* 25 (1969): 1–21. Brinks, *Grabanlagen* [n. 32], pp. 11–47. Nabil M. A. Swelim strongly believes that the Djoser complex (which he identifies as the Netjerykhet complex since he believes Netjerykhet was probably *not* Djoser) represents an early culmination of stone building in Egypt rather than its beginning; an intermediate phase between the Khasekhemwy and Djoser complexes allowed for the development of new building techniques. See Swelim, *Some Problems on the History of the Third Dynasty*, Archaeological and Historical Studies 7 (Alexandria: Archaeological Society of Alexandria, 1983), p. 21. This theory cannot be easily dismissed; the unidentified funerary complex of Nebka (Sanakht) might fill the gap (although it should be noted that Swelim accepts neither the equation Nebka = Sanakht nor the view that the funerary complex is unidentified).

40. This structure may follow Memphite traditions such as the "white walls" of Memphis, which were the funerary enclosures of the kings of the Second and early Third Dynasties.

41. A structure with three stepped sides is known as early as the reign of King Adjib (Saqqara 3038). See Walter B. Emery, *Great Tombs of the First Dynasty* 1 (Cairo: Government Press, 1949), pp. 8, 82–94, pls. 21–35. However, the steps of this structure formed an actual staircase leading to the top of the building, and it cannot be compared to the stepped structure of pyramids, where a considerable distance in height existed between each of the inclined levels.

42. It is difficult to see a connection to the mound- or step-shaped constructions observed in the core of some First Dynasty tombs or to the Saqqara tombs of the Second Dynasty kings, which were apparently still flat.

43. Lauer, *La pyramide à degrés* [n. 39], 1:72; Lauer, "Premier temple," *BIFAO* 80 (1980): 45–67; Rainer Stadelmann, *Die grossen Pyramiden von Giza* (Graz: Akademische Druck- u. Verlaganstalt, 1990), p. 66.

44. The Djoser complex marks the culmination and end of the development of an early dynastic architectural form that had led to sophisticated architectural structures such as the building attached to the north side of the Step Pyramid. After a caesura of several generations we see in the reign of Sneferu the emergence, and under his successors the evolution, of the actual pyramid temple. See Ricke, *Bemerkungen AR* [n. 4], 2:101–2.

45. Ricke, *Bemerkungen AR*, 1:96–99, believes they represent the governmental throne rooms of Upper and Lower Egypt. Lauer, *Histoire monumentale* [n. 39], pp. 163–69, remains undecided.

46. Firth and Quibell, *Step Pyramid* [n. 39], pp. 69, 114–15, pl. 66. Examples of such statues from the Middle Kingdom onward confirm their affiliation with the *Sed*-festival.

47. Ibid., p. 113, pls. 57–58. For a similar base that may date to the Second Dynasty, see Dietrich Wildung, *Fünf Jahre Neuerwerbungen der Staatlichen Sammlung Ägyptischer Kunst München, 1976–1980* (Mainz: von Zabern, 1980), pp. 6–7.

48. Ricke, *Bemerkungen AR*, vol. 1.

49. Lauer, *Histoire monumentale*, pp. 209–11. One has to bear in mind, however, that all these complexes were left unfinished and that more interior structures may have been planned.

50. Following Vercoutter, *L'Égypte* [n. 37], 1:248.

51. A relief, probably from Huni's cult complex, is preserved. See Christiane Ziegler, *Catalogue des stèles, peintures et reliefs égyptiens de l'Ancien Empire et de la Première Période Intermédiaire* (Paris: Réunion des musées nationaux, 1990), pp. 54–57.

52. See Swelim, *Some Problems* [n. 39], who assumes nine royal funerary complexes: Nebka (Horus Khaba), Djeser-sa (Horus Sa), Teti (Horus Ba), Horus Sanakht, Horus Netjerykhet (whom most other scholars identify as Djoser), Djeserty (Horus Sekhemkhet), Nebkara, Neferka, and Huni (Horus Qahedjet?).

53. On Meidum, see Alan Rowe, "The Eckley B. Cox, Jr., Expedition Excavations at Meydûm, 1929–30," *Museum Journal* 22 (1931): 5–84; Vito Maragioglio and Celeste Rinaldi, *L'architettura delle piramidi menfite* (Rapallo: Canessa, 1964–77), 3:6–53. See also I. E. S. Edwards, *The Pyramids of Egypt*, rev. ed. (Harmondsworth: Penguin; New York: Viking Penguin, 1985), pp. 74–101; Stadelmann, *Die ägyptischen Pyramiden* [n. 38], pp. 80–105.

54. Rowe, "Cox Expedition Excavations," *Museum Journal* 22: 30–34.

55. Direct identification of the pyramid with the king seems unlikely. See K. P. Kuhlmann, "Die Pyramide als König? Verkannte elliptische Schreibweisen von Pyramidennamen des Alten Reiches," *ASAE* 68 (1982): 223–35. For an opposing view see Pierre Montet, "Reines et pyramides," *KÊMI* 14 (1957): 92–101, and others. An allusion to a certain degree of identification may be seen in the decoration of the pyramidions of Amenemhat III from Dahshur and of Khendjer from Saqqara, where a vertical inscription can be either read "viewing the beauty of Re" or interpreted as the face of the king looking out from the pyramid. See Dieter Arnold, *Der Pyramidenbezirk des Königs Amenemhet III. in Dahschur*, vol. 1, *Die Pyramide*, AVDAIK 53 (1987), p. 16 and pl. 38.

56. Dietrich Wildung, "Zur Deutung der Pyramide von Medum," *RdÉ* 21 (1969): 135–45, emphasizes aspects of the sun cultus, interpreting the pyramid as a predecessor of the sun temples of later dynasties.

57. W. M. Flinders Petrie, *Meydum and Memphis (III)*, BSAE 18 (1910), p. 2, pl. 2.

58. Barry J. Kemp, *Ancient Egypt: Anatomy of a Civilization* (London and New York: Routledge, 1989), p. 62, emphasizes the complete disappearance of the "sed-festival architecture," whereas Brinks, *Grabanlagen* [n. 32], pp. 115–21, tries to demonstrate a continuous development from the Djoser type to the pyramid temples of the Fourth Dynasty. The marked break in tradition cannot be denied, but at the same time elements of *Sed*-festival architecture reappear frequently in royal funerary architecture.

59. Hornung, *Conceptions of God* [n. 16], pp. 135–42.

60. A god's *ba* cannot be translated simply as his "soul"; the *ba* was the manifestation of his power. See Louis V. Žabkar, *A Study of the Ba Concept in Ancient Egyptian Texts*, SAOC 34 (1968); Žabkar, "Ba," *LÄ* 1:588–90.

61. Edwards, *Pyramids* [n. 53], pp. 102–63; Stadelmann, *Die ägyptischen Pyramiden* [n. 38], pp. 105–58.

62. There is no evidence that the numerous royal statues found in the Djoser complex received a cultus. However, in the First Dynasty tomb of King Djer at Abydos and at mastaba 3505 at Saqqara (time of King Qa'a) remains of wooden statues were recorded. See William Stevenson Smith, *A History of Egyptian Sculpture and Painting in the Old Kingdom*, 2d ed. (London: Geoffrey Cumberlege, 1949), p. 9.

63. The oldest statue chambers (*serdabs*) in private tombs are those in the mastabas of Khabausokar and Hesyra and in no. 3070 at Saqqara, all of which date to the transitional period between the Third and Fourth Dynasties.

64. Royal reliefs first appear on a temple gate of Khasekhemwy at Hierakonpolis and in the two groups of three stela niches in the underground apartments of the Step Pyramid and in the southern tomb of Djoser.

65. They are found at the mastabas of Hesyra, Khabausokar, and Akhetaa at Saqqara. See Hans Goedicke, "Das Verhältnis zwischen königlichen und privaten Darstellungen im Alten Reich," *MDAIK* 15 (1957): 57–67.

66. Ahmed Fakhry, *The Monuments of Sneferu at Dahshur* (Cairo: Government Printing Offices, 1959), 1:75–83, 98–104; Maragioglio and Rinaldi, *Architettura* [n. 53], 3:84–90.

67. Rainer Stadelmann, "Scheintür oder Stelen im Totentempel des AR," *MDAIK* 39 (1983): 237–41.

68. Maragioglio and Rinaldi, *Architettura*, 3:132–34; Rainer Stadelmann, "Die Pyramiden des Snofru in Dahschur," *MDAIK* 39 (1983): 230–34; Stadelmann, *Die ägyptischen Pyramiden* [n. 38], p. 104.

69. Jean-Philippe Lauer, "Le temple funéraire de Khéops," *ASAE* 46 (1947): 245–59; Lauer, "Note complémentaire sur le temple funéraire de Khéops," *ASAE* 49 (1949): 111–23; Maragioglio and Rinaldi, *Architettura*, 4:60–64.

70. Ricke, *Bemerkungen AR* [n. 4], 2:60–62.

71. See the chapters on "*Lichthof*" and "*Tornische*" in Diethelm Eigner, *Die monumentalen Grabbauten der Spätzeit in der Thebanischen Nekropole*, Untersuchungen der Zweigstelle Kairo 6 (Vienna: Österreichischen Akademie der Wissenschaften, 1984), pp. 116–23.

72. See George Andrew Reisner, *A History of the Giza Necropolis* (Cambridge: Har-

vard University Press, 1955), 2:4–5, figs. 5–7; Selim Hassan, *The Great Pyramid of Khufu and Its Mortuary Chapel*, Excavations at Gîza 10, Season 1938–39 (Cairo: Government Printing Offices, 1960), pp. 20–24, pls. 5–8; Hans Goedicke, *Re-used Blocks from the Pyramid of Amenemhet I at Lisht*, MMA Egyptian Expedition 20 (New York: MMA, 1971), pp. 8–23.

73. Georges Goyon, "La chaussée monumentale et le temple de la vallée de la pyramide de Khéops," *BIFAO* 67 (1969): 49–69. Recent attempts to excavate in the area by Zahi Hawass failed because of the opposition of the landowners.

74. Maragioglio and Rinaldi, *Architettura* [n. 53], 5:6–41. *Per-weru* (literally, "house of the great") is the ancient name for the entrance hall of pyramid temples.

75. Uvo Hölscher, *Das Grabdenkmal des Königs Chephren*, Veröffentlichungen der Ernst von Sieglin-Expedition 1 (Leipzig: J. C. Hinrichs, 1912); Maragioglio and Rinaldi, *Architettura* [n. 53], vol. 5.

76. In general see Ricke, *Bemerkungen AR* [n. 4], 2:86–102.

77. Bernhard Grdseloff, *Das ägyptische Reinigungszelt: Archäologische Untersuchung* (Cairo: IFAO, 1941); Ricke, *Bemerkungen AR*, 2:171–81. For embalming installations, see now Edward Brovarski, "The Doors of Heaven," *Orientalia* 46 (1977): 107–15; and James K. Hoffmeier, "The Possible Origins of the Tent of Purification in the Egyptian Funerary Cult," *SAK* 9 (1981): 167–77.

78. Posener-Kriéger, *Archives*, vols. 1–2 [n. 5].

79. See also Stadelmann, "Die ḫntjw-š" [n. 13], p. 160 n. 3.

80. Posener-Kriéger, *Archives*, 2:562.

81. Wendy Wood, "A Reconstruction of the Triads of King Mycerinus," *JEA* 60 (1974): 82–93.

82. These monumental platforms stood high above the water and were connected to the temple by a processional road. The Theban tomb of Amenmose depicts a ceremony during which the statue of the king, standing on a "podium" in the harbor in front of the temple gate, greeted the barque of the god. See Dieter Arnold, *Die Tempel Ägyptens: Götterwohnungen, Kultstätten, Baudenkmäler* (Zurich: Artemis and Winkler, 1992), fig. on p. 115.

83. For the meaning of these misnamed "Osiride" statues, see here note 135. Ricke, *Bemerkungen AR* [n. 4], 2:48–55, favors a reconstruction with seated statues of the king.

84. Stationary barques of hard stone are known from temples of the New Kingdom and later periods.

85. Ricke assumes that these two barques were placed in the two lateral chambers of the second unit. However, these narrow chambers are only 1.40 m wide and could not have contained large objects.

86. On the Abusir Papyri, see Posener-Kriéger, *Archives* [n. 5], 1:59–76, 2:550–53. The Ramesseum Papyri, dating to the reign of Senwosret I, contain forty-six scenes giving illustrations and instructions for the performance of a ritual. See Sir Alan Gardiner, *The Ramesseum Papyri* (Oxford: Griffith Institute, 1955). On the Mansions, see Luc Gabolde, "Les temples 'mémoriaux' de Thoutmosis II et Toutânkhamon," *BIFAO* 89 (1989): 175.

87. Compare Paul Barguet, "Un groupe d'enseignes en rapport avec les noms du roi," *RdÉ* 8 (1951): 10–11.

88. Ricke, *Bemerkungen AR* [n. 4], 2:54. A relief block with prisoners of war, which was found in the valley area (Hölscher, *Grabdenkmal* [n. 75], p. 110, figs. 162–63),

would fit thematically into the decoration of the causeway or of the pyramid temple court.

89. George A. Reisner, *Mycerinus: The Temples of the Third Pyramid at Giza* (Cambridge: Harvard University Press, 1931); Maragioglio and Rinaldi, *Architettura* [n. 53], 6:30–133.

90. See Ricke's reconstruction in *Bemerkungen AR,* 2: frontispiece.

91. Shepseskaf also introduced an offering chapel to his own tomb.

92. See Wood, "Reconstruction," *JEA* 60 (1974): 82–93.

93. Following Vercoutter, *L'Égypte* [n. 37], 1:264.

94. Gustave Jéquier, *Le mastabat faraoun* (Cairo: IFAO, 1928); Maragioglio and Rinaldi, *Architettura,* 6:134–67; Hans Wolfgang Müller, "Gedanken zur Entstehung, Interpretation und Rekonstruktion ältester ägyptischer Monumentalarchitektur," in *Ägypten Dauer und Wandel,* SDAIK 18 (1985), pp. 21–22.

95. Ricke, *Bemerkungen AR,* 2:30, 36. For details, see Peter Janoši, "Die Pyramidenanlagen der Königinnen des Alten und Mittleren Reiches" (Doctoral diss., University of Vienna, 1988), pp. 195–98.

96. Ricke, *Bemerkungen AR,* 2:30–35.

97. For example, see the story of the Papyrus Westcar, which describes the half-earthly origin of the kings of the Fifth Dynasty.

98. Despite suggestions by some scholars, there are no clear examples of false doors in the pyramid complexes of the Fourth Dynasty kings who preceded Shepseskaf. The area of the sanctuary of the Khufu pyramid temple is completely destroyed, but its elongated shape suggests five parallel statue shrines instead of a transverse hall with a false door in the center of a broad rear wall. In the pyramid temple of Khafre, five parallel, monumental statue or barque shrines are surrounded by a corridor with a 6 m wide recess in the rear wall. This flat niche is considered by many to be the frame for a false door, but such an assumption cannot be accepted. First, the width of the recess would require a false door with a proportional height of 12–18 m. Second, the function of a false door demands that it open out of a tumulus (mastaba or pyramid), so it would not have been placed in a wall with no connection to a tomb. This second argument also applies to the mortuary temple of Menkaure, which retains no trace of a recess for a false door in the rear wall of its central statue chamber.

99. Jean-Philippe Lauer, "Le temple haut de la pyramide du roi Ouserkaf à Saqqarah," *ASAE* 53 (1955): 119–33; Maragioglio and Rinaldi, *Architettura,* 7:10–43.

100. Goedicke, *Re-used Blocks* [n. 72], pp. 68–74 (redated to Userkaf based on a comparison with a similar, inscribed block found in 1991 at Lisht North by the Egyptian Expedition of the Metropolitan Museum); W. Stevenson Smith, *The Art and Architecture of Ancient Egypt,* rev. ed. with additions by William Kelly Simpson (New York: Penguin, 1981), pp. 126–29.

101. Smith, *Art and Architecture,* pp. 126–29.

102. Herbert Ricke, *Das Sonnenheiligtum des Königs Userkaf,* vol. 1, BeiträgeBf 7 (1965); Werner Kaiser, "Zu den Sonnenheiligtümern der 5. Dynastie," *MDAIK* 14 (1956): 104–16.

103. See Erich Winter, "Zur Deutung der Sonnenheiligtümer der 5. Dynastie," *WZKM* 54 (1957): 222–33.

104. Rainer Stadelmann has shown ("Das vermeintliche Sonnenheiligtum im Norden des Djoserbezirkes," *ASAE* 69 [1983]: 373–78) that there was no sun cul-

tus in the Djoser complex. The Harmakhis temple of Khafre at Giza, which can also be considered a kind of solar temple, was always isolated from the rest of the cult complex of the king.

105. Most of the funerary temples of this period have been excavated and published:

Sahure: Ludwig Borchardt, *Das Grabdenkmal des Königs S'a3ḥu-Re*ᶜ, vol. 1, *Der Bau*, Ausgrabungen 6 (1910), pp. 40–67; Maragioglio and Rinaldi, *Architettura* [n. 53], 7:44–111.

Neferirkare: Ludwig Borchardt, *Das Grabdenkmal des Königs Nefer-îr-ke³-Re*ᶜ, Ausgrabungen 5 (1909); Maragioglio and Rinaldi, *Architettura*, 7:112–75.

Niuserre: Ludwig Borchardt, *Das Grabdenkmal des Königs Ne-user-Re*ᶜ, Ausgrabungen 1 (1907), pp. 50–96; Maragioglio and Rinaldi, *Architettura*, 8:8–63.

Djedkare: Vito Maragioglio and Celeste Rinaldi, *Notizie sulle piramidi di Zedefrâ, Zedkarâ Isesi, Teti* (Turin: Artale, 1962), pp. 29–33; Maragioglio and Rinaldi, *Architettura*, 8:74–82.

Unas: A. Labrousse, J.-Ph. Lauer, and J. Leclant, *Mission Archéologique de Saqqarah*, vol. 2: *Le temple haut du complexe funéraire du roi Ounas*, BdÉ 73 (1977).

Teti: J.-Ph. Lauer and J. Leclant, *Mission Archéologique de Saqqarah*, vol. 1, *Le temple haut du complexe funéraire du roi Téti*, BdÉ 51 (1972).

Pepi I: Audran Labrousse, *Regards sur une pyramide* (Paris, 1992). Jean Leclant, *Recherches dans la pyramide et au temple haut du pharaon Pépi Iᵉʳ, à Saqqarah* (Leiden: Nederlands Instituut voor het Nabije Oosten, 1979). The temple of Merenre is the only one awaiting investigation.

Pepi II: Gustave Jéquier, *Le monument funéraire de Pepi II*, vol. 2, *Le temple* (Cairo: IFAO, 1938).

106. Dieter Arnold, *The Pyramid of Senwosret I*, MMA Egyptian Expedition 22 (New York: MMA, 1988), pp. 56–57.

107. The only major differences are found in the number and arrangement of the storerooms and in the method used to connect the causeway to the *per-weru* hall. For a structural analysis of these buildings, see Brinks, *Grabanlagen* [n. 32].

108. The pyramid temples of Sahure, Djedkare, and Unas have granite palm columns; that of Niuserre has granite papyrus columns; all others have granite, quartzite, and limestone pillars.

109. The gods are shown with three different types of chapels, the Upper Egyptian *per-wer*, the Lower Egyptian *per-nu*, and the *seh-neṭer* type. See Borchardt, *Ne-user-Re*ᶜ [n. 105], pp. 92–94, fig. 71; Ludwig Borchardt, *Das Grabdenkmal des Königs S'a3ḥu-Re*ᶜ, vol. 2: *Die Wandbilder: Text und Abbildungsblätter*, Ausgrabungen 7 (1913), pp. 36–38, pls. 19–21; Jéquier, *Pépi II* [n. 105], 2: pls. 46–60; William C. Hayes, *The Scepter of Egypt*, vol. 1, *From the Earliest Times to the End of the Middle Kingdom* (New York: MMA, 1953), p. 188.

110. Dieter Arnold, "Rituale und Pyramidentempel," *MDAIK* 33 (1977): 10–11.

111. The areas around the entrances to the pyramids of Sahure, Neferirkare, and Niuserre have not yet been investigated.

112. Janoši, "Pyramidenanlagen" [n. 95], pp. 275–78.

113. Remains of a satellite pyramid(?) have been found at the pyramid of Meidum. That of the Bent Pyramid is well preserved. However, no satellite pyramid was built for the northern pyramid of Sneferu. Remains of the subsidiary pyramid of Khufu were discovered in 1992. That of Khafre is completely destroyed. Menkaure built two queen's pyramids and one satellite pyramid. Userkaf had his satellite pyramid in the southwest corner of his complex. From Sahure on, all subsidiary pyramids stand in front of the southeast corner of the main pyramid. Senwosret II was apparently the last king to build a subsidiary pyramid.

114. Secondary burials have a long tradition in Egyptian history. The theory that the kings of the first dynasties built contemporary tombs at Abydos and Saqqara has been mentioned above. Djoser and Sekhemkhet owned two extensive burial installations in their funerary complexes at Saqqara; whether the satellite pyramids of the Fourth to Sixth Dynasties served the same purpose is unknown. Later, the kings of the Middle and New Kingdoms also had secondary burials, for example, at Abydos. Even the royal tombs of the New Kingdom in the Valley of the Kings are clearly divided into two distinct burial systems. The origin of these practices may lie in differing predynastic burial customs from such areas as Hierakonpolis, Abydos, Memphis, Heliopolis, Buto, and Sais.

115. Brinks, *Grabanlagen* [n. 32], terms the secondary pyramid a "*Sed*-festival funerary monument" (*Sedfestgrabmal*).

116. Samuel A. B. Mercer, *The Pyramid Texts in Translation and Commentary,* vols. 1–4 (New York: Longmans, Green, 1952); Jean Leclant, "Les textes des pyramides," in *Textes et langages de l'Égypte pharaonique, cent cinquante années de recherches, 1822–1972: Hommages à Jean-François Champollion,* BdÉ 64/2 (1973), 2:37–52.

117. Kurt Sethe, *Übersetzung und Kommentar zu den altägyptischen Pyramidentexte,* vols. 1–6 (Glückstadt and Hamburg: Augustin, 1935–62); Siegfried Schott, *Mythe und Mythenbildung im Alten Ägypten,* Untersuchungen zur Geschichte und Altertumskunde Aegyptens 15 (Leipzig: J. C. Hinrichs, 1945), pp. 1–6 and passim; Hermann Kees, *Der Götterglaube im Alten Aegypten,* Mitteilungen der Vorderasiatisch-Ägyptischen Gesellschaft 45 (Leipzig: J. C. Hinrichs, 1941; reprint, Berlin: Akademie-Verlag, 1983), pp. 183–86 and 241; James P. Allen, *The Inflection of the Verb in the Pyramid Texts,* Bibliotheca Aegyptia 2 (Malibu, Ca.: Undena, 1981), p. 512; Hartwig Altenmüller, "Pyramidentexte," *LÄ* 5:19–20.

118. For example, Siegfried Schott's controversial *Bemerkungen zum ägyptischen Pyramidenkult,* BeiträgeBf 5 (1950), pp. 131–252.

119. Jürgen Osing, "Zur Disposition der Pyramidentexte des Unas," *MDAIK* 42 (1986): 131–44.

120. I. E. S. Edwards, *Studies in Honor of Cyril Aldred,* forthcoming. The kings who preceded Khufu seem to have been buried in wooden coffins, not stone sarcophagi, suggesting that the conception of the king's rebirth from a granite coffer was new.

121. The corresponding spells of the Pyramid Texts cover the walls of the eastern half of the crypt (burial chamber).

122. See, for example, Erik Hornung, *Ägyptische Unterweltsbücher* (Zurich and Munich: Artemis, 1972; 2d ed., 1984), pp. 25–30; Hornung, *Tal der Könige: Die Ruhestätte der Pharaonen* (Zurich and Munich: Artemis, 1982), pp. 103–86; trans. by David Warburton under the title *The Valley of the Kings: Horizon of Eternity* (New York: Timken, 1990), pp. 71–124, 135–164; Hornung, *Die Nachtfahrt der Sonne: Eine altägyptische Beschreibung des Jenseits* (Zurich and Munich: Artemis & Winkler, 1991).

123. The only representation of a royal Egyptian funeral is that of Tutankhamun, which appears not in a funerary temple but in the extraordinary decorative program of his tomb. See Hornung, *Tal der Könige,* p. 199, fig. 156 [*Valley of the Kings,*

p. 175, fig. 126]. There are numerous detailed representations of funeral processions and ceremonies in private tombs. See Settgast, *Bestattungsdarstellungen* [n. 12], and Hartwig Altenmüller, "Bestattungsritual," *LÄ* 1:745–65. These representations show that the private funeral ceremonies were actually performed in and around the tombs.

124. The three other royal meals mentioned in the Pyramid Texts were apparently served in heaven, where the king traveled with the sun during the remainder of the day.

125. Ricke, *Bemerkungen AR* [n. 4], 2:35–86; Posener-Kriéger, *Archives* [n. 5], 2:501–4, 544.

126. Relief fragments from the following pyramid temples also exist: Khufu, Khafre, Userkaf, Neferirkare, Niuserre, Djedkare, Unas, Teti, and Pepi I. Some come from later buildings where the blocks were reused. Considering the enormous wall space of the affiliated temples, the small number of extant fragments does not permit a comprehensive reconstruction of the temples' decorative programs. See Smith, *Sculpture and Painting* [n. 62], pp. 157–59, 176–85, 202–5; Goedicke, *Re-used Blocks* [n. 72]; Smith, *Art and Architecture* [n. 100], pp. 98, 126–29, 133–34. See note 105 for a list of publications describing these temples.

127. See Dieter Arnold, *Wandrelief und Raumfunktion in ägyptischen Tempeln des Neuen Reiches,* MÄS 2 (Berlin: Bruno Hessling, 1962).

128. Such statues were found in the following pyramid temples:

Neferefre: Wooden figures of foreign prisoners were found by Miroslav Verner; see Jean Leclant, "Fouilles et travaux en Égypte et au Soudan, 1984–1985," *Orientalia* 55 (1986): 253 and fig. 24.

Niuserre: Borchardt, *Ne-user-Reʿ* [n. 105], pp. 41–42 and fig. 24.

Djedkare: see Maragioglio and Rinaldi, *Architettura* [n. 53], 8:82.

Unas: Labrousse, Lauer, and Leclant, BdÉ 73 [n. 105], p. 131.

Teti: Lauer and Leclant, BdÉ 51 [n. 105], p. 84 no. 64 and fig. 73; pp. 98–99, no. 16; and pl. 32B.

Pepi I: J.-Ph. Lauer and J. Leclant, "Découverte de statues de prisonniers au temple de la pyramide de Pépi I," *RdÉ* 21 (1970): 55–62, figs. 1–6 and pls. 8–10.

Pepi II: Gustave Jéquier, *Le monument funéraire de Pépi II,* vol. 3, *Les approches du temple* (Cairo: IFAO, 1940), pp. 27–29 and pls. 47–48.

129. Following Vercoutter, *L'Égypte* [n. 37], 1:290, 316.

130. Dieter Arnold, "Vom Pyramidenbezirk zum 'Haus für Millionen Jahre'," *MDAIK* 34 (1978): 1–8.

131. Dieter Arnold, *Der Tempel des Königs Mentuhotep von Deir el-Bahari,* vol. 2, *Die Wandreliefs des Sanktuares,* AVDAIK 11 (1974), pls. 11, 19, 25, 30–33.

132. The oldest examples are found in the *Sed*-festival chapel court of the Djoser complex. See above and Firth and Quibell, *Step Pyramid* [n. 39], pp. 114–15, pl. 66.

133. Ibid., pls. 10, 12.

134. Arnold, *Senwosret I* [n. 106], pp. 58–63 with pls. 27–37; pp. 87–88, 94.

135. For example, the Mansions of Millions of Years of Hatshepsut, Thutmose III, Ramesses II, and Ramesses III. Colossal Osiride statues of Senwosret I have also been found at Karnak and Abydos. See Christian Leblanc, "Piliers et colosses de type 'osiriaque' dans le context des temples de culte royal," *BIFAO* 80 (1980): 69–89; Leblanc, "Le culte rendu aux colosses 'osiriaques' durant le Nouvel Empire," *BIFAO* 82 (1982): 295–311.

136. J. de Morgan, *Fouilles à Dahchour en 1894–1895* (Vienna: Adolphe Holzhausen, 1903), pp. 38–39.

137. Sir Flinders Petrie, Guy Brunton, and M. A. Murray, *Lahun II*, BSAE 33 (1923), p. 5. It is interesting to note that the paneled enclosure wall, which was abandoned after the Third Dynasty, reappears at the pyramid of Senwosret II, suggesting the archaistic tendencies seen more distinctly in the reign of the succeeding king. For the valley temple, see ibid., pp. 39–40.

138. Erich Lüddeckens, ed., and Ursula Kaplony-Heckel, *Ägyptische Handschriften*, vol. 1, Verzeichnis der orientalischen Handschriften in Deutschland 19/1 (Wiesbaden: Steiner, 1971), nos. 3, 42, 73, 81, 107–8, 271, 287, 307, 311, 421.

139. Dieter Arnold, "Das Labyrinth und seine Vorbilder," *MDAIK* 35 (1979): 2–5.

140. The two major components, the mortuary temple and the statue temple (which Ricke calls *Totenopfertempel* and *Verehrungstempel*), had already been locally separated and arranged in the same way in the Fifth Dynasty pyramid complex of Userkaf.

141. For a reconstruction drawing, see Dieter Arnold, *Building in Egypt: Pharaonic Stone Masonry* (New York: Oxford University Press, 1991), pp. 224–25, fig. 5.12. The valley temple has recently been re-excavated; see Josef Wegner, "Old and New Excavations at the Abydene Complex of Senwosret III. South Abydos: Burial Place of the Third Senwosret?" *KMT* 6,2 (Summer 1995): 58–71.

142. D. Randall-MacIver and A. C. Mace, *El Amrah and Abydos, 1899–1901*, Memoirs 23 (London: EEF, 1902), pp. 57–60; E. R. Ayrton, C. T. Currelly, and A. E. P. Weigall, *Abydos III*, Memoirs 25 (London: EEF, 1904), pp. 11–28.

143. Arnold, *Amenemhet III* [n. 55], 1:61–64.

144. Alan B. Lloyd, "The Egyptian Labyrinth," *JEA* 56 (1970): 81–100.

145. Pliny, *Natural History*, trans. D. E. Eichholz, Loeb Classical Library (Cambridge: Harvard University Press, 1962), 36.19.87–88.

146. Strabo, *The Geography of Strabo*, trans. Horace Leonard Jones, Loeb Classical Library (New York: G. P. Putnam's Sons, 1932), 17.1.37.

147. For a good late example of the chapels of the gods, see Naville, *Osorkon II* [n. 31], pls. 7–8, 12, 29, 31.

148. W. M. Flinders Petrie, G. A. Wainwright, and E. MacKay, *The Labyrinth, Gerzeh and Mazghuneh*, BSAE 21 (1912), pls. 23–29.

149. Firth and Quibell, *Step Pyramid* [n. 39], pls. 74, 77, 79, 79A.

150. *Memnonia* 1 (1990/91): frontispiece.

151. Other examples are: Amenemhat I from el-Lisht (see here fig. 33; Egyptian Museum, Cairo Jd'E 40484); Senswosret I (unidentified building, Open-Air Museum Karnak); Senwosret III and Amenemhat-Sobekhotep from Medamud (Rémy Cottevieille-Giraudet, *Rapport sur les fouilles de Médamoud, 1931: Les monuments du Moyen Empire*, FIFAO 9/1 [Cairo, 1933]; here fig. 36); Amenemhat III from Bubastis (Shafik Farid, "Preliminary Report on the Excavations of the Antiquities Department at Tell Basta, Season 1961," *ASAE* 58 [1964]: pl. 10); Amenhotep I from Qurna (H. E. Winlock, "A Restoration of the Reliefs from the Mortuary Temple of Amenhotep I," *JEA* 4 [1917]: 11–15); Merneptah from Memphis (W. M. Flinders Petrie, *The Palace of Apries, Memphis II*, BSAE 17 [1909], pl. 21); Pylon of Ramesseum (unpublished); Temple of Ramesses III at Medinet Habu (The Epigraphic Survey, *Medinet Habu*, vol. 5, *The Temple Proper*, Part I: The Portico, the Treasury, and Chapels adjoining the First Hypostyle Hall with marginal material from the Forecourt, OIP 83 [1957], pl. 251); Bubastis (Naville, *Osorkon II* [n. 35], pls. 17, 33).

152. Following Jürgen von Beckerath, *Handbuch der ägyptischen Königsnamen,* MÄS 20 (Munich and Berlin: Deutscher Kunstverlag, 1984), p. 159.

Chapter 3: New Kingdom "Mortuary Temples" and "Mansions of Millions of Years"

1. Adolf Erman, *Die Welt am Nil: Bilder aus dem alten Ägypten* (Leipzig: J. C. Hinrichs, 1936), p. 56; italics added.

2. Amelia B. Edwards: *A Thousand Miles up the Nile,* 2d ed. (London: Routledge and Sons, 1890; reprint, London: Century, 1982), p. 434. Edwards's writings and lectures were highly influential in developing British interest in Egyptology. She was a prime mover in founding the Egypt Exploration Fund, and at her death in 1892 her will established a professorship for Sir Flinders Petrie.

3. Edwards refers here to the opinion of Auguste Mariette (1821–1881), a French Egyptologist, who as curator at the Louvre went to excavate in Egypt and then persuaded the Khedive, Said Pasha, to intervene to protect the country's monuments from theft and destruction and to found the forerunner of the present Cairo Museum. Actively excavating in many places in Egypt to expand its collections, he laid the foundations for the Egyptian Antiquities Organization.

4. Edwards, *A Thousand Miles,* p. 435.

5. Ibid., p. 436.

6. The earliest European travelers, accustomed to finding castles and palaces of eighteenth-century kings and nobles as the most prominent monuments in their home countries, quite naturally assumed that these impressive structures in Egypt had served the same purpose. The pyramids, of course, were excepted, for classical authors had affirmed that they were royal tombs. When texts mentioned a town as the abode of a divinity, the visitors expected to find temples.

7. Edwards, *A Thousand Miles,* p. 434.

8. Harold H. Nelson, "The Identity of Amon-Re of United-with-Eternity," *JNES* 1 (1942): 127–55.

9. Ibid., pp. 136–37, figs. 3–23, reproducing the essential hieroglyphic inscriptions.

10. The form *ḥwt nṯr* is mainly found in monumental inscriptions dating from the reign of Sety I. Significant examples are found in Nelson, "Identity of Amon-Re," *JNES* 1 (1942): 136, figs. 3, 5; and 137, figs. 17, 19.

11. Ibid., p. 137, figs. 20–21 (Ramesses II); p. 136, fig. 9, and p. 137, fig. 22 (Ramesses III).

12. Ibid., p. 136, figs. 3, 5–6, 8; p. 137, figs. 17, 19.

13. Nelson clearly struggled with his translations; see ibid., pp. 127–28 n. 3.

14. Ibid., p. 137, figs. 17, 19.

15. Ibid., p. 137, fig. 17. I have twice added words in brackets, in the first instance where Nelson's text reproduction indicated a lacuna (i.e., a damaged part of the text). There the missing word must have denoted the particular section of the temple dedicated to Ramesses I. A parallel text (ibid., fig. 18) suggests that the word might have been *mnḳb,* "chapel," so I have filled that in. In the second case, there was obviously a sign omitted in the written text that must have been a preposition relating the part dedicated to Ramesses I to the whole temple, so I have supplied "within."

16. Ibid., p. 137, fig. 19, middle line.

17. A clear example is to be found in Sir Alan Gardiner, "Tuthmosis III Returns Thanks to Amūn," *JEA* 38 (1952): 14, n. 8: "The expression 'Mansion of Millions of Years' seems elsewhere always to refer to a funerary temple or cenotaph . . . , and I therefore doubt whether the Festival Hall at Karnak can here be meant." Eberhard Otto, *Topographie des thebanischen Gaues,* Untersuchungen zur Geschichte und Altertumskunde Aegyptens 16 (Berlin: Akademie-Verlag, 1952), p. 48, insists that the designation as "Mansion of Millions of Years" was characteristic of all the "commemorative temples" on the west side of Thebes. He proposed replacing the terms "funerary temple" and "mortuary temple" by "commemorative temple," believing the last to correspond better with the ritual function of these buildings.

18. Nelson, "Identity of Amon-Re," *JNES* 1 (1942): 127–55. In this article, Nelson limited his comments on related evidence from other than these three Ramesside temples to occasional remarks in footnotes.

19. Auguste Mariette-Bey, *Karnak: Étude topographique et archéologique* (Leipzig: J. C. Hinrichs, 1875), pl. 8r.

20. Hieroglyphic writing does not permit us to decide whether the word *pr,* "house," is only a parallel designation for "mansion" named later in the text or whether it should be translated "estate." On the *k3,* see Chapter 4. For the vizier *ʾIj-mr,* see Labib Habachi, "New Light on the Vizier Iymeru, Son of the Controller of the Hall, Iymeru," Supplement *BIFAO* 81 (1981): 29ff.; Habachi, *The Sanctuary of Heqaib,* Elephantine IV, AVDAIK 33 (1985), pp. 67–68; Anthony Spalinger, "Sobekhotep IV.," *LÄ* 5:1044, top.

21. Kurt Sethe, *Urkunden der 18. Dynastie,* 2d ed., Urkunden des ägyptischen Altertums IV.1 (Berlin: Akademie-Verlag, 1961), 25; C. R. Lepsius, *Denkmaeler aus Aegypten und Aethiopien III: Denkmaeler des Neuen Reichs* (Berlin: Nicolaische Buchhandlung, 1849; reprint, Geneva: Éditions de Belles-Lettres, 1972), sheets 3a, 3b.

22. Wolfgang Helck, *Urkunden der 18. Dynastie,* Urkunden des ägyptischen Altertums IV.17–22 (Berlin: Akademie-Verlag, 1955–58), pp. 1680–81; Lepsius, *Denkmaeler* III, 71a, 71b.

23. Adolf Erman and Hermann Grapow, eds., *Wörterbuch der Aegyptischen Sprache im Auftrage der Deutschen Akademien* (Leipzig: J. C. Hinrichs, 1926–31), 5:101. On *nḥḥ* and *ḏt* as terms for "eternity," see Chapter 4.

24. For examples, see Hellmut Brunner, *Die südlichen Räume des Tempels von Luxor,* AVDAIK 18 (1977), pls. 44, 46. In other cases, instead of "millions of years" the god offers "millions of jubilee festivals"; ibid., pl. 76. In pl. 77, the promise of millions of years is clothed in a different literary form: "I give you valor and victory, all the land, your years by the millions, hundred thousand lives." In pl. 74, the gift of the gods is expressed in writing as well as in emblematic form. Characteristic for Egyptian culture is the fact that the emblematic form is found at a considerably earlier date than the expression in writing; Dieter Arnold, *Der Tempel des Königs Mentuhotep von Deir el-Bahari,* vol. 2, *Die Wandreliefs des Sanktuares,* AVDAIK 11 (1974), frontispiece.

25. Sethe, *Urkunden* IV.1, p. 26; E. R. Ayrton, C. T. Currelly, and A. E. P. Weigall, *Abydos III,* Memoirs 25 (London: EEF, 1904), pls. 50, 52.

26. See Barry J. Kemp, "Abydos," *LÄ* 1:28–41; and J. Gwyn Griffiths, "Osiris," *LÄ* 4:623–33.

27. See Claude Vandersleyen, "Tetischeri," *LÄ* 6:458–59.

28. Raymond O. Faulkner, *A Concise Dictionary of Middle Egyptian* (Oxford: Griffith Institute, 1962), p. 105, records five different writings of the word.

29. William Kelly Simpson, *The Terrace of the Great God at Abydos: The Offering Chapels of Dynasties 12 and 13*, Publications of the Pennsylvania-Yale Expedition to Egypt 5 (New Haven: Peabody Museum, Yale University; Philadelphia: University Museum, University of Pennsylvania, 1974); David O'Connor, "The 'Cenotaphs' of the Middle Kingdom at Abydos," in *Mélanges Gamal Eddin Mokhtar* 2, BdÉ 97/2 (1985), pp. 161–77.

30. Ayrton et al., *Abydos III*, pls. 51–52, 61. A recent discussion, not seen at the time this chapter was prepared, is Stephen Harvey, "Monuments of Ahmose at Abydos," *Egyptian Archaeology* 4 (1994): 3–5.

31. Ayrton et al., *Abydos III*, pl. 61.

32. Unless some of the royal tombs of Dynasties 1 and 2 are to be considered as cenotaphs, their existence at Abydos is not attested before the Middle Kingdom. Comparable to cenotaphs in their function, however, are the *ka*-houses (*ḥwt-k3*) created by royal decrees at Coptos in Dynasties 6–8; see Hans Goedicke, "Koptosdekrete," *LÄ* 3:740.

33. See Kent Weeks, "Königsmumien," *LÄ* 3:535–38.

34. The Marquis of Northampton, Wilhelm Spiegelberg, and Percy E. Newberry, *Report on Some Excavations in the Theban Necropolis during the Winter of 1898–9* (London: Constable, 1908); Howard Carter, "Report on the Tomb of Zeser-Ka-Ra Amenhetep I," *JEA* 3 (1916): 147–54; Phillipe Derchain, "Débris du temple-reposoir d'Aménophis Ier et d'Ahmes Nefertari a Draᶜ Abou'l Nagaᶜ," *KÊMI* 19 (1969): 17–21.

35. George Foucart, *Tombes thébaines, Nécropole de Dirâᶜ Abu'n-Nága: Le tombeau d'Amonmos*, MIFAO 57.3,1 and 4 (1935), pls. 4, 6.

36. Jaroslav Černý, "Le culte d'Amenophis Ier chez les ouvriers de la Nécropole thébaine," *BIFAO* 27 (1927): 159–203 with 9 pls.

37. Otto, *Topographie* [n. 17], p. 57.

38. The case is quite similar to the one already mentioned above (see text between notes 12 and 13). How could a building be "united with life"? The name would make considerably more sense if the predicate was related to the king: "Aakheperkare is united-with-life," or even better "Aakheperkare has entered life." Faulkner, *Concise Dictionary* [n. 28], p. 202, offers a wide choice of possible translations for the verb *ḥnm*. The best solution might be "Aakheperkare is receiving life," remembering the frequent relief scenes showing a god extending the sign of life to the pharaoh.

39. The variety of titles is assembled in Otto, *Topographie*, pp. 115–16.

40. On the royal *ka*, see also Chapter 4.

41. Bernard Bruyère, *Deir el Médineh, année 1926: Sondage au temple funéraire de Thotmès II*, FIFAO 4.4 (1952), pp. 49–50.

42. Ibid., pls. 7–8. Representations of later times no longer show the barques with royal statues being dragged on sledges; rather they are carried by priests, and the statues in their shrines are hidden by veils.

43. Since this passage was written, I have become aware of the article by Luc Gabolde, "Les temples 'mémoriaux' de Thoutmosis II et Toutânkhamon," *BIFAO*

89 (1989): 127–78 and pls. 13–24, where he discusses parallel representations identified on blocks reused in the Second Pylon at Karnak.

44. Jürgen von Beckerath, "Mentuhotep II.," *LÄ* 4:66–68; also Dieter Arnold, *Der Tempel des Königs Mentuhotep von Deir el-Bahari* I, AVDAIK 8 (1974).

45. The situation is best illustrated by a model exhibited at The Metropolitan Museum of Art in New York; see William C. Hayes, *The Scepter of Egypt* (New York: MMA, 1990), 2:83, fig. 45.

46. Ibid., 2:90, fig. 49, where the upper part of one of these figures is illustrated.

47. On the peristyle courtyard, see Chapter 4.

48. On false doors, see Chapter 4.

49. Rainer Stadelmann, "Tempelpalast und Erscheinungsfenster in den Thebanischen Totentempeln," *MDAIK* 29 (1973): 221–42. Stadelmann, pp. 229–31, refers to a room in the southeast corner of Hatshepsut's upper terrace that has an opening like a window to the peristyle court. He believes the room to be a precursor of the palace buildings with a Window of Appearance found in the later New Kingdom temples of Western Thebes.

50. On the question of how long the cultus in these temples was maintained, scholarly opinion is divided. Dieter Arnold, *Die Tempel Ägyptens: Götterwohnungen, Kultstätten, Baudenkmäler* (Zürich: Artemis & Winkler, 1992), p. 35, believes it ceased after a few generations. Otto, *Topographie* [n. 17], p. 51, believes it continued for a very long time after a king's death. It is rather unlikely, however, that the cultus in Hatshepsut's temple continued for many years after her reign. And the cultus of Amenhotep III in his temple behind the colossi most probably ended with the Eighteenth Dynasty, although alienated agricultural lands of the temple's estate are still listed with the king's name in administrative documents of the Twentieth Dynasty; Jac J. Janssen, *Late Ramesside Letters and Communications*, Hieratic Papyri in the British Museum 6 (London: British Museum, 1991), pp. 43–47. Some scholars believe that the cultus of Amenhotep III was then revived, but they wrongly attribute the throne name Nebma῾atre to him rather than to Ramesses VI, who adopted the same name.

51. The earlier presence of all these elements cannot be proved because of most temples' regrettable state of preservation.

52. Arthur E. P. Weigall, "A Report on the Excavation of the Funeral Temple of Thoutmosis III at Gurneh," *ASAE* 7 (1906): 121–41; and "Note additionnelle," *ASAE* 8(1907): 286.

53. Herbert Ricke, *Der Totentempel Thutmoses' III.*, BeiträgeBf 3/1 (1939).

54. For the titles of the priests, see ibid., pp. 37–38, and Otto, *Topographie*, pp. 109–110.

55. See note 17 above.

56. Gardiner, "Tuthmosis III," *JEA* 38 (1952): 6.

57. Paul Barguet, *Le temple d'Amon-Rê à Karnak: Essai d'exégèse*, RAPH 21 (1962), pp. 283–84.

58. Faulkner, *Concise Dictionary* [n. 28], p. 165, proposes as possible translations of ḥwt ῾3t "palace," "administrative center," "temple," and "tomb-chapel," a rather wide choice.

59. Barguet, *Temple d'Amon-Rê*, pp. 192–97.

60. Ibid., pp. 198–201.

61. See text at notes 162–63 and 182–83.

62. Otto, *Topographie* [n. 17], p. 61.

63. Otto (ibid.) takes "Amun" to be the subject of the predicate *dsr*, "is sacred," and then supplies a preposition to link *dsr* with *3ht*, "horizon." I prefer to understand *dsr 3ht* as "sacred horizon," "Amun" as genetival, and the whole expression as a predicate whose subject is an elliptic *hwt*, yielding "(The Mansion) is the sacred horizon of Amun."

64. The inscription is broken off, and the missing word is supplied in brackets because the complete formula "of millions of years" occurs in other inscriptions from this site; Jadwiga Lipińska, *Deir el-Bahari II: The Temple of Thutmosis III, Architecture* (Warsaw: Paustwowe Wydawoictwo Naukowe, 1977), pp. 50–52.

65. Wolfgang Helck, "Kiosk," *LÄ* 3:442, B. Another term frequently used in connection with these structures is "way station" (German *Barkenstation*), which refers to their function; see Dieter Arnold, "Deir el-Bahari III," *LÄ* 1:1023, 5.

66. For an earlier example, see note 95 and the discussion in the text thereafter. On the portable divine barque, see also Chapters 1 and 4.

67. On the portable royal barque, see Chapter 4.

68. On the festival, see Chapter 4.

69. I am reminded of a curious report by Herodotus, *History*, 2.63 (see *Herodotus*, trans. A. D. Godley, Loeb Classical Library [London: William Heinemann; and New York: G. P. Putnam's Sons, 1931], 1:348–51). He describes a procession of a god in Papremis where there was fighting between two groups of people—those seeking to hinder the procession's progress and those trying to force its way through.

70. Gardiner, "Thutmosis III," *JEA* 38 (1952): 6–23.

71. Gerhard Haeny, *Basilikale Anlagen in der ägyptischen Baukunst des Neuen Reiches*, BeiträgeBf 9 (1970). The chapter concerning the *Akh-menu* (pp. 7–17) still follows the older tradition by calling the whole complex *"Festtempel"* and its central hall *"Festsaal,"* though opposing the views then generally accepted. On the *Sed*-festival (royal jubilee), see Chapters 1 and 2.

72. Barguet, *Temple d'Amon-Rê* [n. 57], pp. 284–340.

73. For Amenhotep II, see Erik Hornung, "Amenophis II.," *LÄ* 1:203–6.

74. For the Louvre object, see Wilhelm Spiegelberg, "Varia," *Recueil de travaux rélatifs à philologie et à l'archéologie égyptiennes et assyriennes* 16 (1894): 30; and 19 (1897): 88–89. Helck, *Urkunden* IV [n. 22], p. 1355, lines 6–9, suggests in a note that the cartouche of Thutmose might erroneously have been read as Amenhotep's, but Hayes, *Scepter* [n. 45], 2:141–42, confirms the early reading based on a similar beaker and other objects of Amenhotep II in The Metropolitan Museum of Art in New York. For *i'b-3ht*, see Siegfried Schott, *Das schöne Fest vom Wüstentale: Festbräuche einer Totenstadt*, AAWLM, Jahrgang 1952/11, p. 108, no. 69, and p. 123, no. 117.

75. W. M. Flinders Petrie, *Six Temples at Thebes, 1896* (London: Bernard Quaritch, 1897), pp. 4–6 and pls. 22–23.

76. For the titles of priests, see Otto, *Topographie* [n. 17], p. 110; Wolfgang Helck, *Materialien zur Wirtschaftsgeschichte des Neuen Reiches 1–6*, AAWLM (1960–69), 1:(97) 879–(99) 881.

77. Petrie, *Six Temples*, pp. 7–9 and pls. 22, 24.

78. In the early 1980s, the site was reinvestigated by an Italian expedition, but I have no information on the results.

79. Otto, *Topographie*, p. 112, and Helck, *Materialien*, 1:(98) 880–(99) 881. The oriental palanquin conveyed living persons—in Egypt, only used by the living king and his highest officials, in some cases also for gods; see Erman and Grapow,

Wörterbuch [n. 23], 5:52, 1, "Tragsessel (des Königs und des Osiris)." But the priests appointed to attend the palanquin of Menkheperure lived more than two hundred years after the king's death. This seeming contradiction can be explained by the fact that some divine images were occasionally transported on palanquins. The image most frequently represented on a *knj* is that of Amenhotep I; see Foucart, *Tombes thébaines* [n. 35], MIFAO 574 (1935), pl. 6.

80. Helck, *Urkunden* IV [n. 22], p. 1681, lines 10–14; the plural of *hwt* occurs three times in these lines. The first definitely refers to "quarries," and the second, doubtless to "mansions"; but there is no clue for the translation of the third, thus leaving several possibilities for interpretation.

81. For a full treatment of the temple of Luxor, see Chapter 4. For the parallel inscription of Ahmose, see text at note 22 above.

82. For the famous colossi of Memnon, see Labib Habachi, "Die beiden Kolosse im Osten des Tempels," in Habachi and Haeny, *Zur Ausstattung des Tempels—Statuen, Reliefreste, Inschriften,* BeiträgeBf 11 (1981), pp. 43–54.

83. Helck, *Urkunden* IV, p. 1648, lines 6–18; Wilhelm Spiegelberg, in Petrie, *Six Temples* [n. 75], p. 24 and pls. 12–13.

84. Helck, *Urkunden* IV, pp. 1648–1650; Spiegelberg, in Petrie, *Six Temples,* p. 24 and pl. 12, lines 9–10.

85. Best illustrated in Gerhard Haeny, *Untersuchungen im Totentempel Amenophis' III.,* BeiträgeBf 11 (1981), figs. 7a-e (p. 44), 13 (p. 84), and 16 (p. 110).

86. Herbert Ricke, "Ein Sokartempel?" in *Der Totentempel Amenophis' III.—Baureste und Ergänzung,* BeiträgeBf 11 (1981), pp. 31–37. Since then, it has been discovered that all the limestone blocks Ricke thought to belong to the Sokar temple really came from a single huge gateway. See Horst Jaritz and Susanne Bickel, "Une porte monumentale d'Amenhotep III," *BIFAO* 94 (1994): 277–85.

87. Otto, *Topographie* [n. 17], pp. 112–14; the list presented by Ricke in BeiträgeBf 11 (1981): 33–35 includes only the personnel of Sokar.

88. Haeny, *Untersuchungen,* BeiträgeBf 11 (1981), folding pl. 5b, lines 21–22.

89. Brunner, *Die südlichen Räume* [n. 24]. pl. 63. The phrase ends an address of the goddess Renenutet, who accompanies the king with offerings to Amun. So her words, "your Divine Temple of a Million of Years," are directed to the god. In pl. 73, the temple is clearly attributed to Amun, whereas in the next scene (pl. 74), it is the king who, on entering the temple, receives millions of years—from Montu, Mut, and another goddess. Is the temple of Luxor Amun's temple of millions of years, because there the king is to receive a life of millions of years from Amun and from the gods in his retenue? The extant texts just do not permit a decision.

90. See The Epigraphic Survey, *Reliefs and Inscriptions at Luxor Temple,* vol. 1: *The Festival Procession of Opet in the Colonade Hall,* OIP 112 (1994); and William J. Murnane, "Opetfest," *LÄ* 4:574–79.

91. "*Opet*" was the reading of the Egyptian word *ipt* by early Egyptologists; it is still traditionally used. '*Ipt* designates an isolated, secluded place and is here best understood to mean "innermost sanctuary." In referring to Luxor, *ipt* is often accompanied by the adjective *rsjt,* "southern," pointing to Luxor's location in relation to Karnak.

92. See Chapter 4; also, Brunner, *Die südlichen Räume,* pp. 9–12.

93. Murnane, "Opetfest," *LÄ* 4:577–78, n. 15 refers to the main pictorial representations of the festival and mentions that the reliefs of Tutankhamun in the Luxor temple were later usurped by Haremhab and completed by Sety I.

94. Expecting further finds, the reconstruction has so far been made only on photographic plates. Pierre Lacau and Henri Chevrier, *Une chapelle d'Hatshepsout à Karnak* 1–2 (Cairo: SAE and IFAO, 1977).

95. The sixth course on both sides of the shrine depicted the offerings presented at the god's return. In view of the systematic arrangement of the themes, it may fairly be assumed that the offering scenes of the fourth course concerned rites performed when the processions had reached their destination, the temples of Luxor and Deir el-Bahri respectively. See Lacau and Chevrier, *Chapelle d'Hatshepsout*, pp. 153–204 and pls. 7–10.

96. For a detailed description of the layout of the temple of Luxor, see Chapter 4.

97. See Brunner, *Die südlichen Räume* [n. 24], fig. 1, p. 9, for a plan of the platform for Amun's shrine and pls. 115–43 for the wall reliefs of the central room.

98. The texts in the wide hall inscribed beside the sun boats are seriously disfigured. Inspite of several attempts, their meaning has only recently been recovered, after the finding of a clearer version; see Maria Carmela Betrò, *I testi solari del portale di Pascerientaisu (BN 2)*, Università degli studi di Pisa, Missioni archeologiche in Egitto, Saqqara 3 (Pisa: Giardini, [1990]). I am grateful to Hellmut Brunner for indicating this publication to me.

99. For parallels to the hymns, see the list in Betrò, *I testi solari*, pp. 19–23; for sun barques, see below.

100. Helck, *Urkunden* IV [n. 22], p. 1655, lines 1–4; Spiegelberg, in Petrie, *Six Temples* [n. 75], p. 25 and pl. 12, lines 23–25.

101. Lepsius, *Denkmaeler* [n. 21], Text V, pp. 233–34, 237. For Khonsu, see Hellmut Brunner, "Chons," *LÄ* 1:960–63.

102. Amenhotep III is never shown with the additional mark of Khonsu, his sidelock of youth.

103. Illustrated in Arielle P. Kozloff and Betsy M. Bryan, *Egypt's Dazzling Sun: Amenhotep III and His World* ([Bloomington, Indiana]: Cleveland Museum of Art and Indiana University Press, 1992), fig. IV.28, p. 108. The feature is not restricted to Soleb, but also found at Luxor: fig. IV.10, p. 87, where the king is wearing the *ḥnw*-crown. For Theban examples of earlier reigns, see Hans Goedicke, *Problems concerning Amenophis III* (Baltimore: Halgo, 1992), figs. 6–8.

104. Peter Pamminger, "Amun und Luxor—Der Widder und das Kultbild," *BeitrSudanF* 5 (1992): 99–115. The arguments sustaining my opinion will be presented in a separate article.

105. A. H. Gardiner, "The Inscription of Amenhotep," in W. M. Flinders Petrie, G. A. Wainright, and A. H. Gardiner, *Tarkhan I and Memphis V*, BSAE 23 (1913), pp. 33–36 and pls. 79–80; Helck, *Urkunden* IV [n. 22], pp. 1793, line 13, to 1801, line 5.

106. The bracketed words fill a broken part of the text and are supplied from parallel passages later in the text; Petrie et al., *Tarkhan I and Memphis V*, pl. 79, lines 1–2; Helck, *Urkunden* IV, p. 1793, lines 16–18.

107. Petrie et al., *Tarkhan I and Memphis V*, pl. 79, lines 13–14; Helck, *Urkunden* IV, p. 1795, lines 5–7.

108. Petrie et al., *Tarkhan I and Memphis V*, pl. 79, line 18, and pl. 80, lines 19–20; Helck, *Urkunden* IV, pp. 1795, line 18, to 1796, line 4.

109. Petrie et al., *Tarkhan I and Memphis V*, pl. 80, line 21; Helck, *Urkunden* IV, p. 1796, lines 9–11.

110. Otto, *Topographie* [n. 17], p. 115; Hayes, *Scepter* [n. 45], 2:306, fig. 191.

111. Gabolde, "Temples 'mémoriaux,'" *BIFAO* 89 (1989): 127–78 and pls. 13–24.

112. Otto, *Topographie*, p. 115; Uvo Hölscher, *The Excavation of Medinet Habu II: The Temples of the Eighteenth Dynasty*, OIP 41 (1939), pp. 63–115.

113. Georges Legrain, *Répertoire généalogique et onomastique du Musée du Caire* (Geneva: Société Anonyme des Arts Graphiques, 1908), p. 196, no. 333.

114. Epigraphic Survey, *Medinet Habu*, vol. 6, *The Temple Proper* 2, OIP 84 (1963), pl. 447. See also William J. Murnane, *United with Eternity: A Concise Guide to the Monuments of Medinet Habu* ([Cairo]: Oriental Institute, University of Chicago, and American University in Cairo, 1980), p. 54, fig. 38; Nelson, "Identity of Amon-Re," *JNES* 1 (1942): pl. 4 (facing p. 130).

115. In Room III, Nelson, "Identity of Amon-Re," *JNES* 1(1942): 131 and fig. 5, p. 136; in Room V, Champollion-le-Jeune, *Monuments de l'Égypte et de la Nubie*, vol. 2 (Paris: F. Didot Frères, 1835–45; reprint, Geneva: Éditions de Belles-Lettres, [1970]), pl. 151, 3.

116. Erman and Grapow, *Wörterbuch* [n. 23], 3:5, gives a wide variety of possible translations, but in the context of Sety's temple it may be a revival of the older term that designated buildings for commemorative rites of the late Old Kingdom and the Middle Kingdom, e.g., the cenotaphs of Abydos.

117. This translation is adapted from Nelson, "Identity of Amon-Re," *JNES* 1 (1942): 131–32 and fig. 7, p. 136. Nelson does not render the last sentence, and it is therefore uncertain how he would have interpreted the word *k3*. As it is left without a determinative, it can have a wide variety of meanings; possible are "spirit," "essence," "force," and even "food" (food offerings).

118. Louis-A. Christophe, "La salle V du temple de Sethi Ier à Gournah," *BIFAO* 49 (1950): 117–80. For a brief description of the temple's layout, see below.

119. Ibid., p. 127. On the royal *k3*, see Chapter 4.

120. Ibid., pp. 172, 175.

121. Ibid., pp. 121–26.

122. Epigraphic Survey, *Medinet Habu*, vol. 4, *Festival Scenes of Ramses III*, OIP 51 (1940), pl. 244.

123. Ibid., pls. 231–32, lower registers.

124. Nelson, "Identity of Amon-Re," *JNES* 1 (1942): 134, fig. 2. See also Epigraphic Survey, *Reliefs and Inscriptions at Karnak*, vol. 1, *Ramses III's Temple within the Great Inclosure of Amon* 1, OIP 25 (1936), pl. 21a, lower register.

125. Nelson, "Identity of Amon-Re," *JNES* 1 (1942): 133–34 and fig. 2.

126. Ibid., p. 133 and pl. 5 (facing p. 131). I have no translation to offer for the words represented by the ellipsis.

127. Two earlier examples of the phenomenon have been mentioned only in passing. They deserve special mention here. The temple of Hatshepsut at Deir el-Bahri included a room decorated with rows of offering-bearers marching toward a false door devoted to her father, Thutmose I. And the *Akh-menu* of Thutmose III at Karnak had a small room inscribed on three sides with figures of seated kings, each marked with the name of a noted predecessor.

128. For the Great Hypostyle Hall, see Haeny, *Basilikale Anlagen* [n. 71], pp. 29–61. Although I am aware of differing opinions, I still maintain my version.

129. Champollion-le-Jeune, *Monuments de l'Égypte et de la Nubie: Notices descriptives* (Paris: F. Didot Frères, 1844–49; reprint, Geneva: Éditions de Belles-Lettres, [1973]), 1:694, 696–97.

130. The various opinions voiced in this discussion are presented in Haeny, *Basilikale Anlagen*, pp. 58–61.

131. On the south wall of the hall, decorated by Ramesses II, this king is represented several times offering to the Osiris Sety I; see Barguet, *Temple d'Amon-Rê* [n. 57], pp. 66–68: west side, regs. 3d, 2e, and 1a; east side, regs. 3d, 2e, and 1a. It should also be remembered that two Mansions of Millions of Years were later erected in the wide courtyard in front of the Great Hypostyle Hall.

132. Extensive excavations have been carried out around the temple by Rainer Stadelmann, director of the German Archaeological Institute in Cairo. Several preliminary reports have been published in *MDAIK,* but so far only two volumes of the final publication, one describing the finds made in the excavation and one presenting the reliefs of the solar court. For a plan, see Dieter Arnold, *Wandrelief und Raumfunktion in ägyptischen Tempeln des Neuen Reiches,* MÄS 2 (Berlin: Bruno Hessling, 1962), pl. 10.

133. The central chapel on the north side features the important reliefs discussed above (see text at notes 118–21).

134. For this type of false door, see Gerhard Haeny, "Scheintür," *LÄ* 5:570, §3.

135. The reliefs of this court are published in Jürgen Osing, *Der Tempel Sethos' I. in Gurna,* AVDAIK 20 (1977), pp. 38–53 and pls. 24–36.

136. Henri Gauthier, *Dictionnaire des noms géographique contenus dans les textes hiéroglyphiques* (Cairo: IFAO, 1925–31), 4:92. For the goldsmith, see Jocelyne Berlandini, "Varia Memphitica II (II–III)," *BIFAO* 77 (1977): 44, with a reference to C. W. Lunsingh Scheurleer, "Gemeentemuseum te 's-gravenhage," *Jaarbericht van het Vooraziatisch—Egyptisch Gezelschap 'Ex Oriente Lux'* 2/7 (1940): 551 and pl. 17.

137. Published by Herbert E. Winlock, *Bas-Reliefs from the Temple of Rameses I at Abydos,* MMA Papers 1.1 (New York: MMA, 1921); Winlock, *The Temple of Ramesses I at Abydos,* MMA Papers 5 (New York: MMA, 1937). These two publications have been combined and reprinted with drawings and translations; see Winlock, *The Temple of Rameses I at Abydos* (New York: MMA and Arno, 1973).

138. Winlock, *Temple of Ramesses I* (1937), pp. 12–15 and pl. 2. See also Siegfried Schott, *Der Denkstein Sethos' I. für die Kapelle Ramses' I. in Abydos,* Nachrichten der Akademie der Wissenschaften in Göttingen, Philologisch-historische Klasse, Jahrgang 1964/1 (Göttingen: Ruprecht & Classen, 1964), pp. 9–12.

139. Schott, *Denkstein,* pp. 14–16; also Henri Gauthier, "Une statue de Ramsès Ier défunt originaire d'Abydos," *ASAE* 31 (1931): 193–97.

140. Schott, *Denkstein,* pp. 21–22 and pl. 2; also Gauthier, "Statue," *ASAE* 31 (1931): 193–97.

141. Hayes, *Scepter* [n. 45], 2:341; Otto, *Topographie* [n. 17], pp. 66, 112; Ludwig Borchardt, *Statuen und Statuetten von Königen und Privatleuten* 2: *Catalogue général des Antiquités égyptiennes du Musée du Caire Nos 1–1294* (Berlin: Reichsdruckerei, 1925), pp. 154–55 and pl. 109 (604); Gaballa ʿAly Gaballa, "Some Nineteenth Dynasty Monuments in Cairo Museum," *BIFAO* 71 (1972): 129–33 with fig. 1.

142. Rainer Stadelmann, "Totentempel und Millionenjahrhaus in Theben," *MDAIK* 35 (1979), p. 303 n. 9, counts the temples of Abu Simbel among the Mansions of Millions of Years but offers no textual reference in proof. But see K. A. Kitchen, *Ramesside Inscriptions: Historical and Biographical* (Oxford: B. H. Blackwell, 1968–), 3:203–4, spec. 204,2: Rock Stela No. 9, of Ramesses-ʿAsha-Hebsed. I thank Erich Winter for this reference. For location and earlier references, see Bertha Porter and Rosalind L. B. Moss, *Topographical Bibliography of Ancient Egyptian Hieroglyphic Texts, Reliefs, and Paintings VII* (Oxford: Clarendon, 1951), p. 117(9).

143. Labib Habachi, *Features of the Deification of Ramesses II*, ADAIK 5 (1969), pp. 2–10 (esp. 3).

144. Ibid., pl. 5b.

145. Ibid., pp. 8–9 with fig. 8, and pl. 5a.

146. Ibid., pp. 8–9 with fig. 7, and pls. 4a, 4b.

147. Bettina Schmitz, "Statuennamen," *LÄ* 5:1267–70.

148. For the first kind of proof, see Habachi, *Features*, pp. 28–35 with figs. 17–21; for the second, see Helck, *Materialien* [n. 76], 1:(226) 1008–(233) 1015.

149. For a survey of the types of Osiride pillars, see Christian Leblanc, "Piliers et colosses de type 'osiriaque' dans le contexte des temples de culte royal," *BIFAO* 80 (1980): 69–89 and pls. 19–22.

150. Lepsius, *Denkmaeler* III [n. 21], sheets 191m, 191n. Also A. Rosenvasser, "La excavación de Aksha," *Ciencia e investigación* 20/11 (November 1964): 494.

151. Habachi, *Features*, pp. 14–15 with fig. 10.

152. Ibid., pp. 14–15 with fig. 11. For the example of Abu Simbel, see text preceding note 145.

153. Aylward M. Blackman, *The Temple of Derr*, TIN (1913), p. 66, pl. 28.1. The same inscription is found in Kitchen, *Ramesside Inscriptions* [n. 142], 2:743, lines 4–6.

154. Lepsius, *Denkmaeler* III, sheet 181. For sun barques, see the index.

155. Habachi, *Features*, pp. 12–13 and pl. 6.

156. In both two- and three-dimensional ancient Egyptian representations, the king is frequently shown with the attributes of Tatenen, but—as far as I see—their significance has never been explained.

157. Habachi, *Features*, p. 12 and pl. 2b.

158. For Beit el-Wali's being an exception, see ibid., pp. 11 and 43. For reliefs and inscriptions of the temple, see Herbert Ricke, George R. Hughes, and Edward F. Wente, *The Beit el-Wali Temple of Ramesses II*, University of Chicago Oriental Institute Nubian Expedition 1 (Chicago: Oriental Institute, University of Chicago, 1967).

159. Nelson, "Identity of Amon-Re," *JNES* 1(1942): 129, n. 7 refers briefly to this temple. *T3-wr* is the name of the nome in which Abydos is situated, and the name of the Abydos temple parallels the name of the king's western temple at Thebes.

160. The statue group is illustrated by K. P. Kuhlmann, "Der Tempel Ramses' II. in Abydos," *MDAIK* 38 (1982), pl. 102a.

161. For a plan, see ibid., p. 359.

162. For a recent interpretation of the temple's rooms, see ibid., pp. 355–62.

163. The literary text is Papyrus Anastasi II:1, 1–5, found in Alan H. Gardiner, *Late-Egyptian Miscellanies*, BiAe 7 (1937), p. 12; for the stela, see Gardiner, "The Stele of Bilgai," *ZÄS* 50 (1912): 49–57 with pl. 4.

164. Petrie, *Six Temples* [n. 75], pp. 11–13.

165. For a preliminary report on the reinvestigation, see Horst Jaritz, "Der Totentempel des Merenptah in Qurna," *MDAIK* 48 (1992): 65–91. For the name and designation, see Otto, *Topographie* [n. 17], p. 112.

166. Published in Henri Chevrier with Étienne Drioton, *Le temple reposoir de Séti II à Karnak* (Cairo: SAE and Imprimerie Nationale, Boulac, 1940), with separate plans and plates.

167. On the triple barque shrine and way station, see Chapter 4.

168. Chevrier and Drioton, *Temple reposoir*, p. 48.

169. Ibid., pp. 25–26.

170. Ibid., p. 31 and fig. 1.

171. Ibid., figs. 6–10.

172. See Kenneth A. Kitchen, "Tausret," *LÄ* 6:244–45.

173. Petrie, *Six Temples* [n. 75], pp. 13–17.

174. Hayes, *Scepter* [n. 45], 2:358; Sir Alan Gardiner, "Only One King Siptaḥ and Twosre not His Wife," *JEA* 44 (1958): 12–22 (esp. 20).

175. Gardiner, "Stele of Bilgai," *ZÄS* 50 (1912): 49–57 with pl. 4.

176. For the possible location of a temple of "Amun of Ramesses II" at Tanis, see above.

177. Epigraphic Survey, *Medinet Habu* 1–8, OIP 8–9, 23, 51, 83–84, 93–94 (1930–70), which presents photographic views and drawings of reliefs and inscriptions; and Epigraphic Survey, *The Excavation of Medinet Habu* 1–5, OIP 21, 41, 54–55, 66 (1934–54).

178. Besides the articles referring to various particular features, only two major studies of the complex have to my knowledge been presented—one a summary for the general public of the Epigraphic Survey's findings (Murnane, *United With Eternity* [n. 114]), and the other a critical review of the function of some of the rooms (Barbara Switalski Lesko, "Royal Mortuary Suites of the Egyptian New Kingdom," *AJA* 73 [1969]: 453–58). I thank Erich Winter for the latter reference. That I cannot agree with all of Lesko's arguments will become evident in the following pages.

179. Rainer Stadelmann, "Medinet Habu, A + B," *LÄ* 3:1255–58.

180. Gerhard Haeny, "Zum Hohen Tor von Medinet Habu," *ZÄS* 94 (1967): 71–78.

181. For Window of Appearance, see Dieter Arnold, "Erscheinungsfenster," *LÄ* 2:14; for the "Palace," see Uvo Hölscher, *The Excavation of Medinet Habu* 3, *The Mortuary Temple of Ramses III* 1, OIP 54 (1941), pp. 37–48 and pls. 25–30. A different interpretation of the "Palace" is proposed by Stadelmann, "Tempelpalast" [n. 49], *MDAIK* 29 (1973): 221–42.

182. For a comparison of the temple plans, see Hölscher, *Excavation of Medinet Habu*, 3:22–25 with pl. 2; also, Stadelmann, "Totentempel," *MDAIK* 35 (1979): 303–21 with figs. 1–2.

183. "Papyrus Harris I," *LÄ* 4:707. A hieroglyphic transcription is given by W. Erichsen, *Papyrus Harris I*, BiAe 5 (1933); an English translation is published in James Henry Breasted, *Ancient Records of Egypt: Historical Documents from the Earliest Times to the Persian Conquest*, vol. 4, *The Twentieth to the Twenty-Sixth Dynasties* (Chicago: University of Chicago Press, 1906; reprint, New York: Russell & Russell, 1962), pp. 87–206. A new edition of Papyrus Harris I, not seen at the time this chapter was prepared, is Pierre Grandet, *Le Papyrus Harris I (BM 9999)*, 2 vols., BdÉ 109/1–2 (1994).

184. Papyrus Harris I: 3,11 and 29,8 (see Erichsen, *Harris I*, pp. 4 and 34; Breasted, *Ancient Records*, pp. 113 §189, 148 §274).

185. Apart from *m ḥḥ n rnpwt*, Papyrus Harris I uses the same terms in the same order to describe several other temples as it does to describe Medinet Habu, so it is difficult to avoid the conclusion that they all had the same function.

186. Wolfgang Helck, "Ramses IV.," *LÄ* 5:120–23 (esp. nn. 6–7, 9); for Ramesses V, see Kenneth A. Kitchen, "Ramses V–XI.," *LÄ* 5:124 and n. 7.

187. For *ḥwt nb-m3ˁt-rˁ*, compare Helck, *Materialien* [n. 76], 1:(99) 881, "Wirtschaftliche Bemerkungen," and 1:(115) 897, no. 31, "Ramses VI."

188. For Ramesses VI–XI, see Kitchen, "Ramses V–XI.," *LÄ* 5:124–28; also Helck, *Materialien,* 1:(115) 897. For Sheshonq I, see Helck, *Materialien,* 1:(115) 897, no. 34, who quotes Ricardo A. Caminos, "Gebel Es–Silsilah No. 100," *JEA* 38 (1952): 46–61 (esp. 57, about line 50), but this should not be accepted without considering the arguments adduced by Charles F. Nims, "Places about Thebes," *JNES* 14 (1955): 115, n. 45.

189. Henri Frankfort, *Kingship and the Gods: A Study of Ancient Near Eastern Religion as the Integration of Society and Nature* (Chicago: University of Chicago Press, 1948), p. vii. Frankfort's actual text reads: "The creations of the primitive mind are elusive. Its concepts seem ill defined, or, rather, they defy limitations." To speak of the ancient Egyptians as having a primitive mind would be a mistake.

190. See Wolfhart Westendorff, "Leben und Tod," *LÄ* 3:951–54.

191. Otto, *Topographie* [n. 17], pp. 44–82, "Theben-West."

192. Gabolde, "Temples 'mémoriaux.'" *BIFAO* 89 (1989): 127–78 and pls. 13–24.

193. See note 183 above.

194. Oral expression left no trace, of course, and is therefore inaccessible to present study.

195. Lesko, "Mortuary Suites," *AJA* 73 (1969): 453–58.

196. Because of limited space, only one example may be given from among the almost constant alterations in art forms that one could illustrate. For changes in the Osiride figures in front of pillars, see Leblanc, "Piliers et colosses," *BIFAO* 80 (1980): 69–89 and pls. 19–22.

197. We have occasionally met both terms in the course of our investigation.

198. For example, Kozloff and Bryan, *Egypt's Dazzling Sun* [n. 103], pp. 106, 108; and Barguet, *Temple d'Amon-Rê* [n. 57], p. 291.

199. For example, Wolfgang Helck, "Zum Kult an Königsstatuen," *JNES* 25 (1966): 32–41 (esp. 40); Eberhard Otto, "Zwei Bemerkungen zum Königskult der Spätzeit," *MDAIK* 15 (1957): 193–207 (esp. 204); Dietrich Wildung, "Königskult," *LÄ* 3:533–34.

200. For example, Michel Gitton, "Ahmose Nofretere." *LÄ* 1:102–9; Erik Hornung, "Amenophis I.," *LÄ* 1:201–3; Goedicke, *Problems concerning Amenophis III* [n. 103], pp. 52–69 (esp. 52). Goedicke denies outright that Amenhotep III was deified within the borders of Egypt itself.

Chapter 4: The New Kingdom "Divine" Temple: The Example of Luxor

1. Much of the information presented here results from discoveries made by me during my twelve years' experience in Luxor as field director of the Epigraphic Survey of the Oriental Institute of the University of Chicago. This chapter synthesizes several of the most important directions of my research over a ten-year period. Some of my interpretations remain highly speculative, but most of my ideas have been tested before professional audiences and adjusted in response to their criticism.

According to Dieter Arnold, *Die Tempel Ägyptens: Götterwohnungen, Kultstätten, Baudenkmäler* (Zurich: Artemis & Winkler, 1992), pp. 29–39, Egyptian temples are to be classified as dedicated to a god, dedicated to a king, solar shrines, barque chapels, and *mammisis* (divine birth houses). In most developed temples, however, elements of such "pure types" are found in varying proportions. At Thebes, the major divine (or, god's) temple is Karnak, the earthly house of the celestial Amun-Re. Luxor Temple—like Karnak, located on the east bank of the Nile—has been regarded as devoted primarily, if not exclusively, to the cultus of Amun-Re (although the exact relationship between Karnak and Luxor has long been a question). My recognition of the importance of the divine king as object of the cultus at Luxor necessitates a reassessment of this widely held view. The crux, as we shall see, lies in correctly understanding the function of *ka*-chapels and the Mansions of Millions of Years, where king and god merged. In Chapter 3, Gerhard Haeny shows that the major temples on Thebes's west bank were *not* exclusively mortuary in character and that Mansions of Millions of Years also existed on the east bank. Luxor Temple was a Mansion of Millions of Years; so it and the so-called mortuary temples of the west bank were complementary. For the references to Luxor as a *ḥwt/ḥwt-nṯr/st nyt ḥḥw ỉm rnpỉwt*, see Hellmut Brunner, *Die südlichen Räume des Tempels von Luxor*, AVDAIK 18 (1977), pl. 63.4; Ch. Kuentz, *La face sud du massif est du pylône de Ramsès II à Louxor*, Collection Scientifique (Cairo: CEDAE, 1971), pl. 17; K. A. Kitchen, *Ramesside Inscriptions: Historical and Biographical* 2 (Oxford: B. H. Blackwell, 1979), pp. 623.6, 627.12. It is not so easy as we once thought to distinguish divine from royal temples in the New Kingdom, as Haeny emphasizes; nor is the distinction particularly useful.

2. The Egyptian name for Luxor Temple was *'Ip3t-rsyt*, "The Southern Residence Apartments (or Southern Sanctuary)." See Brunner, *Die südlichen Räume*, pp. 10–12; Peter Pamminger, "Amun und Luxor—Der Widder und das Kultbild," *BeitrSudanF* 5 (1992): 93–95. Vowels were not written in the hieroglyphic scripts, so to pronounce Egyptian words we must insert vowels into their consonantal skeletons. Thus, *"Opet"* represents *'Ip3t*. It must be understood, however, that the vocalizations of this and other Egyptian words are scholarly conventions.

The *ka*, long recognized as a constituent element of divine and human being, occurs most frequently in mortuary contexts, where a reference to the soul would be expected. The idea of the soul was a complicated one in ancient Egyptian religion, however. This presentation concentrates on the nonfunerary aspects of the *ka*. The *ka* was particularly important in Egyptian kingship theory, where it symbolized divine ancestry. My own ongoing study of the subject, discussed below, indicates that each major family line could be traced back to the family's own *ka*, or mythic lineage ancestor. The term *ka* (*k3*) comes from the same root as words for "bull" (*k3*), "vulva" (*k3t*), and "food" (*k3w*), and the translation "generative, reproductive, or life-sustaining power" (referring to the collective fertility and vitality of an extended family or clan across the ages) fits most contexts.

3. The Egyptians' sense of god-given superiority implied the pharaoh's right to rule over the whole world, of which the land of Egypt was the center. Egyptians originally thought of non-Egyptians as nonhuman. Only gradually, as Egyptians' horizons expanded, did they come to recognize the humanity of others.

4. *M3ꜥ* is the root of the noun *m3ꜥt* (*maꜥat*). Dictionaries list the simple root as an adjective-verb meaning "to be(come) true, just, righteous." The term "adjective-verb" (German: *Eigenschaftsverbum*) signifies a class of words used not only as adjectives but also as verbs denoting acquisition or possession of an adjective's quality. The antonyms of *m3ꜥt* are *ỉsft*, "wrongdoing," *grg*, "falsehood," and *d̠wỉt*, "evil." For *m3ꜥ-ḫrw* in funerary contexts, the translation "vindicated" or "blessed" may be preferable. The old-fashioned "deceased" is certainly incorrect.

5. See Emily Teeter, *The Presentation of Maat: The Iconography and Theology of an An-*

cient Egyptian Offering Ritual, SAOC 57 (1997). For further discussion and analysis, see Chapter 1.

6. The king assumed the role of the god by reiterating some of the god's creative gestures, utterances, or actions. The Ritual of Amenhotep I facilitated the merging of the various forms of the god Amun and the union of king and god. Lanny Bell, "Luxor Temple and the Cult of the Royal *Ka*," *JNES* 44 (1985): 283–85; Bell, "Aspects of the Cult of the Deified Tutankhamun," in *Mélanges Gamal Eddin Mokhtar*, vol. 1, BdÉ 97/1 (1985), p. 41.

7. For further discussion and analysis, see Chapter 1.

8. The halo in Christian art is a similar sign.

9. The sun is commonly drawn directly over the divine king's head. According to the conventions of Egyptian art, the sun is *one* with him, shining forth through him. The Window of Appearance was a ceremonial balcony in a palace or temple. There, on state occasions, the king gave audiences, often accompanied by the queen and sometimes accompanied by other members of the royal family (e.g., during the reign of Akhenaten). From it he received foreigners and their tribute and rewarded and promoted his retainers and other officials.

10. Two Egyptian words are in play here: *nḥḥ* and *ḏt*. Both define overlapping aspects of eternity or infinity, and both are connected with the redemptive aspect of sacred time that permits escape from the constraints of secular time's relentless forward flow. *Nḥḥ* properly signifies cyclical time, a regular or periodic return to the original starting point at the completion of each cycle or revolution; *ḏt* refers to the stability of the changeless or timeless realm of Osiris as Lord of the Dead and stresses the coinciding of beginning and end, first and last.

11. For further discussion, see Chapter 1.

12. The literary text known as The Prophecies of Neferti (Dynasty 12) announced that the advent of King Amenemhat I, whose Horus-name was *Wḥm-msiwt*, was the coming of a savior. For the text in English translation, see Miriam Lichtheim, *Ancient Egyptian Literature*, vol. 1, *The Old and Middle Kingdoms* (Berkeley: University of California Press, 1973), pp. 139–45.

13. I capitalize "King" when I refer to the institution of divine kingship or the abstraction of kingship rather than to a particular human ruler. We should also note here that the private *ka* is never depicted as an individualized protective spirit, whereas the divine or royal *ka* can be depicted in that way and personalized by appending a name.

14. See Chapter 1. Rejuvenation is also a major feature in the *Opet*-festival, described below.

15. See Florence D. Friedman, "Aspects of Domestic Life and Religion," in *Pharaoh's Workers: The Villagers of Deir el Medina*, ed. Leonard H. Lesko (Ithaca and London: Cornell University Press, 1994), pp. 179 n. 52, 111–17; and Dieter Wildung, "Ahnenkult," *LÄ* 1:111–12. Also, in general, Helen Hardacre, "Ancestors: Ancestor Worship," in *The Encyclopedia of Religion*, ed. Mircea Eliade (New York: Macmillan; London: Collier Macmillan, 1987), 1:263–68. Most recently, Lanny Bell, "Ancestor Worship and Divine Kingship in the Ancient Nile Valley," in *Egypt in Africa*, ed. Theodore Celenko (Indianapolis: Indianapolis Museum of Art, 1996), pp. 56–58.

16. An heir had the duty to bury his father properly. To ensure the succession after the death of a king and a brief, symbolic interregnum, the new king had to take possession of his predecessor's corpse and attend to its burial.

17. See Bell, in *Mélanges Gamal Eddin Mokhtar*, vol. 1 [n. 6], pp. 31–35. To the references cited there, add Beate George, "'Gottesschatten' = Götterbild in Widdergestalt," *Die Welt des Orients* 14 (1983): 130–34. For a depiction of Amenhotep III as the shade or shadow of Amun-Re in the lunette at the top of the back pillar of the statue representing that king's *ka*-statue from the Cachette of Luxor Temple (see note 135 below), see Mohammed El-Saghir, *Das Statuenversteck im Luxortempel*, Zaberns Bildbände zur Archäologie 6 (Mainz: von Zabern, 1992), p. 22.

18. Louis V. Žabkar, *A Study of the Ba Concept in Ancient Egyptian Texts*, SAOC 34 (1968); and William A. Ward, *The Four Egyptian Homographic Roots B-3: Etymological and Egypto-Semitic Studies*, Studia Pohl: Series Maior 6 (Rome: Biblical Institute Press, 1978), pp. 67–88.

19. Gertie Englund, *Akh–une notion religieuse dans l'Égypte pharaonique*, BOREAS 11 (1978); Florence Dunn Friedman, "On the Meaning of Akh (*3ḫ*) in Egyptian Mortuary Texts" (Ph.D. diss., Brandeis University, 1981); R. J. Demarée, *The 3ḫ iḳr n Rᶜ-Stelae: On Ancestor Worship in Ancient Egypt*, Egyptologische Uitgaven 3 (Leiden: Nederlands Instituut voor het Nabije Oosten, 1983). See also Jan Assmann, "Death and Initiation in the Funerary Religion of Ancient Egypt," trans. M. Grauer and R. Meyer, in *Religion and Philosophy in Ancient Egypt*, ed. William Kelly Simpson, YES 3 (1989), pp. 136–37, first published in German in *Sehnsucht nach dem Ursprung: Zu Mircea Eliade*, ed. H. P. Duerr (Frankfurt: Syndikat, 1983), pp. 336–59.

20. See Chapter 1. For Egyptian letters to the dead, see the English translations of Edward F. Wente, *Letters from Ancient Egypt*, ed. Edmund S. Meltzer, Society of Biblical Literature Writings from the Ancient World 1 (Atlanta: Scholar's Press, 1990), pp. 210–20. Two of these specifically address the recipient as an *3ḫ iḳr*, as Thomas Dousa has called to my attention.

21. Every Egyptian had a *ka*, so the royal *ka* was only a particular manifestation of the general *ka*-device. The idea of divine kingship and its justification seem to have arisen out of the ancient Egyptian kinship system or lineage patterns. See the section "Divine Kingship and the Royal *Ka*" below.

22. In New Kingdom Egypt, the father's line predominated in matters of legitimacy and inheritance. The Egyptian understanding of conception and of the physiology of egg and sperm seems to have included the idea that the mother's primary contribution to reproduction was the physical matter from which each infant was made. The *ḥmwst*-spirit, rarely attested but probably associated with the maternal side of the family, was apparently the counterpart of the paternal side's *ka*-spirit; but nothing certain can yet be said about the *ḥmwst*-spirit's role in the kinship system. Material on these concepts was presented in my lecture "Family Priorities and Social Status: Preliminary Remarks on the Ancient Egyptian Kinship System," delivered to a plenary session of the Sixth International Congress of Egyptology at Turin, September 1–8, 1991; an abstract of it is published in *Sesto Congresso Internazionale di Egittologia: Abstracts of Papers* (Turin: International Association of Egyptologists, 1991), pp. 96–97.

23. Much more will be said about the *ka* in this chapter.

24. The generally drab appearance of most temples today is due to their ruinous condition. They have lost the gold plate or leaf that covered the tops of obelisks, the tips of flag masts, and parts of the walls; the brilliant paints and polychrome faience tiles or glass inlays that adorned the walls; and the elaborate furnishings that filled the chambers.

25. For details, see Chapter 1.

26. The pylon—a pair of high, battered (trapezoidal) towers—served as a backdrop for flag masts, obelisks, colossal statues, and guardian sphinxes. Staircases inside the masonry afforded access to the towers' tops, where astronomical observations were made. The towers, or wings, were linked by a bridge decorated with solar images. As noted in Chapter 1, the pylon symbolized the two mountain peaks that flanked the eastern horizon at the mouth of the tunnel or cavern from which the sun daily arose.

27. Before the construction of the Aswan High Dam, the Nile flooded the land of Egypt (its alluvial plain) each year. This annual inundation was probably the single most important influence on the ancient Egyptians' worldview. They likened the flood to the return of the waters of chaos. Whenever the land of Egypt lay completely covered by water, it symbolically ceased to exist. As the flood withdrew, the highest point of land reappeared first—a singular mound in the midst of seemingly limitless waters, the center of a universe being created anew. As the waters receded farther, the peasants returned to their fields, and normal life resumed. Significantly, the first mound was also regarded as the place of first sunrise. For occurrences of the term *sp tpy* (literally, "first occasion [or happening]"), especially with reference to Luxor Temple, see Bell, "Luxor Temple," *JNES* 44 (1985): 290 n. 217a; and Siegfried Morenz, *Egyptian Religion,* trans. Ann E. Keep (London: Methuen; Ithaca: Cornell University Press, 1973), pp. 166–71.

28. Such stelae are found in tombs as well as temples.

29. Gerhard Haeny, "Scheintür," *LÄ* 5:563–74.

30. To clarify terminology, "barges" were great riverine craft, and "barques" were scale-model boats carried on the shoulders of priests and placed on barges for transport. Boats, in their various forms, were the most important means of transportation in Egypt. The gods traveled by boat on ritual journeys through this world; they also sailed or punted across the heavens.

31. For further discussion of divine statues and for discussion of such other topics as the priesthood, daily temple rituals, the temple as principal place of divine manifestation, and the temple as economic institution, see Chapter 1.

32. Although we know more about the state-fostered mythology of kingship than we know about the practical ways in which it influenced or determined the sociopolitical and economic realities of life, the general citizenry must have seen kingship (and to some extent the rule of each individual king) as crucial to their welfare, for the system of government could not have survived for millennia without the support of its subjects. A three-thousand-year police state is inconceivable.

33. In the course of this chapter, several contingent questions will be addressed. By what mechanism(s) was human/divine intercourse promoted within the temple? How did the congregation, forbidden to approach the holy of holies, experience divine presence? How were the awesome and mysterious happenings inside the sanctuary communicated to the populace?

34. Tomb and temple inscriptions written in formal hieroglyphs—especially those presented in deliberately obscure priestly cryptographic style—were composed in an archaistic language. Interpreting them required a specialist's knowledge. (Modern students of Middle Egyptian, the classic language of the ancient monuments, cannot read most inscriptions in Greco-Roman temples, where the enigmatic style was most fully developed and became the norm.) Scribes in the Egyptian civil bureaucracy were trained primarily in the cursive hieratic script, which was used for copying literary works and for writing (in a language more closely resembling everyday speech) current reports, accounts, and letters. Today, Egyptologists teach their students hieroglyphics before introducing them to hieratic, exactly the opposite of ancient educational practice.

35. See Jaroslav Černý, "Egyptian Oracles," in *A Saite Oracle Papyrus from Thebes in the Brooklyn Museum,* ed. Richard A. Parker, BES 4 (1962), pp. 35–48.

36. Egyptian religion never developed into true monotheism, but I use god in the singular to refer to the abstraction of divinity or the ineffability of deity, as well as to a particular god manifest in a cultic image.

37. Such objects and beliefs about them have existed in many cultures and are familiar to historians of religion and cultural anthropologists. See John S. Strong, "Relics," in *The Encyclopedia of Religion,* ed. Eliade [n. 15], 12:275–82.

38. *Talfest* is a German word and means "valley festival." This name for the celebration is used by many English-speaking Egyptologists. For treatments of the festival, see Siegfried Schott, "The Feasts of Thebes," in Harold H. Nelson and Uvo Hölscher, *Work in Western Thebes 1931–33,* Oriental Institute Communications 18 (Chicago: University of Chicago Press, 1934), pp. 73–74; Schott, *Das schöne Fest vom Wüstentale: Festbräuche einer Totenstadt,* AAWLM, Jahrgang 1952/11; Jean-Claude Golvin and Jean-Claude Goyon, *Les bâtisseurs de Karnak* ([Paris]: Presses du CNRS, 1987), pp. 49–51; Janusz Karkowski, "Notes on the Beautiful Feast of the Valley as Represented in Hatshepsut's Temple at Deir el-Bahari," in *Fifty Years of Polish Excavations in Egypt and the Near East: Acts of the Symposium at the Warsaw University 1986* (Warsaw: Centre Professeur Kazimierz Michałowski d'Archéologie Méditerranéenne de l'Université de Varsovie and Centre d'Archéologie Méditerranéenne de l'Académie Polonaise des Sciences, 1992), pp. 155–66; Silvia Wiebach, "Die Begegnung von Lebenden und Verstorbenen im Rahmen des thebanischen Talfestes," *SAK* 13 (1986): 263–91; Saphinaz-Amal Naguib, "The Beautiful Feast of the Valley," in *Understanding and History in Arts and Sciences,* ed. Roald Skarsten et al., Acta Humaniora Universitatis Bergensis 1 (Oslo: Solum Forlag, 1991), pp. 21–32; Martha Bell, "Regional Variation in Polychrome Pottery of the Nineteenth Dynasty," in *Cahiers de la céramique égyptienne,* vol. 1, ed. Pascale Ballet (Cairo: IFAO, 1987), pp. 56–57, 72–75 (notes); Claude Traunecker, "Décor, textes et interprétation," in Traunecker, Françoise Le Saout, and Olivier Masson, *La chapelle d'Achôris à Karnak—Texte,* Recherche sur les grandes civilisations: Synthèse 5 (Paris: Éditions A.D.P.F., 1981), pp. 134–37. See also Arne Eggebrecht, "Brandopfer," *LÄ* 1:848–50. In understanding the significance of important details of this festival, I have been greatly assisted by the suggestions of Jo Ann Scurlock.

39. In ancient Egypt, as in many societies, the family was more important than the individual. Individuals could not survive death intact, but families could endure forever, defeating death through lineage.

40. The dead, after their anthropoid coffins had been sealed away in burial chambers, were represented by statues.

41. One of Hathor's most important epithets is Mistress of Drunkenness.

42. In describing rites of passage, anthropologists speak of three stages: the period of an individual's detachment from the group (separation), the time of transition and ambiguity (liminality), and the period of attachment to a new group (incorporation). Egyptians were separated from the world of the living by death. In funerals, the deceased were made ready to join the community of the next world. But they did not depart permanently from the society of this world. In ancestor cultuses, they were reincorporated, from beyond the grave, into their earthly families.

43. *Ankh*-bouquets are so named because they mediated life force and were sometimes fashioned in the shape of the hieroglyphic sign for "life" ($^c n\underline{h}$).

44. Cf. my lecture on this subject, "Mythology and Iconography of Divine Kingship in Ancient Egypt," delivered at the Brooklyn Museum in a symposium cosponsored by the American Research Center in Egypt, on December 4, 1993; it is summarized in detail by David Moyer, "Symposium: Temples, Tombs, and the Egyptian Universe," *KMT: A Modern Journal of Ancient Egypt* 5 (Summer 1994): 64, 78–79. The most recent treatment of the whole topic is *Ancient Egyptian Kingship,* ed. David O'Connor and David P. Silverman, Probleme der Ägyptologie 9 (Leiden: E. J. Brill, 1995). I have not attempted to present the conclusions of this book in the present chapter.

45. The integration of politics and religion is discussed in Chapter 1. The king was high priest in every temple throughout the land, at least in theory.

46. The divine birth of three New Kingdom monarchs was depicted at Thebes: Hatshepsut, at Deir el-Bahri; Amenhotep III, at Luxor; and Ramesses II, at the Ramesseum (fragments of his scenes are preserved only on decorated blocks reused at Medinet Habu). See Hellmut Brunner, *Die Geburt des Gottkönigs: Studien zur Überlieferung eines altägyptischen Mythos,* 2d ed., ÄgAbh 10 (1986), pp. 7–8, 222, 230–32 and pls. 16–17, 25. For the conception scene itself, see Barry J. Kemp, *Ancient Egypt: Anatomy of a Civilization* (London and New York: Routledge, 1989), p. 199. See also William J. Murnane, "Le mystère de la naissance divine du roi," in *DHA* 101, pp. 54–57.

47. See Chapter 1. In the mythology, Osiris was murdered by his brother Seth, who took Osiris's place as king. Then Horus avenged his father and became the king himself. The triumph of Horus over his uncle Seth is the subject of "The Contendings of Horus and Seth." For an English translation of that story, see William Kelly Simpson, ed., *The Literature of Ancient Egypt,* new ed. (New Haven and London: Yale University Press, 1973), pp. 108–26, or Miriam Lichtheim, *Ancient Egyptian Literature,* vol. 2, *The New Kingdom* (Berkeley: University of California Press, 1976), pp. 214–23.

48. See, for example, the study by Benjamin C. Ray, *Myth, Ritual, and Kingship in Buganda* (New York and Oxford: Oxford University Press, 1991); chapter 7 is entitled "Buganda and Ancient Egypt: Speculation and Evidence."

49. For the use of this terminology, see L. Bell, "Luxor Temple," *JNES* 44 (1985): 293–94; see also Morenz, *Egyptian Religion* [n. 27], pp. 37–40.

50. Godhood tended to be passed to a male in the same family (roughly, same dynasty), but not inevitably so. The new, "divinely born" king might not have been king-designate, or in the direct line of succession, or even a male—most notably, Hatshepsut!

51. The king was divine *only* to the extent that he acted *in loco dei.* He remained capable of great human error and mischief. That there were two aspects to his nature explains Egyptians' ambivalent attitude toward their king. For evidence of the humanity of the king, see Georges Posener, *De la divinité du pharaon,* Cahiers de la Société Asiatique 15 (Paris: Imprimerie Nationale, 1960).

52. Of course, this myth tells us very little about the practical processes involved in selecting a king after the death of his predecessor, particularly after an assassination or at a change in dynasties. However, the paradigmatic story of Horus and Seth may shed some light on the situation. There are other clues that a struggle for dominance probably occurred regularly between competing strongmen: the factionalism, interdynastic rivalries, and intradynastic struggles that erupted during times of trouble (especially in the intermediate periods) and the military training and background that most New Kingdom monarchs possessed. Coregency—in which, paradoxically, two legitimate Horus kings reigned simultaneously—was an extreme measure used occasionally to guarantee one's successor.

53. We find, for example, the human Ramesses II worshiping the divine Ramesses II.

54. It appears that a close connection existed between royal dogma and everyday beliefs regarding the functioning of the *ka,* and my specialized theory of the royal *ka* helps to elucidate the mechanisms that determined familial rights and social obligations in the Egyptian population as a whole. Material on this subject was presented in my lecture "The Meaning of the Term *Ka* in The Instructions of Ptahhotep," delivered at the annual meeting of the American Research Center in Egypt held in St. Louis, April 12–14, 1996; an abstract of it is published in *Program and Abstracts* ([New York]: American Research Center in Egypt, 1996), pp. 30–31. For "The Instruction of Ptahhotep" in English translation, see Lichtheim, *Ancient Egyptian Literature* 1 [n. 12], pp. 61–80.

55. The impression that the arms are upraised results from the absence of perspective in Egyptian art. The *ka*-arms should be seen as outstretched, embracing a person protectively, from behind (cf. fig. 44). See Craig C. Dochniak, "The Horus Falcon's Wings on the Seated Statue of Khafre as a Zoomorphic Substitution for the Ka Hieroglyph," *VA* 8 (1992): 69–73.

56. The standard is the royal *mdw-špsy* discussed in Appendix II, item 3.

57. Being nurtured by a goddess betokened the king's adoption into the divine family, an act of incorporation or aggregation par excellence. Egyptians must also have thought that mother's milk, the food of babies, could make adults young again.

58. The glorified mummy was called *sˁḥ,* "ennobled."

59. For our present purpose, the most detailed and complete plan of Luxor Temple is found in Ludwig Borchardt, "Zur Geschichte des Luqsortempels," *ZÄS* 34 (1896): pl. 7 (after p. 138). For an introduction to the temple, see William J. Murnane, "Pour visiter le temple," in *DHA* 101, pp. 12–16.

60. The ancient town of Luxor became the core of the modern village of Luxor, which grew up around three sides of the temple, eventually invading it. Most of the encroachment was removed from the temple grounds by expropriation and excavation at the end of the nineteenth century.

61. Georges Daressy supposed that a Middle Kingdom temple had existed at Luxor, but he was cautious about the actual evidence. Daressy, *Notice explicative des ruines du temple de Louxor* (Cairo: Imprimerie Nationale, 1893), pp. 1–2; and "Le voyage d'inspection de M. Grébaut en 1889," *ASAE* 26 (1926): 8. Ludwig Borchardt, "Luqsortempels," *ZÄS* 34 (1896): 122, accepted Daressy's evidence at face value. However, the two granite architrave blocks inscribed for King Sobekhotep II (Dynasty 13) that Daressy's excavation found in front of the entrance to the portico ("hypostyle") of Amenhotep III are most probably Middle Kingdom pieces that originated at Karnak and were brought to Luxor only at a much later date, for reuse in building activities there.

62. Borchardt, "Luqsortempels," *ZÄS* 34 (1896): 122–23. See also Brunner, *Die südlichen Räume* [n. 1], pls. 5–7, 10, 20–21 and pp. 84, 14.

63. El-Saghir, *Das Statuenversteck* [n. 17], pp. 69–71. For Amenhotep II at Luxor, see Charles C. Van Siclen III, "Amenhotep II, Shabako, and the Roman Camp at Luxor," *VA* 3 (1987): 158–60.

64. See below for further discussion of the way stations.

65. For a sketch plan showing the locations of suggested Thutmoside structures at Luxor, see Van Siclen, "Amenhotep II," *VA* 3 (1987): 159–60.

66. For this pylon, see Michel Azim, "Le grand pylône de Ramsès II," in *DHA* 101, pp. 33–38. See also Thierry Zimmer, "Destination nouvelle pour l'obélisque," in *DHA* 101, pp. 86–89; Mahmud Abd El-Razik, "Some Remarks on the Great Pylon of the Luxor Temple," *MDAIK* 22 (1967): 68–70. A Kushite kiosk (Dynasty 25) once stood before the pylon; see below.

67. Two seated statues were put in place early in the reign of Ramesses II; Kuentz, *Face sud* [n. 1], pls. 21, 26 (scène 16a), and El-Razik, "Great Pylon," *MDAIK* 22 (1967): 69–70. (For the depiction of the statues, see n. 125.) About twenty-five years later, in time for the king's first *Sed*-festival or jubilee, four standing statues were added. The eastern obelisk and at least remnants of all six statues can be seen there today. A few of the statues are in relatively good condition. The western obelisk was taken to Paris and now stands in the Place de la Concorde. A period of five years elapsed between its removal from Luxor Temple (1831) and its dedication in Paris (1836).

68. The two rows of columns support a narrow canopylike roof, which shades both the walls circumscribing the court and the fringes of its open space. A peristyle colonnade often bounds the edges of a large temple court.

69. Barque shrines were small chapels for housing a portable divine barque, which rested on a plinth near the center of the room. They were constructed either in temples or at sacred resting places along processional routes (way stations or barque stations). In a temple, a barque shrine might be nested within another chamber, called a barque sanctuary. Such free-standing barque chapels were often open-ended. They had stone side walls, but at both ends they had only wooden doors, which opened into the relatively cramped interior space. Various rituals were performed in front of the barque while it rested in its shrine or sanctuary.

70. In the northeast quadrant of the court, towering over visitors on the floor of the peristyle and dating to a relatively modern archaeological stratum, is a mosque (founded in the thirteenth century C.E.) dedicated to Abu el-Haggag, an important local Muslim saint (fig. 56, no. 21). The threshold of the mosque's original door—now severed from all connecting pathways and clearly unused—marks the level to which debris had accumulated in the court before it was cleared by the Egyptian Antiquities Organization (the major part of the work having been completed in 1954). The dressed stone foundations on which the mosque rests are the walls of an unexcavated seventh-century C.E. Byzantine church that was intruded into the "pagan" court.

71. See Frank J. Yurco, "La première cour et ses colosses royaux," in *DHA* 101, pp. 39–40; Christine Strauss-Seeber, "Zum Statuenprogramm Ramses' II. im Luxortempel," in *Tempel und Kult*, ed. Wolfgang Helck, ÄgAbh 46 (1987), pp. 24–42.

72. As the temple was configured at the end of Dynasty 18, the very first structures entered might have been mudbrick. If so, these have disappeared without a trace. Many people are baffled by the shift in axis as one moves from the Eighteenth Dynasty temple to Ramesses II's peristyle court and pylon. The explanation for the anomaly seems simple. The ceremonial road from Karnak to Luxor approached the facade of the Eighteenth Dynasty temple at an oblique angle. Had the architects of Ramesses II extended the temple's axis in a straight line, the entrance would no longer have intersected with the avenue of sphinxes. Instead the avenue would have ended in the ungated east tower of the pylon. The ceremonial route was probably too sacred to be redirected, so the architects accommodated its path by swinging both the pylon and the front of the peristyle eastward to meet the road, sacrificing the rectangularity of the court. See Labib Habachi, "The Triple Shrine of the Theban Triad in Luxor Temple," *MDAIK* 20 (1965): 96–97.

73. See W. Raymond Johnson, "Honorific Figures of Amenhotep III in the Luxor Temple Colonnade Hall," in *For His Ka: Essays Offered in Memory of Klaus Baer,* ed. David P. Silverman, SAOC 55 (1994), pp. 133–34; Johnson, "Images of Amenhotep III in Thebes: Styles and Intentions," in *The Art of Amenhotep III: Art Historical Analysis,* ed. Lawrence Michael Berman ([Bloomington, Indiana]: Cleveland Museum of Art and Indiana University Press, 1990), pp. 29–32. Cf. Betsy M. Bryan, "Designing the Cosmos: Temples and Temple Decoration," in Arielle P. Kozloff and Betsy M. Bryan, *Egypt's Dazzling Sun: Amenhotep III and His World* ([Bloomington, Indiana]: Cleveland Museum of Art and Indiana University Press, 1992), pp. 89–90. See also Françoise Traunecker, "L'architecture de la grande colonnade," in *DHA* 101, pp. 42–45.

74. The colonnade of Luxor Temple is the single most important extant monument from the reign of Tutankhamun. It presents unequivocal evidence that he returned to the orthodoxy of Amun-Re's traditional cultus after the Amarna interlude. See Epigraphic Survey, *Reliefs and Inscriptions at Luxor Temple,* vol. 1, *The Festival Procession of Opet in the Colonnade Hall,* OIP 112 (1994).

75. Excavation has revealed that the pavement beneath the sun court's southernmost inner columns covers the eastern and western ends of a dedicatory inscription on the northern face of the core temple's stone platform (or socle—a kind of pedestal upon which the oldest part of the temple was built). This conclusion is confirmed by the observation that the stones of the sun court's walls are not bonded to those of the core temple's portico. Both data demonstrate that the sun court was a secondary construction. See Daressy, *Notice explicative* [n. 61], p. 51.

76. See fig. 56, nos. 30 (Amun-Re), 29 (Mut), and 28 (Khonsu). These arrangements were the ones made for the barques in the reign of Amenhotep III. For the alterations during the reign of Ramesses II, see below.

77. For the kiosk, see Jean Leclant, *Recherches sur les monuments thébains de la XXVe Dynastie dite éthiopienne,* BdÉ 36 (1965), pp. 134–39 and pl. 80. See further Van Siclen, "Amenhotep II," *VA* 3 (1987): 161–64; Arnold, *Die Tempel Ägyptens* [n. 1], p. 128 (plan). For the Roman camp, see Michel Reddé, "Le camp de Louqsor dans l'architecture militaire du Bas-Empire," in Mohammed El-Saghir et al., *Le camp romain de Louqsor,* MIFAO 83 (1986), pp. 27–31.

78. The doorway was cut through the wall by the Egyptian Antiquities Organization around 1954, when it reopened the ancient axial way that Roman construction had blocked.

79. Brunner, *Die südlichen Räume* [n. 1], pl. 1. See also Mahmud Abd El-Raziq, *Die Darstellungen und Texte des Sanktuars Alexanders des Grossen im Tempel von Luxor,* AVDAIK 16 (1984).

80. Mahmud Abdel-Raziq, *Das Sanktuar Amenophis III im Luxor-Tempel,* Studies in

Egyptian Culture 3 (Tokyo: Waseda University, 1986). The original decorations, like all work from the reign of Amenhotep III, were severely damaged by agents of Akhenaten. For the most part, the restorations of the damaged decorations made in plaster at the end of Dynasty 18 and the beginning of Dynasty 19 have not survived, and the extent of the Amarna-age destruction is fully exposed. Fragments of the original red granite barque stand of Amenhotep III have been identified in Labib Habachi, "Sethos I's Devotion to Seth and Avaris," *ZÄS* 100 (1974): 99 and n. 17.

81. Peter Pamminger, "Die sogenannte 'Thebanische' Götterneunheit," *SAK* 19 (1992): 254. An Ennead was a group or cycle of nine gods. Since nine was considered a large number, the term could be extended to include groups of more than nine.

82. Many modifications have been made to the back wall of the barque sanctuary, most in ancient times. The open doorway that is now there seems to be modern. See William J. Murnane, "False Doors and Cult Practices inside Luxor Temple," in *Mélanges Gamal Eddin Mokhtar* 2, BdÉ 97/2 (1985), pp. 145–46.

83. Brunner, *Die südlichen Räume,* pls. 57, 60. For the form of the cult statue, see n. 159.

84. See Thomas Schuller-Götzburg, "Der Kultweg in den südlichen Räumen des Tempels von Luxor," *VA* 2 (1986): 145–49; Schuller-Götzburg, *Zur Semantik der Königsikonographie*, Beiträge zur Ägyptologie 9 (Vienna: Institute für Afrikanistik und Ägyptologie der Universität Wien, 1990).

85. Brunner, *Die südlichen Räume,* pp. 10–11, 79–82; Brunner, "Die Sonnenbahn in ägyptischen Tempeln," in *Archäologie und Altes Testament: Festschrift für Kurt Galling,* ed. Arnulf Kuschke and Ernst Kutsch (Tübingen: J. C. B. Mohr, 1970), pp. 27–34. Brunner's detailed study of the decorative reliefs in the temple of the *Opet*-sanctuary has revealed the solar nature of the second axis.

86. It was common practice for a single temple to have both a barque shrine for the resident god and an interconnected sanctuary for the resident god's statues. Luxor's arrangement—in which the visiting god had the barque shrine and the resident god had the sanctuary—is noteworthy. Jean-Claude Dégardin, "Procession de barques dans le temple de Khonsou," *RdÉ* 35 (1984): 191–95, suggests a similar arrangement at the Khonsu temple. A popular cult place related to the worship of the divine king as the royal *ka* was located on the exterior of the southern outer wall of Luxor Temple, directly behind the *Opet*-sanctuary.

87. L. Bell, "Luxor Temple," *JNES* 44 (1985): 251–94; cf. L. Bell, "Le culte du *Kâ* royal," in *DHA* 101, pp. 57–59. Three descriptions of Luxor Temple which appeared shortly after these articles incorporated their conclusions: Kemp, *Ancient Egypt* [n. 46], pp. 206–9; Arnold, *Die Tempel Ägyptens* [n. 1], pp. 127–32; Bryan, in Kozloff and Bryan, *Egypt's Dazzling Sun* [n. 73], pp. 82–90. Another recently published work, however, rejects these conclusions: Hans Goedicke, *Problems concerning Amenophis III* (Baltimore: Halgo, 1992), esp. pp. 96–100, 68.

88. Cf. the comments of Brunner, *Die südlichen Räume* [n. 1], p. 77. It is my study of the treatment of the royal *ka* at Luxor Temple that has allowed me to define the divine nature of the king displayed there. See also Thomas Schuller-Götzburg, "Zur Vergöttlichung Amenophis III. in Ägypten," *GM* 135 (1993): 89–95.

89. The *Opet*-festival was distinct from the royal jubilee (the *Sed*-festival [*ḥeb-sed*] or Thirty-Year Festival), although the two were conceptually related.

90. Because the *Opet*-festival was primary in establishing and maintaining the kings' divine status, many pharaohs made it a point to preside in person rather than through a deputy.

91. Luxor Temple was apparently regarded as the birthplace of Amun-Re of Karnak. Cf. Claude Traunecker, "Amon de Louqsor," in *DHA* 101, p. 64; Pamminger, "Amun und Luxor," *BeitrSudanF* 5 (1992): 114–15.

92. The first day of the first month of the solar/sidereal (i.e., astronomical) calendar (averaging 365¼ days) always fell at the heliacal rising of the star Sirius in mid-July, the month when the Nile's flooding actually began.

93. Today, the Islamic lunar calendar operates in this way.

94. Today, the Jewish lunar calendar operates similarly, adding a thirteenth month in seven of every nineteen years so that the New Year always falls in September or early October.

95. Somewhat after the prehistoric lunar calendar had been modified, a schematic civil year was instituted that averaged out the solilunar years of 354 days (twelve months) and of 383–84 days (thirteen months) and the successive heliacal risings of Sothis. This calendar consisted of 12 months of 30 days divided into 3 seasons of 4 months, with 5 epagomenal days tacked onto the end for a total of 365 days. The first day of the first month of the 365-day civil calendar, the start of the season called Inundation (*ỉ3ḥ̣ịt*), coincided exactly with day 1/1 of the solar/sidereal calendar during only the first four years in each cycle of 1460 years (the Sothic cycle). The ancient Egyptians made no attempt to reconcile this discrepancy by adjusting their civil calendar; instead, to bring the lunar and civil months back together again, a second revised lunar calendar was devised that related to the civil year rather than to the solar/sidereal year. For a convenient summary, see Richard A. Parker, "The Calendars and Chronology," in *The Legacy of Egypt*, 2d ed., ed. J. R. Harris (Oxford: Oxford University Press, 1971), pp. 13–21. See also Chapter 1.

96. For the data, see Siegfried Schott, *Altägyptische Festdaten*, AAWLM, Jahrgang 1950/10, pp. 84–87.

97. For representations of barque processions in New Kingdom temples, see Lanny Bell, "Only One High Priest Ramessenakht and the Second Prophet Nesamun His Younger Son," *Serapis: The American Journal of Egyptology* 6 (1980): 20 (1–6) and 22 n. 169; L. Bell, in *Melánges Gamal Eddin Mokhtar* [n. 6], p. 39. To these references, add Janina Wiercińska, "La procession d'Amon dans la décoration du temple de Thoutmosis III à Deir el-Bahari," *Études et Travaux XIV*, Travaux du, Centre d'Archéologie Méditerranéenne de l'Académie Polonaise des Sciences 28 (Warsaw: Éditions scientifiques de Pologne, 1990), pp. 61–90.

98. Highlights of the material that follows were included in a full-day lecture and discussion period on "The *Ka* of Amenhotep III: The Decoration, Cult, and Significance of Luxor Temple," presented at the invitation of Professor Dr. Rolf Gundlach on June 10, 1991, in the Seminar für Ägyptologie at Johannes Gutenberg-Universität in Mainz. Condensed versions were delivered during the next two days at the Institut für Ägyptologie, Universität Würzburg, and the Ägyptologisches Institut, Universität Heidelberg.

99. The north-south axis led to the Seventh through Tenth Pylons. For the apparent skewing of the axis through the Ninth and Tenth Pylons, see the explanation presented in note 72.

100. Cf. Pamminger, "Amun und Luxor," *BeitrSudanF* 5 (1992): 115.

101. Paul Barguet, *Le temple d'Amon-Rê à Karnak: Essai d'exégèse*, RAPH 21 (1962), pp. 157–210, 283–99; Gerhard Haeny, *Basilikale Anlagen in der ägyptischen Baukunst des Neuen Reiches*, BeiträgeBf 9 (1970), pp. 13–17; Golvin and Goyon, *Bâtisseurs* [n. 38], pp. 44–48. Just as the agents of Alexander the Great renewed the barque shrine of Amenhotep III at Luxor Temple in Alexander's name, so they also restored the shrine of the divine Thutmose III in the *Akhmenu*. It seems they paid special attention to the starting point and culminating point of the *Opet*-festival procession.

102. A damaged inscription in the Festival Hall of Thutmose III seems to be directly linked with the boatmen's chant that accompanied the transport of divine barges (best known from the later Tutankhamun reliefs in the Luxor colonnade). The reign of Hatshepsut was encompassed entirely within the early years of Thutmose III, so it is hardly surprising that the same hymn of praise should occur both in his Festival Hall and among the inscriptions of her dismantled barque sanctuary at Karnak, the Chapelle Rouge. Barguet, *Temple d'Amon-Rê*, pp. 172–76, 293–94; Pierre Lacau and Henri Chevrier, *Une chapelle d'Hatshepsout à Karnak*, 2 vols. (Cairo: SAE and IFAO, 1977 and 1979), 1:187–88.

103. William J. Murnane, "La grande fête d'Opet," in *DHA* 101, pp. 22–25. The design of the reliefs and the execution of most of them date to the reign of Tutankhamun. The west wall depicts the procession from Karnak to Luxor, while the east wall depicts the return trip, the events being essentially the same but in reverse order.

104. See L. Bell, in *Mélanges Gamal Eddin Mokhtar*, vol. 1 [n. 6], pp. 31–37.

105. The main sanctuary is now almost completely destroyed, but it would have been located in the so-called Court of the Middle Kingdom. Refer to the plans of Haeny, *Basilikale Anlagen*, BeiträgeBf 9 (1970), p. 6; J. Lauffray, *Karnak d'Égypte: Domaine du divin* (Paris: Éditions du CNRS, 1979), p. 48, fig. 33 (F). On the route from the main sanctuary to the *Akhmenu*, see Chapter 3. For the probability that the king's *ka*-statue did not have its own barque until at least the reign of Amenhotep III, see the statement and citation in note 108.

106. In the time of Amenhotep III, the Third Pylon was the westernmost on Karnak's east-west axis. For changes in the *Opet*-festival procession's land route occasioned by the construction of the Third Pylon, see Bryan, in Kozloff and Bryan, *Egypt's Dazzling Sun* [n. 73], pp. 94–99.

107. Although Amenhotep III laid the foundations for the Tenth Pylon, between the reigns of Hatshepsut and Haremhab the southern exit from Karnak was the Eighth Pylon (fig. 65, no. 4, constructed by Hatshepsut), so the Khonsu Temple lay well outside Karnak-proper. From Haremhab onward, the southern exit was the Tenth Pylon (fig. 65, no. 5), so the Khonsu Temple lay within the Karnak enclosure. The Khonsu Temple that one visits today dates to Dynasty 20, but its predecessor doubtless stood at or very near the same location. See Bryan, in Kozloff and Bryan, *Egypt's Dazzling Sun*, p. 99. It should be noted, however, that no conclusive on-site evidence attests the existence of the earlier version of the temple that I have postulated here; cf. Françoise Laroche-Traunecker, "Données nouvelles sur les abords du temple de Khonsou," in *Cahiers de Karnak VII: 1978–1981* (Paris: Éditions Recherche sur les Civilisations, 1982), pp. 330–32.

108. The evidence from the Khonsu Temple is discussed by Dégardin, "Procession," *RdÉ* 35 (1984): 191–95. The earliest known representation of a royal barque dates to the reign of Tutankhamun; see L. Bell, "Luxor Temple," *JNES* 44 (1985): 261–62. By the time of Amenhotep III, each member of the Theban triad had his or her own barque, usually resident in his or her temple's barque sanctuary. Evidence from the reign of Hatshepsut, however, suggests that at that time only Amun-Re had his own barque and barge, for the barques of Khonsu and Mut are not represented, nor are barque sanctuaries or shrines for them attested this early. The only piece of possibly contradictory evidence known to me is an unpublished scene from a wall in Hatshepsut's temple at Deir el-Bahri, where the barques of Mut and Khonsu *are* represented; cf. L. Bell, "Ramessenakht," *Serapis* 6 (1980): 22 n. 169, item 3. However, that wall was heavily damaged under Akhenaten and restored in the post-Amarna period. During the wall's restoration, the depiction was "modernized" by adding the barques of Khonsu and Mut; Karkowski, in *Fifty Years of Polish Excavations* [n. 38], p. 61. The fragmentary reliefs of Thutmose III at Deir el-Bahri also show the barque of Amun-Re alone; see Hubert J. Górski, "La barque d'Amon dans le décoration du temple de Thoutmosis III à Deir el-Bahari," *MDAIK* 46 (1990): 99–100. So I continue to believe that during the reigns of Hatshepsut and Thutmose III Khonsu and Mut rode with Amun-Re in his barque's covered naos. See William J. Murnane, "Opetfest," *LÄ* 4:578 n. 17. (On a similar matter, the date of the barges of these gods, see Murnane, "The Bark of Amun on the Third Pylon at Karnak," *JARCE* 16 [1979]: 19; and C. Traunecker, in Traunecker, Le Saout, and Masson, *Chapelle d'Achôris* [n. 38], pp. 98–100.) Because Hatshepsut's procession featured only one divine barque, her *Opet* way stations would each have had a single chapel, not a triple one like the Luxor barque shrine of Ramesses II. See Herbert Ricke, *Das Kamutef-Heiligtum Hatshepsuts und Thutmoses' III. in Karnak: Bericht über eine Ausgrabung vor dem Muttempelbezirk*, BeiträgeBf 3/2 (1954), pp. 40–41; and Lanny Bell, "Luxor Update," *Oriental Institute News & Notes* 90 (September-October 1983): 5. Ricke theorized that structural changes were made in Way Station I so that it could accommodate the barque of Mut as well as that of Amun-Re. His hypothesis remains unconfirmed, and the date when the modifications were made, uncertain.

109. The Temple of Mut always lay outside Karnak-proper, that is, beyond Karnak's southernmost pylon (see note 107). Like Luxor Temple, its sanctuary was oriented toward Karnak.

110. The sanctuary of Kamutef and Way Station I of Hatshepsut opened opposite each other on either side of the processional way. Decorative fragments from the largely destroyed sanctuary date its construction to Hatshepsut also. For both these shrines, see Ricke, *Das Kamutef-Heiligtum*. "Kamutef" means "Bull of his Mother." As a fertility god, Kamutef begot himself by impregnating his mother, so he transcended the limits of any single generation in an endless cycle of rebirth and renewal. He was the Theban version of the national fertility god, Min of Coptos, whose chief cult center was located about twenty-two miles north of Luxor.

111. See Luc Gabolde, "L'itinéraire de la procession d'Opet," in *DHA* 101, pp. 27–28.

112. The existence of this landing is indicated by the remains of a spur road that headed toward the river from a junction northwest of the Temple of Mut; see Mohammed El-Saghir, "The Great Processional Way of Thebes (The Avenue of the Sphinxes at Luxor)," in *Sesto Congresso Internazionale di Egittologia: Atti* ([Turin]: [International Association of Egyptologists], 1992), 1:181–87. See also Christian E. Loeben, "Der Zugang zum Amuntempel von Karnak im Neuen Reich: Zum Verständnis einer zeitgenössischen Architekturdarstellung," in *The Intellectual Heritage of Egypt: Studies Presented to László Kákosy by Friends and Colleagues on the*

Occasion of His Sixtieth Birthday, ed. Ulrich Luft, Studia Aegyptiaca 14 (Budapest: La Chaire d'Égyptologie de l'Université Eötvös Loránd de Budapest, 1992), pp. 393–401. Before the discovery of this road, it was assumed that the barque of Amun-Re was loaded aboard his barge from the harbor in front of the First Pylon at Karnak; Golvin and Goyon, *Bâtisseurs* [n. 38], pp. 56–58; Arnold, *Die Tempel Ägyptens* [n. 1], p. 110. However, Kemp, *Ancient Egypt* [n. 46], p. 203, shows the barque of Khonsu going separately to the river from its temple. See also the comments of C. Traunecker, in Traunecker, Le Saout, and Masson, *Chapelle d'Achôris* [n. 38], pp. 98–100. For the remains of the Karnak river installation, see Lauffray, *Karnak d'Égypte* [n. 105], pp. 90–97; and C. Traunecker, in Traunecker, Le Saout, and Masson, *Chapelle d'Achôris,* pp. 89–98.

113. Going upstream to Luxor, against the current, the barges usually sailed with the prevailing north wind. On the return trip to Karnak, the craft usually drifted downstream with the current, in which case the sails were struck and sailors manned the oars.

114. At least some of the onlookers must have been seized by ecstatic fits.

115. The paved, sphinx-lined roadway that one sees today postdates Hatshepsut's reign considerably. It represents part of the extensive restoration work undertaken by Nectanebo I (Dynasty 30), shortly before Alexander the Great imposed his rule over Egypt. Nonetheless, because Hatshepsut's temple at Deir el-Bahri was approached along a sphinx-lined causeway, I find it quite conceivable that sphinxes flanked the Karnak-Luxor road in her time.

116. Lacau and Chevrier, *Chapelle d'Hatshepsout,* vol. 2 [n. 102], pl. 7. We know the sites of Way Stations I (the northernmost) and VI (the southernmost). Station I was located just north of the Temple of Mut (fig. 65, no. 11); its scanty remains have been identified and studied. VI was located at or near the Luxor site of Ramesses II's triple barque shrine (fig. 56, no. 4). Remains from Way Stations II through V have not yet been found. When the official religion of an area changes, it is common practice to preserve ancient holy sites in a new, but nonetheless sacred, form. For example, the mosque of Abu el-Haggag (fig. 56, no. 21) was built on top of the Byzantine church, which had been erected in the peristyle court of Ramesses II. So I think the ancient site of Way Station V stood very near the present site of the mosque of Maqeshqesh (figs. 65, no. 12; 61).

117. On the Temple of Mut, see Richard A. Fazzini, "Report on the 1983 Season of Excavation at the Precinct of the Goddess Mut," *ASAE* 70 (1984–1985): 294 and n. 3, 304 and n. 1.

118. Lacau and Chevrier, *Chapelle d'Hatshepsout,* vol. 2, pls. 7 (south), 9 (south); 1:153–69, 173–91.

119. Golvin and Goyon, *Bâtisseurs* [n. 38], p. 49; see further, Pamminger, "Amun und Luxor," *BeitrSudanF* 5 (1992): 115. For directional symbolism in the set course of the *Opet*-festival procession and its representation at Luxor, cf. also Edward James Walker, "Aspects of the Primaeval Nature of Egyptian Kingship: Pharaoh as Atum" (Ph.D. diss., University of Chicago, 1991), pp. 56–58.

120. The use of the river route by Thutmose III is suggested by the link between his Festival Hall and the boatmen's chant (cf. n. 102). Nothing extant from the reign of Thutmose III or Amenhotep III proves that the monarch ever took a route other than the river. Nonetheless, it seems likely that Thutmose III, at least, would have continued occasionally to use the land route.

121. See Murnane, "Bark of Amun," *JARCE* 16 (1979): 11–27.

122. Cf. Lanny Bell, "Les parcours processionnels," in *DHA* 101, pp. 29–30.

123. On the question of the orientation, see Alexander Badawy, *A History of Egyptian Architecture: The Empire (the New Kingdom) from the Eighteenth Dynasty to the End of the Twentieth Dynasty 1580–1085 B.C.* (Berkeley and Los Angeles: University of California Press, 1968), p. 186. Note also that the barque shrines of Sety II and Ramesses III in the first court of Karnak Temple (fig. 65, nos. 8, 9) are clearly oriented at right angles to the processional route along which they were built (fig. 65, no. 13). See also the orientation of Hatshepsut's Way Station I in relationship to her processional road (note 110).

124. For this principle, see Dieter Arnold, *Wandrelief und Raumfunktion in ägyptischen Tempeln des Neuen Reiches,* MÄS 2 (Berlin: Bruno Hessling, 1962), p. 128.

125. Below the large reliefs, a smaller register shows files of royal children and other offering bearers approaching the facade of the Luxor pylon, drawn as it looked for the first jubilee (*Sed*-festival) of Ramesses II. See Abd El-Razik, *MDAIK* 22 (1967): 69–70. These reliefs may suggest that the large group of participants in the shore procession that accompanied the flotilla entered the peristyle court through the pylon while those in the flotilla itself entered the court through the western gateway. On the other hand, the pylon may simply designate Luxor Temple as the goal of the procession. In the representation of the pylon in this register, the six seated and standing colossi of Ramesses II are shown in profile. Egyptian art rarely showed figures full faced. The most notable exceptions were depictions of Hathor and the hieroglyph *ḥr,* which was used for the noun "face" and the preposition "upon."

126. Stone elements originally belonging to Hatshepsut's way station were incorporated into Ramesses II's triple barque shrine. See Daressy, *Notice explicative* [n. 61], p. 36; Borchardt, "Luqsortempels," *ZÄS* 34 (1896): 125–26; F. W. von Bissing, "Über die Kapelle im Hof Ramesses II im Tempel von Luxor," *Acta Orientalia* 8 (1930): 129–32; Habachi, "Triple Shrine," *MDAIK* 20 (1965): 93–97. The name and epithets of Amun-Re originally carved on the blocks were defaced during the reign of Akhenaten and subsequently recarved, proving that Hatshepsut's structure was still standing both during and after his reign. Furthermore, the text of restoration may be datable to Ramesses II. The restorer added to the original inscription—found on a large block now lying on the floor of the Amun-Re chapel (fig. 58)—a redundant star hieroglyph for *dw3,* "adore," a word already denoted in the composition by the gesture of kneeling *paʿet*-figures. The same star hieroglyph is placed before kneeling anthropomorphic *rekhyet*-figures (fig. 69) and *paʿet*-figures (fig. 70) on the exterior of the people's gate (fig. 56, no. 9), decoration clearly datable to Ramesses II.

127. See von Bissing, "Kapelle," *Acta Orientalia* 8 (1930): 147. See further L. Bell, "Luxor Update" [n. 108], 4–5; L. Bell, "La reine Hatchepsout au temple de Louqsor," in *DHA* 101, pp. 25–26.

128. The *rekhyet* are also mentioned in a formalized (conventional or stereotypical) *rekhyet*-inscription dating to Hatshepsut that is found in the portico of the triple shrine on one of the reused column bases from her way station. See L. Bell, "Luxor Temple," *JNES* 44 (1985): 275–76 n. 128. To visualize how the four columns of the triple barque shrine of Ramesses II might have been arranged in Hatshepsut's barque shrine, see Ludwig Borchardt, *Ägyptische Tempel mit Umgang,* BeiträgeBf 2 (1938), pl. 21 and pp. 95–98.

129. This was suggested to me by Erik Hornung in a 1992 conversation.

130. The Egyptians' penchant for symmetry implies a missing fourth series.

131. A rebus is an artful intertwining or decorative arrangement of hieroglyphic and other pictorial elements. At first glance, a rebus looks like a picture, but it is meant to be read as a phrase or clause. The use of rebuses was fairly common in ancient Egypt, where writing and art were never really separated.

132. However, it must be noted that the cartouche of the king faces in the same direction as the birds that represent the people, as Mechthild Schade-Busch and Peter Pamminger have called to my attention.

133. The *rekhyet*-figures occur on the easternmost (outermost) row of north-south columns on the east side of the court and on both rows of east-west columns on the southeast side of the court.

134. In one of the inscriptions on the people's gate that declares their adoration of Ramesses II, part of the king's cartouche cuts through or overlaps the name "Amun-Re" (fig. 71). I suggest that the Ramesside sculptor started copying one of Hatshepsut's *rekhyet*-inscriptions devoted to Amun-Re, absentmindedly carved "Amun-Re" instead of substituting "Ramesses II," and had to correct his mistake by plastering it in and carving the king's name over it (the ancient plaster has long since fallen out). Ramesses II would have had no qualms about substituting his name for the name of the god with whom he so closely identified himself.

135. A larger-than-life-sized red quartzite representation of what must have been the main Luxor *ka*-statue of Amenhotep III was found buried in the western half of that king's sun court (fig. 56, no. 11), in the Luxor Cachette; El-Saghir, *Das Statuenversteck* [n. 17], pp. 21–27, and Bryan, "Royal and Divine Statuary," in Kozloff and Bryan, *Egypt's Dazzling Sun* [n. 73], pp. 132–35. The size, design, decoration, and inscriptions of this figure of the standing king on a sledge all suggest that it was a reproduction of the principal *ka*-statue. The latter normally would have been inaccessible to the people, probably residing in the chapel that opens off the southwest corner of the Chamber of the Divine King (fig. 56, no. 27). Presumably the reproduction was fashioned so that a version of the image would be accessible to the people.

136. Cf. Henry George Fischer's review of Epigraphic Survey, *Medinet Habu* 5: *The Temple Proper*, vol. 1, *AJA* 63 (1959): 195–98.

137. Haeny, *Basilikale Anlagen* [n. 101], p. 91, n. 55; cf. Haeny, "Scheintür," *LÄ* 5:570. "False doors" are discussed above.

138. The staffs are examples of Amun-Re's portable *mdw-špsy* standard, which would occasionally have stood or been brought here. Cf. Appendix II, item 3.

139. The present reliefs date to Alexander the Great, but they probably replaced virtually identical ones of Amenhotep III. See Abd El-Raziq, *Darstellungen und Texte* [n. 79], p. 55. See also Murnane, "False Doors" [n. 82], pp. 135–48; and Murnane and L. Bell, "La présence divine à Louqsor," in *DHA* 101, pp. 60–61.

140. For this concept and terminology, see Emily M. Ahern, *The Cult of the Dead in a Chinese Village* (Stanford: Stanford University Press, 1973), p. 67. Jo Ann Scurlock called this reference to my attention.

141. For this manner of depicting the statues, see note 125 above.

142. "*Iunmutef*" means "Pillar of his Mother" and stresses the priest's supportive role.

143. Close similarities in garb and function existed between the *Iunmutef*-priest and the mortuary *Sem*-priest (for the latter, see the Index). Some similarity in function also existed between the *Iunmutef*-priest and the priest-mediator, or master of initiation, who guided neophytes, or novices, through rites of passage.

144. See L. Bell, "Luxor Temple," *JNES* 44 (1985): 266–70; Pamminger, "Amun und Luxor," *BeitrSudanF* 5 (1992): 110–14. Cf. Bryan, in Kozloff and Bryan, *Egypt's Dazzling Sun* [n. 73], pp. 86–87, 108.

145. The badly damaged staff was identified by Christian Loeben, who kindly called it to my attention.

146. Pilasters are large, engaged rectangular pillars or solid masonry piers that jut out from the surface of the wall into which they are set and protrude a bit into the court's open space.

147. This moment in the procession would also have afforded court officials, foreign dignitaries, and other important bystanders an excellent opportunity openly to proclaim their loyalty or pledge their allegiance to the "new" king and his regime.

148. Dieter Arnold's classic study *Wandrelief und Raumfunktion* [n. 124] has demonstrated this for Egypt's New Kingdom temples in general; for Luxor Temple in particular, see his pp. 121–23.

149. For details of the architectural alterations and their significance, see L. Bell, "Luxor Temple," *JNES* 44 (1985): 262–63; cf. note 76 above.

150. Khonsu rested to the west of the north-south axis, in a chapel next to the staircase leading up to the roof of the temple (fig. 56, no. 30). Mut was placed in the westernmost of the two chapels located to the east of the north-south axis (fig. 56, no. 29).

151. It is likely that the barques of Mut and Khonsu went as far as the Offering Vestibule (fig. 56, no. 25) before returning to their own chapels.

152. For details, see L. Bell, "Luxor Temple," *JNES* 44 (1985): 265–72.

153. The rites of the king's water purification and introduction to god were components of numerous rituals, not just those of the *Opet*-festival. For rites connected with the presentation of New Year's water, see Claude Traunecker, "Les rites de l'eau à Karnak d'après les textes de la rampe de Taharqa," *BIFAO* 72 (1972): 195–236.

154. See Richard H. Wilkinson, *Reading Egyptian Art: A Hieroglyphic Guide to Ancient Egyptian Painting and Sculpture* ([New York and London]: Thames and Hudson, 1992), p. 49. For this gesture as indicative of adoption, see Hans Peter Hasenfratz, "Zur 'Seelenvorstellung' der alten Ägypter: Anmerkungen zu altägyptischer Anthropologie und ihrer geistesgeschichtlichen Bedeutung," *Zeitschrift für Religions- und Geistesgeschichte* 3 (1990): 205–6. Christian Guksch called this reference to my attention.

155. One scene in the chamber portrays Amenhotep III with the ram's horn, symbolizing his possession of the royal *ka* (fig. 48). This pose is depicted several times on the obelisks of Hatshepsut (fig. 50) and in scenes from her Chapelle Rouge; see Lacau and Chevrier, *Chapelle d'Hatshepsout* [n. 102], vol. 2, pls. 2, 3, 11; 1:61–67, 234–56. For a statue from the Luxor Cachette showing the seated god placing his hands on the shoulder and back of the head of the king (Haremhab), who stands in front of the god with his back to him, see El-Saghir, *Das Statuenversteck* [n. 17], pp. 65–68. For a fragment of another such statue, see W. K. Simpson, "The Head of a Statuette of Tutʿankhamūn in the Metropolitan Museum," *JEA* 41 (1955): 112–14.

156. For the theme of coronation and rebirth, see Assmann, in *Religion and Philosophy in Ancient Egypt* [n. 19], ed. Simpson, pp. 140–42.

157. For details, see L. Bell, "Luxor Temple," *JNES* 44 (1985): 276–78.

158. For a detailed discussion of the reciprocity of offerings, see Chapter 1.

159. See Gerhard Haeny, "Zum Kamutef," *GM* 90 (1986): 33–34. For discussion of the cultic form of Amenemopet in the time of Amenhotep III, see Brunner, *Die südlichen Räume* [n. 1], p. 10. See further, Pamminger, "Amun und Luxor," *Beitr-SudanF* 5 (1992): 93–140.

160. Reinhard Grieshammer, "Mundöffnung(sritual)," *LÄ* 4:223–24. The Opening of the Mouth ritual is apparently depicted twice in the rooms of Amenemopet (fig. 56, no. 19); Brunner, *Die südlichen Räume*, pls. 118, 106. Cf. Murnane, "Le mystère de la naissance divine du roi," *DHA* 101, pp. 56–57; Bryan, in Kozloff and Bryan, *Egypt's Dazzling Sun* [n. 73], pp. 86–87. Furthermore, an offering list (Winfried Barta's type A/B) inscribed near these scenes has the peculiar form primarily associated with Opening of the Mouth rites. An adjacent offering list (Barta's type D, which occurs four other times at Luxor Temple under Amenhotep III) is associated with the deified king as well as Amun-Re, with divine statues in procession during the *Opet*-festival and Valley Festival, and with the Ritual of Amenhotep I; see Brunner, *Die südlichen Räume*, pls. 57 (A/B), 60 (D); Barta, *Die altägyptische Opferliste von der Frühzeit bis zur griechisch-römischen Epoche*, MÄS 3 (Berlin: Bruno Hessling, 1963), pp. 78–82, 94–96, 104–7, 129–40, 162–63, 166; Barta, "Opferliste," *LÄ* 4:587–89. For a somewhat different interpretation of the significance of these offering lists, see Pamminger, "Amun und Luxor," *BeitrSudanF* 5 (1992): 96, 114–15. Cf. also Chapter 1.

161. For Amenemopet and Amun-Re as manifestations of a single god, see Dirk van der Plas, "The Veiled Image of Amenapet," in *Effigies Dei: Essays on the History of Religions*, ed. van der Plas, Studies in the History of Religions (Supplements to *Numen*) 51 (Leiden: E. J. Brill, 1987), pp. 5–6. Egyptians believed that energy was lost in the creative process of distinguishing one entity from another and that the additional energy necessary to keep the cosmos going could be generated through temporary refusion.

162. Pamminger, "Amun und Luxor," *BeitrSudanF* 5 (1992): 93–140. Pamminger cites the relief in the Hypostyle Hall at Karnak, where Amun-Re, wearing the ram's horn, is depicted as the source of the Nile's inundation waters (135–36 n. 276). See Harold Hayden Nelson, *The Great Hypostyle Hall at Karnak*, vol. 1, part 1: *The Wall Reliefs*, ed. William J. Murnane, OIP 106 (1981), pls. 36–38, 258; cf. L. Bell, "Luxor Temple," *JNES* 44 (1985): 270, n. 92. In line with Pamminger's thesis, it is surely no mere coincidence that this figure is associated with the towing of the god's barge during the *Opet*-festival; see Epigraphic Survey, *Reliefs and Inscriptions at Karnak*, vol. 1, *Ramses III's Temple within the Great Inclosure of Amon* 1, OIP 25 (1936), p. ix. For further references to the Nubian origins of the ram of Amun, see Joyce L. Haynes, *Nubia: Ancient Kingdoms of Africa* (Boston: Museum of Fine Arts, 1992), p. 35; and Goedicke, *Problems concerning Amenophis III* [n. 87], pp. 53–69, 99–100 n. 279.

163. El-Saghir et al., *Camp romain* [n. 77], pls. 1, 20; cf. Jean-Claude Golvin et al., "Le camp romain," in *DHA* 101, figs. on pp. 69, 75.

164. C. Traunecker, "Amon de Louqsor," in *DHA* 101, pp. 61–64; C. Traunecker, in Traunecker, Le Saout, and Masson, *Chapelle d'Achôris* [n. 38], pp. 130–34, 138–42, 145–46; van der Plas, in *Effigies Dei* [n. 161], pp. 3–5, 7; William J. Murnane, *United with Eternity: A Concise Guide to the Monuments of Medinet Habu* ([Cairo]: Oriental Institute, University of Chicago, and American University in Cairo Press, 1980), pp. 76–77. Cf. Lanny Bell, "Medinet Habou: Centre administratif de Thèbes-Ouest," in *DHA* 136, p. 66.

165. Jean-Claude Goyon, "An Interpretation of the Edifice," in Richard A. Parker et al., *The Edifice of Taharqa by the Sacred Lake of Karnak,* BES 8 (1979), p. 82; C. Traunecker, in Traunecker, Le Saout, and Masson, *Chapelle d'Achôris,* pp. 130–34, 138–42, 145–46; Christiane M. Zivie, "Recherches sur les textes ptolémaïques de Médinet Habou," in *L'égyptologie en 1979: Axes prioritaires de recherches* (Paris: Éditions du CNRS, 1982), 2:106–9. The thirty-day month of the ancient Egyptian calendar was divided into three ten-day weeks or "decades." The Decade Festival was celebrated once a week (i.e., every ten days).

166. Winfried Barta, "Kematef," *LÄ* 3:382–83. The importance of the snake here lay in the facts that it lives in an underground hole (or "cavern") and that it sheds its skin, making it a symbol of regeneration.

167. The importance of the Appearance of Amun-Min-Kamutef in the Luxor calendar is confirmed by the discovery of two previously unrecognized tableaux depicting it, one in the reassembled fragments of the "lost colonnade" (the broken-down upper registers of the colonnade walls) and the other among the badly damaged reliefs preserved in situ in the Chamber of the Divine King (plastered over in the Roman Period to receive painted decoration but now partially re-exposed). See Johnson, in *For His Ka* [n. 73], ed. Silverman, pp. 139–41. L. Bell, "Luxor Temple," *JNES* 44 (1985): 265; cf. Al. Gayet, *Le temple de Louxor,* vol. 1, *Constructions d'Aménophis III, Cour d'Aménophis, Salle hypostyle, Salle des Offertoires, Salle du* lever *et Sanctuaire de Maut,* MMAF 15 (Paris: Ernest Leroux, 1894), pl. 18 (figs. 68–70), and pp. 56–57. With these finds, representations of the Amun-Min-Kamutef Festival have been identified at four separate spots in Luxor Temple, almost as many as in the whole of Karnak.

168. A representation of the festival is found on the back (inner face) of the east wing of the pylon; see Kuentz, *Face sud* [n. 1].

169. As with all scientific reconstructions, this hypothesis is subject to criticism and modification as I and others examine and evaluate my conclusions and adduce additional evidence. The broader the conceptual argument, the greater the potential for finding further evidence. The success of an hypothesis must be measured by its internal consistency, its experiential probability, and its ability to account for all the relevant data and to identify and integrate related phenomena. In 1991, I expressed to Rolf Gundlach of the Johannes Gutenberg-Universität in Mainz my disappointment that scholars had not yet begun to dismantle my preliminary version of this hypothesis (see "Luxor Temple," *JNES* 44 [1985]: 251–94). He responded, gratifyingly, that to tear down so complex a proposal scholars would have to go beyond objecting to individual details to constructing a better overall theory. If I am someday convinced that a better solution for the puzzle of Luxor Temple has been found, I will gladly embrace it.

170. My understanding illumines the meaning of the ubiquitous offering formula *n k3 ny NN,* "To the *ka* of So-and-so"(that is, "To the Lineage of So-and-so"), and of the common royal epithet *ḫnty k3w ʿnḫw nbw,* "Foremost of the *Ka*s of All the Living" (that is, "Head of All the Clans").

171. I have previously addressed some of the issues involved in Akhenaten's relationship with Luxor Temple in "Luxor Temple," *JNES* 44 (1985): 291–93.

172. "Contra-temple" is the term used to describe a chapel that abuts the back wall of a larger, more important temple to which it is related. Inscriptional evidence specifically linking the contra-temple at East Karnak to Amun-Re-Who-Hears-Prayers is lacking until the reign of Ramesses II. Likewise, inscriptional evidence specifically linking Re-Harakhti to East Karnak is lacking until the reign of Ramesses II. But the preparation by Thutmose III to erect here the Unique Obelisk, the only unpaired monumental obelisk in all of Egypt, indicates that the cultus of Re-Harakhti was already associated with the site during his reign. One of the Aten temples at East Karnak was called the *ḥwt-bnbn*, a name borrowed from the venerable solar sanctuary of Heliopolis, where stood a single obelisk-like stone, the *benben*.

173. Rather inconsistently, several of the traditional gods were apparently tolerated as manifestations of the Aten, for neither their names nor their images were violated by those the king assigned to "clean up" the old temples and accessible tombs by defacing "false" gods.

174. Other members of the royal family, most notably Queen Nefertiti, seem also to have served as intermediaries with god.

175. See notes 14, 89.

176. We do not possess a detailed chronology of Akhenaten's early activities in Thebes, so we cannot say to what extent he at first attempted to salvage Karnak's existing temples by modifying them and incorporating their established rituals into his new schema. Neither can we say for sure when he started closing them. But whether the Amun Temple at Karnak remained open in some underutilized form or was closed completely, it would have played no important role in the king's new ideas.

177. These objects were the subject of my illustrated lecture "The *ʿnḫ*-bouquet, the *mdw-špsy*, and the Transmission of the Divine Life Force: Communication between the Sanctuary and the 'Profane' World," presented at the invitation of Professor Dr. Erika Endesfelder and Professor Dr. Steffen Wenig during the symposium "Tempel am Nil—Struktur und Funktion" at Humboldt-Universität (Bereich Sudanarchäologie-Meroitistik und Ägyptologie) in Berlin, October 22–26, 1990.

178. Later than the New Kingdom, in the first millennium B.C.E., Egyptians poured water over a god's statue, collected the runoff (now magically infused with divine healing power), and gave it to patients to drink. In the Ptolemaic Period (but probably beginning much earlier), women wanting to become pregnant gouged at exterior temple walls (particularly those near cultic foci or special power points) and patiently collected grains of sandstone, which they mixed with water and drank. In later periods, they even gouged at interior, decorated walls. Among peasant women, this practice continued until the late nineteenth century C.E., when the Egyptian Antiquities Organization acted to preserve the monuments. Today, some peasants wanting to become pregnant bathe at the bottoms of the enclosed temple staircases ("Nilometers") that were built around wells reaching down to the sacred ground waters.

179. Johanna Dittmar, *Blumen und Blumensträusse als Opfergabe im alten Ägypten*, MÄS 43 (Munich and Berlin: Deutscher Kunstverlag, 1986), especially pp. 125–32.

180. *ʿnḫ*-bouquets are also attested for Min, Isis, and Montu in the Ptolemaic Period. Cf. ibid., p. 126.

181. See Paule Posener-Kriéger, "Wag-Fest," *LÄ* 6:1135–39.

182. M. Bell, in *Cahiers de la céramique égyptienne* [n. 38], ed. Ballet, 1:56–57, 72–75 (notes); cf. Arielle P. Kozloff, "Jewelry," in Kozloff and Bryan, *Egypt's Dazzling Sun* [n. 73], p. 435.

183. Ph. Derchain, "La couronne de la justification: Essai d'analyse d'un rite ptolémaïque," *CdÉ* 30 (1955): 225–87.

184. Helmut Satzinger, "Der heilige Stab als Kraftquelle des Königs: Versuch einer Funktionsbestimmung der ägyptischen Stabträger-Statuen," in *Jahrbuch der Kunsthistorischen Sammlungen in Wien* 77 (Vienna: Anton Schroll, 1981), pp. 9–43; Catherine Chadefaud, *Les statues porte-enseignes de l'Égypte ancienne (1580–1085 avant J.C.), Signification et insertion dans le culte du Ka royal* (Paris: n.p., 1982). Cf. Satzinger's review of Chadefaud in *BiOr* 41 (1984): 375–85, where he compares their work. See also Pamminger, "Amun und Luxor," *BeitrSudanF* 5 (1992): 110–11.

185. Probably *all* the offerings redistributed from the altars carried some imprint of divine presence.

Chapter 5: Temples of the Ptolemaic and Roman Periods: Ancient Traditions in New Contexts

1. Henri Stierlin, "Le dernier legs de l'Egypte antique," in Serge Sauneron and Henri Stierlin, *Derniers temples d'Egypte: Edfou et Philae* (Paris: Chêne, 1975), pp. 103–13.

2. Jan Quaegebeur, "Documents égyptiens et rôle économique du clergé en Égypte hellénistique," in *State and Temple Economy in the Ancient Near East*, ed. Edward Lipinski, OLA 5–6 (1979), 2:714.

3. For some of the temples, the work started under the Nectanebos.

4. Dabod is now re-erected in Madrid; Kalabsha, near the Aswan Dam; and Dendur, in New York. For a description of the rescue of these Nubian temples, see Torgny Säve-Söderbergh, ed., *Temples and Tombs of Ancient Nubia: The International Rescue Campaign at Abu Simbel, Philae and Other Sites* (London: Thames and Hudson—Unesco, 1987).

5. Hieroglyphs were incised as late as 394 C.E. on Philae.

6. The temples are rightly entitled to the term "Greco-Roman." Naphtali Lewis, in his examination of Egyptian society under the Ptolemaic and Roman rulers, points out that in the sectors of governmental structure, social politics, administration, army, and economy, the changes between Ptolemaic patterns or practices and Roman patterns or practices were so fundamental as to render the term "Greco-Roman" misleading. See "'Greco-Roman Egypt': Fact or Fiction?" in *Proceedings of the Twelfth International Congress of Papyrology*, ed. Deborah H. Samuel, American Studies in Papyrology 7 (Toronto: A. M. Hakkert, 1970), pp. 1–14. The Egyptian temples stand out, however, having an exceptional continuity through the Ptolemaic and Roman periods.

7. Very little has yet been discovered that can be attributed to Greek-Hellenistic influences. Among the well-known instances are the zodiacal ceilings in the temple of Hathor in Dendera and the temple of Khnum at Esna. Zodiacs do not occur until the Ptolemaic Period; from then on they are relatively frequent, especially in the Roman Period. They are found alone or in association with decans, planets, and constellations; see O. Neugebauer and Richard A. Parker, *Egyptian Astronomical Texts III: Decans, Planets, Constellations and Zodiacs (Text)*, BES 6 (1969), p. 4.

8. A survey is given by Claude Traunecker, "Krypta," *LÄ* 3:823–30. The temple at Dendera has as many as twelve crypts.

9. The same type of facade can be seen in the tomb of Petosiris at Hermopolis

Magna. The term "naos" designates a sanctuary and can refer either to a small repository of the statue of god or to the temple proper, i.e., to the halls and rooms situated behind the pronaos. In this chapter the word is used in the latter sense.
10. The so-called double-temple of Kom Ombo had two sanctuaries, one for Sobek and the other for Horus.
11. E. Baldwin Smith, *Egyptian Architecture as Cultural Expression* (New York and London: D. Appleton–Century, 1938), pp. 179–83.
12. François Daumas, *Les mammisis des temples égyptiens,* Annales de l'Université de Lyon, Lettres 32 (Paris: Société d'Édition "Les Belles Lettres," 1958). Daumas, *Les mammisis de Dendara* (Cairo: IFAO, 1959); Émile Chassinat, *Le mammisi d'Edfou,* MIFAO 16/1–2 (1910, 1939); Hermann Junker and Erich Winter, *Das Geburtshaus des Tempels der Isis in Philä,* DÖAW Sonderband, Philä 2 (Vienna: Hermann Böhlaus Nachfolger, 1965).
13. Precursors are birth rooms in earlier temples. See Lanny Bell, "Luxor Temple and the Cult of the Royal *Ka*," *JNES* 44 (1985): 251–94. For a discussion of the relationship between the birth temples and the New Kingdom birth rooms, see François Daumas, "Geburtshaus," *LÄ* 2:462–75. The earliest birth temple that has survived is at Dendera and dates from the time of Nectanebo I (381–364 B.C.E.). See F. Daumas, "La structure du mammisi de Nectanébo à Dendara," *BIFAO* 50 (1952): 133–55.
14. John Ruffle, *Heritage of the Pharaohs: An Introduction to Egyptian Archaeology* (Oxford: Phaidon, 1977), p. 103.
15. The temples had their individual cosmogonies but shared certain traditions.
16. Dendera, especially, offers interesting material. Johannes Dümichen, *Baugeschichte des Denderatempels und Beschreibung der einzelnen Theile des Bauwerkes* (Strassburg: Trübner, 1877); Sylvie Cauville, "Les inscriptions dédicatoires du temple d'Hathor à Dendera," *BIFAO* 90 (1990): 83–114; Constant De Wit, "Inscriptions dédicatoires du temple d'Edfou," *CdÉ* 36 (1961): 56–97 and 277–320; Sylvie Cauville and Didier Devauchelle, "Le temple d'Edfou: Étapes de la construction et nouvelles données historiques," *RdÉ* 35 (1984): 31–55.
17. See, however, Eve A.E. Reymond, *The Mythical Origin of the Egyptian Temple* (Manchester: Manchester University Press; and New York: Barnes & Noble, 1969).
18. Barry J. Kemp: "As to where the measurements in cubits of the primeval temples came from, we just cannot tell. They could be records of buildings which had been erected on the site at various times since, say, the Middle Kingdom, or they could be the result of a symbolic numbers game carried out by the Ptolemaic priests themselves" (*Ancient Egypt: Anatomy of a Civilization* [London and New York: Routledge, 1990], p. 101).
19. A special interest attaches to Arsinoe II, who after her death became an object of cultic attention. See Jan Quaegebeur, "Reines ptolémaïques et traditions égyptiennes," in *Das ptolemäische Ägypten: Akten des Internationalen Symposions 27.—29. September 1976 in Berlin,* ed. Herwig Maehler and Volker Michael Strocka (Mainz: von Zabern, 1978), pp. 245–62; Quaegebeur, "Documents concerning a Cult of Arsinoe Philadelphos at Memphis," *JNES* 30 (1971): 239–70; Quaegebeur, "Ptolémée II en adoration devant Arsinoé II divinisée," *BIFAO* 69 (1971): 191–217.
20. Quaegebeur, in *Das ptolemäische Ägypten,* ed. Maehler and Strocka, pp. 245–62.
21. An example is the catalog of these items engraved on the sanctuary in the temple of Edfu.
22. "Welch eine Freude, das alles zu ermitteln und zusammenzustellen und

welch eine nützliche Wissenschaft!," Adolf Erman, *Die Religion der Ägypter: Ihr Werden und Vergehen in vier Jahrtausenden* (Berlin and Leipzig: de Gruyter, 1934), p. 325.

23. For a discussion about whether the scenes and texts were distributed according to previously designed patterns, see Erich Winter, "Zwei Beobachtungen zur Formung der ägyptischen Tempelreliefs in der griech.-röm. Zeit," in *Religions en Égypte hellénistique et romaine, Colloque de Strasbourg 16–18 Mai 1967* (Paris: Presses Universitaires de France, 1969), pp. 119–25; Winter, "Weitere Beobachtungen zur 'grammaire du temple' in der griechisch-römischen Zeit," in *Tempel und Kult*, ed. Wolfgang Helck, ÄgAbh 46 (1987), pp. 61–76; and Eleni Vassilika, *Ptolemaic Philae*, OLA 34 (1989), pp. 7–8; cf. Maria-Theresia Derchain-Urtel, "Die Bild- und Textgestaltung in Esna—eine 'Rettungsaktion'," in *Religion und Philosophie im alten Ägypten: Festgabe für Philippe Derchain*, ed. Ursula Verhoeven and Erhart Graefe, OLA 39 (1991), pp. 107–21.

24. Ph. Derchain, "Un manuel de géographie liturgique à Edfou," *CdÉ* 37 (1962): 31–65; Dieter Kurth, *Den Himmel Stützen: Die "Tw3 pt"-Szenen in den ägyptischen Tempeln der griechisch-römischen Epoche*, Rites Égyptiens 2 (Brussels: Fondation Égyptologique Reine Élisabeth, 1975). See also Erich Winter, *Untersuchungen zu den ägyptischen Tempelreliefs der griechisch-römischen Zeit*, DÖAW 98 (Vienna: Hermann Böhlaus Nachfolger, 1968).

25. "Die Spätzeit . . . wird redselig." *Der Götterglaube im alten Ägypten* (Leipzig: J. C. Hinrichs, 1956; Berlin: Akademie-Verlag, 1983), p. 415.

26. "Angst des Vergessens" (ibid.).

27. Erman, *Die Religion der Ägypter*, pp. 367–68.

28. Jan Assmann, "Der Tempel der ägyptischen Spätzeit als Kanonisierung kultureller Identität," in *The Heritage of Ancient Egypt: Studies in Honour of Erik Iversen*, ed. Jürgen Osing and Erland Kolding Nielsen, Carsten Niebuhr Institute of Ancient Near Eastern Studies Publications 13 (Copenhagen: Museum Tusculanum Press, 1992), pp. 9–25. The temple was thus regarded as a canon, but "this canon . . . took the form not of a collection of books but of a temple" (p. 9).

29. On the cult, see the material below. On the last point, see, e.g., Jan Assman, "Die Macht der Bilder: Rahmenbedingungen ikonischen Handelns im Alten Ägypten," *Visible Religion: Annual for Religious Iconography* 7 (1990): 1–20.

30. For a bibliographical index see Jean-Claude Grenier, *Temples ptolémaïques et romains: Repertoire bibliographique*, BdÉ 75 (1979). For bibliographical surveys of the work on texts, see Erich Winter (Philae), Adolphe Gutbub (Kom Ombo), Serge Sauneron (Esna), Jacques Vandier (Tod), François Daumas (Dendera), and Philippe Derchain (secondary temples), in *Textes et langages de l'Égypte pharaonique, cent cinquante années de recherches 1822–1972: Hommage à Jean-François Champollion*, BdÉ 64/1–3 (1973–74), 3:229–77.

Dendera: Auguste Mariette, *Dendérah: Description générale du grand temple de cette ville*, 6 vols. (Paris: A. Franck, 1870–1875); Émile Chassinat, *Le temple de Dendara* 1–5 (Cairo: IFAO, 1934–1952); Émile Chassinat and François Daumas, *Le temple de Dendara* 6–8 (Cairo: IFAO, 1965–1978); Daumas, *Le temple de Dendara* 9 (Cairo: IFAO, 1987); Daumas, *Les mammisis de Dendara* (Cairo: IFAO, 1959); Daumas, *Dendara et le temple d'Hathor*, RAPH 29 (1969). A good popular guide is Sylvie Cauville, *Le temple de Dendera*, Bibliothèque Générale 12 (Cairo: IFAO, 1990).

Esna: Serge Sauneron, *Esna I—VI, VIII* (Cairo: IFAO, 1959–1975, 1982).

Edfu: Maxence de Rochemonteix and Émile Chassinat, *Le temple d'Edfou I—II/1*,

MMAF 10–11/1 (Paris: Société Asiatique, 1894–1897); Chassinat and de Roche-monteix, *Le temple d'Edfou II/2—III*, MMAF 11/2, 20 (1918, 1928); a second, cor-rected edition of *Le temple d'Edfou I—II*, MMAF 10–11, was published by IFAO in 1984–1990, ed. Sylvie Cauville and Didier Devauchelle; Chassinat, *Le temple d'Ed-fou IV—XIV*, MMAF 21–31 (1929–34); Cauville and Devauchelle, *Le temple d'Edfou XV*, MMAF 32 (1985); Chassinat, *Le mammisi d'Edfou*, MIFAO 16/1–2 (1910, 1939); Dieter Kurth, ed., *Edfu: Studien zu Ikonographie, Textgestaltung, Schriftsystem, Gram-matik und Baugeschichte* (Wiesbaden: Harrassowitz, 1990). A good popular guide is Cauville, *Edfou*, Bibliothèque Générale 6 (Cairo: IFAO, 1984).

Kom Ombo: J. de Morgan et al., *Catalogue des monuments et inscriptions de l'É-gypte antique II—III* (Vienna: Holzhausen, 1895–1909); Adolphe Gutbub, *Textes fondamentaux de la théologie de Kom Ombo*, BdÉ 47 (1973).

Philae: Georges Bénédite, *Le temple de Philae*, MMAF 13/1–2 (1893, 1895); Her-mann Junker, *Der grosse Pylon des Tempels der Isis in Philä*, DÖAW Sonderband, Philä 1 (Vienna: Holzhausen, 1958); Junker and Winter, *Das Geburtshaus* [n. 12]; Gerhard Haeny, "A Short Architectural History of Philae," *BIFAO* 85 (1985): 197–233; Vassilika, *Ptolemaic Philae* [n. 23].

Deir el-Medina: Bernard Bruyère, *Rapport sur les fouilles de Deir el Médineh (1935–1940)*, FIFAO 20/1 (1948).

Medamud: Étienne Drioton, *Rapport sur les fouilles de Médamoud 1925–1926: Les inscriptions*, FIFAO 3/2 and 4/2 (1926, 1927); F. Bisson de la Roque et al., *Rapport sur les fouilles de Médamoud (1925–1932)*, FIFAO 3/1, 4/1, 5/1, 6/1, 7/1, 8/1–2, and 9/1 (1926–1933).

Dabod, Dendur, and Kalabsha: F. Daumas and Ph. Derchain, *Debod: Textes hiéro-glyphiques et description archéologique* (Cairo: CEDAE, [1960]); Günther Roeder, *De-bod bis Bab Kalabsche 1–2*, TIN (1911); Friedrich Zucker, *Debod bis Bab Kalabsche 3*, TIN (1912); Aylward M. Blackman, *The Temple of Dendur*, TIN (1911); Hassan el-Achirie, *Le temple de Dandour*, vol. 1, *Architecture* (Cairo: CEDAE, 1972); M. Aly, F.-A. Hamid, and Ch. Leblanc, *Le temple de Dandour*, vol. 2, *Dessins* (Cairo: CEDAE, 1979); F. Ibrahim and Ch. Leblanc, *Le temple de Dandour*, vol. 3, *Planches pho-tographiques et indices* (Cairo: CEDAE, 1975); Henri Gauthier, *Le temple de Kalab-chah*, TIN (1911, 1914); F. Daumas and Ph. Derchain, *Le temple de Kalabcha* (Cairo: CEDAE, [1960]); Karl Georg Siegler, *Kalabsha: Architektur und Baugeschichte des Tempels*, AVDAIK 1 (Berlin: Gebr. Mann, 1970); Dieter Arnold, *Die Tempel von Kal-absha* (Cairo: Deutsches Archäologisches Institut, 1975). On the re-erection of this temple, see Hanns Stock and Karl Georg Siegler, *Kalabsha: Der grösste Tempel Nu-biens und das Abenteuer seiner Rettung* (Wiesbaden: F. A. Brockhaus, 1965); and G. R. H. Wright, *The Ptolemaic Sanctuary of Kalabsha: Its Reconstruction on Elephan-tine Island*, Kalabsha 3, AVDAIK 3/1 (1987).

31. This seems to have been conditioned by an accentuation of the pictographi-cal side of the script. See Erik Hornung, "Hieroglyphen: Die Welt im Spiegel der Zeichen," *Eranos Jahrbuch* 55 (1986): 422.

32. Select bibliography: H. W. Fairman, "Notes on the Alphabetic Signs Em-ployed in the Hieroglyphic Inscriptions of the Temple of Edfu," *ASAE* 43 (1943): 191–310; Fairman, "Ptolemaic Notes," *ASAE* 44 (1944): 263–77; Fairman, "An In-troduction to the Study of Ptolemaic Signs and Their Values," *BIFAO* 43 (1945): 51–138; Adolphe Gutbub, "Jeux de signes dans quelques inscriptions des grands temples de Dendérah et d'Edfou," *BIFAO* 52 (1953): 57–101; C. De Wit, "Some Val-ues of Ptolemaic Signs," *BIFAO* 55 (1955): 111–21; Serge Sauneron, "L'écriture ptolémaïque" and "La grammaire des textes ptolémaïques," in *Textes et langages* [n. 30], 1:45–56, 151–56; Barbara Watterson, "The Use of Alliteration in Ptolemaic," in *Glimpses of Ancient Egypt: Studies in Honour of H. W. Fairman,* ed. John Ruffle, G. A. Gaballa, and Kenneth A. Kitchen (Warminster: Aris & Phillips, 1979), pp. 167–69; Adolphe Gutbub, "Remarques sur l'épigraphie ptolémaïque: Kom Ombo, spécialement sous Philométor," in *L'égyptologie en 1979: Axes prioritaires de recherches* (Paris: Éditions du Centre National de la Recherche Scientifique, 1982), 2:79–95; Serge Sauneron, *Esna VIII: L'écriture figurativa dans les textes d'Esna* (Cairo: IFAO, 1982); Dieter Kurth, "Die Lautwerte der Hieroglyphen in den Tempelinschriften der griechisch-römischen Zeit—Zur Systematik ihrer Herleitungsprinzipien," *ASAE* 69 (1983): 287–309; François Daumas et al., *Valeurs phonétiques des signes hiéroglyphiques d'époque gréco-romaine,* 3 vols., Institut d'Égyptologie, Université Paul Valéry (Montpellier: Université de Montpellier, Publications de la Recherche, 1988–1990); Friedrich Junge, "Zur 'Sprachwissenschaft' der Ägypter," in *Studien zu Sprache und Religion Ägyptens zu Ehren von Wolfhart Westendorf,* vol. 1, *Sprache,* ed. Friedrich Junge (Göttingen: [n.p.], 1984), pp. 257–72.

33. The scribes intentionally used graphic polyvalence to denote a plurality of meanings. For example, the sign of the falcon has the values *bjk* (falcon), *nb* (lord), *ḥr* (Horus), and in certain contexts they are all included.

34. Cf. François Daumas, "L'interprétation des temples égyptiens anciens à la lumière des temples gréco-romains," in *Cahiers de Karnak VI, 1973–1977* (Cairo: Centre Franco-égyptien d'Étude des Temples de Karnak, 1980), pp. 261–84. See, for instance, Maurice Alliot's study of the ritual proceedings, *Le culte d'Horus à Edfou au temps des Ptolémées,* 2 vols., BdÉ 20/1–2 (1949, 1954).

35. Derchain, "Kalabcha," *CdÉ* 37 (1962): 31–65; Paul Barguet, "La cour du Temple d'Edfou et le Cosmos," in *Livre du Centenaire 1880–1980,* MIFAO 104 (1980), pp. 9–14; Dieter Kurth, *Die Dekoration der Säulen im Pronaos des Tempels von Edfu,* GOF 11 (1983); Françoise Labrique, "Observations sur le temple d'Edfou," *GM* 58 (1982): 31–48; Sylvie Cauville, *Essai sur la théologie du temple d'Horus à Edfou I,* BdÉ 102/1 (1987); Erik Hornung, "Symmetrie," *LÄ* 6:129–32.

36. John Baines, *Fecundity Figures: Egyptian Personification and the Iconology of a Genre* (Warminster: Aris & Phillips; Chicago: Bolchazy-Carducci, 1985).

37. Its chapels on the roof have vanished, but the building is intact; and so is its richly inscribed and decorated surrounding wall, the only one found among the remains of Egyptian temples. This wall is a valuable source for our knowledge of Egyptian religious thought.

38. Of special interest is the focus on the theology of divine rule.

39. Sylvie Cauville, "Le panthéon d'Edfou à Dendera," *BIFAO* 88 (1988): 7–23.

40. Alliot, BdÉ 20 [n. 34], 1:251–65, 219–39.

41. The water for libations was taken from a well underneath the wall and brought along the ambulatory into the Chamber of the Nile.

42. The sanctuary was an independent structure having its own roof.

43. For Dendera, see Marie-Eve Colin, "Le Saint des Saints (ou le sanctuaire des barques) du temple de Dendara à travers ses inscriptions dédicatoires," in *Hommages à François Daumas,* Institut d'Égyptologie, Université Paul Valéry (Montpellier: Université de Montpellier, Publication de la Recherche, 1986), 1:109–31.

44. The shrine dates from the time of Nectanebo II.

45. Khepri is the name of the sun god as he comes out of the night sky, *nnt*. His iconographic form is a beetle.

46. Cauville and Devauchelle, *Edfou* [n. 30], 1:26, lines 4–6. There is a wordplay on *ḫpr*, "come into being," *ḫprw*, "image, form," and *ḫprr* or *ḫprj*, name of the god who comes into being while causing the world to come into being—the solar Creator.

47. Alliot, BdÉ 20 [n. 34], 1:84–98; H. W. Fairman, "Worship and Festivals in an Egyptian Temple," *BRL* 37 (1954): 180–81. For the discussion concerning the sequence of the rites, see Winfried Barta, "Kult," *LÄ* 3:844–45.

48. For New Kingdom precursors, see Hellmut Brunner, "Die Sonnenbahn in ägyptischen Tempeln," in *Archäologie und Altes Testament: Festschrift für Kurt Galling,* ed. Arnulf Kuschke and Ernst Kutsch (Tübingen: J. C. B. Mohr, 1970), pp. 27–34.

49. Behdet is a name of Edfu. The distinguishing icon of "the god of Behdet" is the winged sun disk. *ʿpj* is the coming sun. The Two-Temples name refers to the temple's function of representing Egypt. De Rochemonteix and Chassinat, *Edfou* [n. 30], 1:379, lines 5 and 16–17.

50. Cf. the descriptions of the sun god's passage through a series of gates in such literature as The Book of Gates and The Amduat; see Erik Hornung, *Das Buch von den Pforten des Jenseits,* 2 vols., AH 7–8 (1979, 1980); Hornung *Das Amduat: Die Schrift des verborgenen Raumes,* 3 vols., ÄgAbh 7/1–2, 13 (1963, 1967). See also Hellmut Brunner, "Die Rolle von Tür und Tor im Alten Ägypten," *Symbolon: Jahrbuch für Symbolforschung* n.f. 6 (1982): 37–59.

51. Erhart Graefe, "Der 'Sonnenaufgang zwischen den Pylontürmen'," *Orientalia Lovaniensia Periodica* 14 (1983): 55–79.

52. The two images are intertwined in many temple texts.

53. Fairman, "Worship and Festivals," *BRL* 37 (1954): 168; Chassinat and de Rochemonteix, *Edfou* [n. 30], 3:355, line 6, and Chassinat, *Edfou,* 5:5, line 5.

54. Here, Mesen is a name of the temple. The morning hymn; Cauville and Devauchelle, *Edfou* [n. 30], 1:13.

55. And, vice versa, the sun god's coming onto the horizon can be likened to the opening of doors or gates. Jan Assmann, *Der König als Sonnenpriester: Ein kosmographischer Begleittext zur kultischen Sonnenhymnik,* ADAIK 7 (1970), pp. 21, 48.

56. At Edfu, there were three ways of bringing light into the temple: through the doors; through small apertures in the roof or high up on the walls, directing shafts of sunlight to particular spots in the dark interior (the sanctuary of the High Seat had no openings except the door); and through artificial illumination, the candle/torch representing the sunlight (Alliot, *Le culte d'Horus* [n. 34], BdÉ 20, 1:62–63, with a reference to Moret's study of the Karnak ritual, p. 63 n. 5). There has been a debate concerning the time at which the doors lying on the axial road were opened; see Fairman, *BRL* 37 (1954): 176–77; cf. Alliot, BdÉ 20, 1:4–5.

57. Cauville and Devauchelle, *Edfou,* 1:13.

58. For this meaning of the structure, see Kurth, *Den Himmel Stützen* [n. 24]; Kurth, *Dekoration* [n. 35].

59. These were identified, for example, in the morning hymn.

60. James P. Allen, *Genesis in Egypt: The Philosophy of Ancient Egyptian Creation Accounts,* YES 2 (1988), pp. 5–7.

61. For examples of an underworld location, see L. Kákosy's references to Dendera, "Temples and Funerary Beliefs in the Graeco-Roman Epoch," in *L'égyptologie en 1979* [n. 32], 1:118–19.

62. We see this in the morning hymn "Wetjeset [name of the temple] which lifts you skyward, your mother Isis protecting you" (Cauville and Devauchelle, *Edfou*, 1:18, line 34) and in the decoration of ceilings, e.g., the ceiling of the Pure Hall, in which the sky is depicted as a woman bending over the moving sun god in all his shapes, from child to aged man (ibid., pl. 33c).

63. Cauville and Devauchelle, *Edfou*, 1:16, line 13; A. M. Blackman and H. W. Fairman, "A Group of Texts Inscribed on the Façade of the Sanctuary in the Temple of Horus at Edfu," in *Miscellanea Gregoriana* (Rome: Poliglotta Vaticana, 1941), p. 406.

64. Cauville and Devauchelle, *Edfou*, 1:379, lines 5–18.

65. Chassinat, *Edfou* [n. 30], 5:29, line 10; Alliot, *Le culte d'Horus* [n. 34], BdÉ 20, 2:500 n. 6.

66. See, for example, Chassinat, *Edfou*, 4:11, line 5: "His *ba* having come, it united with his temple"; cf. also the equation of the *ba* and the winged Beetle in the morning hymn on the sanctuary of the High Seat, Cauville and Devauchelle, *Edfou*, 1:14, line 1; 15, lines 16 and 31; 16, line 1; 17, lines 16 and 31.

67. Jean-Claude Goyon, "La littérature funéraire tardive," in *Textes et langages* [n. 30], 3:77–81.

68. See, for example, Papyrus Bremner-Rhind 28, 20–21, dating from the early Ptolemaic Period: "Thus spake the Lord of All: When I came into being, 'Being' came into being. I came into being in the form of Khopri who came into being on the First Occasion; I came into being in the form of Khopri when I came into being, and that is how 'Being' came into being." R. O. Faulkner, trans., "The Bremner-Rhind Papyrus—IV," *JEA* 24 (1938): 41. Similar phrases are known already from Middle Kingdom texts.

69. Jan Assmann, *Ägypten: Theologie und Frömmigkeit einer frühen Hochkultur* (Stuttgart: Kohlhammer, 1984), pp. 243–49; James P. Allen, "The Natural Philosophy of Akhenaten," in *Religion and Philosophy in Ancient Egypt*, ed. William Kelly Simpson, YES 3 (1989), p. 91.

70. Sauneron, *Esna* [n. 30], 5:158–59, 213, 358–72; Derchain-Urtel, in *Religion und Philosophie* [n. 23], ed. Verhoeven and Graefe, pp. 113–14.

71. Mariette, *Dendérah* [n. 30], 1:62–63.

72. Hermann Junker, *Der Auszug der Hathor-Tefnut aus Nubien* (Berlin: Königl. Akademie der Wissenschaften, 1911).

73. "Soleil femelle": Philippe Derchain, *Hathor Quadrifons: Recherches sur la syntaxe d'un mythe égyptien*, Uitgaven van het Nederlands Historisch Archaeologisch Instituut te Istanbul 28 (Istanbul: Nederlands Historisch Archaeologisch Instituut in het Nabije Oosten, 1972), p. 37.

74. Assimilated to the solar boat, the boat of Hathor acquires the two aspects of morning boat and evening boat; Colin, in *Hommages à François Daumas* [n. 43], 1:112–13 n. 52.

75. Translated by Louis V. Žabkar, *Hymns to Isis in Her Temple at Philae* (Hanover and London: University Press of New England, 1988), p. 80.

76. Ibid., p. 58. The Uraeus is an hypostasis of Re's vanquishing function.

77. Ibid., p. 91.

78. For the metaphoric values of gold, see François Daumas, "La valeur de l'or dans la pensée égyptienne," *Revue de l'Histoire des Religions* 149, no. 1 (1956): 1–17; Sydney Aufrère, *L'univers minéral dans la pensée égyptienne*, vol. 2, BdÉ 105/2 (1991), pp. 353–92.

79. Alliot, *Le culte d'Horus* [n. 34], BdÉ 20, 1:68; Daumas, *Les mammisis des temples égyptiens* [n. 12], pp. 151–58; Daumas, "Structure" [n. 13], *BIFAO* 50 (1952): 153–55.

80. Žabkar, *Hymns*, p. 58.

81. At Dendera, even Osiris is drawn into this solar theology: "Osiris . . . the glorious serpent, he comes as *j3ḥw* to unite with his form in his sanctuary; he comes flying from the sky as the falcon with shining feathers, and the *bas* of the gods follow him. He flies as falcon to his chapel in Dendera." Hieroglyphic text in Mariette, *Dendérah* [n. 30], 4:44a.

82. Porphyry, *De abstinentia* 4.6–8, in Pieter Willem van der Horst, *Chaeremon: Egyptian Priest and Stoic Philosopher*, ÉPRO 101 (1984), pp. 16–23.

83. Porphyry, *De abstinentia* 4.6, in van der Horst, *Chaeremon*, p. 17.

84. See, among others, P. W. van der Horst, "The Way of Life of the Egyptian Priests according to Chaeremon," in *Studies in Egyptian Religion Dedicated to Professor Jan Zandee*, ed. M. Heerma van Voss et al., Studies in the History of Religions 43 (Leiden: Brill, 1982), pp. 61–71.

85. Porphyry, *Epistula ad Anebonem* 2.12–13; see van der Horst, *Chaeremon*, pp. 14–15.

86. Sylvie Cauville, *La théologie d'Osiris à Edfou*, BdÉ 91 (1983).

87. Leiden Papyrus I 350, IV 15–16. See J. Zandee, "De Hymnen aan Amon van Papyrus Leiden I 350," *OMRO* 28 (1947): 80–81; cf. Hornung, *Das Buch von den Pforten des Jenseits* [n. 50], Scenes 56 and 57, 1:305–12 and 2:210–14.

88. The ritual integration of life and death was a conspicuous feature of the tomb sanctuaries as well.

89. François Daumas, "L'architecture et son décor," in *L'Égypte du crépuscule*, vol. 3 of *Les Pharaons*, ed. Jean Leclant (Paris: Gallimard, 1980), p. 54. Cf. Jan Assmann, who sees in the series of walls a fear of profanation (*Profanationsangst*) and finds in the feature a reflection of the closed, self-reserved mentality that regarded all non-Egyptians as unclean, a mentality that was particularly prominent in the Ptolemaic and Roman periods; "Der Tempel der ägyptischen Spätzeit," in *Heritage of Ancient Egypt* [n. 28], ed. Osing and Nielsen, p. 11.

90. In Ptolemaic temples, texts from the Book of the Dead are inscribed in diverse places. In the temple at Deir el-Medina, the judgment scene is even represented; see Kákosy, in *L'égyptologie en 1979* [n. 61], 1:125.

91. For a closer study of the comprehensive chaos-cosmos imagery of the temple, see Ragnhild Bjerre Finnestad, *Image of the World and Symbol of the Creator: On the Cosmological and Iconological Values of the Temple of Edfu*, Studies in Oriental Religions 10 (Wiesbaden: Harrassowitz, 1985).

92. The Laboratory of Edfu is particularly richly inscribed.

93. François Daumas, "Les propylées du temple d'Hathor à Philae et le culte de la déesse," *ZÄS* 95 (1968): 1–17.

94. An excellent exposition of the concept that the gods of the world constitute the diversified being of the Creator is given by Erik Hornung, *Der Eine und die Vielen: Ägyptische Gottesvorstellungen* (Darmstadt: Wissenschaftliche Buchgesellschaft, 1971). Translated by John Baines under the title *Conceptions of God in Ancient Egypt: The One and the Many* (Ithaca: Cornell University Press, 1982; London: Routledge & Kegan Paul, 1983).

95. Blackman and Fairman, in *Miscellanea Gregoriana* [n. 64], pp. 408 (17) and 422 (110); Cauville and Devauchelle, *Edfou* [n. 30], 1:16, line 14.

96. Blackman and Fairman, in *Miscellanea Gregoriana*, pp. 409–10, 423–28.

97. An exposition of the theme of divine immanence as developed by the temple and its cult is given in Finnestad, *Image of the World*.

98. There is an inherent connection between taking form and coming into being; see John Baines, "*Mswt* 'manifestation'?" in *Hommages à François Daumas* [n. 43], 1:43–50.

99. See Hornung, *Conceptions of God*, p. 165, a reference to Plutarch: Egyptian gods are "neither unbegotten nor imperishable"; p. 152; and p. 160, the Egyptians saw rejuvenation and regeneration as the true meaning of death (= *Der Eine und die Vielen*, pp. 159, 144–45, 153–54).

100. Alliot, *Le culte d'Horus* [n. 34], BdÉ 20, 1:205–49; Daumas, *Les mammisis des temples égyptiens* [n. 12], pp. 236–84; Sauneron, *Esna* [n. 30], 5:2–28; Hartwig Alt-enmüller, "Feste," *LÄ* 2:171–91; Altenmüller, review of Robert Hari, *La tombe thébain du pére divin Neferhotep (TT 50)*, *Orientalistische Literaturzeitung* 83 (1988): 398–402.

101. Over forty celebrations are documented for Edfu; Fairman, "Worship and Festivals" *BRL* [n. 47], 37 (1954): 182.

102. E.g., Jan Assmann, "Das ägyptische Prozessionsfest," in *Das Fest und das Heilige: Religiöse Kontrapunkte zur Alltagswelt*, ed. Jan Assmann and Theo. Sundermeier, Studien zum Verstehen fremder Religionen 1 (Gütersloh: Gütersloher Verlagshaus Gerd Mohn, 1991), pp. 105–22.

103. $Ḥʿw$ is a pregnant word in the temple cult. The semantic field of the word is comprehensive, but there is a basic reference to sunrise. Regarding the wider area of the word's application, see Margit Schunck, *Untersuchungen zum Wortstamm ḥʿ*, Habelts Dissertationsdrucke: Reihe Ägyptologie 5 (Bonn: Habelt, 1985).

104. On birth houses: Daumas, *Les mammisis des temples égyptiens*; Sauneron, *Esna*, 5:185–88. On Osiris festivals: Émile Chassinat, *Le mystère d'Osiris au mois de Khoiak* 1–2 (Cairo: IFAO, 1966 and 1968). Source material is especially abundant from Philae and Dendera.

105. On the latter, see Chassinat and Daumas, *Dendara* [n. 30], 6:158, line 2.

106. The Nile's role in the temple cult is conspicuous in daily as well as festival ritual. The Nile is frequently represented in decoration, in the form of the god Hapy. Liturgical and cosmological inscriptions draw a religious ideology of the Nile. That these features are more than a picturesque homage to the Nile becomes clear when we examine the integration of the temples into Egyptian society.

107. Fairman, "Worship and Festivals," *BRL* 37 (1954): 185–86; Alliot, *Le culte d'Horus* [n. 34], BdÉ 20, 1:303–433. In the Ptolemaic Period there was a synodal decree that festival processions include statues of the royal ancestors (ibid., 1:358–60); Eddy Lanciers, "Die ägyptischen Priester des ptolemäischen Königskultes," *RdÉ* 42 (1991): 135–37; cf. the discussion by Erich Winter, "Der Herrscherkult in den ägyptischen Ptolemäertempeln," in *Das ptolemäische Ägypten* [n. 19], ed. Maehler and Strocka, pp. 147–60.

108. Cf. Daumas, *Dendara et le temple d'Hathor* [n. 30], pp. 65, 69. At Esna, the ceremony was celebrated in a kiosk erected in front of the hypostyle; Sauneron, *Esna* [n. 30], 5:56–57, 123. As for Philae, see Žabkar, *Hymns to Isis* [n. 75], p. 121.

109. Sauneron, *Esna*, 5:56–57, 130–32. The kiosk of the temple at Dendera is still to be seen.

110. Aufrère, *L'univers minéral* [n. 78], 2:383.

111. The conceptual connection between the sun's daily and annual uniting with the image sometimes makes it difficult to identify the precise ritual context that pertains to the uniting; compare hymns inscribed in the sanctuary at Philae that invoke Isis to come to her house and to "unite herself" with her sanctuary images.

The texts have references to the consecration of the temple, but Žabkar suggests that they may also refer to the annual reconsecration rite and to the daily temple ritual of which these hymns may be a part. His suggestion seems likely. See *Hymns to Isis*, p. 89. On the mortuary cultus, see Erik Hornung, *Das Buch der Anbetung des Re im Westen (Sonnenlitanei)* 1–2, AH 2–3 (1975, 1976), 1:178 and 2:83, 137–38.

112. The time for performing the rite varied from temple to temple. At Dendera, the rite took place in the morning; Chassinat and Daumas, *Dendara* [n. 30], 7:179, line 8, and 8:113, line 16; Daumas, *Dendéra et le temple d'Hathor*, pp. 63–66. At Esna, it may have taken place late in the morning; Sauneron, *Esna*, 5:130. At Edfu, the rite seems to have coincided with the sun in zenith, i.e., at noon; Alliot, BdÉ 20 [n. 34], 1:347–48, and Fairman, "Worship and Festivals" [n. 47], *BRL* 37 (1954): 184–86. At Kalabsha, it was perhaps performed in the afternoon; François Daumas, "Neujahr," *LÄ* 4:470. For the ceremonies at Philae, see Žabkar, *Hymns to Isis*, p. 121.

113. Suggested by Daumas, in *L'Égypte du crépuscule* [n. 89], p. 51. For Edfu, Alliot, BdÉ 20, 1:353–54.

114. See Alliot, BdÉ 20, 2:565–676; and Fairman, *BRL* 37 (1954): 189–92.

115. Sacred falcons were also reared and celebrated at Dendera and Philae. See Hermann Junker, "Der Bericht Strabos über den heiligen Falken von Philae im Lichte der ägyptischen Quellen," *WZKM* 26 (1912): 42–62.

116. Fairman, *BRL* 37 (1954): 190.

117. On the names, see Chassinat, *Edfou* [n. 30], 6:93, line 11, and 102, line 9.

118. Alliot, BdÉ 20, 2:677–822; Fairman, *BRL* 37 (1954): 192–96.

119. Chassinat, *Edfou*, 13: pls. 494–514; 6:60, line 6–90; 13: pls. 518–33; 6:108, line 15–132, line 5; H. W. Fairman, "The Myth of Horus at Edfu—I," *JEA* 21 (1935): 26–36; A. M. Blackman and H. W. Fairman, "The Myth of Horus at Edfu—II," *JEA* 28 (1942): 32–38; 29 (1943): 2–36; and 30 (1944): 5–22; H. W. Fairman, *The Triumph of Horus: An Ancient Egyptian Sacred Drama* (London: Batsford, 1974); cf. É. Drioton, *Le texte dramatique d'Edfou*, *ASAE* supp. 11 (1948); Constant De Wit, "Les inscriptions des lions-gargouilles du temple d'Edfou," *CdÉ* 29 (1954): 29–45; De Wit, "Inscriptions dédicatoires," *CdÉ* 36 (1961): 56–97, 277–320; J. Gwyn Griffiths, "Egyptian Nationalism in the Edfu Temple Texts," in *Glimpses of Ancient Egypt* [n. 32], ed. Ruffle et al., pp. 174–79.

120. The mythological theme of combat-and-victory belongs to the universal repertoire of the temples. See Heike Sternberg, *Mythische Motive und Mythenbildung in den ägyptischen Tempeln und Papyri der griechisch-römischen Zeit*, GOF 14 (1985).

121. Alliot, *Le culte d'Horus* [n. 34], BdÉ 20, 2:442–560; Fairman, "Worship and Festivals," *BRL* 37 (1954): 196–200.

122. H. W. Fairman and many with him interpret the festival as a celebration of the marriage between Hathor and Horus. Claas Jouco Bleeker, challenging this interpretation, sees the festival as a celebration of the sun-eye that reunites with her father, a motif found in the texts to the festival [see *Hathor and Thoth: Two Key Figures of the Ancient Egyptian Religion*, Studies in the History of Religions 26 (Leiden: Brill, 1973), pp. 95–101]. This motif, however, belongs to a wider scheme of regeneration. There is good reason to regard the Festival of the Reunion as an Egyptian version of the divine marriage.

123. A. M. Blackman and H. W. Fairman, "The Significance of the Ceremony of Ḥwt Bḥsw in the Temple of Horus at Edfu," *JEA* 35 (1949): 98–112; and 36 (1950): 63–81.

124. For a general presentation of the various kinds of priests, see Serge Sauneron, *Les prêtres de l'ancienne Egypte,* 2d ed. (Paris: Perséa, 1988), pp. 60–79. His first edition has been translated into English by Ann Morrissett: *The Priests of Ancient Egypt* (New York: Grove; London: Evergreen, 1960), pp. 56–75.

125. See Erich Fascher, Προφήτης: *Eine sprach- und religionsgeschichtliche Untersuchung* (Giessen: A. Töpelmann, 1927), pp. 76–100. Cf. Hermann Kees, "Der berichtende Gottesdiener," *ZÄS* 85 (1960): 138–43.

126. On the position of women in Egyptian cultus, see Aylward M. Blackman, "On the Position of Women in the Ancient Egyptian Hierarchy," *JEA* 7 (1921): 8–30; Hans Bonnet, *Reallexikon der ägyptischen Religionsgeschichte* (Berlin: de Gruyter, 1971), pp. 607–8; Gay Robins, *Women in Ancient Egypt* (London: British Museum Press, 1993) pp. 142–56; Françoise Dunand, "Le statut des *hiereiai* en Égypte romaine," in *Hommages à Maarten J. Vermaseren,* ÉPRO 68/1 (1978), pp. 352–74.

127. Recruitment involved a combination of inheritance, purchase of office, and selection by the group of priests.

128. Jan Quaegebeur, "The Genealogy of the Memphite High Priest Family in the Hellenistic Period," in *Studies on Ptolemaic Memphis,* Studia Hellenistica 24 (Louvain: n.p., 1980), pp. 43–81; E. A. E. Reymond, *From the Records of a Priestly Family from Memphis,* vol. 1, ÄgAbh 38/1 (1981); Quaegebeur, in *State and Temple Economy* [n. 2], ed. Lipinski, 2:707–29.

129. S. Sauneron, "Les conditions d'accès à la fonction sacerdotale à l'époque gréco-romaine," *BIFAO* 61 (1962): 55–57.

130. Walter Otto, *Priester und Tempel im hellenistichen Ägypten* (Leipzig and Berlin: Teubner, 1905), 1:83–86.

131. On the *pastophoroi,* see ibid., 1:94–98; Hans-Bernhard Schönborn, *Die Pastophoren im Kult der ägyptischen Götter,* Beiträge zur Klassischen Philologie 80 (Meisenheim am Glan: Anton Hain, 1976). At the smaller temples some of these offices were probably combined in one person. Also, priests could be borrowed from other temples; see, for example, J. A. S. Evans, "A Social and Economic History of an Egyptian Temple in the Greco-Roman Period," in Yale Classical Studies 17 (New Haven: Yale University Press, 1961), pp. 205–6.

132. The custom of carrying out liturgical service in rotation continued in the late temples. The priests were on duty for one month and off duty for three months. The traditional number of rotating groups, called by the Greeks *phylai,* was four. In the decree of Canopus (238 B.C.E.), Ptolemy III Euergetes introduced a fifth, thus returning to the division prevailing in the Old Kingdom; cf., conveniently, Paule Posener-Kriéger, *Les archives du temple funéraire de Néferirkarê-Kakaï,* BdÉ 65/2 (1976), 2:565–74. See also Jan Quaegebeur, "Documents" [n. 19] *JNES* 30 (1971): 250.

133. For Edfu, Alliot, *Le culte d'Horus* [n. 34], BdÉ 20, 1:181–98; cf. Gutbub, *Kom Ombo* [n. 30], pp. 146–47. These norms were also written outside the temple; see Maria-Theresia Derchain-Urtel's study of mortuary stelae belonging to priests in Dendera and Edfu: *Priester im Tempel: Die Rezeption der Theologie der Tempel von Edfu und Dendera in den Privatdokumenten aus ptolemäischer Zeit,* GOF 19 (1989). See also, J. Quaegebeur, "Sur la 'loi sacrée' dans l'Égypte gréco-romaine," *Ancient Society* 11/12 (1980/1981): 227–40; Walter Otto, *Priester und Tempel im hellenistichen Ägypten* (Leipzig and Berlin: Teubner, 1908), 2:238–43.

134. Alliot, BdÉ 20, 1:142–43, 185.

135. See Assmann, in *Heritage of Ancient Egypt* [n. 28], ed. Osing and Nielsen.

136. Otto, *Priester und Tempel* [n. 130], 1:87–90.

137. The artists and decorators were under the supervision of the House of Life.

138. Alan H. Gardiner, "The House of Life," *JEA* 24 (1938): 157–79; Philippe Derchain, *Le papyrus Salt 825 (B.M. 10051), rituel pour la conservation de la vie en Égypte,* Mémoires de l'Académie Royale de Belgique, Classe des Lettres 58/1 (Brussels: Palais des Académies, 1965); Manfred Weber, "Lebenshaus I. (*pr - ʿnḫ*)," *LÄ* 3:954–57.

139. A selection of books with special relevance for the liturgy of the temple was placed in a room in the temple; at Edfu, this room can still be seen in the pronaos. On its walls are inscribed lists of the titles of these books. See, for example, Vilmos Wessetzky, "Die Bücherliste des Tempels von Edfu und Imhotep," *GM* 83 (1984): 85–89.

140. Otto, *Priester und Tempel,* 1:89–90.

141. See, e.g., Garth Fowden, *The Egyptian Hermes: A Historical Approach to the Late Pagan Mind* (Cambridge: Cambridge University Press, 1986).

142. Under Roman rule, the Egyptian clergy were no longer a body that could deal with the ruler, and the state sought to restrict their influence outside the temples.

143. Discontent and opposition against the Ptolemies' social-economic policy could be supported by Egyptian priests; see Willy Peremans, "Les revolutions égyptiennes sous les Lagides," in *Das ptolemäische Ägypten* [n. 19], ed. Maehler and Strocka, p. 47. But there is material to document cooperation; see Dorothy J. Crawford, "Ptolemy, Ptah and Apis in Hellenistic Memphis," in *Studies on Ptolemaic Memphis* [n. 128], pp. 1–42; and Quaegebeur, "Documents," *JNES* 30 (1971): 239–70. See also the discussion by Griffiths, in *Glimpses of Ancient Egypt* [n. 119], ed. Ruffle et al., pp. 174–79.

144. Winter, in *Das ptolemäische Ägypten* [n. 107], ed. Maehler and Strocka, pp. 147–60.

145. On the king's role: Ludwig Koenen, "Die Adaptation ägyptischer Königsideologie am Ptolemäerhof," in *Egypt and the Hellenistic World,* ed. E. van 't Dack, P. van Dessel, and W. van Gucht, Studia Hellenistica 27 (Louvain: n.p., 1983), pp. 143–90; Françoise Dunand, "Fête, tradition, propagande: Les cérémonies en l'honneur de Bérénice, fille de Ptolémée III, en 238 a.C.," in *Livre du Centenaire 1880–1980,* MIFAO 104 (1980), pp. 287–301. From the New Kingdom onward, dead kings could be venerated in the temple of a god, but the *dynastic* cult was something new. It was promulgated at the synod of Canopus in 238 B.C.E.

146. Jan Quaegebeur, "The Egyptian Clergy and the Cult of the Ptolemaic Dynasty," *Ancient Society* 20 (1989): 93–116.

147. Winter, in *Das ptolemäische Ägypten,* ed. Maehler and Strocka; see the discussion among the scholars on p. 159; also Lanciers, *RdÉ* 42 (1991): 119 with n. 22.

148. The cult is particularly often reflected in the decoration of the temple of Edfu; Winter, in *Das ptolemäische Ägypten,* ed. Maehler and Strocka, pp. 147–60.

149. Ibid., p. 154.

150. Source material from outside the temples complements this picture. In demotic documents, Berenice II is entered as *t3 pr-ʿ3.t brnjg3,* "the female pharaoh Berenice"; P. W. Pestman, *Chronologie égyptiennes d'après les textes démotiques (332 av. J.-C.–453 ap. J.-C.),* Papyrologica Lugduno-Batava 15 (Leiden: Brill, 1967), p. 28; Quaegebeur, in *Das ptolemäische Ägypten* [n. 19], ed. Maehler and Strocka, p. 255.

Arsinoe II was titled *nswt-bjtj*, "female pharaoh of Upper and Lower Egypt," and wore a crown corresponding to the king's double crown; see Quaegebeur, "Ptolémée II," *BIFAO* 69 (1971): 204–6; Quaegebeur, in Maehler and Strocka, pp. 258, 262; Quaegebeur, "Arsinoé Philadelphe, reine, 'roi' et déesse, à Hildesheim," *GM* 87 (1985): 73–78.

151. Chassinat and Daumas, *Dendara* [n. 30], vol. 1, pls. 17–29.

152. See the Amarna iconography of Akhenaten and Nefertiti. Nefertiti is also depicted alone, even in the conventional pharaoh-slaying-his-enemies pose; with her weapon in one hand, she grasps the tufts of hair of the enemy with the other. See Julia Samson, *Nefertiti and Cleopatra, Queen-Monarchs of Ancient Egypt* (London: Rubicon, 1985), p. 25 and fig. 7, with reference to pl. 23, 2 in Ray Winfield Smith and Donald B. Redford, *The Akhenaten Temple Project,* vol. 1, *The Initial Discoveries* (Warminster: Aris & Phillips, 1976). An exposition of the underlying conception of rulership is given by Lana Troy in *Patterns of Queenship in Ancient Egyptian Myth and History,* BOREAS 14 (1986).

153. There was no dynastic cultus. However, there was a "prophet of Caesar"; see Winter, in *Das ptolemäische Ägypten* [n. 107], ed. Maehler and Strocka, p. 158 and n. 3.

154. Leon Mooren, "Macht und Nationalität," in *Das ptolemäische Ägypten* [n. 19], ed. Maehler and Strocka, pp. 51–57.

155. Erwin R. Goodenough, "The Political Philosophy of Hellenistic Kingship," in Yale Classical Studies 1 (New Haven: Yale University Press, 1928), pp. 55–102.

156. Ibid., p. 66. See also Koenen, in *Egypt and the Hellenistic World* [n. 145], ed. van 't Dack, van Dessel, and van Gucht, pp. 168–69.

157. Regarding the economic role of the temples, see Quaegebeur, in *State and Temple Economy* [n. 2], ed. Lipinski, 2:707–29; see also Evans, in Yale Classical Studies 17 [n. 131], pp. 143–283, and Janet H. Johnson, "The Role of the Egyptian Priesthood in Ptolemaic Egypt," in *Egyptological Studies in Honor of Richard A. Parker,* ed. Leonard H. Lesko (Hanover and London: University Press of New England, 1986) pp. 70–84.

158. Dimitri Meeks, "Les donations aux temples dans l'Égypte du Ier millénaire avant J.-C.," in *State and Temple Economy,* ed. Lipinski, 2:605–87. In Ptolemaic times, the land was the king's by eminent domain. The cultivators were assigned to work on the temple estates. At the beginning of the Ptolemaic Period, the temples lost their right to manage their own land, but by the end they had strengthened their position. Under the Romans, the temples were deprived of their relative autonomy.

159. Dimitri Meeks, *Le grand texte des donations au temple d'Edfou,* BdÉ 59 (1972). In the ideology of the temple, the lands registered to the temple were owned by the god, but both god and king were called "lord of the land" (*nb t3wj*), thereby legitimating the power of the king. Economic realities centered around the question of who had the right to use the land and who had the right to appropriate its products. On these matters there is widespread disagreement, and with good reason. The right kind of sources are scarce, and it is difficult to sort out how the categories "private" and "public" might be applied to the Ptolemaic era. Such categories belong to our time, place, and political/economic system, not theirs.

160. For the "reversion of the offerings," see A. M. Blackman,"The King of Egypt's Grace before Meat," *JEA* 31 (1945): 68; Alliot, BdÉ 20 [n. 34], 1:104–5.

161. To what extent the kings themselves *actually* visited the temples is an open question; there is poor documentation.

162. Otto, *Priester und Tempel* [nn. 130, 133], 1:262–82; 2:81–113; Sherman LeRoy Wallace, *Taxation in Egypt from Augustus to Diocletian* (Princeton: Princeton University Press, 1938; reprint, New York: Greenwood, 1969), pp. 238–54; Elizabeth H. Gilliam, "The Archives of the Temple of Soknobraisis at Bacchias," in Yale Classical Studies 10 (New Haven: Yale University Press, 1947), pp. 179–281. The temples were not treated uniformly; endowments and taxation varied.

163. The "High Priest of Alexandria and All Egypt," who held the highest authority over the temples, was a Roman civil official.

164. About the question of who financed the building program, see Quaegebeur, in *State and Temple Economy* [n. 2], ed. Lipinski, 2:713–15.

165. E.g., Serge Sauneron: "the Ptolemies had little but scorn for the Egyptian cults and regarded the priests with the interested eye of a breeder who sees his cattle growing fat"; *Priests of Ancient Egypt* [n. 124], p. 105 (= *Les prêtres*, 2d ed., p. 114). And: "the Ptolemies needed the clergy, which exercised a certain influence on the masses of people, and contributed to supporting the myth of the Macedonian-Pharaoh" (p. 106 (= *Les prêtres*, 2d ed., p. 114).

166. For example, Juvenal, *Satire* 15. See, among others, *Juvenal and Persius*, rev. ed., trans. G. G. Ramsay, Loeb Classical Library (Cambridge: Harvard University Press; London: William Heinemann, 1979), pp. 288–301.

167. Koenen, in *Egypt and the Hellenistic World* [n. 145], ed. van 't Dack, van Dessel, and van Gucht, pp. 152–70.

168. Wilfried Swinnen, "Sur la politique religieuse de Ptolémée Ier," in *Les syncrétismes dans les religions grecque et romaine, Colloque de Strasbourg (9–11 Juin 1971)* (Paris: Presses Universitaires de France, 1973), pp. 115–33.

169. The rich mixture of cults can be seen, even in the early period of Ptolemaic rule, in centers like Memphis and especially in towns designed for both non-Egyptian settlers and Egyptian inhabitants, for example in the Faiyum.

170. The Hellenization of the cult of Serapis, under Ptolemy I, apparently aimed at presenting a god that could be venerated by both Egyptian and Greek populations. See Günther Hölbl, "Serapis," *LÄ* 5:870.

171. On the vitality: Reinhold Merkelbach, "Ein ägyptischer Priestereid," *Zeitschrift für Papyrologie und Epigraphik* 2 (1968): 7–30; Fowden, *Egyptian Hermes* [n. 141]. In the mortuary field, some interesting syncretistic developments can be noted, such as the mummy portraits. See Hilde Zaloscer, *Porträts aus dem Wüstensand: Die Mumienbildnisse aus der Oase Fayum* (Vienna and Munich: Anton Schroll, 1961); Klaus Parlasca, *Mumienporträts und verwandte Denkmäler* (Wiesbaden: Steiner, 1966); Günter Grimm, *Die römischen Mumienmasken aus Ägypten* (Wiesbaden: Steiner, 1974). Cf. also the tombs in Alexandria. On Egyptian influence on the Greeks, see Dorothy J. Crawford's study, *Kerkeosiris: An Egyptian Village in the Ptolemaic Period* (Cambridge: Cambridge University Press, 1971), pp. 86–92.

172. See note 7. Philippe Derchain sees Greek influence in the presentation of Horus's victory on the walls of the Edfu temple; "Miettes," *RdÉ* 26 (1974): 7–20.

173. L. Kákosy, "Probleme der ägyptischen Jenseitsvorstellungen in der Ptolemäer- und Kaiserzeit," in *Religions en Égypte* [n. 23], pp. 59–68.

174. François Daumas, "Sur trois représentations de Nout à Dendara," *ASAE* 51 (1951): 373–400. On an equally solid basis one might suggest that the double and triple figures of the sky goddess may have been a graphic way of representing a process of expansion. This issue requires clarification.

175. Jean Yoyotte, "Bakhthis: Religion égyptienne et culture grecque à Edfou," in *Religions en Égypte*, pp. 127–41.

176. See Derchain-Urtel, *Priester im Tempel* [n. 133].

177. Again we are faced with a continuum; this practice has ancient antecedents. See John Baines, "Society, Morality, and Religious Practice," in *Religion in Ancient Egypt: Gods, Myths, and Personal Practice,* ed. Byron E. Shafer (Ithaca: Cornell University Press; London: Routledge, 1991) pp. 179–86, 195–98; Hellmut Brunner, "Persönliche Frömmigkeit," *LÄ* 4:951–63.

178. François Daumas, "Le sanatorium de Dendara," *BIFAO* 56 (1957): 35–57. "Incubation" is a technical term denoting the practice of sleeping in a temple in order to experience healing dreams.

179. On prayer: Hellmut Brunner, "Gebet," *LÄ* 2:454, and n. 35; Dietrich Wildung, "Götterbilder, volkstumliche verehrte," *LÄ* 2:672–74; Wolfgang Helck, "Torgötter," *LÄ* 6:637; Charles F. Nims, "Places about Thebes," *JNES* 14 (1955): 110–23. For traditions in earlier times, see W. Spiegelberg, "Das Tor des Beke (*Bkj*)," *ZÄS* 65 (1930): 123–24. Also, the functions of the so-called contra-temple in Karnak; see Paul Barguet, *Le temple d'Amon-Rê à Karnak*, RAPH 21 (1962), pp. 300–306. For selected references to settling legal disputes at the gates: Serge Sauneron, "La justice à la porte des temples," *BIFAO* 54 (1954): 117–27; Hellmut Brunner, "Tür und Tor," *LÄ* 6:782 with notes.

180. Remarks in the works of Greek and Roman authors show that the native Egyptians adhered to their own religious traditions; see J. Gwyn Griffiths, *Plutarch's De Iside et Osiride* ([Swansea]: University of Wales Press, 1970). See also Françoise Dunand, *Religion populaire en Égypte romaine*, ÉPRO 76 (1979), pp. 92–100.

181. The development of Christianity in Egypt was slower than contemporary Christian authors might lead us to conclude. Egyptian religious traditions as well as Greco-Roman ones were active in the later Roman Empire. For a description of Alexandrian developments, see Garth Fowden, "The Pagan Holy Man in Late Antique Society," *Journal of Hellenic Studies* 102 (1982): 33–59.

182. Theofried Baumeister, *Martyr Invictus*, Forschungen zur Volkskunde 46 (Münster: Regensberg, 1972); Wolfgang Schenkel, *Kultmythos und Märtyrerlegende: Zur Kontinuität des ägyptischen Denkens*, GOF 5 (1977); William M. Brashear, "Horos," in *Reallexikon für Antike und Christentum* 16 (Stuttgart: Anton Hiersemann, 1992), pp. 574–97; Wolfgang Kosack, *Die Legende im Koptischen: Untersuchungen zur Volksliteratur Ägyptens*, Habelts Dissertationsdrucke: Reihe Klassische Philologie 8 (Bonn: Habelt, 1970); Adolf Erman, "Ein koptischer Zauberer," *ZÄS* 33 (1895): 43–46; Angelicus M. Kropp, *Ausgewählte koptische Zaubertexte* 1–3 (Brussels: Fondation Égyptologique Reine Élisabeth, 1930–1931); Florence D. Friedman, *Beyond the Pharaohs: Egypt and the Copts in the 2nd to 7th Centuries A.D.* ([Providence]: Museum of Art, Rhode Island School of Design, 1989); Winifred S. Blackman, *The Fellāḥīn of Upper Egypt: Their Religious, Social and Industrial Life Today* (London: Harrap, 1927).

183. The contribution of the temples to the formation of the cross-cultural theological traditions of early Christianity has not received proper attention, but Siegfried Morenz has raised the question of continuity for the roots of trinitarian formulas, in *Ägyptische Religion*, Die Religionen der Menschheit 8 (Stuttgart:

Kohlhammer, 1960), pp. 270–73 (translated by Ann E. Keep under the title *Egyptian Religion* [Ithaca: Cornell University Press; London: Methuen, 1973], pp. 255–57), and in *Die Begegnung Europas mit Ägypten*, Sitzungsberichte der Sächsischen Akademie der Wissenschaften zu Leipzig, Philologisch-historische Klasse 113/5 (Berlin: Akademie-Verlag, 1968), p. 104; see also W. Westendorf, "Altägyptische Dreieinigkeit und christliche Trinität," *Sonderforschungsbereich 13 Orientalistik, Arbeitsbericht 1974* (Göttingen: Universität Göttingen, 1974), pp. 235–38.

Ability to read hieroglyphic and hieratic texts was still a precondition for becoming a priest in the second century C.E. See J. Vergote, "Clément d'Alexandrie et l'écriture égyptienne," *CdÉ* 16 (1941): 23; Sauneron, "Fonction sacerdotal," *BIFAO* 61 (1962): 55–57.

184. L. S. B. MacCoull, "Christianity at Syene/Elephantine/Philae," *Bulletin of the American Society of Papyrologists* 27 (1990): 151–62. Philae, actually the whole Aswan region, was a Christian pilgrimage site in the sixth and seventh centuries C.E. (ibid., pp. 160–61).

185. Procopius, *De bello Persico* 1.19.36–37; see *Procopius I*, trans. H. B. Dewing, Loeb Classical Library (London: William Heinemann; New York: Macmillan, 1914), pp. 188–89. See also MacCoull, *Bulletin of the American Society of Papyrologists* 27 (1990): 153.

DYNASTIC CHRONOLOGY WITH NAMES OF RULERS AND PERIODS MENTIONED IN THE TEXT

Dates are approximate.[1] The margin of error rises to as much as one to two centuries for the early third millennium B.C.E. For Dynasties 3–13, the margin of error is up to sixty years; for Dynasties 15–31, up to ten years. After 332 B.C.E., most dates are exact to within one year. Overlaps in dynasties' dates indicate competing dynasties; overlaps in monarchs' dates indicate co-regency.

Predynastic Period		c. 5000–3185
Early Dynastic Period	(Dynasties 1–3)	c. 3185–2630
First Dynasty	c. 3185–2930	
Menes/Narmer		
Aha		
Djer		
Djet		
Meritneith		
Den/Udimu		
Semerkhet		
Adjib		
Qaʻa		

[1]Through the Old Kingdom, the chronology follows Jean Vercoutter, *L'Égypte et la vallée du Nil* (Paris: Presses Universitaires de France, 1992), 1:200, 222, 248, 264, 290, 316. For the First Intermediate Period and later, the chronology follows, for the most part, Jürgen von Beckerath, *Handbuch der ägyptischen Königsnamen*, MÄS 20 (Munich and Berlin: Deutscher Kunstverlag, 1984), pp. 159–65.

Second Dynasty	*c. 2930–2715*	
Hetepsekhemwy		
Raneb		
Ninetjer		
Sekhemib		
Peribsen		
Khasekhemwy		

Third Dynasty	*c. 2715–2630*	
Nebka (Horus Sanakht)		
Djoser (Horus Netjerykhet)		
Djoserteti (Horus Sekhemkhet)		
Horus Khaba (?)		
Huni (Horus Qahedjet)		

Old Kingdom (Dynasties 4–8) **c. 2630–2160**
Fourth Dynasty *c. 2630–2510*
  Sneferu
  Khufu
  Djedefre
  Khafre
  Menkaure
  Nebka (?)
  Shepseskaf

Fifth Dynasty *c. 2510–2350*
  Userkaf
  Sahure
  Neferirkare
  Shepseskare-Ini
  Neferefre
  Niuserre-Izi
  Djedkare-Isesi
  Unas

Sixth Dynasty *c. 2350–2195*
  Teti
  Pepi I Merire
  Merenre
  Pepi II Neferkare

First Intermediate Period (Dynasties 9–11) **c. 2160–1994**
Ninth and Tenth Dynasties *c. 2160–2040*
Eleventh Dynasty *c. 2160–1994*

Middle Kingdom (Dynasties 11–13) **c. 2040–1650**
Eleventh Dynasty (all Egypt) *c. 2040–1994*
  Nebhepetre Mentuhotep c. 2065–2014

Twelfth Dynasty *1994–c. 1781*
  Amenemhat I 1994–1964
  Senwosret I 1974–1929
  Amenemhat II 1932–after 1898
  Senwosret II 1900–after 1881

Senwosret III	1881–after 1842		
Amenemhat III	1842–1794		

Thirteenth Dynasty		*c. 1781–1650*	
Amenemhat Sobekhotep			
Sobekhotep II			
Khendjer			
Sobekhotep IV			

Second Intermediate Period (Dynasties 15–17) **c. 1650–1540**
HYKSOS PERIOD (Dynasties 15–16) *c. 1650–1540*
Seventeenth Dynasty *c. 1650–1550*

Kamose	c. 1555–1550		

New Kingdom (Dynasties 18–20) **1550–1075**
Eighteenth Dynasty *1550–1291*

Ahmose	1550–1525
Amenhotep I	1525–1504
Thutmoside Period	
Thutmose I	1504–1492
Thutmose II	1492–1479
Thutmose III	1479–1425
Hatshepsut	1479–1458
Amenhotep II	1428–1397
Thutmose IV	1397–1387
Amenhotep III	1387–1350
Amarna Period	
Amenhotep IV/Akhenaten	1350–1334
Semenkhkare	1334–1333
Tutankhamun	1333–1323
Ay	1323–1319
Horemhab	1319–1291

RAMESSIDE PERIOD (Dynasties 19–20)
Nineteenth Dynasty *1291–1185*

Ramesses I	1291–1289
Seti I	1289–1278
Ramesses II	1279–1212
Merneptah	1212–1202
Seti II	1199–1193
Siptah	1193–1187
Tausert	1193–1185

Twentieth Dynasty *1185–1075*

Ramesses III	1184–1153
Ramesses IV	1153–1147
Ramesses V	1147–1143
Ramesses VI	1143–1135
Ramesses VII	1135–1127
Ramesses VIII	1127–1126
Ramesses IX	1126–1108
Ramesses X	1108–1104
Ramesses XI	1104–1075

Third Intermediate Period
Twenty-first Dynasty
Twenty-second Dynasty
  Sheshonq I   945–924

  Osorkon II   883–850

Twenty-third Dynasty

Twenty-fifth (Kushite) Dynasty

(Dynasties 21–25)   **1075–653**
1075–945
945–718

820–718

c. 775–653

Late Period
Twenty-sixth (Saite) Dynasty

Twenty-eighth Dynasty
Twenty-ninth Dynasty
Thirtieth Dynasty
  Nectanebo I   380–362

  Nectanebo II   360–342

(Dynasties 26–31)   **664–332**
664–525

404?–399
399–380
380–342

Greek-Roman-Byzantine Period   **332 B.C.E.–642 C.E.**
Macedonian Dynasty
  Alexander the Great   332–323
  Philip Arrhidaeus   323–317

332–305 B.C.E.

Ptolemaic Dynasty
  Ptolemy I Soter   305–282
  Ptolemy II Philadelphus   285–246
  Ptolemy III Euergetes   246–222
  Ptolemy IV Philopator   222–205

  Ptolemy XII Neos Dionysos   80–58, 55–51
  Cleopatra VII Philopator   51–30
  Ptolemy XV Caesarion   36–30

305–30 B.C.E.

Roman Period

  Tiberius   14–37 C.E.
  Caligula   37–41
  Claudius   41–54
  Nero   54–68

  Vespasian   69–79
  Titus   79–81

  Trajan   98–117

  Decius   249–251

30 B.C.E.–323 C.E.

Byzantine Period

  Theodosius I   379–395

  Justinian   527–565

323–642 C.E.

INDEX

Page references for endnotes are given immediately after the text page on which the note number appears; for example, if a note on page 253 further explains the text on page 23, then 253 is listed immediately after 23.

Amenhotep III: (*cont.*) 126; temple of (Western Thebes), 101–2, 273; time of, 116. *See also* Luxor Temple

Amun: at Abydos, 112; chthonic, 178; cultus of, 3, 253, 28; domain of, 88–89, 115, 117, 119–20; as father of king, 93, 101, 105–7; ithyphallic form of, 97, 102, 104; of Karnak, 93, 96, 99, 108–9, 121–22; and king, 102, 105; of Luxor (Amenemopet), 104, 121, 156–57, 174, 176–79; priests and priestesses of, 14, 16, 18, 96, 100; prominence of, 251; ram-headed, 105; in temple names, 88–89, 92–93, 98, 101; temple of (Karnak), 97, 99, 101, 119, 282, 158, 160, 176, 181; of United-with-Eternity, 108–9. *See also* Amun-Re; Barque: of Amun (Amun-Re); Barque shrine; Creator: Amun(-Re) as; Gerf Hussein; Luxor Temple; Min-Amun-Re; Procession: of Amun (Amun-Re); Ram's Horn: downward-curved; Statue: of Amun; Wadi el-Sebuʿa

Amun-Min-Kamutef, 178. *See also* Kamutef; Min-Amun-Kamutef

Amun-Re: cultus of, 3, 290, 183; at Deir el-Bahri, 74–76; domain of, 158; as father of king, 96, 107, 138–40, 144, 158, 161, 170, 173–74, 179–80; of Karnak, 99, 282, 156–57, 176, 178–79; and king, 104–5, 107–9, 111, 284, 141, 143, 147, 170, 181; at Luxor, 156–64, 167–70, 173–76, 179–80; temple of (Teuzoi), 17; at temples of Ramesside kings, 115–18, 120. *See also* Amun: temple of (Karnak); Barque: of Amun (Amun-Re); Creator: Amun(-Re) as; Luxor Temple; *mdw-špsy* standard; Min-Amun-Re; *Opet*-festival; Procession: of Amun (Amun-Re); Ram's Horn: downward-curved; Re; Statue: of Amun-Re

ankh (ʿnḫ), 23–24, 92–93, 181, 183–84

ankh-bouquet, 137–38, 183

ankh-sign, 272, 105, 107, 113–14, 116, 183

Apophis, 129, 210, 213

Apotropaic rite and scene, 5, 25–27, 55, 63

Appearance of god, 207, 210–16, 220–21. *See also* Coming out of god; Seeing god

Architecture, symbolic, 2, 4–8, 244–45, 258, 31–35, 46, 72, 84–85, 202, 211, 215–16. *See also* Temples: symbolism of

Arsinoe II, 303, 314

Arsinoe III, 229

atef-crown, 98–99, 107, 118, 141

Aten, 159, 181–83

Axial way (processional path), 5, 8, 133, 197, 200, 208, 210–11, 213–14

Ay, 103, 106, 123, 153, 177

ba (b3), 47, 263, 130–31, 212, 308–9, 216, 221

Barque: of Amun (Amun-Re), 3, 95, 103, 108–12, 116–17, 119, 121–23, 160–61, 293–95, 173–74, 176; of a god, 6, 27, 36, 259, 264, 134, 285, 136–37, 181, 183, 206, 208–9; of Khonsu and of Mut, 103, 110–11, 119, 121, 160–61, 293–95, 173, 298, 176; of a king, 53, 57–58, 89, 93, 272, 98–99, 116–18, 158, 160–61, 173, 176; of Ramesses II, 109, 121; of Ramesses III, 110; of Re, 122; of Sety I, 119; of sun, 104, 117. *See also* Boat burial; Boat journey

Barque sanctuary (chamber, chapel), 289, 291, 95, 111–12, 122, 174, 206, 208, 210, 216. *See also* Luxor Temple: barque sanctuary of

Barque shrine: definition of, 289; as a type of temple, 242, 281. *See also* Barque (way) station (chapel, kiosk); Karnak: Sety II barque shrine at; Luxor Temple: barque shrine of (triple), barque shrines of (southern)

Barque stand, 289, 154, 206, 208

Barque (way) station (chapel, kiosk): definition of, 289; for Festival of the Valley, 3; for *Opet*-festival, 103, 148; for other processions, 27–28, 221, 310; of Thutmose III, 98–99, 274. *See also* Hatshepsut: barque stations of; Roof shrine

Beer, 17, 23, 257, 28, 226

Behdet, god of, 201, 307, 207, 210

Beit el-Wali, 117–18

Berenice II, 313

Biban [Bab]-el-Molûk. *See* Valley of the Kings

Binary opposition, 20–21, 252, 25

Birth: and death, 202; of god, 4, 26, 220–21; and the *ka*, 180; symbol of, 5, 244, 130. *See also* Death: and rebirth; King: begetting and birth of; Luxor Temple: Birth Room of; Rebirth

Birth house, 242, 281, 190, 303, 194–95, 217, 219, 221

Boat burial, 36, 259–60

Boat journey: by god, 26, 34, 36, 259, 39, 51, 285; by *ka*-statue, 57. *See also* Barque; *Opet*-festival: procession during; Procession

Body (corpse, ḫ3wt), 130–32, 283

Body of the Creator: temple as, 244, 7–8, 217, 219; world as, 8, 217

Book of the Dead, 10, 212, 309

Bread, 17, 23–24, 257, 28, 183–84, 226

Bull (beef, ox), 7, 247, 17, 23–24, 26–27

Calendar, 2, 242, 25, 256, 157–58, 292, 300, 180. *See also* Festival calendar

Sokar, 11, 26, 256, 51, 71, 73, 98–99, 102, 216, 221. *See also* Ptah-Sokar; Ptah-Sokar-Osiris

Solar (sun) temple, 11, 242–43, 39, 57, 60, 63, 266, 281

Soleb, 104–5, 116, 126

Space, 1–2, 241–42, 6–7, 244, 133, 234

Sphinx avenue, 55, 93, 105. *See also* Karnak: sphinx avenue at; Luxor Temple: sphinx avenue at

Square antechamber, 35, 48, 64–65, 67–69, 266, 77–78, 81–82

Star, 7, 26, 204, 217

Statue: of Akhenaten, 182; of Amenhotep III, 101; of Amun, 93, 95, 98, 101, 120–21, 156, 176; of Amun-Re, 74, 156; of Djoser, 43, 263, 268; of god, 6–8, 244–45, 10–15, 17, 22–23, 27, 81, 118–19, 134, 136, 156, 181, 205, 211, 217, 220–21, 310, 223–24; of Khafre, 51, 54, 57; of king, 5–6, 244–45, 13, 15, 25–26, 255, 257–58, 264, 70, 72, 81, 90, 93, 272, 123, 125–26, 134, 136, 310; of king and gods, 52, 58, 81; of king as Osiris, 79, 268, 87, 95; meaning of, 202; of Mentuhotep, 74–75; of prisoner of war, 73, 268; of private person, 5–6, 244–45, 25, 255, 263, 105, 125, 136; of Ptah, 251; of Ramesses I, 115; of Ramesses II, 116, 151, 289, 155, 296; of Ramesses III, 121; of Sety I, 107; of Sneferu, 47; of Thutmose III, 99; of Userkaf, 60. *See also* ka-statue

Statue chapel (hall, room, sanctuary, shrine) within a pyramid (or statue cult) temple, 48–50, 53, 57–58, 60, 64–65, 67, 72–73, 78

Statue cult temple, development of, 61. *See also* Pyramid (statue cult, upper) temple

Statue cultus: private, 47; royal, 57, 84, 93, 123, 126

Statue shrine (within a statue chapel or sanctuary of the divine image), 6, 13, 22–23, 47, 50, 72, 104, 134, 206, 306, 208, 210. *See also* Door: of statue shrine

Statue temple. *See* Valley (statue, lower) temple

Subterranean crypt: of Greco-Roman temples, 189, 302, 216, 221; of Late Period, 7

Sun, 5, 8, 71, 158, 177, 202, 204, 307, 210, 216–17, 221, 310, 223, 226

Sun cultus, 45, 63, 265–66

Sun disk, 101, 116–18, 181, 200–201, 307, 211

Sun god, 4, 253, 47, 71, 95, 104, 138, 144, 156, 206–7, 306–7, 210–12, 308. *See also* Courtyard: with altar for sun god; Creator: the solar

Sunrise, 2, 242, 244, 8, 22, 71, 129, 285, 204, 206, 220

Sunset, 2, 242, 8, 71, 129, 204

Swamp (marsh), 6, 8, 133

Symbol, 19–21, 251, 23, 255, 202. *See also* Mortuary cultus, ritual, and symbol; Solar (sun) temple

Tausert, 120

Tefnut, 15, 217

Temples: as center of culture and learning, 191, 194, 196–98, 304, 202–3, 227–28; closing of all, 237; economic role of, 3, 8–9, 246, 248, 15–16, 25, 27, 36, 191, 226–27, 232–34, 314; founding of, 7, 26; lay personnel of, 8–9, 228; overview of, 1–9, 132–35; presence of god in, 215–17, 219–20, 235–36; symbolism of, 5–8, 244–45, 132–35, 285, 203–7, 210–11, 215–19. *See also* Architecture, symbolic; Body of the Creator: temple as; Common people; Divine cult complex; Estate; Priest; Priestess; Royal cult complex; Scribe; *specific temples, temple types, and architectural components*

Teti, 48, 63, 65, 74

Thebes: and Edfu, 232; festivals of, 26, 256, 136–37, 158; gods of, 294; kings at, 74; necropolis of, 74, 86–87, 91–92, 99–100, 103, 120–24, 137, 183; priests of, 9, 14, 16, 18, 138; private tombs of, 132, 137, 184; temples of, 3, 242, 84, 106, 112; west bank of, 3, 242, 50, 86–89, 92–95, 273, 99–101, 110, 115, 119–22, 137, 178, 186. *See also* Amun; Amun-Re; Khonsu; Montu; Mut; *individual Theban temples and other sites on map 3*

Thinite Period. *See* Dynasty 1; Dynasty 2; Dynasties 1–2

Third Intermediate Period, 16. *See also* Dynasty 21; Dynasty 22; Dynasty 23; Dynasty 25

Thoth, 11, 22, 24, 26, 256, 105, 107, 120, 170

Thutmose I, 14, 92–93, 95, 277

Thutmose II, 14, 93, 100, 123

Thutmose III: cultus of, 147; and Hatshepsut, 93, 95, 144, 161; and *Opet*-festival, 103, 148–49, 293, 162; and priests, 13–14; sanctuary rebuilt by, 121; temples of, 95–99, 102, 104, 277, 123, 125. *See also* Akhmenu (Akh-menu); Barque (way) station; Mansion of Millions of Years; *Sed*-festival; Statue

Thutmose IV, 14, 100

Time, 1–2, 242, 244, 129–30, 283, 133

Trajan, 190, 219

Tura, 89, 100–101

Tutankhamun: funeral of, 267; inscribed name of, 123; and *Opet-festival*, 162; orthodoxy of, 290; and Ptah, 251; tomb of, 106, 148, 177. *See also* Luxor Temple: colonnade of (Tutankhamun)

Unas, 256, 36, 63–64, 70–71, 74
United-with-Eternity, 88, 107–10, 121–22. *See also* Medinet Habu: and Ramesses III
United-with-Thebes, 88, 109, 115. *See also* Ramesseum
Upper temple. *See* Pyramid (statue cult, upper) temple
Userkaf, 59–63, 74, 269
Userma͑atre-Meryamun, 88. *See also* Ramesses III
Userma͑atre-Setepenre, 25, 88, 115–20. *See also* Ramesses II

Valley of the Kings (Biban-el-molûk), 267, 87–88, 92, 106, 148, 177
Valley (statue, lower) temple: of Amen-emhat III (Hawara), 35; of Bent Pyramid, 47–49, 51; decoration of, 36; of Dynasties 5–6, 63, 72; and *ka*-statue, 57; of Khafre, 51–52, 54–55, 58; of Khufu, 51; of Meidum, 48; of Menkaure, 52, 58; at Saqqara, 45; of Senwosret II, 80, 269; of Senwosret III (Abydos), 80; tradition of, 52, 264

w3ḥ-collar (garland), 137, 183
w3s-scepter, 105, 107
w͑b, 174
W͑b-priest, 11–13, 248–49, 15–17, 100, 106, 160, 178
W͑bt-priestess, 12–13, 15, 18
Wadi el-Sebu͑a, 117–18
Wadjit, 14, 42, 75
Water, 6, 243, 9, 13, 15, 22, 253–54, 72, 100, 107, 112, 129, 132–33, 285, 160, 173–74, 298, 301, 306, 226. *See also* Chaos; Creation: waters of; Foundation; Libation; Lustration; Nile River; Nonexistent; Nun; Purification
Window of Appearance, 273, 121, 129, 283, 223